C000050889

GRASSROOTS ACTIVIS
EVOLUTION OF TRAN
JUSTICE

The families of the disappeared have long struggled to uncover the truth about their missing relatives. In so doing, their mobilization has shaped central transitional justice norms and institutions, as this groundbreaking work demonstrates. Kovras combines a new global database with the systematic analysis of four challenging case studies – Lebanon, Cyprus, South Africa and Chile – each representative of a different approach to transitional justice. These studies reveal how variations in transitional justice policies addressing the disappeared occur, explaining why victims' groups in some countries are caught in silence while others bring perpetrators to account. Conceiving of transitional justice as a dynamic process, Kovras traces the different phases of truth recovery in post-transitional societies, giving substance not only to the *why* but also to the *when* and *how* of this kind of campaign against impunity. This book is essential reading for all those interested in the development of transitional justice and human rights.

Iosif Kovras is a senior lecturer in comparative politics at the City University of London. His research interests include comparative politics, post-conflict transitional justice and human rights.

GRASSROOTS ACTIVISM AND THE EVOLUTION OF TRANSITIONAL JUSTICE

The Families of the Disappeared

IOSIF KOVRAS

City University of London

CAMBRIDGE
UNIVERSITY PRESS

CAMBRIDGE
UNIVERSITY PRESS

University Printing House, Cambridge CB2 8BS, United Kingdom

One Liberty Plaza, 20th Floor, New York, NY 10006, USA

477 Williamstown Road, Port Melbourne, VIC 3207, Australia

4843/24, 2nd Floor, Ansari Road, Daryaganj, Delhi – 110002, India

79 Anson Road, #06–04/06, Singapore 079906

Cambridge University Press is part of the University of Cambridge.

It furthers the University's mission by disseminating knowledge in the pursuit of education, learning, and research at the highest international levels of excellence.

www.cambridge.org
Information on this title: www.cambridge.org/9781107166653
DOI: 10.1017/9781316711262

First published 2017

Printed in the United Kingdom by Clays, St Ives plc

A catalogue record for this publication is available from the British Library.

ISBN 978-1-107-16665-3 Hardback
ISBN 978-1-316-61770-0 Paperback

Στη Δήμητρα πάντα

CONTENTS

List of Figures   *page* ix
List of Tables   x
Acknowledgments   xi

1 Introduction   1

PART I   **Methods and Theory**   15

2 Methodological and Theoretical Innovations in
the Use of Databases in Transitional Justice   17

PART II   **Global and Historical Perspectives**   59

3 The Daughters of Antigone in Latin America: Argentinian
Mothers   61

4 "Forensic Cascade": The Technologies and Institutions of
Truth   84

5 The "Missing" Tale of Human Rights   111

PART III   **National Perspectives**   127

6 Institutionalized Silences for the Missing in
Lebanon   129

7 Cyprus: The Bright Side of a Frozen Conflict   154

8 Truth Commissions and the Missing: South Africa's
"Unfinished Business"   181

9 Poetic Justice: The Chilean *Desaparecidos*   208

10 Conclusions: Five Lessons for Transitional
Justice   233

List of Interviews   245
Bibliography   251
Index   278

FIGURES

2.1 Geographic Diffusion of Enforced Disappearances
   (1975–2009)   *page* 28
2.2 Distribution of Transitional Justice Policies in Dealing with the
   Disappeared   30
2.3 Passage of Time, Opportunities and Truth Recovery   40
2.4 Timing of Truth Recovery for the Disappeared   43
2.5 Phase-Based Truth Recovery for the Disappeared   49
4.1 The Impact of Technologies of Truth on Contemporary Transitional
   Justice   90
6.1 Disappeared in Lebanon   134
9.1 Disappeared in Chile   211

ix

TABLES

2.1 Type of Settlement and Type of Truth Recovery for the
    Disappeared   *page* 33
2.2 Type of Violence and Truth Recovery   44
2.3 Distribution of Countries According to Levels of Truth
    Recovery   55
4.1 Evolution of Truth Commissions   106
4.2 A Dialectic Relationship: Truth Commissions and Exhumations
    (1981–2009)   108
6.1 Perpetrators and Victims' Groups in Lebanon   136

x

ACKNOWLEDGMENTS

The idea for this book was sparked by a family story. After the forced expulsion of the (Greek) Christian Orthodox population from Turkey in 1922, my great-grandfather went missing for more than a year. The whole family fled from Asia Minor to the Aegean island of Lesbos and considered him dead, a casualty of the violence. Although he was later found alive, this position puzzled me, not least because it clashed with my research experience on the missing and disappeared. By the 1970s, the families of the missing in conflict in contexts like Cyprus or Lebanon saw their loved ones not as casualties but as victims of violence; a moral order was fractured, and they deemed themselves agents with legal rights. I was interested in probing this radical normative shift in the understanding of victimhood. I was convinced that the mobilization of the families – particularly in Latin America – was the critical factor in transforming moral expectations into concrete policy outcomes, and wanted to test my theory. The book is the culmination of my efforts to account for this extremely interesting historical, legal and political normative shift.

The book would not have been possible without the support of three universities who offered vibrant intellectual environments to cultivate certain arguments. The seeds were planted during a wonderful year at the Seeger Center for Hellenic Studies at Princeton University. I am very grateful to Dimitri Gondicas for providing the ideal conditions to take the first steps of this stimulating intellectual journey. I am equally indebted to the Institute for the Study of Conflict Transformation and Social Justice at Queen's, Belfast, and its director, Hastings Donnan. During two very productive years at Queen's, I wrote the bulk of the book. Last but by no means least, the immense support I received from colleagues at the Department of International Politics at City University of London gave me the necessary push to finish. I am also indebted to my students for bringing the necessary fresh and critical perspective to develop further some of the arguments developed in this book.

For the assistance in collecting excellent data from Chile and Lebanon, as well as for detailed comments on the politics of the two countries, I am particularly indebted to Cath Collins, Boris Hay, Isidora Vasquez and Jessica Boutanios. I am deeply indebted to Elizabeth Thompson for helping me edit previous versions of the manuscript.

The scope and the quality of the book have greatly benefited from the thoughtful feedback, advice and support of good friends and colleagues. My heartfelt thanks go to Paloma Aguilar, Timofey Agarin, Amnon Aran, Jay Aronson, John Brewer, Bruce Clark, Evi Chatzipanagiotidou, Derek Congram, Gemma Collantes-Celador, Tom Davis, Antonis Ellinas, Paco Ferrandiz, Christopher Gandrud, Stefanie Grant, Adrian Guelke, Alexis Heraclides, Nadia Hilliard, Iolanda Jaquemet, Stathis Kalyvas, Nikolas Kyriakou, Alexander Lanoszka, Evan Liaras, Neophytos Loizides, Louise Mallinder, Natasa Mavronikola, Shaun McDaid, Claire Moon, Anastasia Nesvetailova, Stefano Pagliari, Yiannis Papadakis, Ronen Palan, Inderjeet Parmar, Madura Rasaratnam, Tony Robben, Adam Rosenblatt, Paul Sant-Cassia, Nukhet Sandal, Nicos Trimikliniotis, Ayse Uskul, Sarah Wagner and Chrystalla Yiakinthou. I would like to sincerely thank the three anonymous reviewers for their insightful comments. Special thanks go to my editor at Cambridge University Press, Elizabeth Spicer, for believing in this book and for being supportive at all stages of its preparation.

I am indebted to Kieran McEvoy. Kieran has been extremely generous with his time in developing some of the central ideas and concepts in this book. Working with him broadened my horizons. Last, but definitely not least, I cannot thank enough Neophytos Loizides. He has been a wise mentor for almost ten years and has offered me his unconditional support at all steps in my career. I cannot thank him enough for being such an inspiring role model.

My family and my closest friends have given me unqualified emotional support throughout the ups and downs of the past few years. I am indebted to Christos, Andromachi, Efpraksia, Simoni, Manolia, Andreas, Mitsos and Phyllis. The book is dedicated to my partner Dimitra, not only for her endless supply of patience, smiles and emotional intelligence that helped me finish this book but also for her ability to help me keep sight of the bigger picture in life.

1

Introduction

The Puzzles

In September 1973, the Chilean army deposed the newly elected socialist President Salvador Alliende and imposed a repressive military dictatorship that lasted until 1990. In the first 3 years, the regime systematically abducted, secretly detained, tortured and killed thousands of suspected leftist militants, students and union members. In an effort to remove potential "threats" to the regime, the bodies were often thrown into the ocean to ensure that their remains would never be recovered. Just a year later, in the summer of 1974, the Turkish army invaded the small Mediterranean island of Cyprus and has since occupied the northern part. During the invasion, approximately 1500 Greek Cypriots went missing, allegedly at the hands of the Turkish army or Turkish-Cypriot paramilitary groups. This was nothing new for Cyprus; a decade earlier (1963–1967), approximately 500 Turkish Cypriots had been abducted by Greek-Cypriot paramilitary groups. Lebanon has a similar experience of disappearances. Approximately 17,000 persons have gone missing throughout its long civil war (1975–1990). Most disappeared within the first 2 years of the civil war, but it became a strategic tool of the paramilitary groups to keep their own groups obedient and to minimize collaboration, so people continued to disappear even after the conflict ended.

By the 1970s and 1980s, disappearances in the context of political repression or internal conflict had become endemic to political violence and had diffused globally. In South Africa, for example, approximately 2000 persons went missing during apartheid – particularly between the mid-1970s and 1990s – mostly at the hands of the agents of the repressive government or during intra-communal violence.

Apart from the temporal overlap, an obvious thread linking these cases is the use of disappearances to instill terror. Less obvious, perhaps, is the result of this strategy; simply stated, the families of the missing are uniquely traumatized. Are their loved ones dead or alive? If they are dead, where are they buried? In the absence of conclusive evidence, the families remain in limbo. This leads to a fourth commonality: in all cases cited above, the families mobilized in an effort to uncover the truth. And the movements were stubborn and persistent – often lasting for decades.

In Lebanon, even during the war, relatives' associations were established; at the end of the conflict, the mobilization became more visible – the families set up a tent in front of the UN headquarters in Beirut, they lobbied politicians and, more recently, they joined forces with international actors. Similarly, in Cyprus, Greek-Cypriot mothers of the missing, dressed in black and carrying photos of their lost children, have held annual rallies in the buffer zone since 1974. They have also established an extremely influential relatives' association. Some families have taken their cases to the European Court of Human Rights and established influential alliances with European Union and Council of Europe institutions. By the same token, the families of the missing in South Africa gained international attention through the Truth and Reconciliation Commission (TRC). Meanwhile, in Chile, the mobilization of the families was so innovative and influential that it became a global example for other human rights movements. Even in the early stages of the military junta, the families were openly carrying photos of their disappeared relatives, established links with international advocacy groups and never ceased to demand the truth.

Despite similarities in the repertoire of mobilization, the four countries have ended up with radically different transitional justice outcomes. The families in Lebanon remain trapped in silence, unable to bring perpetrators to justice or to uncover the remains of their loved ones. In contrast, the relatives in Cyprus have made pivotal gains. Although the island remains divided and no political solution has been achieved to this date, a bi-communal committee has managed to unearth more than half of the 2000 missing persons. This form of "forensic" truth is crucial for the families; they are finally able to bury and mourn their loved ones, despite a significant delay. The mobilization of the families in Chile was even more effective; since the early 2000s, approximately 800 individuals have been investigated, some indicted and even convicted of the charges related to the crime of disappearances. This contrasts with the experience of the families in South Africa. The absence of a blanket amnesty and the institutional role of relatives in the TRC may have increased their global visibility but were not sufficient conditions for the families' mobilization to prosecute perpetrators.

The comparative experience of the four countries raises a set of empirical and theoretical puzzles, the solving of which could benefit our understanding of transitional justice. First, in what ways has the mobilization of victims' groups, particularly families of the missing, contributed to the development of contemporary transitional justice norms and institutions? Obviously, the impact of mobilization has not been uniform across the globe, pointing to an overlapping mystery: why are victims' groups in some countries caught in silence, even after the passage of several decades, while other groups bring perpetrators to account? In effect, what explains global variations in transitional justice policies dealing with specific human rights abuses, in this case, the missing?

The extant literature does not provide an authoritative response. In explaining why certain post-conflict societies adopt a more proactive set of policies to deal with the violent past than others, some early literature has emphasized the importance of the distribution of political power during transitions (Huntington 1993; O'Donnel, Schmitter & Whitehead 1986). Formulating policies to deal with human rights abuses is easier in a "victor's peace," and more difficult in negotiated peace settlements/transitions. In the latter cases, the need to maintain stability, ensure security and democratize the main institutions requires a smooth reintegration of potential spoiler groups, most often the army or the paramilitary groups. The prospect of prosecuting culprits increases the risk of derailing the peace process or democratization unless there is a significant presence of international institutions driving transitional justice policies (Cobban 2006; Newman 2004; Vinjamuri 2010; Zalaquett 1991). As such, negotiated transitions usually necessitate amnesty laws, which in turn become a major obstacle in the path of victims who are claiming their rights. As Vinjamuri and Snyder put it, "Justice does not lead, it follows" (2004:6). Scholars emphasizing the pragmatic constraints to transitional justice implicitly acknowledge the impact of timing on transitional outcomes, but this has not been fully explored. For example, in his classic study, Huntington argues that "justice comes quickly or not at all"; in other words, as time passes, the window of opportunity for addressing human rights issues closes (1993:228). Yet a growing number of countries, like Chile, have started to revisit their violent past – some have waited many years but are doing it all the same. Although the above school of thought explains the original decision to remain silent, it provides limited insights into *why* (or *when*) societies revisit transitional justice settlements.

The "justice cascade" argument is probably better placed to shed light on the conditions enabling victims' groups to tear down the obstacles created by amnesties and publicly acknowledge the truth (Sikkink 2011). Kathryn Sikkink tells the fascinating story of how the emergence and global diffusion of accountability norms paved the way for a growing number of countries to prosecute perpetrators of human rights violations (Lutz & Sikkink 2001; Sikkink & Walling 2007). The indictment of previously untouchable heads of state, such as Serbian leader Milosevic or Guatemalan General Ríos Montt, is part of a cascade of human rights accountability (Lutz & Reiger 2009). Similarly, the exclusion of heinous crimes against humanity, including enforced disappearances, from amnesty laws (Bell 2008) has created novel avenues for victims' groups to prosecute perpetrators and investigate the conditions under which disappearances took place.

Although the justice cascade argument can explain how a favorable international normative framework might pave the way for truth recovery, it says little about why certain societies remain resistant to this norm. When primary emphasis is placed on external influences and actors, the repertoire of domestic actors is necessarily reduced. More importantly, the argument sheds limited light on the timing and the conditions that allow victims' groups to move toward retributive justice. This reflects three broader gaps in the mainstream literature: a lack of systematic knowledge of the role of timing in transitional justice outcomes, a simplistic view of victims' groups as receivers rather than makers of norms and a methodological dialogue of the deaf between global large-n approaches seeking to establish causality and idiographic qualitative analyses.

First, the role of timing (and sequencing) has not been adequately explored in the literature (see Dancy, Kim & Wiebelhaus-Brahm 2010; Olsen, Payne & Reiter 2010). Most theories are built on a static and narrow conceptualization of transitional justice which focuses exclusively on the period of the transition or its immediate aftermath (Thoms, James & Roland 2010). As such, they fail to explain why a number of countries revisit transitional justice settlements, often with a delay. The phenomenon of "post-transitional justice," or delayed justice, has been gaining currency over the past decade in countries such as Chile, Spain and Brazil; yet, few longitudinal studies have been carried out to explain *why* and *when* societies renegotiate transitional justice settlements (Aguilar 2008; Collins 2010; Kovras 2014; Skaar 2011). Equally puzzling and not yet addressed is why certain societies remain resistant to post-transitional justice norms. Despite the passage of time and the persistent mobilization of the families, some countries are unable to break the silence and circumvent the amnesty laws.

Most analyses, both quantitative and qualitative, take a "snapshot" of processes of transitional justice. In this book, my objective is to sketch a more dynamic picture of truth recovery for the missing. Building on an established body of literature in the social sciences (Mahoney 2000; Pierson 2000; Thelen 2000), I will highlight and account for the temporal aspect of transitional justice. To do so, I will draw on a novel global database of countries with those gone missing as a result of political violence since 1975. I will couple this with an in-depth comparative analysis of four cases with divergent transitional justice outcomes.

A second important gap in the literature is the simplistic approach to victims' groups. Although transitional justice emerged in an effort to restore relations broken by violence, with victims taking center stage in the literature, the role of victims in shaping transitional justice policies is still understudied (Bouris 2007; McEvoy & McConnachie 2012).[1] Mainstream literature has a narrow scope, often treating widely divergent victims' groups as a single homogeneous group with uniform transitional justice preferences and needs. Yet different groups have different or even conflicting transitional justice preferences. For example, how can relatives of the missing have the same or even similar transitional justice preferences as internally displaced persons or refugees? The latter two are more likely to be interested in material forms of reparation. Based on a simplistic and often erroneous view of victims, most analyses focus on a predetermined set of generic transitional justice policies (e.g. trials, truth commissions, amnesties, reparations, etc.), ignoring crucial mechanisms tailored to deal with specific crimes of the past. For example, according to all available empirical evidence, identifying the remains of the missing is probably the most pressing need (ICRC 2013; Robins 2013), yet exhumations have been excluded from transitional justice policies. Taking a "disaggregated" approach (Hafner-Burton & Ron 2009), then, the book challenges the narrow scope of the literature. Different groups have different transitional justice preferences.

---

[1] The literature of transitional justice has benefited from a more recent qualitative turn toward "victim-centered" studies. This is predicated on three key objectives: paying closer attention to victims' voices, understanding their needs and assessing how effective transitional justice policies are in addressing these needs. On critical approaches to victimhood, see, for example, Stover and Shigekane (2004), Gready and Robins (2014), McEvoy and McConnachie (2012), Wagner (2008) and Nettelfield (2010).

In a related issue, there is an implicit understanding of victims as powerless groups who have been morally wronged, as simply the recipients of transitional justice. This deprives them of political agency and fails to appreciate a long history of political activism behind landmark transitional justice outcomes. As will be explained in Chapters 3–5, without the historical mobilization of the families of the missing, a number of key transitional justice norms or mechanisms would not have been available. These include the growing use of forensic sciences in "unearthing" the violent past, the use of truth commissions in documenting past crimes and the emergence of key contemporary transitional justice norms, such as the "right to know" the truth.

One of the unique contributions of the book is its effort to probe the overlooked role of organized victims' groups in the evolution of contemporary transitional justice norms and institutions, by considering the specific case of the families of the missing. It deploys the social movements literature (McAdam, Tarrow & Tilly 2001; McEvoy & McGregor 2008; Tarrow 1998), highlighting the importance of the "political opportunities" available to families in their struggle for truth and acknowledgment. This, coupled with their clever use of framing strategies (Snow & Benford 1992, 2000; Snow et al. 1986), considerably augmented the repertoire of their mobilization.

Any effort to address the puzzles I have identified has been inhibited by what I call a methodological dialogue of the deaf. Most qualitative analyses provide in-depth accounts of how individual countries deploy particular transitional justice arrangements or assess their success in reaching their declared objectives. Yet the obvious "cherry picking" in the case selection precludes any effort to build new testable theories (Backer 2009). Largely as a result of this idiographic scope of qualitative studies, a recent quantitative trend has sought to develop global databases in order to identify causal relations, determine what drives transitional justice outcomes and evaluate the impact of these policies on the quality of emerging democracy and respect for human rights (Kim 2012; Olsen, Payne & Reiter 2010; Sikkink & Walling 2007; Wiebelhaus-Brahm 2010). That said, most quantitative approaches are static. Based on a problematic assumption that causal structures are uniform across time, they freeze a relationship at a particular point in time (Mahoney 2000; Pierson 2000; Thelen 2000). In effect, most quantitative approaches decontextualize and depoliticize very complex processes, and this delimits our understanding of how societies deal with their violent past. It is not only important to determine why a particular transitional justice policy is implemented, we also need to know *how* and *when*. All perspectives have something valuable to offer, but their inability to communicate inhibits our effort to provide a comprehensive analytical picture of transitional justice processes.

I applaud the growing emphasis in the literature on the study of databases and have created a new database, titled Disappeared and Missing Database (DIMIDA). The database includes countries with disappearances and missing persons as a result of political violence since 1975. In this book, I use it to critically engage with the theoretical and methodological utility of databases in the study of sensitive questions of human rights in transitional justice. I draw on a mixed-methods research design to bridge the growing gap in the literature between large-n analyses and small-n case-studies (Lieberman 2010). I show how historically oriented replication databases could test and refine existing theories, create new analytical categories, map geographical and temporal trends and, most significantly, pave the way for qualitative analysis by minimizing bias in case selection. Drawing on both the global database and the systematic analysis of four challenging cases (Lebanon, Cyprus, South Africa and Chile), each representative of a different approach to transitional justice, I highlight the interplay between global influences and the repertoire of mobilization of domestic truth seekers.

Central Argument

As the preceding discussion makes clear, this book identifies global variations in transitional justice policies on the missing. It offers a new analytical framework to explain the timing and sequencing of different transitional justice mechanisms to accommodate the problem of the missing. Building on the temporal aspect of truth recovery, it explains how some societies often renegotiate transitional settlements at different post-transitional periods while others do not. Drawing on an innovative research design, it combines global perspectives gleaned from the analysis of the above-mentioned database, with the systematic analysis of Lebanon, Cyprus, South Africa and Chile, each challenging case of negotiated transition with distinct transitional justice outcomes. In spite of the absence of a political settlement in Cyprus, the island's two communities have cooperated on the sensitive issue of the missing and unearthed more than half of the 2000 missing. Despite similar background conditions, Lebanon has not overcome the obstacles set by amnesty law to establish "forensic truth." Meanwhile, the mobilization of the families of the missing in Chile was so effective that it not only catalyzed the establishment of a number of truth recovery mechanisms tasked with documenting the conditions behind the disappearances but also led to the prosecution of perpetrators and the gradual erosion of the amnesty law. Finally, although it is one of the most celebrated cases in the literature, the South African Truth and Reconciliation Commission did not pave the way for accountability measures.

The book explains the timing and sequencing of different transitional justice policies in dealing with the problem of the missing, looking specifically at the activation of the families. Separating truth recovery for the missing into distinct phases, it shows the relative impact of different factors across each phase. First, in the early period after a negotiated transition, amnesty laws and concerns about security and stability inhibit truth recovery initiatives. To cross this initial phase of "institutionalized silence," most families prioritize a "forensic" form of truth, such as humanitarian exhumations and identification of the dead. They do so because this process is likely to satisfy their most pressing humanitarian need – to find and bury their loved ones according to cultural and religious rituals and, hence, to begin to mourn. In the presence of amnesties, however, a society's ability to cross this "forensic" phase of truth depends on a minimum level of security and stability, not to mention the provision of institutional "carrots" to tempt perpetrators to come forward with valid information that could lead to burial sites. These incentives may include immunity from prosecution, anonymity and confidentiality. While the "forensic" stage is often the end of the truth recovery process for countries emerging from conflict, most post-authoritarian societies that link exhumations to truth commissions open a new chapter of "broader" truth recovery. In countries where the passage of time is followed by the democratization of institutions, new opportunities become available for a criminal investigation of the conditions behind the initial disappearances, and such investigations can be considered "broader" truth recovery. Forensic evidence from the graves coupled with the documentation of patterns of abuses by truth commissions greatly facilitates the struggle of families for retributive justice.

What I have referred to as the repertoire of mobilization is pivotal in determining whether families reach this "broader" stage of truth recovery or remain at "forensic" truth – if, indeed, they get that far. An effective repertoire will include the successful deployment of domestic and international legal tools, the formation of influential alliances and the addition of the issue of the missing to the political agenda. However, consolidating the minimum level of security required to create the conditions for perpetrators to point to gravesites and, thus, to get from the original stage of "institutionalized silence" to implementing a policy of exhumations ("forensic truth"), let alone "broader truth," is determined by the conditions of the transition, something the families cannot control.

As this short introduction suggests, the book's framework eschews the static picture of the missing painted by most quantitative approaches. Its findings promise to shed some much-needed light on the timing and sequencing of transitional justice mechanisms in dealing with the problem of the missing.

Book Outline

The book is divided into three parts. Part I critically engages with the methodological and theoretical utility of databases in the study of transitional justice, drawing on the new global database on disappearances mentioned above. Part II presents a historical narrative explaining how the mobilization of the families of the missing has shaped contemporary transitional justice norms and institutions. Part III compares the national experiences of four countries with different transitional justice policies to deal with the problem of the missing to probe the generalizability of the argument. Both Parts II and III draw on rich empirical evidence, including interviews with families of the missing, members of relatives' associations and other stakeholders in all four cases, as well as international forensic and legal professionals with excellent knowledge of the problem of the missing.

Chapter 2 introduces a global database of countries with disappeared or missing persons as a result of political violence since mid-1970s. It critically engages with the theoretical and methodological utility of quantitative analyses of databases in the study of sensitive questions of human rights. At the same time, it deploys the database on the missing to illustrate how databases can expand the scope of small-n comparative analyses in transitional justice, including theory testing, minimizing selection bias in case selection, creating meaningful descriptive categories, mapping global trends and refining theory. The chapter also explains how the nature of violence (conflict vs. state repression) determines the type of truth recovery. Societies emerging from civil wars face more complex challenges and, in the absence of international intervention, it becomes almost impossible to implement a mechanism of broader truth recovery. Finally, the chapter uses the findings from the database to explain the rationale of case selection of Lebanon, Cyprus, South Africa and Chile. These four challenging cases of negotiated transitions or frozen conflicts are illustrative of four different approaches to transitional justice. The case studies are explored in detail in Chapters 6–9.

Chapter 3, the first chapter in Part II, discusses the history of contemporary mobilizations around the missing. Any analysis of the mobilization of families must obviously start with the "big bang" of transitional justice in Argentina. Accordingly, Chapter 3 investigates why the struggle of the Argentinian "Mothers" and "Grandmothers" to recover the truth about their relatives was far more effective than the struggle of families in other countries facing similar challenges in the same period. The chapter narrates the powerful story of transformation of bereaved Mothers into agents of radical change. Drawing on a number of psychological, cultural and religious explanations, it shows how the unique nature of the crime left families in an "ambiguous" state of loss that set the stage for a relentless struggle to uncover the truth for their loved ones. Using the analytical toolkit of contentious politics, it shows that families not only deployed existing political opportunities but also created new ones. The chapter points to the establishment of alliances with influential domestic and transnational actors and the strategic use of motherhood as a global symbol of undeserved suffering/victimhood. It shows how mobilization was pivotal in framing the problem of the disappeared in general and the "Mothers," in particular, as "ideal" victims of undeserved suffering, a framing quickly deployed by other relatives' movements around the world.

While Chapter 3 explains why the effective mobilization of relatives in Latin America brought the crime of the missing onto the center stage of international politics, Chapters 4 and 5 go farther and illustrate how the families' struggle for truth has influenced contemporary transitional justice norms and institutions. They identify four key mechanisms through which relatives have shaped transitional justice. To begin, Chapter 4 shows how the forensic struggle for truth gradually created an international epistemic community of forensic experts; this not only helped thousands of families reach closure through the identification of their loved ones, but it greatly facilitated the quest for justice by providing "hard" incriminatory evidence from graves in courts, often critical to secure a conviction. In the chapter, I argue, this "forensic cascade" enabled a subsequent "justice cascade" to gain global currency. I also maintain that the emergence and global diffusion of truth commissions is intrinsically related to the struggle of families of the missing for truth; for example, the mandates of the first commissions focused almost exclusively on documenting the specific crime. The chapter also explains how the diffusion of the tools of truth seeking has benefited the struggle for justice in societies with well-entrenched cultures of silence and denial.

Chapter 5 goes on to show how the relentless legal battle against the impunity imposed by amnesty gradually created a robust international legal framework around the problem of enforced disappearances, thereby shaping much of the contemporary vocabulary of human rights and transitional justice, including the "right to know" the truth. It identifies the mobilization of victims' groups (in this case, the families) as a catalytic factor in the "justice cascade" and the design of transitional justice in societies emerging from conflict.

Chapter 6 opens Part III, and it begins the book's movement into its four case studies. The chapter explores the interesting and understudied problem of missing persons during and after the Lebanese civil war, in an effort to determine why these families never managed to overcome the phase of "institutionalized silence." It looks at a unique feature of the Lebanese experience, namely, the continued instability and lack of security, evident in the use of the practice of disappearances by paramilitary groups years after the official termination of the war. The chapter explains why despite the proactive and ongoing mobilization of relatives, there was no "forensic" form of truth recovery. The Lebanese experience is instructive, yet neglected, as literature reserves a preferential position for "success stories," leaving aside those lessons to be learned from policy "failures." Moreover, as amnesty laws are particularly popular in the Middle East, lessons from Lebanon can shed useful analytical light on why the vast majority of societies in the region have failed to proceed to more comprehensive truth recovery.

Chapter 7 reveals the instructive experience of Cyprus. Despite the absence of a political settlement, the two communities in the island have found and identified more than half of the 2000 persons who went missing during the Cyprus conflict. The chapter enumerates the difficulties involved in overcoming an "institutionalized silence" in post-conflict settings. To this end, it investigates the conditions that transformed the Committee on Missing Persons (CMP) from a defunct body for several decades into the most successful bi-communal project since 2005. It illustrates why Cyprus' quest for (forensic) truth has been more effective than other societies with comparable background conditions, such as Lebanon, and determines the conditions required for the success of "forensic" truth recovery. The chapter explains that despite early mobilization of the relatives, it was impossible for them to overcome the obstacles created by the partition of the island and establish a truth commission or prosecute perpetrators. However, the current wave of exhumations has empowered local bi-communal groups of relatives in their struggle for truth and acknowledgment; their grassroots activities are effectively challenging official discourse about the violent past. Finally, using the comparative experiences of Colombia and Northern Ireland, the chapter asks if this model is exportable to other cases of ongoing or frozen conflict and explains why it is almost impossible for families in negotiated post-conflict settings to demand "broader" truth.

Chapter 8 looks at one of the most celebrated cases in the literature of transitional justice, the South African Truth and Reconciliation Commission (TRC), in a new light. More specifically, it evaluates the TRC's effectiveness in recovering the truth about those who went missing during apartheid. By drawing on the report of the TRC, most notably its reference to the missing as "unfinished business," the chapter is able to identify the limitations of truth commissions. Although it is seen as a success story, the TRC and ensuing fact-finding mechanisms have identified only a small fraction of the missing persons. The chapter asks why, despite the availability of institutional and legal tools to hold perpetrators to account, relatives were unwilling to pursue or ineffective in their quest for retributive justice. South Africa is one of the few outliers; although exhumations and truth commissions were linked, this did not lead to retributive justice. Drawing on cases with similar background conditions, the chapter shows the virtues and vices of truth commissions in dealing with the problem of disappeared.

Chapter 9 narrates the powerful story of the struggle of families of the missing in Chile. Simply stated, their story became a global symbol of resistance. The chapter investigates why despite the fragile (negotiated) transition and the amnesty law, the mobilization of relatives was catalytic, not only in setting up a number of fact-finding bodies but also in gradually annulling the amnesty law applicable to the crime of disappearances. The chapter explains the effectiveness of the families in promoting accountability and shows how they skillfully formed influential alliances, politicized the problem of disappearances and took novel forms of action. It argues that the passage of time enabled democratic consolidation; with this, new institutional tools became available to domestic truth seekers, allowing them to challenge amnesty. It also accounts for the failure of the policy of exhumations, specifically the low identification rates. Although

Latin America is deemed the "champion of human rights," the case of Chile illustrates both the virtues and the pitfalls of judicial-driven approaches to transitional justice.

Chapter 10 sums up the theoretical and policy lessons to be gleaned from the systematic comparative analysis of the case studies. First, it shows how social movements and the mobilization of relatives have shaped contemporary transitional justice, a previously underexplored relationship. It explains how the mobilization of the relatives has critically contributed to the diffusion of accountability norms and enhanced our understanding of the growing phenomenon of the "justice cascade." It argues that the struggle of the families is guided by a gradualist logic of "peeling the onion," where every new demand is based on strategic (legal and political) precedents, creating a form of path dependence. Second, the chapter elaborates on the temporal aspect of transitional justice. It shows how placing transitional justice in time and systematically situating specific moments in a temporal sequence of events can greatly benefit our understanding of transitional justice.

Short Guide to Terms

The book addresses two categories of victims: "missing" and "disappeared," which refer to two distinct legal categories. On the one hand, the term "missing" is used but not defined in international humanitarian law. According to the International Committee of the Red Cross (ICRC 2003:6):

> *Missing persons* or *persons unaccounted for* are those whose families are without news of them and/or are reported missing, on the basis of reliable information, owing to armed conflict (international or non-international) or internal violence (internal disturbances (internal strife) and situations requiring a specifically neutral and independent institution and intermediary).

The term missing is a broader category covered by international humanitarian law, historically founded on the principle of reciprocity.[2] It is based on the assumption that even in times of conflict, two parties have the mutual interest (and obligation) to follow fundamental rules that will enable them to recover their soldiers. As warfare gradually changed and non-combatants went missing in conflicts, international humanitarian

---

[2] I am very grateful to Stefanie Grant for bringing this point to my attention and for all the support on legal issues.

law became applicable to internal conflicts. To this end, more recently, it has been employed widely outside conflict settings.[3]

Enforced disappearance "is considered to be the arrest, detention, abduction or any other form of deprivation of liberty by agents of the State or by persons or groups of persons acting with the authorization, support or acquiescence of the State, followed by a refusal to acknowledge the deprivation of liberty or by concealment of the fate or whereabouts of the disappeared person, which place such a person outside the protection of the law."[4]

In effect, it refers to a complex human rights violation, at times of both peace and armed conflict (Crettol & De La Rosa 2006; Scovazzi & Citroni 2007).[5] The practice of enforced disappearance refers to individuals being kidnapped by agents of repressive states; therefore, the practice is covered by international human rights law. The International Convention against Enforced or Involuntary Disappearances (the "Convention" henceforth) includes enforced disappearances in the list of crimes against humanity. It is important to draw an analytical distinction between the "crime" of enforced disappearances and the "right not to be subject to enforced disappearance."

Despite these fine legal distinctions, it is worth noting that some of the key needs and challenges of families in post-conflict and post-authoritarian settings are similar. In countries with long histories of complex state failure, it is often impossible to determine whether persons go "missing" in contexts of warfare or are "disappeared" by state agents, as in Lebanon, Syria and Libya. Often these categories are rendered meaningless in societies emerging from deep trauma. So the terms "missing" and "disappeared" will be used interchangeably unless explicitly mentioned otherwise. Besides "disappearance" has now become a generic term that is often used quite loosely and tends to include both missing and enforced disappearance.

---

[3] See, for example, the UN Secretary General's 2014 report to the GA UN Doc. A/69/293, August 11, 2014 and its antecedent resolutions.

[4] Article 2, International Convention for the Protection of All Persons from Enforced Disappearance 2006, GA Res.61/177, December 20, 2006, A/RES/61/177;14 IHRR 582 (2007).

[5] "Missing" persons in domestic contexts in peacetime is a completely different category, subject to policing and other mechanisms.

PART I

Methods and Theory

Methodological and Theoretical Innovations in the Use of Databases in Transitional Justice

Transitional justice is a growing but relatively new field of research and, like all new disciplines, is characterized by methodological polyphony and little multi-method synthesis (Backer 2009; Bell 2008; Dancy, Kim & Wiebelhaus-Brahm 2010; Thoms, James & Roland 2010; Wiebelhaus-Brahm 2010). Much of the early literature is dominated by a normative and prescriptive drive to convince readers of the virtues (or vices) of a specific mechanism. Hence, this first wave is rife with qualitative studies of a single case (or a small number of cases) where a specific transitional justice mechanism has been implemented (Buergenthal 1994; Chapman & Ball 2001; Thoms, James & Roland 2010), often in a very specific period of the transition. This narrow approach ignores how societies can successfully deal with problems of human rights, such as the disappeared, in the absence of an "official" transitional justice mechanism. Consider Cyprus, for example; despite the absence of a transition, Greek-Cypriots and Turkish-Cypriots, the two dominant communities on the island, have implemented a policy of exhuming the bodies of the disappeared, thereby addressing the most pressing humanitarian need of thousands of families.

More recently, a second wave of scholarship has emerged. Its objective is to assess the success and impact of different transitional justice mechanisms. Spearheaded primarily, but not exclusively, by political scientists, the new trend is to use global databases of various transitional justice instruments, including trials (Kim and Sikkink 2010), truth commissions (Dancy, Kim & Wiebelhaus-Brahm 2010; Wiebelhaus-Brahm 2010), amnesties (Mallinder 2008) and their combination (Dancy et al. 2014; Gates, Binningsbo & Lie 2007; Olsen, Payne & Reiter 2010). Most such analyses create complex statistical models to establish relations of statistical significance among different variables and draw causal inferences based on large-n studies. In constructing these databases, scholars often draw on high levels of conceptual abstraction in an effort to make key concepts measurable and comparable across the globe (Clark & Sikkink 2013; Landman & Carvalho 2009; McCormick & Mitchel 1997). Despite establishing the overall impact of transitional justice, this research and its concomitant abstractions have sidelined complex and significant political processes, such as the role of victims' groups in shaping or changing political agendas. In turn, the absence of in-depth understanding of complex causal processes has inhibited the development of theoretical frameworks with larger explanatory power.

In brief, the current methodology resembles a "dialogue of the deaf," with some seeing the forest and others seeing the trees – if I can mix my metaphors to make my point. Both strands of the literature are valuable, yet their inability to communicate inhibits the creation of new knowledge.

In the first part of this chapter, I expand on the role of databases in creating new knowledge in transitional justice, in general, and in dealing with the problem of the disappeared, in particular. This is important. The growing influence of quantitative-oriented databases in the field has created misconceptions about the use of the databases in transitional justice and has discouraged scholars who prefer qualitative tools from drawing on this useful instrument.[1] I look at the Cingranelli and Richards' (1999) database (CIRI henceforth), one of the most widely used sources, to understand its strengths and limitations in addressing the problem of the disappeared and missing persons (Cingranelli, Richards & Clay 2014). The analysis highlights the static nature of quantitative studies, which sideline temporal aspects of transitional justice, as well as inherent flaws in the quality of data on sensitive questions of human rights in conflict zones.

As the ensuing part of the chapter makes clear, "qualitative historically oriented" databases could drive the quest for new theoretical knowledge (Lieberman 2010). By introducing a new database of countries with disappearances and missing persons (DIMIDA) as a result of political violence since 1975, I show that qualitative-driven databases, could serve four important functions: mapping geographic trends in the development of a phenomenon; testing theory; refining theory by developing new hypotheses which could then be tested in a small-n comparative analysis; and guiding case selection by minimizing selection bias. To sum

---

[1] For interesting exceptions, see Mallinder and O'Rourke (2016) and Collins, Balardini and Burt (2012).

up, global databases can help test and refine theory, especially when coupled with small-n analysis.

Methodological and Theoretical Utility of Databases in Transitional Justice

A fascinating yet theoretically underdeveloped element in the study of transitional justice is its temporal aspect. Transitions themselves are "critical junctures" taking place in extraordinary times of political change. Also implicit in the study of transition is that decisions made during this period will have an impact on the quality of emerging institutions, norms and practices, albeit in the long term. More importantly, international experience suggests that societies often (re)negotiate the terms years, even decades, after transitions, engendering what might be called "post-transitional justice" (Collins 2011; Kovras 2013). Take Spain, for example; silence on the events of the civil war (1936–1939) characterized the transition to democracy in the 1970s, only to be broken in the 2000s after a delay of 30 years (Aguilar 2008).

We have spent little time probing the role of timing in transitional justice. The time frame of most analyses is limited to "the immediate – we look for causes and outcomes that are both temporally contiguous and rapidly unfolding. In the process we miss a lot" (Pierson 2004:79). This is particularly relevant to the limited scope of large-n databases. By examining the relationship between variables at a single point in time, most statistical analyses offer only a "snapshot" of transitional justice processes (Mahoney 2000:88; Pierson 2000:79). Based on the assumption that "causal structures are uniform through time" (Sewell 1996:263), the temporal aspect of transitional justice often remains unnoticed. This is particularly important in the study of transitions. We need to explain not only *why* a particular outcome takes place but also *when* it occurs and *how*. Charles Tilly argues, "When things happen within a sequence affects how they happen" (1984:14). Placing transitional justice in time, that is, "systematically situating particular moments in a temporal sequence of events and processes," can strengthen our grasp of complex transitional justice processes (Pierson 2000:79).

Mahoney notes, "Causal mechanisms require analyzing data that embody dynamic relations and unfolding processes in a way that does not lend itself to efficient quantification/statistical inference" (2004:89). Understanding "unfolding processes" could shed light on timing in transitional justice, but most statistical processes fail to capture the necessary dynamism. Societies and victims' groups renegotiate the terms of transitional settlements when the time is right – whether 2 years or 30 years after the fact. This book represents one of the first efforts to develop a more dynamic picture of truth recovery by considering the case of the disappeared and the missing.

Another limitation of database-driven analyses in the field is their focus on certain generic transitional justice mechanisms, including trials, truth commissions and amnesties (Gates, Binningsbo & Lie 2007; Hirsch 2009; Kim & Sikkink 2010; Sikkink 2011; Olsen, Payne & Reiter 2010; Wiebelhaus-Brahm 2010). Minimal effort has been made to disaggregate transitional justice into specific human rights problems and consider different groups of victims in post-conflict settings (Hafner-Burton & Ron 2009; Wood & Gibney 2010). After all, the *raison d'être* of transitional justice is to understand how societies address open wounds left by past human rights violations; it makes sense to ask how societies deal with independent categories of victims and whether theoretical assumptions hold true.

Similarly, despite the important insights derived from both detailed small-n analyses and innovative large-n databases, a major problem in the literature is the largely simplistic approach to victims; by treating different victims' groups as a homogenous category, such work implies that all victims have uniform transitional justice preferences. Yet, distinct groups often have contrasting attitudes toward transitional justice policies. The point of reference for most analyses remains the society (at large), without accounting for any deviation in transitional justice priorities among different victims' groups. For example, do relatives of the missing have the same or even similar transitional justice preferences as internally displaced persons or refugees who may be more interested in material forms of reparation? Previous experience and established research highlight the need to recover the whereabouts of the disappeared for their families to reach some form of closure (Blaauw & Lähteenmäki 2002:778; ICRC 2013; Robins 2013).

A third limitation of large-n databases is the inherently flawed approach to measuring sensitive human rights in transitions. Currently, there is a fetishization of numbers in transitional justice and in social sciences in general:

> If something is not measured it does not exist, if it is not counted it does not count. If there are no "data," an issue or problem will not be recognized, defined, prioritized, put on the agenda and debated. Therefore, to

measure something – or at least claim to do so – is to announce its existence and signal its importance and policy relevance.

(Andreas & Greenhill 2011:1)

This is not to diminish the relevance of databases; rich data can greatly benefit our understanding of complex transitional justice processes. Yet, collecting reliable data related to clandestine human rights abuses in contexts of fragile political transitions meets with inherent and inevitable obstacles.

The quality, reliability and validity of data on which most databases are built are important issues that have not been critically analyzed.[2] As an example, consider CIRI, one of the most widely used databases in the field of transitional justice and human rights;[3] some of the most renowned studies in the field have drawn on this database to evaluate the impact of transitional justice on human rights and democracy (i.e. Olsen, Payne & Reiter 2010; Kim & Sikkink 2010). Given the scope of this book, it makes sense to use this because it is one of the few existing databases to include a specific section dedicated to disappearances.[4] Since 1981, every country has been ascribed a grade, ranging from 0 to 2. Countries where not a single incident of enforced disappearance has occurred during a specific year are assigned 2; countries with between 1 and 50 are ranked 1; countries with more than 50 cases receive 0. The primary sources on which this ranking has been established are the Country Reports on Human Rights Practices of the US State Department and the annual reports of Amnesty International.

However, there are several limitations in CIRI's approach to the problem of the missing, in both the measurement of the central concept (i.e. disappearances) and its additive scale.[5] Measuring human rights is an arduous and sometimes callous enterprise (Brysk 1994; Landman &

---

[2] For important exceptions, see Clark and Sikkink (2013); Ron, Ramos and Rodgers (2005); Hafner-Burton and Ron (2009); and Wood and Gibney (2010).

[3] Available at: http://ciri.binghamton.edu/, last accessed January 23, 2015. Another source for developing quantitative datasets is the "Political Terror Scale"; it measures physical integrity rights as well; available at: www.politicalterrorscale.org/, last accessed January 23, 2015.

[4] CIRI defines disappearances as "cases in which people have disappeared, political motivation appears likely, and the victims have not been found."

[5] Another significant conceptual limitation of CIRI is the fact that it does not distinguish between disappearances and missing in conflict, largely treating "enforced disappearances" and "missing persons" as a homogenous group; both categories are considered under the label "disappearances." Yet, this is supported neither by the existing legal framework nor by the relevant literature.

Carvalho 2009). In post-conflict settings, the problem of disappearances and dead bodies carries significant symbolic capital, inhibiting our attempts to accurately measure or classify cases. In fact, certain societies are excluded from CIRI despite having experienced the problem. For example, in Northern Ireland, the fate of 16 people who disappeared in the 1970s and 1980s, presumably as a result of the clandestine activities of the militant republican groups, remains a sensitive issue; yet Northern Ireland, failing to reach the restrictive threshold set by CIRI, is not included in the database (Dempster 2016).

Sensitive questions of human rights, such as missing persons, can become political instruments. It is not uncommon for authoritarian regimes to decrease the official number of victims while NGOs inflate the number to attract international attention or sympathy. Equally, in conflict settings, the "statistics" of victimhood is frequently hijacked by hardliners and used as a symbol promoting their ethnic monopoly of suffering. In short, the task of determining numbers of missing in such volatile contexts as in transitions becomes a herculean one. Alison Brysk got it right when she commented on the creation of a "politics of measurement," as information in conflict-ridden societies is neither neutral nor value free (1994:692). Because of this complex reality, then, datasets, including the prestigious CIRI, do not represent all countries with disappearances as a result of political violence, but only specific countries that satisfy a crude and restrictive threshold set of criteria.

In addition, it is often difficult to determine the precise number of the disappeared from primary sources, let alone using additive scales. Specifically, the use of numerical values to categorize the problem of disappearances in a country as "practiced frequently" (>50 instances), "practiced occasionally" (1–49 instances) and "have not occurred" is hard to justify. Especially in the period 1981–1985, the quality of information included in reports is often vague for several reasons. As Clark (2010) shows, the definition of "disappeared" adopted by Amnesty International was crystallized gradually in the early 1980s. As such, the definition and understanding of "enforced disappearances" adopted by the CIRI's original sources, the annual reports of the US State Department and Amnesty International, make it impossible to accurately and consistently capture the number of the disappeared (Amnesty International 1981). This raises the broader issue of "information effects," exhaustively discussed by Clark and Sikkink (2013). Due to the contemporaneous coding, the quality of human rights data diverges over a long time (Clark & Sikkink 2013; Ramos, Ron & Thoms 2007; Ron,

Ramos & Rodgers 2005). The bureaucratic capabilities of the collecting bodies, the access to data in particularly turbulent countries and the clandestine nature of the crime all affect the quality of data, especially in this early period (1970s–1980s) (Poe, Carey & Vazquez 2001:677). By aggregating indicators, CIRI assumes that a single disappearance is the equivalent of an act of torture, another physical integrity right included in the database, but this is hard to justify or to measure (Cingranelli & Richards 1999; McCormick & Mitchell 1997; Wood & Gibney 2010).

CIRI has also made factual mistakes by establishing its contemporaneous coding on a report that does not take into account the historical context. For example, Cyprus is coded as having incidents of disappearances from 1981 until 1995. Yet, as a result of the de facto partition of the island, it would have been impossible to have any new disappearances after the mid-1970s. As noted above, Northern Ireland had 16 disappearances over the course of the "Troubles" (1969–1998) that were never recorded by CIRI. These two examples highlight the pitfalls of quantitative perspectives, especially their tendency to study human rights problems out of political and historical context.[6]

Finally, even if a database overcomes these obstacles and determines with relative precision, validity and reliability the number of the disappeared in each country, statistical analyses are based on the flawed premise that all cases carry the same explanatory weight. Yet, we all know some cases have been far more influential than others in the study and debates of transitional justice. Take the example of Argentina; as the next chapter will show, the mobilization of relatives shaped contemporary transitional justice norms and institutions. Based on a high level of conceptual abstraction and the assumption that all cases are comparable, some large-n analyses fail to shed light on the complex social and political processes leading to certain outcomes. Essentially, explaining *how* a particular "impact" was reached is as important in the causal chain as determining and measuring the impact itself.

To recapitulate, there are significant methodological flaws inherent to the effort to use statistical tools to analyze databases in transitional justice. This is not to discredit their usefulness. In what follows, I argue databases can be very useful and should not be limited to evaluating the success or impact of specific transitional justice policies. Drawing on DIMIDA, a newly developed database, I show that such databases can augment the scope of analysis by mapping geographic and temporal

---

[6] On this issue, see Munck and Verkuilen (2002) and Herrera and Kapur (2007).

trends, testing theoretical assumptions, refining theory and guiding case selection to pave the way for comparative small-n analysis.

Databases and Theory Development

One of my primary objectives is to explain why certain societies are more effective in deploying policies to recover the truth about the disappeared, while others remain trapped in silence. I develop a new theoretical framework to account for the global variation in truth recovery processes for the missing, as well as the sequencing and timing of different transitional justice mechanisms. In this section, I show how databases can enhance the analytical scope of transitional justice processes, not necessarily by using statistical inference. I introduce DIMIDA, a new global database of countries with disappearances and missing persons as a result of political violence since 1975. I will mention two novelties at the outset. First, its scope diverges from that of most of the existing databases, as it is designed not to draw statistical (causal) inferences. Second, instead of focusing on the mechanisms of justice, it focuses on one of the most pressing problems of human rights in transitions – the disappeared.

The growing use of datasets in the study of transitional justice is heartening but could be expanded by focusing on specific victims' groups and/or human rights offences, while simultaneously probing the generalizability of the findings to challenging case studies. In this book, I stress the utility of a mixed-methods approach, one which combines global perspectives (databases) with local experiences (small-n cases) (Cardenas 2010; Lieberman 2005; Wiebelhaus-Brahm 2010). It is important to illustrate why and how norms diffuse regionally or globally and to underscore why domestic actors deploy or resist external influences.

Drawing on Lieberman's "nested" framework, the first objective is to develop a historically oriented replication database (2010), where data are defined as "systematically collected and theoretically informed containers of facts and observation for consistent set of units over time" (2010:39). In this particular project, the construction of a large-n, qualitative, historically oriented database is followed by a small-n analysis. The premise is not unprecedented. In fact, some pioneering pieces of research in political science draw on a similar framework (Beissinger 2002; Lange 2011; Mansfield & Snyder 2005).[7] Similarly, in his seminal

---

[7] Matthew Lange, in his fascinating exploration of the impact of education on violence, develops a database and tests the findings against the comparative historical analysis of six

research, Wiebelhaus-Brahm (2010) links large-n insights with critical cases to probe the success and impact of truth commissions. Sonia Cardenas (2010), in another fascinating analysis, combines statistical analysis with focused comparison of selected cases to explain variation in compliance with international human rights norms.

The database developed here draws on two primary sources: the US Department of State's Annual Country Reports on Human Rights Practices and Amnesty International's Annual Reports.[8] Since 1981, both sources have incorporated a section with information on disappearances.[9] Before 1981, their annual reports included information about the state of human rights (abuses) in most countries with disappearances, but the absence of a definition of enforced disappearances hinders accurate coding; coding cases in this period calls for extra care.

It is worth noting that DIMIDA draws on the same sources as CIRI. The reason is simple: they remain the two most reliable and consistent sources. Yet, the scope of DIMIDA is different. First, the coding is not contemporaneous – coding each year independently – but historical. So, in cases where insufficient information is available, especially in the early period, when the quality of reporting was often poor, I draw on reports of the same sources in the following years.[10]

The database covers the years 1975–2009. The decision to extend the scope back to 1975, despite potential coding difficulties, reflects the landmark cases of disappearances in Latin America in that period;

---

cases (2011). A similar design is adopted by Mansfield and Snyder (2005) to examine why nascent democracies often go to war shortly after transition.

[8] The reports can be accessed at www.state.gov/j/drl/rls/hrrpt/ and http://amnesty.org/en/annual-report/2013. Lieberman (2010) sets four criteria for the development of historically oriented databases: proximity of observation, transparency of citation, certainty of historical record and attention to valid comparison.

[9] One of the central flaws of the two original sources is that they fail to address the most recent form of disappearances, namely, "extraordinary renditions," the government-sponsored abduction of individuals from one country to another. Being a clandestine and transnational phenomenon, the existing sources fail to capture this important issue. Mindful of this limitation, it should be acknowledged that DIMIDA does not address this important category of disappearances.

[10] In cases of inconsistency or where the information was contradictory in the original reports, the information was triangulated through secondary sources, such as the data included in reports published by UN Working Group on Enforced or Involuntary Disappearances (WGEID) www.ohchr.org/EN/Issues/Disappearances/Pages/DisappearancesIndex.aspx and/or Lexis-Nexis.

excluding them would delimit the analytical scope of the project. After 1975, with the third wave of democratization, more countries began a transition to democracy and the quest for dealing with the past gained currency (Huntington 1993). That said, information published by states and international NGOs often reflects an agenda that may influence their objectivity (Landman & Carvalho 2009). Simply stated, the annual reports published by the US State Department and Amnesty International may be influenced by policy considerations and bureaucratic flaws (Clark & Sikkink 2013). To minimize this bias, I have used the two sources jointly, while any potential shortcomings in terms of bias are outweighed by the consistency of the sources. Besides, the objective of this dataset is to map trends, not make causal inferences; the main concern is securing the reliability and consistency of the sources.

The broad temporal scope of the database (1975–2009) minimizes the possibility of distorting the overall picture. As noted above, I have selected the only two sources to focus exclusively on the problem of the disappeared (implicitly before 1980, explicitly afterward). A number of other databases in transitional justice also privilege these two sources over others (Kim 2012; Sikkink 2011). Overall, the database is reliable, consistent and easily replicable.

A caveat is appropriate here. Any database on the missing and the disappeared would have been incomplete without incorporating exhumations, a key transitional justice tool used to address the problem. It is a state's legal obligation to locate, identify and return remains to the relatives (Article 24.3 of the International Convention for the Protection of All Persons from Enforced Disappearances), while available empirical evidence and clinical practice show identification of the dead body is the most fundamental form of repair for the families, without which it is impossible to reach closure (Boss 2006; ICRC 2013).[11] As no database presently focuses on exhumations, I had to construct a new one.[12] Several

---

[11] Article 24.3 of the Convention says the State has a legal duty "to search for, locate and release disappeared persons, and in the event of death, locate, respect and return their human remains."

[12] Globally, the number of forensic teams undertaking exhumations is specific, so I drew on their resources and conducted personal interviews to determine the countries where they have engaged in exhumations or trained local groups of forensic scientists. These groups include Argentine Forensic Anthropological Team (EAAF), Physicians for Human Rights (PHR), International Commission for Missing Persons (ICMP), Forensic Program of the Human Rights Center at the University of California, Berkeley, as well as annual reports of the International Committee of the Red Cross.

credible databases already offer ample information on trials, truth commissions and amnesties, so I drew on them.[13]

Mapping Global Trends

Social science research in general and transitional justice literature in particular have devalued the analytical power of description. Databases could enrich our analytical understanding of complex transitional justice phenomena (Mallinder & O'Rourke 2016), in this case, by shedding light on the geographical and temporal spread of the problem of the disappeared, the intensity of the crime over the past decades, or the transitional justice preferences in different regions.[14] These issues are seldom tackled by small-n analyses. By identifying regional and temporal patterns, however, we can minimize bias in the case selection, thereby benefiting the quality of an in-depth small-n analysis (Backer 2009; Cardenas 2010).

As suggested above, in human rights crimes, it is often impossible to determine the number of the victims to any degree of accuracy. These numbers are heavily politicized in times of transition, and the clandestine nature of the crime precludes safe conclusions about the intensity of the crime. To get around this problem, I deployed an alternative unit to measure the *intensity of the practice of disappearances*, namely, "country-disappearances-years." When reliable information indicated a country had systematic disappearances for a particular year, I included it in the database, irrespective of the precise number of the disappeared.[15] This paints a representative picture of the intensity of the problem in a country or a region.

---

[13] For amnesties, the most comprehensive database is Amnesty Law Database, available at: http://incore.incore.ulst.ac.uk/Amnesty/about.html, last accessed November 28, 2016; for trials, I drew on Transitional Justice Research Collaborative, available at: https://transitionaljusticedata.com/browse, last accessed November 28, 2016. To identify truth commissions, I drew on the Transitional Justice Research Collaborative database and USIP Truth Commission Digital Collection, available at: www.usip.org/publications/truth-commission-digital-collection, last accessed November 28, 2016. Both offer descriptive data, and it is possible to identify whether their mandate/scope of the mechanism focuses explicitly on the problem of the missing and the disappeared.

[14] A database doing interesting work on mapping trends is Mallinder (2008) and Amnesty Law Database, available at: http://incore.incore.ulst.ac.uk/Amnesty/about.html, last accessed: January 24, 2015. Collins (2013) has developed a systematic database of prosecutions in Latin America, seeking to map trends, not establish relations of statistical significance.

[15] This builds on a similar design by Sikkink (2011:137) on human rights' prosecutions.

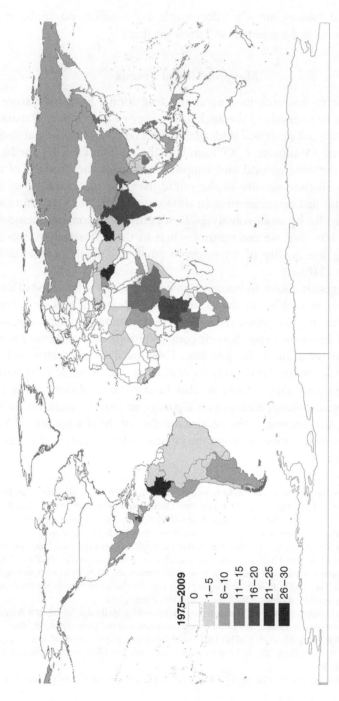

Figure 2.1   Geographic Diffusion of Enforced Disappearances (1975–2009)

Based on my analysis of the database, the map in Figure 2.1 illustrates the global diffusion of disappearances since 1975. The map includes countries with 1–5 years of disappearances, illustrated in light gray, and goes on to sketch countries with more than 20 years of disappearances, such as Colombia (27 years), Afghanistan (22 years) and Iraq (23 years), by gradating to black.

As the map indicates, the crime is an endemic feature of contemporary conflict, with a staggering 67 countries experiencing this specific form of political violence over the past 35 years. In this period, 469 "country-disappearances-years" (almost 13.5 per year) were reported, revelatory of the intensity of the phenomenon. It is also clear that the problem has been diffused to almost all parts of the world experiencing conflict or author-itarian rule, verifying an alarming finding in conflict research that civilians have become a central target of political violence (Fearon & Laitin 2003; Lacina, Gleditsch & Russett 2006; Newman 2004). Most importantly, it shows that any meaningful transition must address this humanitarian problem, as a number of families are trapped in a state of "ambiguous loss" that does not enable them to move forward (Boss 2006).

To understand how post-conflict societies have dealt with this problem over the course of the past decades, consider Figure 2.2, which shows the distribution of tools adopted by societies that have undergone a transition (not all cases).[16] The most popular mechanisms among societies in transi-tion are amnesty laws (34 percent), reflecting the predominant role of stability and security in post-conflict settings (Vinjamuri & Snyder 2004). Yet, a closer look tells a slightly different story. Most societies use amnesties to provide a minimum level of stability – deemed necessary in contexts of negotiated transitions – that usually paves the way for the adoption of another transitional justice tool, most frequently, exhumations (30 per-cent), truth commissions (21 percent), or trials (15 percent). It is equally clear that exhumations are growing in popularity as an institutional means of dealing with the problem of the disappeared. While exhumations have

---

[16] It is frequently difficult to determine the specific year of the transition. Most quantitative analyses – designed to make causal inferences – draw on the Polity IV Project database. However, my purpose is narrow: to determine the year and type of the transition. It was necessary to consider historical and political details on the transition, so I drew on evidence from UPPSALA/PRIO Conflict Termination Dataset, with some information on the conflict termination (peace agreement, ceasefire, victory, etc.), essential to deter-mine the type of transition from civil wars. To determine the type of transition from authoritarian settings, I used the Autocratic Regimes database (Geddes, Wright & Frantz 2014), which offers a short narrative of events leading to the transition. Also available at: http://dictators.la.psu.edu/, last accessed: January 23, 2015.

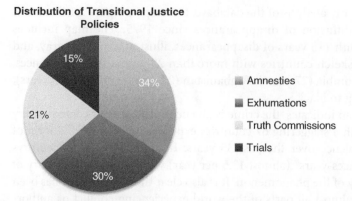

Distribution of Transitional Justice Policies

- Amnesties
- Exhumations
- Truth Commissions
- Trials

Figure 2.2 Distribution of Transitional Justice Policies in Dealing with the Disappeared

been used by almost a third of the societies in transition, this tool is neglected in mainstream transitional justice debates. Simply stated, it deserves more systematic analysis.[17]

Theory Testing

Theory testing is another important function of databases. Small-n approaches usually fall short of testing alternative hypotheses, as certain crucial variables may be absent from specific cases under scrutiny, the problem of "few cases, many variables" (Collier 1993). By way of contrast, databases offer the possibility of testing and ruling out alternative theoretical hypotheses. Although quantitative perspectives dominate the use of databases in the field, a qualitative approach could be beneficial too – reinterpreting existing knowledge, challenging theoretical assumptions and providing greater conceptual clarity. To test this assumption, I will draw on DIMIDA to evaluate the existing theories of transitional justice outcomes.

A key argument in the literature is that accountability constitutes a moral imperative because the suffering of the victims of violence should be acknowledged (Biggar 2003). A transition's failure to promote

---

[17] The literature has overlooked this popular tool, opting to discuss generic mechanisms like trials, truth commission, reparations, lustrations, etc. This tendency to focus on tools/ mechanisms of transitional justice instead of the demands of victims' groups is based on a uniform approach to victims' groups discussed above.

retributive justice conveys the message that a state has failed to perform one of its core duties and is nurturing a culture of impunity (Arthur 2009; Elster 2004; Kaminski, Nalepa & O'Neill 2006; Landsman 1997; Méndez 2001:32; Popkin & Roht-Arriazza 1995). In essence, devising a rigorous policy of prosecuting the perpetrators of gross human rights violations is considered the most effective policy to bring about stability, peaceful transformation and eventually reconciliation (Sikkink 2011; Sikkink & Walling 2007).

More specifically, proponents argue that trials and human rights prosecutions have a "deterrence" function, with the cost of resuming violence becoming prohibitive (Kim 2012; Méndez 2001; Sriram 2012). Kathryn Sikkink (2011), one of the most influential scholars in the field, argues that over the past few decades there has been a "justice cascade," a global diffusion of accountability norms for human rights abuses. States emerging from violence more frequently adopt retributive forms of (transitional) justice, revealing a growing socialization to international norms (ibid.). A gradual eradication of impunity clauses from amnesty laws has reinforced this thesis (Bell 2008).

Other idealist scholars note that because the new model of warfare has shattered inter-communal relations, the objective of societies emerging from mass violence and trauma is not merely the absence of violence but the restoration of relationships fractured by violence. To "break the cycle of hatred" (Minow 2002), societies must devise a policy that will uproot well-entrenched cultures of victimhood embedded in collective identities (Breen-Smyth 2007; Gibson 2006; Hayner 1994; Kelman 1999). The most widely cited transitional justice tool associated with the restorative approach is truth commissions; especially after the global media spotlight on the South African Truth and Reconciliation Commission, it has become a central transitional justice mechanism (Hayner 2002; Wiebelhaus-Brahm 2010). More recently, new localized forms of restorative justice have gained currency – partly as a result of the growing interest of anthropologists in traditional practices of transitional justice (Baines 2010; Quinn 2007).

Other literature considers the role of the type of transition and the distribution of power in determining transitional justice outcomes. In any society emerging from conflict, the main objective is the termination of violence and the maintenance of order, peace and stability (Cobban 2006:24; Vinjamuri 2010). Following this line of thought, the political balance of power between the parties of the conflict determines the transitional justice policy response (Huntington 1993; Olsen, Payne & Reiter 2010). As in most post-conflict settings there is little room for maneuvering, societies often prioritize stability and order, even if this means amnesties/impunity. In particularly fragile transitions where per-petrators retain power, any effort to bring them to justice has the poten-tial to mobilize spoiler groups and derail the peace process (Newman 2002; Vinjamuri & Snyder 2004). In addition, some scholars object to the use of retributive justice as a conflict-resolution mechanism, as this does not provide a "safe exit" strategy for ruthless rulers and warlords, who cling to power, prolonging conflict and increasing human suffering (Vinjamuri 2010). Hence, for "realist" scholars in fragile transitions, amnesties are a frequently used tool for a reason. Besides, amnesty laws often acquire democratic legitimacy through referendums, as illustrated by the instructive experience of Uruguay (Lessa 2012).

To examine the explanatory strengths of each of these perspectives in determining policy outcomes, Table 2.1 groups the countries included in the database according to the type of transition (if applicable) and the type of acknowledgment of the disappeared. Countries are clustered in three groups: (1) those where there has been no transition from the political context that featured disappearances (bottom row – 'No Settlement'); (2) those which have undergone a negotiated transition (middle row – 'Negotiated Settlement'); and (3) those where one of the parties in conflict achieved a victory or a transition through rupture (top row – 'Rupture') (Linz & Stepan 1996).[18]

To specify the policy preferences of societies for truth recovery for the missing persons, I suggest three broad policy options, explored in greater detail as follows: (1) *institutionalized silence* includes those societies adopting only amnesties to address the problem; (2) *Forensic truth recovery* refers to those societies relying exclusively on forensic exhuma-tions (even when coupled with amnesty laws) and (3) *broader truth recovery* includes those countries opting for a more comprehensive approach of documenting patterns of disappearances, including trials and/or truth commissions;[19] this does not exclude the possibility of being coupled with policies of exhumations or amnesties.

---

[18] I have drawn on the UPPSALA/PRIO Conflict Termination Dataset, which provides some information about the conflict termination (i.e. peace agreement, ceasefire, victory, etc.), essential to determine the type of transition from civil wars. To identify the type of transition from authoritarian settings, I have drawn on the Autocratic Regimes database, "New Data on Autocratic Breakdown and Regime Transitions" (Geddes, Wright & Frantz 2014), which offers a short narrative of events leading to the transition.

[19] Commissions of Inquiry are not considered Truth Commissions. They are included in the table only for cases where the mandate is limited to the problem of the disappeared (e.g. Morocco).

Table 2.1 *Type of Settlement and Type of Truth Recovery for the Disappeared*

	Broad Truth Recovery	Forensic Truth Recovery	Institutionalized Silence
Rupture	Algeria (2004–2003)	Ethiopia (1991–1994)	Guinea (2010)
	Chad (1990–1991)	Iraq (2003–2004)★	Nicaragua (1979)
	Cambodia (1998–2003)★	Kuwait (1991–1991)	Nigeria (1999)
	Democratic Republic of Congo (2003–2003)★	Libya (2011–2012)	Sri Lanka (2009)
	Haiti (1994–1995)	Philippines (1986–2000)	Tajikistan (1998)
	Indonesia (1999–2005)★		
	Paraguay (1993–1994)		
	Rwanda (1994–1994)★		
	Timor (1999–2002)★		
Negotiated Settlement	Argentina (1983–1983)	Angola (2002–2003)	Burundi (2006–1993)
	Bolivia (1982–1982)	Georgia (1993–2012)	Lebanon (1991)
	Brazil (1985–2011)	Mexico (2000–2002)	Senegal (2005)
	Bosnia (1995–1996)★	Namibia (1995–2005)	Vietnam (1975)
	Chile (1990–1990)	Nepal (2006–2009)	
	Croatia (1995–1999)★		
	El Salvador (1991–1992)★		
	Guatemala (1995–1997)★		
No Settlement	Morocco (2004)	Colombia (2007)	Afghanistan Sudan
		Cyprus (2004)	Azerbaijan Pakistan
		Iran (2008)	Burma/Myanmar Russia
		Zimbabwe (1999)	China Somalia
			Cuba Syria
			Eritrea Thailand
			Guinea Equatorial Turkey
			India Uganda
			Korea (North) Venezuela
			Laos Yemen

Note: Countries in asterisks indicate cases where international actors played a key role in the design of the transitional justice architecture.

The first and most obvious category includes those countries with a ruptured transition (i.e. a *total victory* or *collapse* of one of the parties in conflict) creating conducive conditions for the winning side to address the past, along with the specific policy mechanisms to do so. In places like Cambodia or Timor (Indonesia), transition is almost immediately followed by some form of official acknowledgment of disappearances, either through exhumations or truth commissions. It is not surprising, then, that the majority of countries with transitions through "rupture" adopt a broader form of truth recovery. And in fact, as the second date in parentheses indicates, the implementation of these tools occurred very soon after the transition. Occasionally, the winning side may decide to remain silent because of its own record of human rights abuses, like post-2009 Sri Lanka or Nigeria, or in cases of interstate war when access to essential information is stored on the other side. Most of the societies on this row have deployed either trials or truth commissions, yet these policies are often coupled with exhumations (forensic truth) and amnesties. The "realist" school of thought that pays attention to the balance of power and the type of transition in determining transitional justice policies is well suited to explain this group of countries.

The second and more puzzling group, the focus of this book, involves cases of negotiated transitions/peace settlements and is found in the middle row of Table 2.1. It becomes evident from the left quadrant that when societies finally decide to tackle the issue of disappearances, they frequently select a broader form of acknowledgment, usually implemented in the immediate aftermath (first 5 years) of the peace agreement or transition to democracy. At first glance, this supports the argument of scholars who underline the necessity of societies to come to terms with the past (Hayner 2002; Minow 2002; Orentlicher 1991). It seems that a significant number of countries have opted for acknowledgment of human rights abuses, despite the fragility of the peace/democratization processes. Still, a more careful look reveals that this applies to societies undergoing a transition after the normative turn of the 1990s, when dealing with the past had become internationally the appropriate way to handle such issues (Sikkink 2011). In that respect, the second date in parentheses, indicating the year a mechanism of acknowledgment/truth recovery was adopted, is interesting: with the exception of Bolivia and Uruguay, these societies established trials or truth commissions only after the 1990s. Even more interestingly, the majority of the cases are from the Americas with no Asian or Middle

Eastern country overcoming the political obstacles created by negotiated transitions.

Paradoxically, the middle and right quadrants, under "negotiated
settlements," seem to verify the "realist" argument that societies decide
to let bygones be bygones when the possibility of opening the book of
the past may derail the fragile transition process. This perspective may
be better suited to address a third group with 'No Settlement', in
particular the cases in the bottom right-hand quadrant. The absence
of a political settlement explains the non-solution of human rights
issues. It would be absurd to expect Turkey or Russia to address these
sensitive and complex human rights issues in the absence of an official
political settlement.[20]

Another central hypothesis explaining variation in policies of truth
recovery in societies emerging from conflict is the presence of external
actors in the transitional justice and peacebuilding strategy (Olsen,
Payne & Reiter 2010). A growing literature shows the presence of
international organizations often paves the way for the implementation
of transitional justice policies (Bell 2008; Méndez 2001; Newman 2002;
UN 2006).[21] External actors facilitate the adoption of transitional
justice mechanisms, either by providing the necessary resources, infrastructure and expertise, as the experience of the International Criminal
Tribunal for the former Yugoslavia (ICTY) shows (Nettlefield 2010), or
by shifting the normative considerations of domestic actors (Lutz &
Reiger 2009; Sikkink 2011).

Hence, another group, marked with an asterisk, found in 'Ruptured'
and 'Negotiated Settlements'. It involves cases where international
actors play a key role in the transitional justice architecture, prescribing
moral scrutiny of past human rights abuses. In all cases where international bodies have been involved in the task of transition or peacebuilding, the issue of disappearances has been addressed in the form of
exhumations or truth commission/trials or, more frequently, both. It is
evident that countries emerging from conflict or authoritarianism
frequently lack the resources or logistical support to undertake

---

[20] For an interesting analysis of a limited number of prosecutions in Turkey, see Mecellem
(2016).
[21] Much criticism considers the role of international actors in transitions (Richmond 2011;
Vinjamuri 2010), but these studies evaluate the impact of the intervention, while I am
interested in the decision to adopt a specific transitional justice mechanism in the first
place. There seems to be a consensus that the presence of international actors catalyzes
outcomes.

exhumations or establish war crimes tribunals, and the tasks devolve onto international actors.

How do we explain this cluster of countries? On the one hand, the idealist school of thought recognizes the moral obligation of international society to reinforce liberal peace. On the other hand, those subscribing to political realism argue that the deployment of foreign security forces and the allocation of abundant resources provide the much-needed stability for democratic consolidation and the absorption of potential turbulence triggered by a policy of dealing with the past. The cases of Iraq, Sierra Leone, the former Yugoslavia, Democratic Republic of Congo and Rwanda are obvious examples. It would have been virtually impossible to exhume almost 17,000 of the 30,000 people who went missing during the war in the Balkans (1992–1995) without the involvement of international organizations (ICMP 2014). Equally, in Iraq, the proactive stance and the available resources of the Coalition Provisional Authority was the catalyst for solving disappearances, predominantly Kurds buried in mass graves during the Al Anfal campaign of 1988 (Stover et al. 2008). The indictment of warlords and domestic leaders for crimes against humanity by the International Criminal Court (ICC) explains the inclusion of cases of protracted conflict in the group of countries with broader truth recovery, such as Sudan or Uganda (Akhavan 2005).

A final hypothesis to be tested is regional learning (Bermeo 1992). Transitional countries may be better able to deal with the disappeared if other countries in the region have already dealt with similar questions. The "justice cascade" argument (Sikkink 2011; Sikkink & Walling 2007) includes this learning feature. Societies not only take normative lessons but they also instrumentally use regional legal tools. Notably, 9 of the 15 countries in this group are from Latin America. Yet, the theory skips a step. How exactly do societies learn from each other? Moreover, learning does not account for the timing when a society jumps from amnesty to truth recovery; nor does it show possible sequences in the selection of transitional justice policies.

So the analysis of databases, even if not statistically significant, has something valuable to tell us about transitional justice processes by testing alternative hypotheses. Probably, the most significant function of databases is the refinement of theory by identifying gaps and exploring these gaps in greater detail.

Refining Theory: A New Conceptual Framework
for the Disappeared

I began this book because I was convinced a number of analytical tools of transitional justice are uncritically deployed in the literature. The term "truth recovery" is a case in point. It has been used to refer to a wide range of different processes (truth-telling), outcomes (report of truth commissions) and units of analysis (individuals and institutions) to become an overstretched concept with minimal explanatory value. Moreover, it is questionable whether "truth" can ever be retrievable in post-traumatic contexts. As illustrated in the following chapters, truth is something more than the aggregation of facts; the "truth" about the missing – where their bodies lie and how they died – does not necessarily overlap with the wider truth about human rights violations.

To overcome the pitfalls of the simplistic approach adopted by much of the literature, I propose a new analytical framework of truth recovery that focuses only on the problem of the disappeared. The framework builds a comprehensive conceptualization of truth, reflected in three levels of truth recovery for the missing/disappeared: institutionalized silence, forensic truth and broader truth.

"Institutionalized silence" refers to those societies emerging from conflict where the only policy response to the problem of the missing is the enactment of an amnesty law (de jure or de facto); this is the narrowest level of truth. The main objective in most transitions is to strengthen stability and security, partly by not pointing a finger at perpetrators. As amnesties are often the only policy response to the human rights abuses of the past, especially at an early stage after transition, this "institutionalized silence" is a common starting point – but it often lasts for decades.

Forensic truth refers to a very narrow level of truth recovery, associated with the process of exhumation, identification and return of remains to the families. All available research findings and previous personal experience from interviewing relatives of the missing suggest identification of the remains, and a proper burial constitutes the most fundamental humanitarian need of families without which it is impossible to start the mourning process (Kovras 2013; Robins 2013). Although we need more systematic research on the subject, surveys, empirical material from different countries and therapists' positions all converge: identification can bring an end to a state of "ambiguous loss" and initiate the mourning process (Boss 2006; ICRC 2013; Robins 2013; UNFICYP 2007). This is a rudimentary yet essential form of truth recovery for the missing and reparation for the relatives. Without this, any form of acknowledgment is minimal. In addition, the recovery of forensic truth corresponds to the legal duty of the state to "take the necessary measures to search for, locate and release disappeared persons and, in the event of death, locate, respect and return their human remains" (Article 24.3 of the Convention). Forensic acknowledgment clearly overlaps with the right of the families "to know the truth" (Scovazzi & Citroni 2007). One of the main advantages of this specific criterion is that it provides a relatively objective measure of truth recovery, as the number of exhumed and identified indicates progress. Moreover, forensic evidence, such as whether the dead body is found blindfolded or with a bullet hole in the back of the head, becomes an important piece in the broader puzzle of past violence. Hence, exhumations/identifications can serve as a representative measure of the effectiveness of transitional justice policies in addressing a narrow, yet pivotal, need of bereaved families.

Broader truth refers to the official processes of carrying out an effective investigation into the conditions leading to the disappearances in the first place. This may take the form of an official fact-finding body, such as a truth commission, or legal mechanisms tasked to hold perpetrators accountable for the crime. This level of truth overlaps with the international legal framework on enforced disappearance mentioned above.[22] Although they adopt different methods of documenting the past, they are both designed to officially investigate and document the conditions of human rights violations, including the disappeared. Once again, broader truth corresponds to two central legal duties of the state; thus, it makes sense to assess a state's handling of its legal obligations. First, the state has a duty to "carry out prompt and impartial investigation of an alleged enforced disappearance" (Article 12.1 of the

---

[22] See Articles 24.2 and 24.4 of the International Convention for the Protection of all Persons from Enforced Disappearances. According to the European Convention of Human Rights, failure to investigate is a breach of the "right to life" (Article 2, para 1 of the Convention), revealing the emergence of a robust international legal framework over the "duty of the state to investigate." For a similar decision, see the European Court on Fourth Interstate Application of the Republic of Cyprus vs. Turkey, May 10, 2001. Application no. 25781/94.

Convention) (Vibhute 2008). Second, it has a "duty to prosecute" perpetrators and an obligation

> to hold a person who commits, orders, solicits or induces the commission of forced disappearance, assists or participates in the commission of an act of enforced disappearance, criminally responsible, and to disallow a subordinate officer to justify his act of enforced disappearance on the ground of superior orders.

> (Article 6; see McCrory 2007)

I am not making a clear-cut distinction among these three levels of truth. Societies often cross over between levels. In fact, one of my central objectives is to explain variations in societies' adoption of transitional justice tools and their movement from one level to another level of truth recovery. Note that the framework is a way to categorize mechanisms for dealing with the problem of the missing; it does not necessarily assess their effectiveness. The levels of truth do not reflect a normative position on which policies are better suited to deal with the missing. In fact, as will become evident in the following chapters, some countries have not climbed the higher rung of this ladder of truth but have still managed to accommodate some of the most pressing demands of the relatives.

The framework is designed to provide an analytically rigorous picture of the different approaches to transitional justice and truth recovery. First, contrary to the almost exclusive focus of the literature on the period of transition or the immediate aftermath, this framework paints a fluid picture, one that explains post-transitional developments. Second and following on the first, it is flexible and dynamic. It sheds light on why the attempts of certain societies to leap high hurdles, such as amnesty laws, are more successful, enabling these societies to reach higher levels of truth. At the same time, it helps us understand why other societies have been less effective or less inclined to take the leap. Third, all the three levels represent different mainstream perspectives to truth recovery for the missing. The flexible framework eschews the simplistic binary approach frequently adopted by quantitative approaches to measuring transitional justice. Such perspectives do not permit nuances or encourage complexities. The analytical framework suggested here gives us room for analytical maneuvering, while remaining consistent. Finally, as illustrated in the case studies, this framework encourages a long-term evaluation of the success of a deployed transitional justice mechanism, one that goes well beyond the period of transition.

Timing and Sequencing in Truth Recovery for the Disappeared

The design of transitional justice in any society reflects a balance between opportunities for and constraints to truth recovery, but this equilibrium is not predetermined. The struggle for truth is a dynamic process, and the passage of time offers novel opportunities for domestic truth-seeking actors, predominantly relatives' associations, to revise a transitional settlement. Figure 2.3 illustrates this point. The graph includes all countries that enacted an amnesty law during transition or are currently in a frozen status (e.g. de facto partition). On the vertical axis, I have included the level of freedom and quality of democracy in each country since its transition. This is based on data in Freedom House, which ascribes every country a mark from 1 to 7 (where 1 stands for the highest score on civil and political liberties and 7 for the lowest). On the horizontal axis, I have calculated the number of years since the transition took place. In the graph, the black triangles indicate countries that have set up either a forensic or broad truth recovery process, while rhombi indicate those with an important international presence in the establishment of truth recovery mechanisms. Squares indicate countries where amnesty law has not been followed by any other policy of truth, and silence prevails, such as Lebanon.

We might expect those societies with greater democratic consolidation to be more effective in their attempts to acknowledge the truth about the

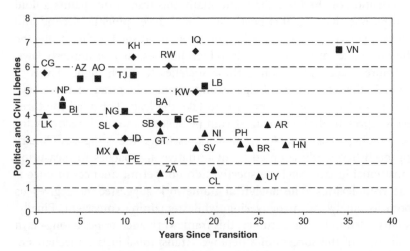

Figure 2.3 Passage of Time, Opportunities and Truth Recovery

disappeared. This hypothesis overlaps with a central premise of the literature of contentious politics (Tarrow 1998; Tilly 1995). That is, the success
of a group's mobilization depends largely on the availability of political
opportunities, such as the presence of elite allies, openness of the political
system and states' capacity for repression (Gamson & Meyer 1996;
McAdam 1999; McAdam, Tilly & Tarrow 2001). In other words, the
democratization of key institutions should open a window of opportunity
for relatives. The bottom right area of the chart suggests this is true; the
families of the missing were effective in their search for the truth in all
societies where institutional tools were available (i.e. stability, democratic
consolidation and civil liberties). In addition, all societies scoring less than
3 (reflecting a relatively high quality of democracy) overcame the obstacles
set by amnesty law by establishing domestic mechanisms of truth recovery,
not by turning to international actors.

As we move upwards on the vertical axis, we see that only in countries
where the international community assumed a proactive role in
the transitional justice architecture were amnesties surpassed.
The remaining societies did not manage to break the silence. In fact,
the experience of several countries, including Lebanon, clearly indicates
that if time passes without simultaneous improvement of the quality of
democracy, the prospect of accommodation remains negligible. Hence, it
is not the amnesty per se that perpetuates silence but the absence of
necessary conditions for the mobilization of the relatives to overcome the
"institutionalized silence"; these conditions include security, democratic
consolidation, and civil and political liberties.

Amnesties constitute the most frequently used tool in transitional
settings. Interestingly, in some societies their deployment blocks truth
recovery while other societies fare better. Amnesties are designed to
perform a specific function, namely to bolster stability in the aftermath
of fragile transitions. Whether this minimum level of stability will be used
by domestic actors to build an inclusive democratic nation and set the
stage for truth recovery is a question that exceeds the role of amnesties in
a transition. Although not conducive to truth recovery, an amnesty law is
clearly not an insurmountable obstacle. Especially in the case of enforced
disappearances where "ongoing crimes" are not subject to statutes of
limitations, amnesties should not be treated as the exclusive or even the
primary cause of silence (Freeman 2009; Mallinder 2008).

Truth recovery is a dynamic process, not necessarily determined by
transitional settlements; societies usually renegotiate these settlements

when political opportunities are present, but this is often a time-consuming enterprise. Cyprus started exhuming graves 30 years after the Turkish invasion (1974), Brazil set up a truth commission only in 2011 (Coelho-Filho 2012) and Chile brought perpetrators to justice 25 years after the crimes (Collins 2011). In Spain, recovery of the victims of the civil war was delayed for almost seven decades (Aguilar 2008). It seems the passage of time creates new opportunities for families to overcome amnesties, at least in countries where key institutions become democratized. This leads to an interesting question: once a country breaks this silence, does it follow a particular sequence in its adoption of transitional justice tools?

To examine in greater detail whether there is a particular sequence and timing in the adoption of truth recovery mechanisms, Figure 2.4 shows on its right-hand vertical axis the average number of years intervening between the transition and the year of adoption of each of the four central policies (i.e. amnesties, trials, truth commissions and exhumations), which appear on the horizontal axis.[23] The left-hand vertical axis shows the number of countries employing each policy. There is a clear element of timing in the decision of the countries to adopt specific transitional justice instruments. The starting point for all countries is the adoption of amnesty laws, deemed pivotal in strengthening stability and security in fragile transitions; in fact, in most countries this predates the transition (−0.62) by half a year. Interestingly, both exhumations and truth commissions take place almost concurrently, on average 3.5 years after the transition. It is worth noting that the number of countries using exhumations exceeds the number setting up truth commissions. Trials remain the most difficult and time-consuming step: it takes on average 10.1 years to prosecute and convict someone for the crime of disappearances, and few countries have brought perpetrators to justice.

---

[23] This draws on a previous example of Olsen, Payne and Reiter (2010). The different nature of the transitional tools deployed here makes it difficult to identify the year of adoption. Some policies, such as amnesty laws or truth commissions, are enacted within a specific year and are easily identifiable. But trials and exhumations are often temporally dispersed, inhibiting the effort to identify the year of adoption. To get around this problem, the year of adoption of exhumations is the first year where evidence suggests a forensic team systematically worked on unearthing graves, even if it was not followed or was interrupted. For trials, it is the first year an individual was convicted on charges related to the crime of disappearance. I abandoned the idea of using the year of indictment, as these prosecutions often lead to acquittal or are even dismissed, thereby making it difficult to suggest that such evidence is sufficient to categorize a country as reaching broader truth.

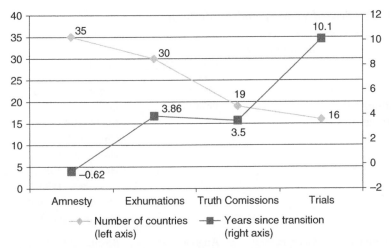

Figure 2.4 Timing of Truth Recovery for the Disappeared

Hence, although most societies have the same starting point, that is, amnesty laws, this is not the end of the process for the majority. As time passes, new opportunities arise, and relatives, as the most political actors, are strategic in prioritizing and framing their demands (Benford 1997; Benford & Snow 2000). They usually begin with the most pressing (humanitarian) demands for finding the whereabouts of their loved ones and, when the time is ripe, proceed to more political or judicial forms of truth recovery. To be sure, transitional justice processes are not linear, and there are ruptures. Broadly speaking, however, truth recovery is driven by a logic of "peeling the onion" with every layer connected to a previous one. This strategic element of truth recovery is explored below.

But does this sequence work in all societies in the same manner? Do families in post-conflict societies have the same opportunities and face the same challenges in recovering the truth, as relatives in post-authoritarian states?

Types of Violence and Levels of Truth Recovery

One of the key findings of my analysis of the database is that the *form of violence* responsible for the creation of the problem of the missing largely *determines the type of truth recovery* a society will pursue after transition. This will become more evident in the analysis of individual cases in Part III of the book. Table 2.2 shows all countries in the database experiencing a transition followed by an amnesty law and conflicts in a "frozen" status,

Table 2.2 *Type of Violence and Truth Recovery*

	Institutionalized Silence	Forensic Truth	Broader Truth
Post-authoritarian Settings		Mexico Philippines	Argentina (1983) Bolivia (1982) Brazil (1985) Chile (1989) Haiti (1994) Honduras (1981) Indonesia (1999) South Africa (1995) Uruguay (1984)
Post-conflict Settings	Georgia Lebanon Nepal Nigeria Sri Lanka Tajikistan Vietnam	Angola Cyprus Iraq Kuwait Namibia	Bosnia (1995)* Cambodia (1997)* Democratic Republic of Congo (2008) * El Salvador (1992)* Guatemala (1997)* Peru (2001) Serbia (1995)* Sierra Leone (2002)*

Note: Countries in asterisks indicate cases where international actors played a key role in the design of the transitional justice architecture.

the two biggest challenges to the recovery of truth. I grouped these countries according to the level of truth recovery: the left column shows societies with amnesty laws that also carried out forensic exhumations and the right column includes countries using a broader mechanism of truth recovery (trials or truth commission) as well as amnesties and exhumations. I then categorized the countries according to the type of violence (post-conflict vs. post-authoritarian). The first date in parentheses refers to the year of transition and the second, if applicable, to the year a transitional justice policy was implemented.

The countries in the top row, the post-authoritarian societies, are especially intriguing. First, amnesty law did not become an insurmountable obstacle in any of them; in fact, all carried out exhumations, often coupled with a policy of broader truth (either trials or truth commissions). The majority proceeded to the setting up of either truth commissions, as in South Africa and Uruguay, or judicial mechanisms of accountability, as in Argentina and Chile. Interestingly, most countries presented in Table 2.2 are located in Latin America. This partly verifies the regional learning argument, as most societies drew on the experiences of their neighbors (Bermeo 1992; Sikkink 2008). The image is radically different in post-conflict transitions. As the bottom left column illustrates, a large number of the countries undergoing a transition from conflict to peaceful democratic consolidation never managed to overcome the obstacles thrown in their path by amnesty. Even more interestingly, as we see in the bottom right quadrant, only those societies where international actors helped shape transitional justice policies (marked with asterisks) reached the level of broader truth. The lone exception is Peru where the impact of regional norms is probably catalytic on explaining the outcome, especially if we consider the timing of the transition (2000s). In most cases, in the absence of external influences, the best post-conflict societies could hope for was forensic truth.

These findings illuminate how the nature of violence can shape the framework within which actors design policies of dealing with the past, not to mention the creation of opportunities available to truth-seeking actors. Most accounts fail to notice that the type of crimes committed during a period of violence often determine post-transitional justice settlements. The logic of abductions in the context of civil wars ranges from instilling terror to cleansing specific areas of the "other," as in the massive waves of disappearances in Mayan-dominated regions in Guatemala (Sanford 2003). Abductions can become a bargaining chip to exchange captured soldiers, as the experience of Lebanon shows. But victims are usually civilians; their abduction is instrumentally used to reach strategic objectives, including preventing defection or collaboration with the enemy (Kalyvas 2006). The tool of abduction can span decades in ongoing conflicts, leading to the institutionalization of lawlessness, as illustrated by Colombia and Afghanistan. Legacies of violence are transmitted over generations, as evident in the recent effort of the grandchildren of the disappeared of the Spanish civil war to uncover the remains of their ancestors (Aguilar 2008; Minow 2002).

This deviates from the logic of disappearances in authoritarian settings, usually used as a counterinsurgency tool against specific targets, including civilian members of militant groups, usually framed as "terrorists" and "security" threats. Such operations are often confined to a particular period, typically the aftermath of a military coup, in an effort to limit resistance. For example, in Chile and Argentina, despite the extremely high numbers of disappearances, the practice was almost terminated in the second or third year of the dictatorships.

In post-authoritarian settings, irrespective of the depth of the trauma, there is a clear-cut cleavage between those who support democracy and those who sympathize with the military; the key cleavage emerges or becomes more salient usually after the emergence of dictatorship and the commission of crimes. This contrasts with deeply divided societies, as these are commonly marked by well-entrenched religious or ethnic cleavages that usually precede conflict. In such contexts, new human rights abuses are framed within the lenses of past atrocities, creating a restrictive and politicized framework within which human rights can be addressed. Therefore, leaders in post-conflict settings are usually guided by "realist" considerations, often prioritizing (negative) peace and stability. But in post-authoritarian contexts, the framework is slightly more flexible, enabling leaders to set up mechanisms of broader truth, including truth commissions or trials. In fact, the restoration of democracy and party politics means that victims' groups – despite facing important obstacles – have more institutional avenues to express their needs, predominantly by establishing influential political alliances. If they are skillful in framing their cause, it becomes possible to introduce their demands to the political agenda. These opportunities are simply absent in societies emerging from conflict.

Another feature distinguishing post-conflict from post-authoritarian settings is the number of parties involved. In contexts of civil wars, there are usually two or more paramilitary groups engaging in disappearances. In fact, it is not uncommon for neighboring countries to use local proxies to carry out human rights abuses, as the experiences of the Democratic Republic of Congo or Lebanon illustrate (Autesserre 2010). The difficulty of assigning responsibilities to myriad actors – especially those that are not present in the country – constrains broader truth recovery. For example, any comprehensive model of broader truth recovery in Cyprus would require the participation of Turkey, and that would entail access to its military archives, an impossible scenario even four decades after the Turkish invasion. In transition from authoritarianism, where one actor, usually the military, is likely responsible for the crime, broader truth is relatively easier. Over time and with democratization, a new leadership emerges in the military. These new leaders will often accept some form of wider truth recovery that allows the military to distance itself from the past and promotes an image more accommodating of popular demands (Bakiner 2010).

Surprisingly, though, a policy of forensic truth may be implemented more easily in post-conflict than post-authoritarian settings. To explain this apparent paradox, it is important to understand the role of perpetrators. In post-authoritarian settings, the military is often the only source of information on burial sites, but the hierarchical decision-making structure of the military institutionalizes a top to bottom silence that blocks forensic truth. In other words, those who made the decisions are not willing to talk. Even if low-ranking officers are eager to share information about gravesites, as the experience of Chile illustrates, it may be impossible for them to break the silence imposed by the higher echelons of the military (see Chapter 9). In post-conflict settings, the larger number of perpetrators and the loose structure of paramilitary groups usually open a window of opportunity for forensic truth recovery, especially when followed by institutional incentives. The crucial difference is that these carrots – usually immunity, anonymity and confidentiality – are offered directly to individual perpetrators, circumventing hierarchical structures. This direct appeal to perpetrators can work even under the least likely conditions, as the experiences of Cyprus, Colombia and Northern Ireland indicate.

At the same time, the challenges and the dilemmas faced by post-conflict societies trying to approach the problem of the missing are greater than those encountered by post-authoritarian societies. The weakness of state institutions, the feeble infrastructure and the priority of boosting economic recovery and accommodating the demands of survivors of the conflict often throw up major obstacles to a more comprehensive form of truth recovery, especially in the presence of negotiated/pacted transitions based on mutual silence (Kovras 2013; Zalaquett 1990). In contrast, state institutions may be weakened during an autocratic regime, but they are usually not annihilated. For example, even during the reign of Pinochet in Chile, the judiciary was still operating (albeit within an extremely confined space), thereby providing an opportunity for relatives to bring their cases to court (Collins 2010). Although none of these lawsuits was effective, the strategy was instrumental in keeping an official paper trail of the crimes, a useful tool in subsequent truth recovery initiatives, such as the truth commission. Finally, in the aftermath of state repression, relatives have more institutional tools available, including the media; they also have better economic prospects and access to political parties to voice their demands.

Admittedly, in contexts of complex political violence, it is difficult to draw such a distinction. It is not uncommon for civil wars to erupt amidst a dictatorial regime, and people may disappear as a result of authoritarian repression or go missing in violence occasioned by civil war. For example, during the Iran–Iraq war, thousands of people went missing on the battlefields of a bloody interstate war; this was followed by Saddam Hussein's use of disappearance as a tool of repression against Kurds in the late 1980s. When the sources of violence overlap, it is often impossible to determine whether people have gone missing because of a civil war or because of an authoritarian state's repressive techniques.

All these point to the different nature of truth recovery in post-conflict and post-authoritarian transitions. Families of the missing, in contexts of ethnic conflict, are guided by a "humanitarian logic" that prioritizes the recovery of the whereabouts of their loved ones. Their ability to push for truth commissions or trials is limited by contextual factors: political opportunities are absent, channels to policy-makers blocked and priorities are shifted toward an elite settlement rather than the needs of grassroots groups. That said, in societies emerging from state repression, in parallel with the humanitarian logic, we find an "instrumental" approach to truth recovery, which indicates each step is a means to a high end (i.e. official acknowledgment of their suffering, justice, etc.).

Phase-Based Theoretical Framework

Figure 2.5 illustrates the timing and sequencing of various transitional justice policies in solving the problem of the disappeared. It proposes a phased-based theory to explain variations in truth recovery in negotiated transitions. Separating truth recovery into distinct phases, the framework shows how the relative impact of different factors varies across each phase. In the early period after a negotiated transition, amnesty laws and concerns about security and stability may inhibit truth recovery efforts. To cross this initial phase of "institutionalized silence," most families prioritize a "forensic" form of truth by exhuming and identifying victims. In the presence of amnesties, the success of societies in crossing to this "forensic" phase of truth depends on the design of institutional incentives offered to perpetrators to come forward with valid information on burial sites; such "carrots" include immunity

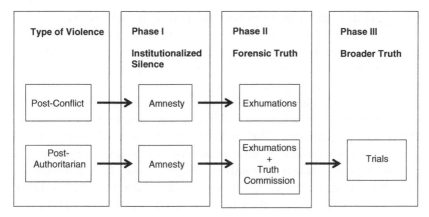

Figure 2.5   Phase-Based Truth Recovery for the Disappeared

from prosecution, confidentiality of information and depoliticization of debates about the disappeared. This "forensic" stage is the end of the truth recovery process for most countries emerging from conflict. The families' struggle for truth is guided by a humanitarian logic that prioritizes finding their loved ones' bodies.

By way of contrast, most post-authoritarian societies that manage to link exhumations to truth commissions proceed to the next phase of "broader" truth recovery. In essence, while the humanitarian demand for recovering the truth is present, the struggle of the families of the disappeared takes on instrumental proportions. That is, for a significant part of the relatives, exhumations are seen as tools that open the door to documenting the crime and eventually to retributive justice. As time passes, new opportunities arise for an official investigation of the conditions behind the disappearances, and the society enters a phase of "broader" truth recovery. Forensic evidence from the graves, coupled with the documentation of patterns of abuses by truth commissions, greatly facilitate the struggle of families for retributive justice. The effectiveness of this "broader" truth recovery depends on the mobilization of families and their effectiveness in deploying domestic and international legal tools, forming influential alliances and politicizing the problem.

The framework transcends the static picture more commonly offered by quantitative approaches and sheds light on the timing and sequencing of transitional justice mechanisms in dealing with the problem of the disappeared. It also illustrates how the nature of violence (conflict vs. state repression) determines the type of truth recovery. Societies emerging from civil wars face more complex challenges, and in the absence of international intervention, it becomes next to impossible to implement a mechanism of broader truth recovery.

To explain when a society overcomes the obstacles set by amnesty law and crosses the threshold of forensic truth, it is important to understand the role of perpetrators. Obviously, the effectiveness of forensic truth depends on the quality of information on the location of graves; as perpetrators are (usually) the only eyewitnesses, they have a monopoly on information. Determining the conditions under which it becomes more probable for perpetrators to come forward with information will determine forensic truth.

Three conditions are particularly important for this level of truth to bear fruit. First, a minimum level of *security and stability* is necessary. As the experience of Lebanon suggests, it is unlikely for perpetrators to participate if the transition is followed by ongoing instability. The continuation of an "embedded security apparatus" and the non-effective demobilization of paramilitary groups exacerbate the situation. In contexts of continued destabilization, sharing contentious information could lead to reprisals against family or community members; thus, even low-ranking paramilitaries are reluctant to divulge information. In the absence of rudimentary conditions of security, it is improbable for perpetrators to point to graves.

A second critical condition is the *design of the policy*. As forensic findings from exhumations constitute incriminatory evidence that may lead to the prosecution of those who share information, some provisions of immunity from prosecution and confidentiality over the management of information are necessary. As Chapter 7 shows, this has been the secret of success of the Committee for Missing Persons (CMP) in Cyprus. We find some evidence of it in Northern Ireland as well. And it has been an effective formula in Colombia; despite the continued violence, since 2005, the Peace and Justice Law has enabled almost 3000 families to bury their loved ones (Latin American Herald Tribune 2014). Part and parcel of the "carrots" offered to perpetrators/eyewitnesses is the confidential and informal processing of information. This means low-profile commissions decoupled from other transitional justice mechanisms have more realistic chances of boosting the credibility and effectiveness of forensic truth. In countries like Chile, where humanitarian exhumations have been led by judges, mechanisms for forensic truth are considerably less effective. A properly designed policy may address the relatives' need for a body, yet this usually requires some form of immunity.

Finally, *depoliticization* of the debates about the missing is necessary. Framing the problem in humanitarian terms is critical, especially in negotiated peace settlements where conflicting parties may prefer to remain silent about the past to maintain a negotiated pact, or in "frozen conflicts" where human rights are instrumentally used to promote political objectives in negotiations. The experience of Cyprus is revelatory. It was only when the problem of the missing was *depoliticized* and *delinked* from political negotiations that the CMP became a winning formula (Kovras 2012). Essentially, when the problem is framed in humanitarian terms, forensic truth gains currency. In addition, the role of international actors is pivotal in the credibility of the humanitarian framing. In short, for forensic truth to take place, perpetrators must be motivated to share information about gravesites; they must feel secure, the issue must be depoliticized and a package of carefully designed incentives (immunity, confidentiality) must be proffered.

In sharp contrast, to cross the threshold of broader truth, the mobilization of families becomes crucial. Although the persistence of the families is a common denominator in all societies, only certain ones have moved toward setting up judicial mechanisms of accountability.

To explain this process, the social movement theory offers the most appropriate analytical framework. Different strands of the social movement literature seek to explain the repertoires of mobilization deployed by contentious groups and what determines their success (Kriesi 1995a; McAdam, Tilly & Tarrow 2001; Meyer 2004). Although most analyses focus on contentious mobilization in consolidated democracies, the analytical insights are relevant in understanding how victims' groups mobilize in democratic transitions. Two clusters of the literature are particularly useful in explaining variations in the outcomes of relatives' mobilization. First, "contentious politics," the dominant framework notes the importance of the availability of (external) political opportunities (Meyer 2004). Political opportunities, such as access to political decision-making (domestic and international), access to influential political actors (i.e. political parties, transnational actors, international NGOs, etc.), as well as levels of state repression (expected to gradually decline with democratization of institutions), are all critical in explaining the consequences of mobilization (Keck & Sikkink 1998; McAdam,

Tarrow & Tilly 2009; Roht-Arriazza & Mariezcurrena 2006; Tarrow 1998; Tilly 1995).[24]

The most significant variable is the degree of *democratic consolidation following authoritarianism*. Democratization of institutions offers necessary new opportunities to domestic truth-seeking actors, especially the families. These include independence of the judiciary, lodging lawsuits in courts of law, unrestricted reporting of experiences in the press and democratization of the military. In the absence of these conditions, it is impossible to uncover broader truth and bring perpetrators to justice.

Although they are necessary, external conditions/opportunities alone are insufficient. This highlights the second important point. Agency is required. For example, families must be able to frame a particular situation as "unjust" and in need of redress (Benford & Snow 2000; Goffman 1974; Klandermans 1997). The framing strategies of victims' groups have received relatively little attention,[25] yet they are important in understanding how demands resonate with different (domestic and international) audiences, including political elites, media, judicial authorities, international NGOs and foreign governments. Families must frame debates about human rights in a way that captures the hearts and minds of actors who will add the issue to the political agenda. In contrast to forensic truth, which requires depoliticization, the objective of relatives is to create influential alliances, convince the public of their undeserved suffering and put pressure on the government to set up authoritative mechanisms to recover broader truth. Creating alliances with such domestic actors as political parties, judges and journalists is pivotal. Access to *international allies*, such as transnational advocacy networks (Keck & Sikkink 1998), is equally key as these allies can offer expertise, logistics and financial support.

Societies linking exhumations with the setting up of a truth commission have a far better chance of bringing perpetrators to justice, in spite of a delay that seems inevitable. As illustrated previously, almost all societies emerging from authoritarianism that coupled exhumation and truth commissions eventually proceeded to criminal investigation of the past too. An interesting exception is South Africa, discussed in detail in Chapter 8. The forensic evidence, coupled with authoritative documentation of patterns of past human rights abuses, inevitably facilitates the

---

[24] For a historical account of the emergence of the transnational civil society, see (Davis 2014)

[25] For exceptions, see Keck and Sikkink (1998), Sikkink (2011), Clark (2010) and Brysk (1994).

struggle of families in court. Although building influential (political) alliances or preparing legal cases is time-consuming, it is a necessary prerequisite for success in court. As the ensuing chapters show, groups of relatives in some countries have skillfully used powerful symbolic images, including vigils, mothers in white/black scarves, bones exhumed from graves, to lend credence to their framing. This symbolic aspect of their mobilization, when coupled with the scientific evidence from the graves and authoritative accounts of patterns of abuses documented by truth commissions, increases the appeal of calls for accountability. In such contexts, relatives are effective in the drive to achieve broader truth recovery.

Three conditions determine the effectiveness of relatives' struggle: a minimum level consolidation of democratic institutions, politicization of the problem of the missing and incriminatory evidence from forensic truth. This highlights the "paradox" of truth recovery: forensic truth is needed for relatives to reach closure, yet the monopoly of information remains in the hands of those persons least inclined to divulge it, the culprits. Perpetrators have more interest in abstaining from retributive/broader truth, yet as time passes, this outcome is determined more and more by the power and effectiveness of the mobilization of relatives. Truth recovery often involves a delicate balance between the relative power of two groups of actors with conflicting objectives, but whose success frequently depends on the political action of the other.

At the beginning of the chapter, I noted a "dialogue of the deaf" in the literature, yet it turns out that different scholars focus on different processes of the broader transitional justice architecture. Realist scholars build their theories by studying primarily societies emerging from conflicts; it is hardly surprising, then, that they prioritize the role of amnesty laws, stability, security, the role of spoilers/perpetrators and elite agreements in peace settlements. These insights are incredibly important in explaining truth recovery in post-conflict settings. At the same time, idealist scholars, usually more optimistic about transitional justice outcomes, seek to account for the "justice cascade" and the diffusion of human rights norms. Accordingly, they build their theories by exploring the experience of societies emerging from authoritarian rule. The two strands shed light on two different, yet interesting, aspects of transitional justice. Understanding their analytical strengths and limitations is important, as certain insights are more relevant in some cases than others.

Being aware of the various vantage points from which transitional justice theories approach key processes is useful to analysts. For example, the process of truth recovery is radically different in post-conflict and post-authoritarian settings. In the former, a "humanitarian" logic of truth recovery delimits the ability of relatives to get something more than exhumations. Realist scholars have done a great job explaining the obstacles to transitional justice, including stability, security, incorporating perpetrators/spoilers, etc. (Vinjamuri & Snyder 2004). In contrast, by focusing on post-authoritarian societies, idealist scholars are better suited to unfold the "incremental logic" of truth recovery and the transformative role of victims' groups in transitions. In short, to overcome the dialogue of the deaf, we must acknowledge these fine differences in angles and incorporate the strengths of each approach.

Case Selection Explained

The analysis so far has showed how the database can help develop a novel and dynamic framework of truth recovery. Yet by depending exclusively on the database, we cannot trace the processes leading to particular outcomes or understand how a country moves from one phase of truth to another. It is necessary to test the validity of the framework in comparative small-n analysis. Qualitative historically oriented databases of events facilitate a careful and transparent case selection that will permit in-depth small-n qualitative analysis. With access to a universe of cases, it becomes easier to identify "crucial cases," outliers or cases that are more representative of specific patterns we want to scrutinize in greater detail (Collier & Mahoney 1996; Gerring 2004; Lieberman 2005; Seawright & Gerring 2007). At the same time, the use of a the database minimizes selection bias.

Table 2.3 is tailored to the problem of the disappeared and is based on the framework of truth proposed here. The four columns represent four different approaches to truth recovery for the disappeared. The first column includes countries with amnesties, and the second column includes societies where amnesty law was followed by exhumations. The third column includes countries where the previous tools were coupled with the setting up of truth commissions, and finally the last column shows countries that took all steps up to trials.

A case from each column is carefully selected to explain: the puzzling variation in transitional justice outcomes and the particular sequencing and timing of transitional justice policies. Although each country is

Table 2.3 *Distribution of Countries According to Levels of Truth Recovery*

Amnesties (Level 1)	Exhumations (Level 2)	Truth Commissions (Level 3)	Trials (Level 4)
Afghanistan	Angola	Brazil	Argentina
Burundi	Colombia	El Salvador*	Bolivia
India	**Cyprus**	**South Africa**	**Chile**
Lebanon	Georgia	Haiti	Honduras
Pakistan	Honduras	Philippines	Croatia*
Senegal	Iraq*	Timor*	DR Congo*
Sri Lanka	Kuwait*	Sierra Leone*	Liberia*
Nicaragua	Libya		Guatemala*
Tajikistan	Mexico		Peru
Guinea	Namibia		Cambodia*
Thailand	Nepal		Serbia* Bosnia*
Vietnam	Zimbabwe		Rwanda*
Yemen			Uruguay

Note: Countries in asterisks indicate cases where international actors played a key role in the design of the transitional justice architecture.

discussed in a separate chapter, the cases are selected to be comparable to facilitate conclusions.

The case selection uses the following criteria. First, I am looking only for cases of negotiated transitions or countries with frozen conflicts – deemed to be the most challenging cases. As the intervention of international organizations in transitions often determines policy outcomes, all cases must be driven primarily by domestic actors. To be sure, international influences/norms are very important and affect domestic processes, but my objective is to exclude cases with the direct involvement of international actors in the design of a peacebuilding structure. Similarly, it is important for the transition – or conflict termination – to have taken place before 2000. After 2000, the intervention of the international community became more proactive in shaping transitional justice. The time lag also permits us to draw safer conclusions about the processes that enabled (or prohibited) the renegotiation of transitional settlements. Most significantly, to probe the generalizability of the findings so far, it is important to select two countries emerging from conflict as well as two societies in the aftermath of authoritarianism. Finally, all cases reflect regional patterns. Four cases meeting these criteria are Lebanon, Cyprus, South Africa and Chile.

The cases are contrasting and represent puzzling variations, thus strengthening the comparative scope of the analysis. Lebanon has had an amnesty law since 1991 and has never managed to get past the first level of "institutionalized silence." The Lebanese experience is representative of a number of countries where the presence of an amnesty law has prohibited other forms of truth from emerging. Despite the proactive efforts of the families of approximately 17,000 disappeared, over the course of the past three decades, there has been no attempt to accommodate their demands. The case of Lebanon is also illustrative of the regional patterns in the Middle East or Asia, where amnesties remain the predominant tool to deal with the disappeared. It makes sense to deploy one of the few cases in the region with an official transition to explain why it was impossible for the county to reach even forensic truth.

The Cypriot experience is puzzling, especially when compared to Lebanon. The countries have similar background conditions, including the involvement of external actors (Turkey and Greece) in the conflict, and a regional proximity and temporal overlap, but Cyprus has crossed to level 2 of truth (forensic truth) and exhumed the missing. Strangely enough, in Cyprus, there has been no official political solution to the conflict. Nevertheless, despite the partition of the island and the "frozen status" of conflict, the two communities have made the CMP a fruitful bicommunal project, although admittedly with a significant delay. Cypriot experience is worth exploring as it could be an instructive model for dealing with sensitive questions of human rights in contexts of ongoing or frozen conflicts.

South Africa is the most representative case of level 3 of truth recovery, with its much celebrated "Truth and Reconciliation Commission." The transition that followed the end of apartheid was based on an amnesty law, which did not preclude exhumations of missing persons or the setting up of the truth commission, mandated to document human rights violations, including kidnappings and disappearances. Moreover, as Africa is the region where the truth commission is the most widely used tool (after amnesties), the South African experience can shed light on regional patterns and show the effectiveness of truth commissions in dealing with the disappeared. Oddly, despite linking truth commissions with exhumations, South Africa is one of only a few post-authoritarian societies not taking the final step to retributive justice. This oddity sheds light on the obstacles societies face when they seek to hold perpetrators accountable.

For its part, Chile is globally one of the most challenging cases. The transition to democracy was based on a very fragile negotiated settlement; Pinochet and the army retained their popularity well after the transition. Yet in spite of the amnesty law and the negotiated nature of the transition, truth-seeking groups managed to reach the highest level of truth, establishing both truth commissions and judicial mechanisms to bring perpetrators to justice, with forensic truth also in place. The Chilean transition took place during the same overall period as the South African one, raising a puzzling question: why were Chile's efforts to bring perpetrators to justice more effective? Finally, Chile is arguably one of the most representative cases of Latin American countries, often characterized as the "global leader in transitional justice" (Forsythe 2011:559). If we exclude cases with international intervention/imposition of trials, all countries achieving level 4 of truth recovery (trials), including Argentina, Guatemala, Peru, Uruguay and El Salvador, are in Latin America. It makes sense, therefore, to use the Chilean experience to evaluate the virtues and vices of the retributive forms of justice in the management of the problem of the missing.

PART II

Global and Historical Perspectives

The Daughters of Antigone in Latin America

Argentinian Mothers

> After my son and his wife disappeared, I never again heard from any of my six
> sisters or my brother. They all avoided us. It has been 17 years since I last saw
> them. They were terrified that the same thing would happen to them.
>
> (Raquel Marizcurrena, cited in Arditti 1999:83)

The terrorizing effect of enforced disappearances described by Raquel
Marrizcurrena is a unique feature of the crime, making it an extremely
useful tool: by disappearing a small number of victims, perpetrators
ensure the compliance of the broader society. Relatives often believe
a reckless move will jeopardize the lives of their loved ones, if they are
still alive; neighbors and friends are equally terrified and distance themselves from the families, fearing for their own safety.

In Argentina, the military leaders deployed disappearances as the main
tool of repression; in the period from 1976 to 1983, they disappeared
10,000–30,000 people. In selecting this technique, they drew on the
experiences of other countries in the region, as for example, Chile.
Public executions in stadiums in Chile shocked and galvanized the
international community (1973–1975). The Argentine military, with
the wisdom of hindsight and responding to international pressures to
comply with human rights practices (Hafner-Burton & Ron 2009:239;
Ron 1997), deployed disappearances as a more clandestine form of
repression. This enabled them not only to gather intelligence through
illegal detention and torture but also to distance themselves from the
crime. In the absence of official registration in prisons or a dead body, the
military could easily deny the existence of the crime in the first place.

To carry out disappearances on a massive scale requires systematic
collaboration among different strands of the state and a high level of
infrastructural support. By acting outside the realm of the rule of law, the
Argentinian military could employ cruel interrogation techniques and find
new ways to execute the disappeared. During the military junta,

approximately 360 clandestine detention centers were operating throughout the country; thousands of people were tortured in them for days or
even weeks, with most later killed (Crenzel 2008:175). A mainstream
practice included sedating the disappeared and throwing them from air-
planes into the ocean or even moving the dead bodies from the detention
centers to a remote public place where an armed confrontation was staged
(Robben 2005a:267). Most frequently, the bodies were given to local
cemeteries with clear instructions to be buried as "N/N" (unidentified) in
mass graves. One of the most traumatic chapters of this repressive era was
the abduction of babies born to mothers during captivity. The military
gave the babies to foster parents, often members of the security services, to
grow up under "Christian" values. In total, approximately 500 babies were
taken from their mothers (Arditti 1999; Penchaszadeh 2011).

This chapter tackles two puzzling questions, both dealing with
Argentina's search for the truth and its impact on other societies with
similar problems. Spain's experience mirrors the Argentinian one in
many ways. In Spain, disappearances were an important tool of
Francoism long after the end of the civil war (Julia 1999; Moreno
1999). A process of child abduction was devised by the Francoist regime,
ostensibly to bring children up according to Christian traditions (Vallejo-
Nájera 1937). But unlike Argentina, Spain did not seek the truth about the
past – at least not until much more recently. Similarly, although the two
communities in Cyprus mobilized to recover the missing persons from
the two waves of inter-violence in the 1960s and the Turkish invasion in
1974, their efforts were futile until the 2000s. Even more interestingly, in
Latin America, a number of societies experienced the problem of the
disappeared in the 1960s and 1970s, including Guatemala, Brazil and
Chile. Yet both regionally and globally, policies to address the problem of
enforced disappearances were developed *only after Argentina did so*.
Therefore, the chapter tackles the question: what made the mobilization
of the families in Argentina so effective, with such a global impact?

A second major question addressed in the chapter is whether the
theoretical framework proffered in this book accounts for transitional
justice outcomes in Argentina. More specifically, what was the sequence
in policies of dealing with the problem of the disappeared? How important is the temporal aspect in explaining the early truth recovery
processes (i.e. exhumations and truth commissions) in contrast to the
relative delay of accountability (i.e. crumbling of the amnesty law)?

The next two parts of the chapter shed light on the repertoire of
mobilization of the families during repression and after the transition,

respectively. To account for the unprecedented mobilization *during* the dictatorship, when domestic political opportunities were blocked, the analysis shows how the symbolic repertoire of the Mothers and Grandmothers created domestic and external opportunities. By re-appropriating the universal symbols of motherhood and family, all of which were part of the claims-making apparatus of the dictators, these grassroots activists not only directly challenged the legitimacy of the regime but also attracted a global sympathetic audience, paving the way for influential transnational alliances. By the time of transition, the mothers had already been established as undisputed global champions of human rights. The restoration of democracy created new political opportunities for them to uncover the truth, including the discovery of powerful domestic and international allies.

Then the chapter examines the role of timing and sequencing in explaining the Argentine experience. Argentina represents the "Big Bang" of transitional justice, with a number of policies implemented a matter of months after transition (i.e. exhumations, truth commission). Still, the overall sequence is consistent with the phase-based framework offered in Chapter 2. The passage of time was contiguous with the demo-cratization of institutions, the skillful establishment of new influential alliances and the effective use of incriminatory evidence from preceding truth recovery mechanisms, including exhumations and documentation of the crime by the truth commission. This led to growing accountability and the gradual erosion and final annulment of the amnesty law. The chapter concludes by summing up the regional and global significance of the struggle of the Mothers and Grandmothers for truth.

Symbolic Politics and Mobilization during Repression

Although the objective of disappearance in Argentina, as elsewhere, was to instill terror and impose silence, it shot back like a boomerang to strike the military. Instead of paralyzing the relatives, the disappearances became a catalyst for the Mothers and Grandmothers to turn their grief into a drive for truth. Hebe de Bonafini, the historic leader of the Mothers in Argentina, puts it eloquently:

> Nothing mattered anymore except that I should find him, that I should go everywhere, at any time, day or night. I didn't want to read anything about what was happening, just search, search. Then I realized we had to look for all of them and that we had to be together because together we were

stronger. We had not previous political experience. We knew no one. We made mistakes at first, but we learnt quickly.

(cited in Fisher 1989:53)

Contentious politics literature helps explain how a small, weak and inexperienced group of relatives gradually evolved into an influential social movement with global impact. It highlights the importance of political opportunities available to a group with a contentious agenda, including but not limited to the availability of influential allies, the openness of the political system and the extent to which the regime represses or facilitates collective claim making (Kriesi 1995b; Tarrow 1998; Tarrow & Tilly 2007:440). However, this framework is most relevant in explaining mobilization outcomes in established democracies. In contrast, in Argentina during the years of military dictatorship, the state repression was so widespread that opportunities were simply blocked, with no room for collective expressions of contentious demands.

The symbolic aspect of the early mobilization was pivotal to its success. Examining the framing strategies of the families can shed light on this. Benford and Snow say:

> Frames are constructed in part as movement adherents negotiate a shared understanding of some problematic condition or situation they define as in need of change, make attributions regarding who or what is to blame, articulate an alternative set of arrangements and urge others to act in concert to affect change.

(2000:615)

Framing generally has two key elements: "diagnostic" framing identifies the source of the problematic/unjust situation and "prognostic" framing identifies the actions to be taken to rectify this injustice (Benford 1993; Klandermans 1997). Framing strategies focus on "gaining attention, then empathy, and then evoking a powerful norm that persuades power-holders, allies or fellow sufferers to mobilize" (Brysk 2013:15).

For the vast majority of the Mothers and Grandmothers, the main problem during repression was the absence of information about the whereabouts of their children. In most cases, they had been kidnapped from their own homes, and the state denied the act. As a 1977 Amnesty International report reveals, the state's official position toward disappearances was that these persons had "gone 'underground,' left the country or were killed in clashes with the security services" (Amnesty International 1977:27). The single most important demand for the families was the recovery of the truth about their relatives; accountability was definitely not on the table (Crenzel 2008:175; Sikkink 2011:64).

After 3 years of the intensive use of disappearances and the elimination of all potential "sub-versive" elements, the state's deployment of this particular tool of terror decreased. In an effort to set itself apart from the earlier period of repression, the government passed a law on the Presumption of Death because of Disappearance in September 1979. The law gave families the opportunity to declare their disappeared relatives dead and, in this way, to deal with pending legal, bureaucratic and financial issues (Joyce & Stover 1992:225). Most families perceived the law as an attempt to cover up the problem, but they quickly added this perception to their diagnostic framing, taking a negative and turning it into a positive.

Identifying the source of the problem was relatively easy, as most families had similar experiences. It was harder to convert this common experience into collective action. It was important to confirm the unjust situation and to establish that an agency ("we") could alter this situation by taking concrete steps (Klandermans 1997). Most institutional channels of expressing discontent were blocked by the military junta. Again, the families simply made a detour around the barrier: despite the absence of political opportunities, the Argentine human rights movement was effective in winning the "hearts and minds" of domestic and international actors (Brysk 1994) using symbolic protests, the systematic documentation of crimes and the internationalization of the mobilization.

In the first period of repression, women used to visit ministries and police stations to inquire about their missing sons and daughters. Because of the clandestine nature of the crime, no records were kept. Frustrated by the inability to get information from the government, on Thursday April 30, 1977, a very small group of 14 mothers with lost children decided to gather in Plaza de Mayo in front of the Presidential Palace (Navarro 1989). When the police told them they could not sit in the square, they started walking together around the square – this was the first (unofficial) march of what soon became known simply as the Mothers of Plaza de Mayo. From that day on, every Thursday at 3:30 pm, the Mothers met to march. The number grew exponentially and the Mothers became one of the most influential groups of victims globally.

Later that year, they formed an official association, *Asociación Madres de Plaza de Mayo* (Association of Mothers of May Square). In October 1977, Mothers whose pregnant daughters had been kidnapped (or were kidnapped with their children) started to search for their grandchildren (Arditti 2002).[1] This smaller group obtained formal status and became the *Asociación Civil Abuelas de Plaza de Mayo* (Association of Grandmothers of May Square).

It is not coincidence that Plaza de Mayo, the square in which they staged their rallies, became an intrinsic part of the names of both associations. Argentines traditionally celebrated the national Independence Day here, attended military parades or listened to Peron's speeches (Brysk 1994). In other words, it was a symbolically and politically charged urban space. Mothers re-appropriated it during the repression to stage their marches, silent vigils and other forms of protest. Global media were inundated with images of their weekly vigils, women carrying photos of their children, with their children's nappies used as white headscarves. Many embroidered their missing children's names on the headscarves. Aida de Suarez remembers the headscarves as markers to help newcomers join the protests:

> The headscarves grew out of an idea of our dear Azucena ... Azucena's idea was to wear as a headscarf one of our children nappies because every mother keeps something like this, which belonged to your child as a baby. It was very easy to spot the headscarves in the crowds and people came up to us and asked us who we were.
>
> (cited in Fisher 1989:54)

The bond the Mothers developed was so strong that even today, more than 35 years after the fall of the regime, they continue to organize vigils and marches around the country (Bosco 2006).

The framing strategies and symbolic repertoires of the Mothers and Grandmothers resonated domestically and internationally. The mobilization of the relatives gained currency because the humanitarian demand was proffered by a socially legitimate actor – the Mothers. Their "moral capital" made the framing credible (Brysk 2013:64). Fortunately, at the early (critical) stages of their mobilization, they were not perceived as a threat by the military; they were simply *locas* (madwomen), and this gave them enough space to take their first critical steps (Navarro 1989:252). At the time, they were careful to highlight their lack of political motivation; they portrayed themselves simply as mothers and housewives in search of their missing children (Robben 2005a:305). Soon, though, their activities began to raise eyebrows among the military,

---

[1] There are approximately 500 recorded cases of abducted minors (Arditti 1999).

and the group was infiltrated by secret agents pretending to be brothers of the disappeared. This led to the disappearance of a number of Mothers. The military later revealed that kissing a Mother was the signal for abduction and, ultimately, an execution (Verbitsky 2005:4). Although the disappearance of Azucena Villaflor de Vincenti, one of the founding members and a leader of the Mothers, was a traumatic event for the group, it did not dissuade them from continuing their struggle (Robben 2005b).

Despite the growing danger, their mobilization remained intact. Alison Brysk explains why their repertoire was so appealing:

> If you have a Nelson Mandela it will get you really far. In Argentina they didn't really have that capacity. They weren't leaders and there weren't people who had international resonance or who could openly speak ... You have to find a way to represent them [the families]. You have to find a way to universalize them. You have to find a way to connect to a larger public with them. The lowest common denominator is the family: every mother's son is the most universal trope you can find. It travels across every culture on earth.

> (Interview No.32)

The symbolic use of motherhood resonated for cultural and religious reasons. The image of a crying mother mourning for her son suggested "Mater Dolorosa," a powerful image in the Catholic tradition (Malin 1994:2000), and showed the public how disappearances caused an enduring trauma. Mothers also directly challenged the dominant discourse of the junta built on the idea of the state as the guarantor of the Christian family; instead, they showed it was responsible for disintegrating the Argentine family (Krause 2004). The humanitarian framing worked: it was commonsensical to both domestic and international audiences (Femenia & Gil 1987).

Perhaps equally important, systematic and painstaking documentation of the repression provided hard evidence for their claims. Family groups were privileged to be supported by human rights organizations seeking to collect evidence related to disappearances. In sharp contrast to other countries in the region like Guatemala, Argentine disappearances took place in urban areas and targeted the middle class (e.g. students, lawyers, leaders of labor unions, intellectuals). Therefore, the domestic human rights movements to recover the truth were composed of people who were eloquent, articulate and very familiar with legal instruments. This proved to be an asset in documenting patterns of crimes during repression and after transition. For example, the Permanent Assembly for Human Rights (APDH) and the Center for Legal and Social Studies (CELS) brought cases to courts and prepared writs for habeas corpus, all critical to compiling a list of disappearances. During the dictatorship, this group gathered information on about 6000 cases of disappeared; their work was later used by the truth commission (Brysk 1994:46). Despite the non-facilitative role of the Catholic Church, SERPAJ (Peace and Justice Service), a religious non-governmental organization (NGO), was also very supportive of the families' mobilization. Its leader Adolfo Pérez Esquivel was awarded the Nobel Peace Prize in 1980. In short, the symbolic mobilization of the Mothers and Grandmothers was complemented by the calculated and systematic documentation of the human rights groups. Both were critical in securing international support. If Mothers won the "hearts" of international advocates, these umbrella organizations won their "minds."

However, this mobilization would not have had such an impact had it not been coupled with external opportunities. The bold and dynamic domestic mobilization took place at a time when significant changes in international politics put normative and human rights issues front and center. Probably the most important shift was the broader normative change in US foreign policy in the Carter administration (1977–1981). During this period, the US State Department set up the Bureau of Human Rights mandated to produce annual reports on human rights for all countries; these were used to guide US foreign policy (Sikkink 2004). The egregious record of the Argentine government on the disappeared could not go unnoticed; in 1977, the Carter administration cut military aid and blocked a $270 million loan (Navarro 1989:254). Stefanie Grant, then head of research for Amnesty International, highlights the significance of the international normative change:

> It is a broader change in 1970s, the unanimous adoption against torture by the General Assembly, it was the time when the Amnesty International gets the Nobel Peace Prize, it's the time of Helsinki Final Act which has human rights in basket III and it's a time when Carter administration comes to power with human rights mandate. So 1976–1977 is a pivotal moment in geopolitical terms.
>
> (Interview No.33)

An overlapping international opportunity for the relatives was the emergence of new transnational actors supportive of grassroots human rights activists. By the mid-1970s, the number of transnational advocacy groups and the budget available to them had grown exponentially (Keck & Sikkink 1998:98). A good example of a powerful transnational ally is Amnesty International. Note the nice overlap between the documentation of individual cases of disappearances by domestic human rights groups, such as CELS and APHD, and the Amnesty International strategy of working on individual cases (Keck & Sikkink 1998:88). In its 1976 visit to Argentina, Amnesty International consolidated thousands of cases of disappearances, made their stories public, and then put pressure on US and European governments to act on this information (Clark 2010).

The nature of the crime and the Mothers' search for their missing children appealed to a global audience who sympathized with the grieving mothers. Hearing the voices of individual victims resonated better than abstract statistics of human rights abuses. The fact that a number of disappeared were citizens of the United States and other European countries did not hurt either; naturally, these governments adopted a proactive stance. Dora de Bazze argues:

> We'd always gone to foreign embassies asking for help because there are
> *Desaparecidos* from 26 countries and we thought they might be able to do
> something. Then we realized that abroad there were people fighting for
> human rights, so we got the addresses of people like Willy Brandt and
> politicians in the US.

> (cited in Fisher 1989:74)

An important external influence was the Interamerican human rights system. Alarmed by the continuous violations of human rights, the Interamerican Commission for Human Rights (IACHR) set up an official visit to Argentina in 1979. Despite the climate of terror occasioned by the military regime, almost 3000 Mothers and Grandmothers queued to offer their testimonies (Navarro 1989:253). In 1980, the Commission issued a landmark report shedding light on patterns of human rights abuses and disappearances. More importantly, for the first time, a regional body captured in an official document the idea that a national government had the duty to investigate and prosecute perpetrators. Ariel Dulitzky, a member of the UN Working Group of Enforced Disappearances and an Argentine national, is clear about the importance of the Commission and its report:

> It was the first time that any human rights body visits a country and in
> a report described to the world what is an enforced disappearance, how is
> the practice carried out in a massive scale, essentially it shed light on a new

phenomenon. When the commission released its report in 1980, gave much credibility to the relatives. It was an international body describing with legitimacy what the relatives were saying from the onset.

(Interview No.34)

To their credit, the Mothers' and Grandmothers' proactive and innovative repertoires of mobilization attracted the attention of these external actors. Although other countries in the region (and abroad) were facing similar challenges, the international community shifted its attention to Argentina as a result of their strenuous efforts. For example, by sending letters and mounting continuous pressure, the Grandmothers convinced the Organization of American States to visit Argentina in 1979; it highlighted the problem of the abducted children in its final report (Arditti 1999:64). The Grandmothers also established connections with the Committee for the Defense of Human Resource in Southern Cone (CLAMOR). Through their activities, they raised awareness of the disappeared in the region and abroad (ibid. 65).

Mobilization after the Transition: New Opportunities and a Split in the Group

The military junta dragged Argentina into a nationalist war with Britain over the contested sovereignty of Malvinas/Falkland Islands in 1982. The resulting military defeat delegitimized the junta and facilitated the return of democracy in Argentina after 6 years of military rule. Contentious politics literature highlights the importance of political opportunities in the struggle of social movements, and the democratic transition created several such opportunities, especially for the Mothers and Grandmothers of Plaza de Mayo. Their political opportunities included the availability of influential (political, judicial and media) allies, the openness of new actors to their demands, and the regime's willingness to facilitate collective claims (Tarrow & Tilly 2007).

Obviously, the most significant change was the return of democracy and electoral politics. The "ruptured" transition discredited the Generals and gave enough room to press for truth recovery. The return of party politics was a unique opportunity for the Mothers and Grandmothers. By time of the transition, they had already become *causes celebres* of international media and had accumulated significant symbolic capital, giving them a privileged position in party politics. Similarly, the surprise victory of Raúl Alfonsín, elected on a proactive agenda of addressing past human rights abuses, gave incredible strength to the families. Only 3 days after taking office, he announced the establishment of a truth commission (National Commission on the Disappearance of Persons [CONADEP]), revealing his understanding of the importance of the problem of the disappeared. Of course, no political party could have turned a blind eye to the problem, especially after the mobilization which de facto introduced the problem to the political agenda. Yet the election of Alfonsín was a significant boost. He was a proactive human rights lawyer and one of the founders of APDH. Prosecutions of top military personnel were part of his electoral campaign.

Another opportunity was the growing independence of the judiciary and the newfound freedom of expression in the media, as families could now bring their cases to court and also publicize their stories. As the human rights groups had systematically documented both patterns of crimes and individual cases, families were poised to take the next step.

Still, the availability of new opportunities and more options created rifts in the relatives over the preferred course of action. Although the government was addressing the issue, not everyone agreed with the methods chosen. Hence, early after transition, we find the first fissures in the "prognostic" framing of transitional justice preferences among different groups of relatives. Although all agreed on the need to find the whereabouts of their loved ones, there was significant disagreement as to the preferred policy instrument of truth recovery. Should it be exhumations, truth commissions or trials?

The first major bone of contention was the mandate and the structure of the truth commission, CONADEP. Presidential Decree No. 187 set it up as an independent body, but most families favored a bicameral commission with subpoena powers. The mandate of the truth commission was tailored to establish the fate of the disappeared by (a) receiving reports on individual cases of abductions, (b) locating the abducted children and (c) publishing a final report with findings and recommendations (Crenzel 2008:179). Many feared CONADEP was a political tool to cover up the problem, and this perception led Adolfo Pérez Esquivel to originally reject an invitation to participate.

Other families perceived CONADEP to be the only realistic opportunity for finding the whereabouts of their children, so they collaborated. The Grandmothers was a proactive group, readily sharing its findings with the commission, and several human rights advocacy groups adopted a similar approach. But the Mothers of the Plaza de Mayo remained reluctant and denounced the commission (Jelin

1994). They adopted an uncompromising attitude, evident in their main motto *aparicion con vida* (bring them back alive). This was the first rift between the Mothers and Grandmothers. Although during repression and immediately after transition, the main demand for all families was to recover the missing, encapsulated in the slogan *donde están* (where are they), as more opportunities appeared, calls for accountability and punitive justice got louder.

A second contentious issue was the policy of exhumations. In the first weeks after the transition, human remains were found in cemeteries and other common graves. In an effort to identify hundreds of remains located in common graves, the government, in conjunction with CONADEP, asked for the support of forensic scientists from the United States. As explained in the next chapter, the American Association for the Advancement of Sciences (AAAS) sent a delegation of leading experts, led by Clyde Snow, now considered the patriarch of forensic science. During their stay, they not only helped unearth a number of graves, but more importantly, they trained a group of local students of anthropology in forensic identification techniques (Stover 1985).

Exhumations polarized the debates among families, however. On the one hand, the official organization of the Mothers of Plaza de Mayo vehemently rejected exhumations as a government plan to cover up the issue. This, coupled with the policy of "presumption of death," which gave families the option to declare their loved ones dead in order to deal with legal and other bureaucratic issues, was perceived to absolve the government of any political, legal and moral responsibility (Robben 2000:105). Mothers were afraid exhumations would depoliticize the issue and deviate from the central objective of the group, which by 1984 had become punitive justice for the perpetrators. As the leader of the group stated, "We reject exhumations, because we want to know who the murderers are – we already know who the murdered are" (cited in Brysk 1994:73).

Of course, opposition to exhumations is not unique to Argentina. The leaders of the Greek-Cypriot association of relatives also rejected a government plan for exhumations in the late 1990s (Kovras & Loizides 2011). Similarly, a segment of the families of the *desaparecidos* in Spain distanced themselves from exhumations, as they considered mass graves part of living memory, while other families – like that of poet Federico García Lorca – were reluctant to support exhumations as this would stir up heated political debates (Ferrándiz 2009; Tremlett 2008).

On the other hand, other family groups, especially the Grandmothers, became strong advocates of exhumations. The Grandmothers were searching not only for their children but also for their grandchildren. Exhumations were far more important to them because they could verify whether abducted grandchildren were dead (i.e. buried with their mothers) or alive, in which case, they could start "searching for life" (Arditti 1999). In essence, "exhumations were no longer a re-experience of the traumatic death of unidentified disappeared but became a means of hope, of recovering abducted grandchildren and reestablishing the violently broken family ties" (Robben 2005a:328). For some families, exhumations became the only instrument to support with hard evidence the existence of the crime and, in this way, challenge the military's official discourse saying the disappeared had fled the country. With dead bodies revealing buried (forensic) secrets, some families saw incriminatory evidence from the graves as a new opportunity to prove the crime. For example, the testimony of Clyde Snow in trials of the military was critical in securing convictions.

The scope of retributive measures to punish perpetrators became the third major point of contention. President Alfonsín devised a balanced policy, one which would shed light on the fate of the disappeared (i.e. CONADEP) and punish the military junta's "big fish," while simultaneously strengthening stability, generally seen as a prerequisite of democratic consolidation (Alfonsín 1993). Ignoring the lower-ranking officers, the government targeted the leaders.[2] Originally, the government let the military tribunals take the lead, but their reluctance to deal with the issue convinced the government of the need to turn to civil courts. In 1985, the Federal Court of Appeals ruled that a civilian court could try the masterminds of the junta. In December 1985, nine leaders of the military junta were convicted for past human right abuses, most related to the crime of disappearances. This was a major victory for the human rights movement; for the first time, dictators were tried in a national court on charges of violating human rights (Sikkink 2008).[3]

However, for many families, this was merely the first step. Most insisted on the need to punish all involved (Osiel 1986). After the trials of the leaders, almost a thousand new complaints were filed by relatives, creating a wave of pending trials that promised to last for years. At the

[2] Decree Law 158/83 of December 12, 1983.
[3] Although the first trials of leaders of a military dictatorship took place in Greece in 1975, the charges were related to treason based on the provocation of the Turkish military intervention in Cyprus.

same time, to show their teeth to the government, the military staged provocative incidents, such as barrack uprisings, jeopardizing the democratization process. The thousands of pro-democracy protesters who supported the government eliminated the prospect of a military coup, but the government deemed it had sufficient evidence to end the apparently uncontrollable wave of trials. In 1986, it enacted the *Punto Final* (Full Stop) law,[4] narrowing the temporal scope; interested parties now had 60 days to bring their case to court. In 1987, it passed the Due Obedience Law, exculpating lower-ranking officers for obeying their superiors' orders.[5] Both laws understandably frustrated the families.

The struggle for accountability became even more difficult with the election of President Menem. There were at least four military uprisings after transition, mostly as a reaction to policies of accountability (Sriram 2004:113). To appease the military and secure stability, Menem issued pardons to the military leaders in 1989.[6] Not surprisingly, for most relatives, these were steps backward. They radicalized and heavily politicized a group of Mothers who considered the margins of liberal democracy too restrictive to accommodate their demands.

The escalating disagreement on the preferred transitional justice policies ("prognostic framing"), particularly the radicalization of a segment of the Mothers, split the movement. It is worth noting that the experience of Argentina challenges a common view of victims in post-conflict settings, whereby all victims are perceived to have uniform transitional justice preferences. Disagreements are not unusual in the politics of victims groups in transitional settings; in fact, divisions over transitional justice policies, political/ideological orientations and/or leadership style are far from uncommon.

At any rate, by 1986, only 3 years after the transition, the Mothers of the Plaza de Mayo had split into two groups (Jelin 1994; Robben 2005a:33). The group led by Hebe de Bonafini adopted a radical stance, opposing the new government and party politics of the new democracy in general. They also objected to most government initiatives in dealing with the problem of the disappeared, including exhumations and the building of memorials, museums and other policies of memory (Bonner 2005). In their view, maintaining a strategy of street protests and a confrontational style was the best way to achieve accountability.

---

[4] Law No. 23492, December 23, 1986.
[5] *Ley de Obedencia Debida* No. 23.521, June 4, 1987.
[6] Decree 1002/98, October 7, 1998 and Decree 2741/90, December 29, 1990.

While during repression there was a unanimous framing of their children as depoliticized victims of the junta, after transition, several Mothers revised this framing. They now emphasized the political/ideological struggle of their children, framing them as radical fighters struggling for a better society. The Mothers led by Bonafini thought this a more appropriate way to keep their children's memory alive. In essence, their struggle was not limited to solving the problem of disappearances but was expanded to include the radical transformation of society.

Mothers led by María Adela Antokoletz adopted a more moderate stance and created a splinter group, the Mothers of Plaza de Mayo "Founding Line" (Robben 2005a:330). They highlighted the need for a less confrontational style with the government, perceiving it as a potential ally. They drew a line between the repertoire of mobilization during repression, when street protest was the only available channel of expression, and mobilization after the return of democracy, when a wide array of opportunities became available (Bosco 2004). In sharp contrast to the "politicized" memory within which Hebe De Bonafini tried to incorporate the disappeared, the "Founding Line" focused on "individual" memories of the disappeared children. This dovetails with the group's memorial practices, such as embroidering the children's names in headscarves, carrying photos and sustaining torture centers as memorials (Bonner 2005; Bosco 2004).

The most fascinating story is the struggle of the Grandmothers, largely because of their innovative strategies and effective outcomes. A distinctive feature of their mobilization was that their framing strategies changed very little after transition. Their primary demand remained the identification of the missing children while simultaneously ensuring the reunion of the grandchildren with their families. Thus, their strategies were more practical, including systematic documentation of individual cases that could potentially lead to future identification. Although they were always part of the broader movement, then, their repertoires often deviated. As they were double victims, having to search not only for their children but also their (kidnapped) grandchildren, they fought on two fronts: they had to identify their dead children and find ways to track and conclusively identify their grandchildren (Nosiglia 2007).

Marta de Baravalle says, "You had to have a lot of patience. We began to make dossiers on each case based on the testimony of the grandmother and with photographs of the child. We took these dossiers to the juvenile courts, to orphanages, to the Ministry of Interior, to the government. . . . [but] we couldn't prove anything" (cited in Fisher 1989:105). They staged demonstrations, they appealed in court and they launched advertisements in major newspapers asking for information. When all attempts failed, they turned to the international community. One of the Grandmothers remembers:

> One day in 1981 I read an article in Diario el Dia, that said scientists had found a way of identifying a person through analysis of the blood ... when I travelled abroad I'd take it with me. I asked scientists and doctors and scientific institutes if this new discovery would help us identify our missing grandchildren.
>
> (cited in Joyce & Stover 1992:226)

Their struggle broke new ground when they put pressure on the scientific community to help them. And this attempt was very successful.

As Chapter 4 explains in greater detail, a delegation of Grandmothers traveled to the United States and discussed with forensic experts whether it would be possible to use their skills to help them establish grandpaternity, even in the absence of the second generation. Victor Penchaszadeh, an Argentine forced into exile because he was a victim of (attempted) kidnapping in 1976, was the critical link in developing the grandpaternity test. He remembers his experience: "I left Argentina because there was an attempt to kidnap me by paramilitary [...] I left Argentina 24 hours later and in 1981 I moved to the States" (Interview No.35). Later he became famous because he was part of the group of geneticists, led by Mary-Claire King, who developed the grandpaternity index that helped dozens of grandchildren to reunite with their biological families (Joyce & Stover 1992). This ultimately led to the creation of a genetic databank;[7] thousands of grandmothers left samples. So far this has allowed 116 children to reunite with their biological families. The growing awareness of the missing children resulted in the creation of a new victims' group, the HIJOS (i.e. Children), composed of abducted children, opening another new chapter in the struggle for truth and acknowledgment in Argentina (see Druliolle 2013).[8]

Equally innovative legal strategies deployed by Grandmothers, discussed below, helped trim the amnesty law. Overall, the Grandmothers' struggle was more effective than the Mothers' efforts in terms of

---

[7] This became a law, No. 23511/87, May 11, 1987; the National Genetics Bank immensely facilitated the initiative of Grandmothers to reunite with their kidnapped grandchildren (Bonner 2005:63).

[8] HIJOS is the most significant association of children of the disappeared, founded in 1999 (HIJOS: Hijos e Hijas por la Identidad y la Justicia contra el Olvido y el Silencio).

catalyzing transitional justice outcomes; the Mothers may have been the "muscle" of the struggle, but the Grandmothers were the "brain." In explaining their impact, it is important to emphasize the moral authority of the grandmothers. Their struggle was targeted on the more sensitive humanitarian issue of recovering abducted minors, a cause engendering the sympathy of even conservative elements in the society, including a segment of the military.

But a crucial question remains. After an initial honeymoon period, by the late 1980s, the new amnesty and pardon laws, coupled with the split in the family movements, had inhibited the struggle for truth and justice. Yet the relatives overcame myriad legal, political and mobilization obstacles to make Argentina a global human rights leader by the mid-2000s. Exactly how did they do this?

Timing, Sequencing and Success

The case of Argentina is the "Big Bang" of transitional justice. Mainstream transitional justice policies dealing with the disappeared were created and implemented in a condensed period of time (1983–1985). With the exception of amnesties that were already a common instrument in transitions, as the next chapters suggest, three novel policy tools were designed to handle the disappeared: exhumations, a truth commission and human rights prosecutions.

Although Argentina represents a landmark case, the sequence of transitional justice policies fits into the phase-based framework presented in Chapter 2. Even before the collapse of the junta, the military passed a self-amnesty law. Then, only a few months after the transition, a policy of exhumations and the setting up of a truth commission (CONADEP) were almost concurrently followed and linked (Robben 2005a:324). In the early stages, CONADEP started collecting evidence without a concrete plan; families could only share information already available to them. When the commissioners realized this approach was counterproductive, they reversed the order and started by asking for evidence from eye witnesses and perpetrators to gain access to more information. After all, the military held a monopoly on information on gravesites. This fits into the theoretical framework posited here: in the early stages of truth recovery, the evidence of the perpetrators is essential to gather a critical mass of evidence and pave the way for later prosecutions.

Consistent with the phase-based framework, once CONADEP published its report, its findings were channeled to the courts. This, coupled with the incriminatory evidence from the graves, secured the conviction of the military leaders in 1985 (Crenzel 2011:1063). Without the sub-stantiated evidence and the testimony of Clyde Snow on incriminatory evidence from graves, it would have been impossible to stage such effective and quick human rights trials. Every new step of truth recovery shed more light on the notorious activities of the military, and this was pivotal in challenging the denial of the crime (Ocampo 1999). In the end, five out of nine military leaders, including Jorge Rafael Videla and Emilio Eduardo Massera, were convicted to life in prison.

However, even in the "Big Bang" case of Argentina, the role of timing is critical if we are to explain the "retributive" phase of truth recovery. More specifically, after the "Big Bang," which triggered a counterreaction from the military and led to the pardons offered by President Menem in 1989, the flurry of transitional justice initiatives stalled. For some family orga-nizations, like the Mothers (led by Bonafini), pardons verified their skepticism of the effectiveness of human rights discourse and main-stream party politics. For many, this heralded the end of the process. Nevertheless, by the mid-2000s, the amnesty was revoked, hundreds of perpetrators were in jail and the most comprehensive policy of retribu-tive justice in any post-authoritarian society in the world was in place. In other words, transitional justice is not a linear process; the passage of time creates opportunities for abrupt changes.

The theoretical framework proffered in these pages explains the long-term and occasionally erratic transitional justice path of Argentina. The passage of time was followed by the gradual democratization of institutions and the stability of the democracy; this, in turn, offered new opportunities to the families – primarily the Grandmothers – to revise previous transitional justice settlements, trim the amnesty law and promote accountability.

For this mobilization to enter the punitive phase of truth recovery, the role of the Grandmothers was critical. The *Abuelas* had a pressing issue to deal with. As a growing number were aging or dying, time was of the essence. For their struggle to be effective, they had to provide conclusive evidence in courts that they were the biological families of the children. And they had to counter the amnesty law.

A new period of truth recovery started in the 1990s. The amnesty laws and pardons blocked most pathways, so the Grandmothers and other human rights groups intensified their efforts and became even more creative in their legal strategy. With the support of CELS, the Grandmothers brought a case to the Inter-American Court of Human

Rights in 1992, the court ruled the amnesty law and the pardons were incompatible with the American Convention of Human Rights. Then, a 1994 amendment of the Argentinian constitution gave international human rights treaties a superior position over domestic law.

In another case, at the Buenos Aires Federal Court of Appeals, the Grandmothers and CELS argued that in spite of the amnesty law that precluded prosecutions, the relatives had a right to know the truth, while the state had a duty to investigate the whereabouts of the disappeared (Mallinder 2009). Decoupling these two duties represented the origins of the "right to truth," a point explored in Chapter 5. The court accepted the argument and established an unprecedented form of "truth trials" where the objective was not to attribute blame but to establish the whereabouts of the disappeared. That was a major victory for the relatives, one largely attributable to the innovative legal strategy of the Grandmothers and the umbrella human rights organizations.

Another legal innovation of the Grandmothers with far more impact was the legal argumentation that the crime of kidnapping minors was excluded from the amnesty law; therefore, the state had a duty to prosecute those responsible (Crenzel 2008:181; Sikkink 2008). That argument was put forward in 1998 by the Grandmothers, again supported by CELS.[9] In a landmark 2001 ruling on the disappearance of an 8-month-old baby, Claudia Poblete, the court deemed the amnesty law null and unconstitutional.[10] The court also demanded an investigation be carried out to find the biological parents or grandparents. The rationale of the ruling was based on the premise that after 1994, crimes against humanity, such as the abduction of minors and enforced disappearances, violated international human rights treaties to which Argentina was party (Mallinder 2009:112).[11] Seeing the writing on the wall, in 2003, the Kirchner administration declared the amnesty law null and void (Mallinder 2009). A massive wave of cases immediately reopened and found their way to the court.

As more families were reunited, this translated into new court cases. Most frequently, the Grandmothers pressed charges on kidnapping and

---

[9] They argued that the court should investigate the role of the defendants (Julio Simon and Juan Antonio Del Cerro) not merely for the abduction of the baby (Claudia Poblete), but also for the disappearance of her parents (Mallinder 2009:111).

[10] Poblete-Hlacziks case, ref. 8586/2000.

[11] Organization of American States (OAS), American Convention on Human Rights, "Pact of San Jose," Costa Rica, November 22, 1969, available at: www.refworld.org/docid/3ae6b36510.html, last accessed: July 6, 2016 Article 1.2.8.15.

forging birth certificates. A significant number of the grandchildren became legally active when they were informed about their (disappeared) biological parents, filing suits against their foster families (Elkin 2008). Some of the 116 grandchildren identified so far even discovered their foster families were responsible for the disappearance, torture and execution of their biological families, a shocking surprise (Penchaszadeh 2015). Maria Ines Garcia, an abducted daughter, now a 29-year-old, puts it succinctly: "There are no words to describe the pain for the disappearance of my parents. It is an anguish that will follow me for the rest of my life" (cited in Biazzini 2013).

An interesting story is that of Estella Carlotto, the leader of the Grandmothers. A 36-year-old man, Ignacio Hurban, was informed by his family that he had been adopted in the late 1970s, so he contacted the genetic databank. The results of his genetic sample matched with two entries, Estela Carlotto and Wilmar Montoya; the remains of the latter had been exhumed from a common grave in 2009 (Penchaszadeh 2015). In this case, DNA evidence illuminated a tragic love story between Estella Carlotto's daughter Laura and Wilmar Montoy; both disappeared and were shot, and their baby was abducted. After 37 years, Estella Carlotto found her grandchild. She says, "I didn't want to die without hugging him" (Goni 2014). Without the DNA database, the systematic documentation and the global publicity, all of which were the result of the mobilization of Las Abuelas, this would not have been possible.

The efficacy of the mobilization of the Grandmothers cannot be underestimated; simply stated, their decision to use the kidnapping of minors led to the annulment of the amnesty law. Without their perseverance and creativity, reaching the phase of punitive justice would have been impossible. Their investigative work, both during repression and after the return of democracy, was significant; they continued to gather circumstantial evidence (i.e. suspicious certificates, personal testimonies of survivors in detention centers), which proved critical in trials in the post-transition period (Penchaszadeh 2011).

Of equal importance, the passage of time offered new opportunities to domestic truth-seekers. The military was gradually democratized and remained loyal to the government, without posing a threat to democracy. The elderly military – who had direct involvement in the coup – were retiring, and the new generation of army leaders was less invested in defending the past. One of the most significant opportunities was the liberalization of the judicial authorities, at both a national and a regional level. Over time, with the democratic consolidation, the judiciary became more independent and trustworthy, eventually becoming a crucial ally to the families. Equally, little by little, the Interamerican human rights system became an independent actor in the struggle for truth. A more progressive interpretation of human rights cases was gradually adopted by the IACHR and skillfully deployed by domestic truth seekers (Huneeus, Couso & Sieder 2010). Ariel Dulitzky is clear: "From being a very weak and dependent institution to become little by little a stronger power within the state ... that opened up a lot of possibilities for the groups of relatives to use the judiciary to challenge political arrangements" (Interview No.34). Put otherwise, and as I will reiterate throughout the book, timing and institutions are the keys.

Conclusion

The mobilization of the Mothers and Grandmothers in Argentina is a stellar example of human rights activism. As Kathryn Sikkink shows, Argentina has been the "exporter" of human rights tactics (Sikkink 2008), and the mobilization is ongoing, some 35 years in (Bosco 2006). Although Chapters 4 and 5 will shed light on the ways this mobilization has influenced transitional justice norms and institutions, it is worth recapitulating its innovations. First, the magnitude of the crime affecting thousands of families put the systematic practice of enforced disappearances squarely in the center of the agenda of international politics, and it became a rallying cry for international human rights organizations and activists around the world. Stefanie Grant, head of research of Amnesty International in the 1970s, is adamant: the Argentine mobilization was critical in drafting a definition of the crime of disappearances (Interview No.33). Second, when confronted by apparently insurmountable domestic obstacles, the Argentine relatives brought their cases to international forums. The establishment of the UN Working Group on Enforced or Involuntary Disappearances can certainly be traced to their struggle (Guest 1990).

As evident in the next chapters, the mobilization of Argentines contributed to the emergence of the norms required to deal with a specific and hitherto undefined human rights problem. For one thing, the concept of the "right to know the truth" can trace its origins to the "truth trials" staged in Argentina in mid-1990s. For another, the Grandmothers' innovative struggle to reconnect with their grandchildren created a new norm, the "right to identity," as stated in the UN Convention on the Rights of the Child.[12]

The influence on other countries in the region facing similar challenges is equally obvious. A significant number – if not the majority – were also facing up to a legacy of disappearances. But they learned strategic lessons from the Argentine mobilization and with their help created regional associations, such as FEDEFAM (Latin American Federation of Associations of Relatives of Detained-Disappeared). In another example, assisted by the Grandmothers, El Salvador set up *Pro-Búsqueda*, a group tasked to trace abducted minors (Arditti 2002). Similar regional associations appeared globally, including the Asian (AFAD) and African (AFASD) federations of families.

All in all, the Mothers and Grandmothers of the disappeared in Argentina helped construct the image of an "ideal victim" in transitional settings. Any Mother seeking the remains of her children is seen as an innocent victim, with the right to truth and justice. The message of the Mothers spoke to all families everywhere. In the past, the missing were merely casualties of repression or conflict, but the Argentine experience transformed the conception of victimhood. The struggle was so influential that most human rights' organizations now try to imitate their winning formula of mobilization. Images of silent vigils, black and white photos and headscarves appear in Lebanon, Philippines, Chechnya and other parts of the world. Even in Spain, the leaders of the memory movement framed their demand for exhuming the executed Republican victims of the civil war (1936–1939) as "disappeared" to gain cultural currency and legal standing (Interview No.44).

In the title to this chapter, I cited Greek myth. Simply stated, Antigone felt obliged to comply with "God's law" and bury her brother Polynikes according to rituals, despite clear orders from the King to leave the body unburied as a punishment for his wrongdoing. Like Antigone, the modern Mothers and Grandmothers of the disappeared left their traditional roles at home to play a public role and challenge the state.[13] In Argentina, they used "motherhood" to deconstruct "the Fatherland," a founding

---

[12] UN General Assembly, *Convention on the Rights of the Child*, November 20, 1989, United Nations, Treaty Series, Resolution 44/25, available at: www.refworld.org/docid/3ae6b38f0.html, last accessed: July 6, 2016.

[13] The power of the Mothers is not surprising, as in the crime of disappearances, the most vulnerable institution is the family (Bouvard 1994:66). In his analysis of the Argentine experience, Robben says the abduction of children from their own homes eroded a basic

tenet of the junta. The problem of the disappeared was strategically used to show how disappearances tore apart families. In this way, they challenged the argument that the military junta was the safeguard of Christian family values. Not least, the call of Mothers and Grandmothers to find the bodies of their children resonated around the world, creating a sympathetic global audience.

It is important to remember that external conditions and the passage of time certainly facilitated the impressive mobilization. More specifically, the fact that a number of countries in Latin America had to deal with the same problem, coupled with linguistic and cultural affinities, created opportunities for relatives. The ease of regional communication also facilitated the attempts of the Mothers and Grandmothers to spread their message. Finally, the gradual democratization of key institutions, particularly the independence of the judiciary, helped curb and then annul the amnesty law.

Yet the final credit goes to the creativity and tenacity of the Mothers and the Grandmothers. As Estella Carlotto says, "If somebody had told me then that I would dedicate my life to searching for the truth and struggling against historical amnesia, I would not believe it" (Arditti 2002:34).

social trust that parents can protect their children (2005b:270–273). That is particularly important for mothers (2005b:305).

4

"Forensic Cascade"

The Technologies and Institutions of Truth

This chapter explains how the innovative mobilization of the families of the disappeared shaped the mechanisms of contemporary transitional justice. It sheds light on two overlapping transitional justice innovations: "technologies of truth," or the application of forensic sciences in human rights investigations, and "institutions of truth," primarily investigative truth commissions. The chapter challenges our understanding of key transitional justice policies by exploring their evolution from the standpoint of victims' groups. It highlights the growing, yet neglected, role of technologies of truth in advancing victims' struggles for acknowledgment, accountability and human rights, and the impact of these technologies on transitional justice. It argues that it is impossible to fully grasp the growing human rights accountability in post-conflict settings, often known as the "justice cascade," without first acknowledging the "forensic cascade." For the first time in human history, science offers a credible way to use undisputable evidence from graves to convict perpetrators of human rights violations. Last but by no means least, it sheds light on the emergence and diffusion of a forensic epistemic community. Here, community refers primarily to scientists (forensic anthropologists or archaeologists, geneticists, etc.) but includes human rights workers.[1]

The first part of the chapter shows how the clandestine nature of the crime of disappearances made the recovery of forensic truth essential to challenge the inherent deniability of the crime and to assist families' attempts to find their loved ones. It then explains how an ensuing "forensic cascade" influenced transitional justice by facilitating the following: the identification of human remains for humanitarian purposes; the use of forensic incriminatory evidence to convict perpetrators; the global spread of truth commissions and the emergence of delayed or post-transitional

---

[1] For other interesting accounts on the evolution of the forensic community of experts, see Rosenblatt (2015), Crossland (2013) and Wagner (2008).

justice. Finally, the chapter explores the symbiotic relationship of the institutions and technologies of truth, illustrating how truth commissions and forensic tools go hand in hand in policies of dealing with the violent past.

Disappearances: A Unique Crime

The crime of enforced disappearances was used instrumentally to terrorize the broader population beyond the immediate victims and their families. Yet certain victims were selected over others because of their alleged political or ideological beliefs or social networks. The "deeply private and personal" act of disappearance (Robben 2000:70) has led to important and visible policy outcomes. At the most fundamental level, the clandestine nature of the crime causes a unique psychological trauma among relatives, whereby deeply wounded persons (and societies) develop mechanisms of repression/dissociation (McNally 2003). Relatives of the disappeared "cannot mourn their losses when others deny that those losses took place" (Robben 2005a:122). After spending decades working with families of the missing, Pauline Boss argues disappearances uproot a fundamental human need for "certainty" (2006). Families are left in a state of ambiguity, with no information on the fate of their loved ones. Are they dead? Are they alive? If they are dead, where are they buried? One of the early reports of Amnesty International perfectly captured the devastating effect on the families.

> It is the crushing reality of loss coupled with the unreality of death that afflicts the families of those who have "disappeared". The result is a form of mental torture brought about by either the suspension of bereavement or the feeling of helplessness – and paralyzing uncertainty about what to do to protect their loved ones
>
> (Amnesty International 1981:109).

A unique feature of the trauma causing great difficulty for the relatives is that the reason for the inability to enter into a mourning process is external (i.e. the absence of a body to mourn), not internal (Boss 2002, 2006). Relatives may be trapped in limbo for decades, making it impossible to start the grieving process, let alone reach closure (Robins 2013:45). The specific nature of the crime leaves them in "frozen" or "ambiguous" grieving (Boss 2006; Blaauw & Lahteenmaki 2002; Frankl 1985; Pérez-Sales, Durán-Pérez & Herzfeld 2000; Walsh 2007:233). This transcends cultures and is evident in both Western and non-Western contexts. As Simon Robins shows in his study of Nepal, the absence of a minimal form of certainty, such as a dead body, traps families in a state of ambiguous loss that prevents mourning (Robins 2011). The inability to mourn, in turn, affects quality of life, causing extreme levels of distress, anxiety and depression (Pérez-Sales, Durán-Pérez & Herzfeld 2000). Families of the disappeared have almost twice as many stress disorder symptoms as relatives of victims of other accidents (Quirk & Casco 1994). Even after the passage of decades, families can remain trapped in a situation of ambiguous loss.

On the one hand, psychological accounts portray individuals who have experienced an enduring trauma, such as the abduction of a loved one, as paralyzed by severe psychological disorders. On the other hand, however, the mobilization of the relatives of the disappeared in certain countries has been the catalyst for landmark social and political developments. How can we explain this apparent paradox? Boss says "searching for meaning" is one of the most efficient ways to overcome a state of "ambiguous loss" (2006). This search for meaning is always relational and socially constructed (Boss 2006; Robins 2011). The existential need to make sense of what has happened has motivated families in many different countries to come together, share their experiences and mobilize to make their stories heard. For example, as will be discussed below, although external conditions, that is, the disappearance of a relative, were important in mobilizing families in Latin America, the common driving force was the search for truth for their loved ones and the public acknowledgment of their suffering. We are all storytellers, and we need to make our stories heard to resist uncertainty, silence, oblivion and denial (Lederach 2005; Minow 2002).

An overlapping cultural account points to the importance of death rituals. In his landmark book *The Work of the Dead*, Thomas Laqueur explains why the dead body matters dearly to their families "everywhere and across time." Simply stated, "it matters because the dead make social worlds" (2015:1). The dead should be construed as

> social beings, as creatures who need to be eased out of this world and settled safely into the next and into memory. How this is done – through funeral rites, initial disposition of the body and often redisposition or reburial, mourning, and other kinds of postmortem attention – is deeply, paradigmatically and indeed foundationally part of our culture.

(2015:6)

Although different cultures have developed different mourning processes, ranging from prolonged communal grieving to swift family funerals, the common thread is the importance of a proper death ritual that enables families to initiate mourning and healing. Having a body to bury is of paramount importance in funeral rituals in African and most Latin American cultures (Castro, Beristain & Rovira 2000; Martin, Arendse & Majhaba 2013). Even in Buddhist and animistic traditions, both of which place secondary emphasis on the dead body, a ritual that symbolically illustrates the end of this cycle of life – such as communicating with spirits to enable passage to the afterlife – is important for families (Robins 2011). Similarly, in Timor, the remembrance of the dead is conditional on a decent funeral (Grenfell 2015). In Greek-orthodox culture, burial marks a rite of passage for the family (Danforth & Tsiaras 1982:50–62). In most cultures, a funeral ritual is seen as a "culturally appropriate farewell ceremony" (Blaauw & Lahteenmaki 2002:769), enabling the living relatives to start their reintegration into human society (Lobar, Youngblut & Brooten 2006:48–49).

In the absence of a body to bury, it is impossible for relatives to even initiate the period of mourning (Stover & Shigekane 2004). A senior source in the Cypriot Committee on Missing Persons (CMP) (who preferred to remain anonymous) with decades of experience dealing with families of the missing said to me: "All humans have two documents that verify their passage into and out of the human community: the birth certificate and the death certificate. In the absence of a death certificate, they are neither members of the human community nor of the (imagined) community of ancestors; they are trapped somewhere between the two" (Interview No.27). Obviously, this view represents a state-centric and largely bureaucratic approach that links the dead body with the death certificate, something that is not culturally important to every society. Yet it also reflects the myriad mundane bureaucratic hurdles created by this ambiguous social and legal status. It is not uncommon for the wives of the disappeared, for example, to be unable to access their husbands' bank accounts, claim their pensions, etc.

The need to mourn loved ones transcends cultures and eras; the strength of this deeply felt and intensely personal need, coupled with a highly public, political and collective quest for justice, explains why relatives of the disappeared simply refuse to give up. But in the case of the disappeared, a personal trauma became a public one when the relatives mobilized, ultimately reshaping our understanding of contemporary human rights. As Antonius Robben argues in his seminal analysis of the relatives' mobilization in Argentina, "Social trauma unleashes powerful political forces" (2005b:284).

Mothers of the disappeared have mobilized to find their loved ones in Kashmir, Turkey, Bosnia, in most Latin American countries and elsewhere. Paul Sant Cassia offers a vivid account of the struggle of two mothers in Cyprus to learn the truth about their husbands (2005). In 1998, two Greek Cypriot women secretly entered a military cemetery and started digging up a mass grave in the hope of finding their beloved husbands missing for more than 20 years (ibid.). This bold and pragmatic act became a symbol of resistance to state discourse, which posited their husbands were missing, not dead. The story quickly attracted significant media attention and initiated a process of exhumations revealing many Greek Cypriots deemed missing were, in fact, buried in Greek-Cypriot cemeteries.

Sant Cassia dubs these determined women "heirs of Antigone" (2005), referring to a woman who felt morally obliged to comply with "God's law" and bury her brother Polynikes according to traditional customs, despite clear orders from the King to leave the body unburied as punishment for his misdeeds. As Chapter 3 shows, the mothers of the disappeared in Argentina, like Antigone, left their traditional roles at home to play a public role and challenge the state.[2] Similarly, the Chilean mothers strategically used "motherhood" to deconstruct "the Fatherland," a founding tenet of Pinochet's regime; by showing how disappearances affect families, they deconstructed the argument that Pinochet could safeguard family values (Thomas 2011).

A key challenge for the families, intrinsic to the unique nature of the crime of disappearances, is the deniability of the practice (Méndez & Vivanco 1990). Repressive regimes can "disappear" their enemies and distance themselves from the crime as there is no *corpus delicti* (body of evidence). Amnesty International explains why disappearances represent the perfect crime: "If there is no prisoner, no body, no victim, then presumably no one can be accused of having done anything" (Amnesty International 1981:91). Ewoud Plate, an advisor to family groups globally, describes enforced disappearances as "the mother of all crimes, because it entails several human rights violations at once" (Interview No.36).

---

[2] The power of the mothers is not surprising, as in the crime of disappearances, the most vulnerable institution is the family. In his analysis of the Argentine experience, Robben says the abduction of children from their homes eroded the basic social trust that parents can protect their children (2005b:270–273). That is particularly important for mothers; interestingly, the role of fatherhood has not been adequately explored (2005b:305).

The practice of disappearances removes the individual from the realm of the law. As Chapter 5 shows, both the families and the transnational human rights groups had to search for the truth in a legal, political and institutional vacuum, because the law did not include provisions for dealing with disappearances. Even leading human rights watchdogs, such as Amnesty International, had difficulty defining the practice. Anne Marie Clark says Amnesty International's effective repertoire of mobilization for other types of human rights violations, such as torture or release of prisoners, could not be extended to disappearances because of the clandestine nature of the crime, which made it difficult to prove the crime has been committed in the first place (Clark 2010).

This is where science entered the scene, and the "forensic cascade" began. Families in countries around the world were mobilizing to identify their loved ones to challenge the authorities' denial and to prove a crime was committed – but they were trapped in a legal limbo. This convinced forensic scientists to step in. Over time, technologies of truth became central to transitional justice and to victims' struggles for acknowledgement, accountability and human rights.

Technologies of Truth in Transitional Justice

Technologies of truth have had a powerful impact on contemporary policies of dealing with the past. As illustrated in Figure 4.1, over the past three decades, they have shaped transitional justice in at least four ways.

Humanitarian exhumations: For the first time in human history, science offers a credible way – particularly after the introduction of the DNA test – to identify the remains of victims of violence and give them back to their families (ICRC 2009:9; London, Parker & Aronson 2013; Moon 2016). "Humanitarian" exhumations are particularly important for certain types of clandestine crimes, such as the disappeared. In the past, any effort to identify human remains buried in common graves was conditional on the testimony of eyewitnesses, most often the perpetrators. Perpetrators have the monopoly on information about gravesites but are understandably reluctant to incriminate themselves. Often they are the only actors able to find the bodies, but at the same time, they are the least inclined to do so. This has left enduring open wounds, even in societies with celebrated transitions, such as South Africa or Chile.

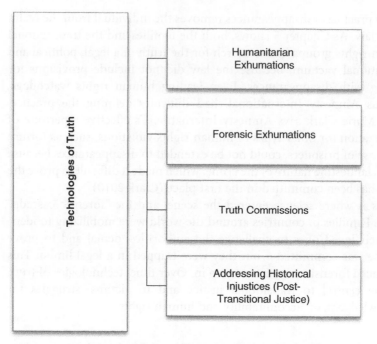

Figure 4.1   The Impact of Technologies of Truth on Contemporary Transitional
Justice

Modern (forensic) technologies of truth have been able to counter this
intransigence, assisting thousands of families around the world to identify the remains of their loved ones, end a prolonged period of ambiguous
loss and start the healing process, both at individual and at societal levels.
In a recent survey in Bosnia and Herzegovina, more than 73 percent of
the relatives of the missing and 80 percent of the broader population said
humanitarian   exhumations   contribute   to   reconciliation   (ICMP
2014:117). Similarly, despite the absence of a political settlement in
Cyprus, with the support of forensic teams, the two communities have
looked back at a painful chapter in the country's history (1963–1974) and
addressed the missing (Loizides 2016). These are not the only countries
so affected; humanitarian exhumations have assisted families around the
world.

Forensic exhumations: Scholarship examining the increase of human
rights prosecutions in transitional settings has isolated a phenomenon

known as a "justice cascade" following Kathryn Sikkink's influential book (Sikkink 2011). There is a parallel "forensic" cascade. When the military leaders of the junta in Argentina, the Serb-Bosnian General Radko Mladic or other leaders of repressive regimes were "disappearing" their enemies, they considered it the crime for which they were least likely to be held accountable. There was no identifiable body, and in some contexts national amnesty laws guaranteed their immunity from prosecution. Yet forensic findings have come back to haunt them. At this point, many have been prosecuted, despite a significant delay.

The use of incriminatory evidence from the graves to assist human rights prosecutions has had a critical impact on transitional justice (Stover & Shigekane 2004:354). Scientists can establish the identity of the dead; they are now able to determine with relative precision the cause of death (e.g. execution, indications of torture). Past trials were frequently restricted to the testimony of eyewitnesses; this was considered circumstantial evidence and, as such, often failed to secure a conviction. Critical factual evidence now convicts the perpetrators of disappearances. Although the lion's share of academic attention has been paid to the political or legal processes behind the growing accountability of wrongdoers and former dictators, technologies of truth have had an enormous impact on the "justice cascade."

The distinction between humanitarian and forensic concerns is often blurred in reality. The very nature of digging graves is open-ended, making it difficult to disentangle humanitarian from prosecutorial needs. For example, in the 1980s, the Argentine Forensic Anthropology Team (EAAF) carried out its first exhumations simply to identify victims, making this a typical case of humanitarian exhumations. At a later stage (2000s), however, the findings from exhumations were used as critical incriminatory evidence to bring perpetrators to justice. Throughout the book, I emphasize the role of timing and sequence in truth recovery – and this is a notable instance. The example also illustrates that forensic evidence derived from humanitarian exhumations is not neutral but can be used as an instrument of justice too.

Truth commissions: Apart from reinforcing accountability, forensic sciences have affected the global spread of truth commissions, another key transitional justice mechanism. Truth commissions emerged in Latin America to document and publicly acknowledge patterns of clandestine human rights violations, mainly the disappeared. Yet as shown below, truth commissions alone cannot assuage the personal need of the families to find their loved ones and bury them according to their cultural and religious rituals. The first time forensic experts were invited to participate in a human rights investigation was to assist the Argentine truth commission (National Commission on the Disappearances of Persons [CONADEP]) to identify the remains of the disappeared and back the findings of the commission with "scientific" evidence; the mere "assertion of death failed to neutralize denial of disappearance, prevented closure, and raised an incessant call for truth" (Robben 2005b:130). The symbiotic relationship between truth commissions and forensic sciences is explored at greater length later in the chapter.

Post-transitional justice: The impact of technologies of truth is not limited to addressing human rights violations in times of transition. A key feature of forensic sciences is their ability to challenge oblivion and denial in societies with long-standing cultures of silence. A growing number of countries have started to revisit traumatic legacies of their distant past, despite a significant delay; this phenomenon is frequently called "post-transitional justice" (Aguilar 2008; Collins 2011; Kovras 2014). To a large extent, forensic tools made this possible. For example, General Franco could not have imagined that a wave of exhumations of thousands of republican *desaparecidos* of the Spanish civil war (1936–1939) would occur in the early 2000s and break the long-standing silence created after the transition to democracy in 1975. Having said that, the struggle of societies to deal with chapters from their past has also propelled new uses of forensic technologies.

The common thread linking all cases mentioned above is that the application of forensic tools has facilitated the struggle of countries to deal with a violent past. Of course, forensic tools can also provoke conflict and divisions among families and victims, and this can happen simultaneously with more positive outcomes. Counting the number of the disappeared or naming the dead are often complex and ambivalent processes, and not every family is content with the way forensic tools are applied (Rosenblatt 2015; Wagner 2008). Overall, however, forensic sciences offer new tools and new opportunities for truth recovery.

Drawing on the theoretical framework of "epistemic communities," the next section traces the genealogy of the "forensic" epistemic community and shows how technologies of truth became a central ingredient in transitional justice. More importantly, it suggests the emergence of these tools is intrinsically linked to the need of families to find their loved ones and their innovative repertoire of mobilization.

Forensic Epistemic Community

Social, political and economic problems in contemporary world politics have become extremely complex. Policy-makers often consult scientists and experts to make sense of this complex reality and to choose among alternative courses of action. A comprehensive theorization of the growing centrality of non-elected professionals in international politics is the concept of "epistemic communities" (Mai'a 2013). In the words of one of the pioneers of this approach, an epistemic community "is a network of professionals with recognized expertise and competence in a particular domain and an authoritative claim to policy-relevant knowledge within that domain or issue-areas" (Haas 1992:3). Experts within a particular community have shared normative and causal beliefs of how the world operates (or ought to operate) and an overlapping scope of policy expertise (ibid.). These groups of experts range from physicians and environmental experts to human rights lawyers and religious actors.

Different versions of this framework have been used in the literature to explain various phenomena in international politics. For example, in a pioneering study, Adler (1992) illustrates how the intensive training of US bureaucrats in game theory enabled the diffusion of the deterrence doctrine across the Iron Curtain to become the guiding principle of bilateral relations during the Cold War. Similarly, Haas (1989) shows how regimes and experts' knowledge facilitated pollution control in the Mediterranean, while Finnemore (1993) explores an equally interesting story, how UNESCO experts socialized individual states into "organizational innovation."

Significant effort has been made to explore the role of epistemic communities in human rights, transitional justice and peacebuilding. For example, Keck and Sikkink (1998) explain the growing importance of transnational advocacy networks, such as human rights lawyers, in assisting domestic groups to overcome obstacles set up by repressive states. Similarly, Hirsch (2007) shows how influential actors closely involved in the South African Truth and Reconciliation Commission (TRC), mostly lawyers and religious actors, actively promoted the specific mechanism as the optimum tool to deal with the past. Finally, Sandal provides a fascinating account of how religious actors have used their influence to catalyze peaceful transitions (2011).

I argue that forensic experts should be considered an epistemic community, an influential one. Interestingly, Clyde Snow, the patriarch of forensic sciences, said in an interview that he considered himself part of such a community: "I am not an activist. I'm a scientist. I'm an expert. If I have a philosophy, it's that I am anti-homicide" (cited in Rosenblatt 2015:18).

Simply stated, communities of experts have a unique opportunity to impact policy in times of uncertainty, especially when policy makers are confused by a novel reality. Adler and Haas explain this ability to make an impact (1992:373). First, in times of uncertainty, such as economic crises or political transitions, they say these communities have a unique opportunity to make a *policy innovation* to reframe how public and policy makers understand a particular issue. This is usually followed by the *diffusion* of a specific policy, through national and international interactions of the members of the community, including workshops, conferences and other unofficial channels of communication. Finally, once the community has managed to effectively define the problem in a particular way, it becomes institutionalized and reaches the stage of "policy persistence," whereby it has become the "orthodoxy" (ibid. 385).

Emergence and Diffusion of Forensics

Historically, the first large-scale operation to deploy forensic tools in a forensic investigation was the exhumation of over 4000 victims of the "Katyn massacre" (Haglund 2001; Hanson 2008). In 1943, in an effort to avoid blame for the execution of thousands of Polish army officers by the Soviet army at Katyn forest, the Nazis carried out a systematic and methodologically sound process of exhumations (Congram 2013). It is a tragic irony that the Nazi regime invented the practice of disappearances and used it in 1941 with the operation "Night and Fog" and yet was the first to use forensic techniques to solve the mystery of disappearances 3 years later – albeit for propaganda purposes. In the future, these techniques would become the key instrument to challenge the practice of disappearances.

Interestingly, in post-World War II Europe, there were no systematic exhumations of human remains (Congram 2013; Rosenblatt 2015).[3] The emergence of forensic truth recovery occurred much later, with the enforced disappearances in Latin America and the affected families' efforts to recover the truth about their loved ones in the 1970s and

---

[3] British pathologist Keith Mant notes a systematic process of exhumations to recover British soldiers buried in common graves in Germany at the end of World War II.

1980s. The type of repression and the disposal of human remains as an intrinsic part of state terror made the need for recovery crucial for these families.

A second reason why forensic exhumations started in Latin America, particularly Argentina, is related to the mobilization of the Grandmothers of the disappeared (*Las Abuelas*). As explained in Chapter 3, the Grandmothers had two overlapping objectives: to search for the bodies of their disappeared children and to find their missing grandchildren, as their daughters often were pregnant when they were abducted. After the restoration of democracy, they sought to determine whether their grandchildren were alive and, if so, whether there was a scientific way to prove grandmaternity/paternity and reconnect with them (Arditti 1999).

In fact, the Grandmothers were the driving force in convincing scientists to use their expertise to find the truth. In the early 1980s, they learned about advancements in genetic sciences. This aroused their curiosity; would it be possible to use these tools to establish grandpaternity/maternity without the presence of the biological parents? Victor Penchaszadeh, an Argentine geneticist living in the United States, became a "bridge figure," helping *Las Abuelas* reach the offices of the American Association for the Advancement of Sciences (AAAS) in Washington (Rosenblatt 2015). One of the pioneers of forensic sciences, Eric Stover, participated in the first mission of the AAAS to Argentina in the early 1980s; he remembers the initial visit of the families and the critical pressure they put on the scientific community:

> They came into my office and they asked: "We have got disappeared children we are trying to find, can you help us do this?" I knew nothing about forensics back then, zero. So I called the National Academy of Sciences in the US and asked them "could you recommend forensic scientists?" and then I contacted various people, including Clyde Snow. And we put this team together and travelled to Argentina.
>
> (Interview No.17)

Clyde Snow and Eric Stover became the leaders of the mission to Argentina to help the Argentine truth commission, CONADEP.

During their first visit, the Grandmothers also met with a leading geneticist, Dr. Mary Claire King, from the University of California, Berkeley. She later developed the grandpaternity/maternity test that helped hundreds of abducted children reconnect with their biological families (Keck & Sikkink 1998:93; Snow, Stover & Hannibal 1989:48).

Luis Fondebrider, a member of the Argentine Forensic Anthropology Team, who participated in these early exhumations is adamant:

> The reason we talk today about forensic science, is because many families and human rights organizations without any knowledge about science and mainly women desperate to know what happened to their loved ones began to ask for help ... helping was not the decision of AAAS, institutions or universities. It was the initiative of families and Mothers in Argentina.
>
> (Interview No.8)

The first visit of the team of AAAS forensic experts to Argentina in 1984 should be considered the starting point of the forensic "epistemic community." One of the first decisions was to set up an intensive 5-week workshop on practices of "identifying human skeletal remains." This was attended mainly by local undergraduate students of anthropology and archaeology, not the professionals one might have expected to show an interest (Snow, Stover & Hannibal 1989:46). As a result of the political insecurity, in the early years after the transition, established local coroners and other professionals were not particularly eager to attend seminars of this nature. However, the approximately 20 local undergraduate students who participated went on to form the EAAF in 1984. EAAF later became the leading forensic team globally (Joyce & Stover 1992; Salama 1992).

Luis Fondebrider, one of the students, says many of his fellow students were activists; accordingly, the impetus behind EAAF was to help families in their struggle for accountability (Interview No.8). In the late 1980s, existing national amnesty laws and the use of pardons made this impossible, however, and EAAF members asked themselves: should they continue their efforts even if exhumations did not lead to prosecutions or should they abandon the project altogether? According to Adam Rosenblatt, an informed observer in the evolution of the forensic epistemic community, gradually and without entirely jettisoning the idea of accountability, EAAF acquired a more family-centric approach, focusing on helping relatives to find their loved ones (Interview No.49).

EAAF quickly became the undisputed champion in forensic investigations for human rights, not only in Latin America but also globally. The transformation of a regional (i.e. Latin American) epistemic community into a global community of experts is intriguing. Although EAAF was founded as a non-profit organization in the specific context of post-junta Argentina, by the mid-1990s, it was active in almost 40 countries.[4] It has now worked in post-conflict societies attracting extensive political, academic and media attention, including Iraq, Cyprus, Democratic Republic of Congo and the former Yugoslavia. It has contributed to the human rights investigations of more than ten truth commissions, including Guatemala and El Salvador, and to trials of human rights perpetrators in a number of countries emerging from conflict (Bernardi & Fondebrider 2007; Binford 1996:124; Blau & Skinner 2005:452; Crossland 2013:129; Drawdy & Katzmarzyk 2016; Fondebrider 2002). Finally, EAAF has led UN peacebuilding missions in Sierra Leone and East Timor (Juhl 2005:26).

EAAF has also provided training for and facilitated the establishment of national forensic teams in numerous countries emerging from conflict, most of which faced the problem of enforced disappearances. For example, the Argentine model was replicated in the Guatemalan Forensic Anthropology Foundation (FAFG), the Chilean Forensic Anthropology Team (GAF), the Peruvian Forensic Anthropology Team (EPAF) and the Latin American Forensic Anthropology Association (ALAF) (Juhl 2005:25–30).[5]

The rapid diffusion of the forensic epistemic community was facilitated by EAAF's key role in forensic investigations and truth commissions in different parts of the world and in training local forensic groups (Interview Nos.4 and 6).[6] The literature of norms theory often asks why certain norms promoted by epistemic communities resonate and diffuse, while others fail (Haas 1989). In this case, the forensic epistemic community gained global currency because it could effectively address

---

[4] EAAF has worked in the following countries: Argentina, Bolivia, Brazil, Chile, Colombia, El Salvador, Guatemala, Haiti, Honduras, Mexico, Panama, Paraguay, Peru, Surinam, Uruguay, Venezuela, Angola, Ethiopia, DR Congo, Ivory Coast, Kenya, Namibia, Sierra Leone, South Africa, Sudan, Togo, Zimbabwe, Iraqi Kurdistan, Morocco, East Timor, Indonesia, Philippines, French Polynesia, Bosnia, Croatia, Cyprus, Kosovo, Republic of Georgia, Romania and Spain. Further information can be found at EAAF's website: eaaf .org, last accessed: March 15, 2015.

[5] EAAF is also involved in identifying Missing in Action (MIA) in Vietnam. They unearth both American and Vietnamese soldiers and are tasked with training a local forensic group of experts in North Vietnam.

[6] As another example of its impact, EAAF was contracted in 2001 by OHCHR to draft a "Model Protocol for the Forensic Investigation of Suspicious Deaths Resulting from Human Rights Violations" (Juhl 2005:26); this was proposed as a law by the Mexican state in the 2000s.

a pressing humanitarian need. Equally important is the fact that it had the potential to promote the top priority in the international peacebuilding architecture of the 1990s, namely, human rights accountability.

In the formative period (1980s), the forensic epistemic community was mostly shaped by the families' cry for truth; it was based in Latin America, and its objective remained largely "humanitarian" as a result of constraints set by national amnesty laws. Yet, by the early 1990s, the community had been transformed as a result of external influences and new opportunities for expansion. It gradually took on a life of its own.[7] Especially after the wars in the Balkans and the Rwandan genocide, a new challenge emerged: to use the incriminatory evidence collected from graves to support the work of the ad hoc international criminal tribunals (Wagner 2008). This normative shift created new opportunities for the emergence of new forensic actors, such as Physicians for Human Rights (PHR), and the establishment of the ICMP. Although EAAF and PHR were established the same year, PHR assumed a proactive forensic investigation agenda in the early 1990s. For example, in 1992, PHR participated in Iraqi Kurdistan and El Salvador missions, playing a major role in the UN Commission of Experts (Juhl 2005).[8]

In the early years after the war in the former Yugoslavia, exhumations became a central ingredient of the ICTY's criminal processes. One of the most pressing problems was the accommodation of the demands of the families of approximately 30,000 persons who went missing during the conflict (Nettelfield & Wagner 2013; Wagner 2008). Originally, limited exhumations took place for the sole purpose of providing incriminatory evidence to the Office of the Prosecutor of ICTY to substantiate charges against perpetrators. According to Stover and Shigekane, the objective of the exhumations of missing in the Srebrenica massacre was to determine the ethnicity and cause of death (e.g. execution and buried blindfolded); identification and return of the remains to the family were not part of the exhumation process (2004:91). However, a fierce reaction from the mothers of the missing in Srebrenica, the region most heavily affected, convinced US President Bill Clinton to establish the most ambitious forensic institutional globally, the ICMP (Congram & Sterenberg 2009;

---

[7] The objective of EAAF was always to support accountability efforts, but it took a long time for these avenues to open. Still, EAAF as well as other groups systematically collected evidence, including statistical analysis of data (see Snow & Bihurriet 1992) for future criminal proceedings.

[8] UN Sec. Council Res. 780, S/Res./780, October 6, 1992.

Crossland 2009:128; Fondebrider 2002; Nettelfield & Wagner 2013; Skinner 2007).[9]

The 1996 creation of ICMP in Bosnia marks a turning point in the global diffusion of forensic technologies of truth. Since 2001, when it started applying the DNA test in Srebrenica, ICMP has identified almost 80 percent of the approximately 7000 missing in the most challenging case of missing persons in Europe (Wagner & Kesetovic 2016). In Bosnia and Herzegovina more broadly, almost 25,000 (70 percent) of the 31,500 persons who went missing during the war have been accounted for, marking the highest identification rate in any post-conflict setting (ICMP 2014).

Apart from the sheer size of the endeavor, ICMP has changed the scope of forensic investigations. While the objective of most exhumations in the past was predominantly humanitarian, namely, to unearth, identify and return the remains to the families, ICMP explicitly linked humanitarian needs with the use of forensic evidence in criminal proceedings. Of course, this reflects the opportunities available to the ICMP. While the Latin American teams started to operate within a context of impunity set by amnesty laws in the 1980s and early 1990s, ICMP was the key instrument in prosecutions by major international actors. Obviously, ICMP did not invent "forensic investigations"; it just did not face the political, institutional and financial constraints EAAF did. According to Kathryne Bomberger, ICMP's Director General, its distinctive feature is that its humanitarian and forensic objectives are seen as identical. She stresses, "We are dealing with a crime, so families of the missing do not only want closure; they want justice" (Interview No.18). In sharp contrast to the highly local response tailored to meet the particular needs of the Argentinean families, ICMP was part of an international intervention that culminated in ICTY in the former Yugoslavia. Still, as noted below, this discourse of justice is partly instrumental to differentiate their agenda from other forensic groups.

Another novel feature of ICMP is its comprehensive forensic toolkit. While EAAF used chiefly classic forensic techniques (archaeological and anthropological) in parallel with DNA, ICMP introduced

---

[9] ICMP has worked in Iraq, Kuwait, Lebanon, Libya, Syria, Turkey, Cameroon, Kenya, Namibia, South Africa, Maldives, Philippines, Thailand, Albania, Cyprus, Greece, Norway, Ukraine, Bosnia, FYROM, Kosovo, Montenegro, Croatia and Serbia. Further information can be found at: www.icmp.org, last accessed: March 15, 2015.

the application of DNA on a massive scale.[10] This stemmed from the magnitude of the problem it had to address, the sheer number of missing persons it had to uncover and the abundant resources available to it. The type of mass graves and the commingled remains in Bosnia made DNA the only feasible way to identify the victims of the war and minimize the prospect of false identifications (Wagner 2008). Additionally, the number of the missing, much higher than in most Latin American countries, and the fact that it took place just a few hundred km from Central Europe meant ICMP had more direct support from affluent European and American political actors (Interview No.41). Hence, ICMP's comprehensive toolkit includes its opportunities and resources, especially in the context of the political, financial and legal constraints faced by Latin American teams.

ICMP and the application of forensic investigations on a massive scale in Bosnia assisted in the diffusion of the forensic epistemic community in another, overlapping way. According to Director of Policy Andreas Kleiser, in the early years of its operation, ICMP outsourced most of its Bosnian operations to other groups of forensic experts from other parts of the world (Interview No.38). Therefore, it is hardly surprising that almost all major groups worked in Bosnia early on, including PHR, International Committee of the Red Cross (ICRC) and EAAF. Bosnia became a rite of passage for a young generation of forensic scientists who used this experience in other post-conflict settings, such as Iraq or Peru (Interview Nos.4 and 8).

This new generation published its findings, reflected on its experiences and participated in conferences, setting the stage for the institutionalization of the forensic community (Rosenblatt 2015). New academic journals and other novel venues appeared, fostering the exchange of ideas. Interestingly, contrary to the widely held assumption in the epistemic community literature that the more institutionalized the community, the more homogenous it becomes, the forensic community is divided on ethical, moral, political and ideological issues (Interview Nos.39 and 46). Despite the divisions, it is highly influential, posing a significant puzzle to the literature.

Since the late 1990s, ICMP has developed its ability to identify human remains and carry out forensic investigations on a large scale. According

---

[10] EAAF and other Latin American teams started their work well before these technologies were fully developed and never had the access to financial and technological resources available to the ICMP.

to Andreas Kleiser, "ICMP is the organization with the largest specialized capacity in this field making use of processing formats tailored to one single type of activity" (Interview No.38). Today, this contribution is not limited to the disappeared; ICMP has a broader impact in a wide array of activities. For example, the development of a DNA database was pivotal in the enormous effort required to identify the remains of victims of the attack against the Twin Towers in New York (Edkins 2011). It is participating in tsunami-affected areas and working on aircraft disasters, and at the time of writing, ICMP is designing a process of identifying refugees and migrants dying in shipwrecks in the EU periphery.

The ICMP story best illustrates the institutionalization of forensic sciences as an independent field in international politics. In December 2014, ICMP officially became a distinct intergovernmental/international organization, based on the understanding that there is "a systemic global challenge that demands a coherent and effective global response."[11]

Although this epistemic community organized around a tool to deal exclusively with the problem of the disappeared, it has expanded its focus to include broader instruments to deal with the past. Although the emergence is directly linked to families' efforts to find their loved ones, its diffusion should also be attributed to the availability of resources and international opportunities. Sponsoring forensic investigations, especially when based on DNA, is costly, and diffusion was possible only when money became available for investments in international peace-building activities (after the 1980s) (Moyn 2010). By the late 2000s, ICMP had become the "hegemon" in forensic investigations, mainly because it was able to draw from a large pool of resources; originally, the US government was the major source, but today, sources are scattered across the globe.

Despite ICMP's growing visibility and policy influence, other forensic groups have continued to flourish. They have expanded geographically and entered new types of human rights investigations. It is worth noting that the two most important groups, EAAF and ICMP, have worked in more than 40 and 24 countries, respectively.[12] Equally impressive, the

---

[11] www.ic-mp.org/news/icmp-established-as-international-organization-in-its-own-right/.

[12] Since its inception, EAAF has worked in the following countries: Argentina, Bolivia, Brazil, Chile, Colombia, El Salvador, Guatemala, Haiti, Honduras, Mexico, Panama, Paraguay, Peru, Surinam, Uruguay, Venezuela, Angola, Ethiopia, DR Congo, Ivory Coast, Kenya, Namibia, Sierra Leone, South Africa, Sudan, Togo, Zimbabwe, Iraqi Kurdistan, Morocco, East Timor, Indonesia, Philippines, French Polynesia, Bosnia,

Forensic Services of ICRC has 30 staff members and has worked in more than 50 countries,[13] while PHR has operated in more than 16 countries.[14] Originally the community was quite small; it was based on personal interactions and frequently changed its institutional affiliations. For example, Eric Stover, who worked on the AAAS mission in Argentina and trained EAAF members, was appointed Executive Director of PHR in the early 1990s (Juhl 2005:30). Similarly, William Haglund became the UN's Senior Forensic Advisor for ICTY and ICTR and later became Director of the international forensic program for PHR. This goes a long way toward explaining the prominent role of PHR in the 1990s. It also illustrates how influential members of this community had the capacity to shape the policy agenda of international organization on specific issues and vice versa. For example, the most significant environmental or humanitarian disasters, such as the 2004 tsunami or the thousands of refugees who die or go missing in their effort to cross the Mediterranean, have been "opportunities" for thematic expansion to new types of investigations.

Paradoxically, another opportunity for the global diffusion of technologies of truth came from the competition of these groups for limited resources. To attract funding, they had to travel around the world and expand the scope of their investigations in societies emerging from conflict. Funding for forensic groups is often attached to providing assistance to "fact-finding" missions; therefore, groups had to shift their agenda to include forensic investigations to get funding.

One of the interesting features of this community is that because the various expert groups are competing for scarce resources, they have developed competing strategies and unique agendas. Although it is difficult to generalize, all main forensic actors have different investigative mandates, objectives and priorities. This is partly attributable to the

Croatia, Cyprus, Kosovo, Republic of Georgia, Romania and Spain. Further Information can be found at EAAF's website: www.eaaf.org, last accessed: March 15, 2015. ICMP has worked in Iraq, Kuwait, Lebanon, Libya, Syria, Turkey, Cameroon, Kenya, Namibia, South Africa, Maldives, Philippines, Thailand, Albania, Cyprus, Greece, Norway, Ukraine, Bosnia, FYROM, Kosovo, Montenegro, Croatia and Serbia. Further info can be found at: www.icmp.org, last accessed: March 15, 2015.

[13] Staff members of the "forensic services" come from an international roaster including 18 from Latin America (Argentina, Chile, Colombia, Guatemala, Mexico and Peru), 6 from Europe (Austria, Cyprus, France, Germany, Greece and Ireland), 4 from North America (United States and Canada) and 2 from Africa (South Africa and Kenya).

[14] PHR has participated in operations in Brazil, Guatemala, Iraqi Kurdistan, former Yugoslavia, El Salvador, Rwanda, Israel, South Korea, Czech Republic, Cyprus, Georgia, Abkahzia, Afghanistan, Nigeria and Thailand (Blau & Skinner 2005:453; Juhl 2005).

historical context within which each emerged. ICRC emerged as the key humanitarian actor, engaging in post-conflict (both intra-state and inter-state) settings, and as such, it developed a humanitarian approach to dealing with the missing (Drawdy & Katzmarzyk 2016; Tidball-Binz 2006). ICRC does not focus on judicial processes, so it can avoid being labeled partisan, as this might affect its capacity to intervene as a neutral actor in future conflicts. For EAAF, which emerged as an independent (non-profit) NGO to deal with the problem of the disappeared in the aftermath of authoritarianism in Latin America, the concept of account-ability is more central (members are activists); still, the main objective remains the support of the families. An informed participant told me about working with a forensic colleague from EAAF in an African country; the colleague in question was willing to participate in exhu-mations only if this did not lead to any further financial or psychological costs for the families (Interview No.46). As illustrated above, for more recently established bodies, such as ICMP, the element of justice is at the core of their activities. This is hardly surprising, as ICMP was tasked to deal with a different type of violence (ethnic cleansing) in a different region at the height of "liberal peace," where accountability had become the Holy Grail of peacebuilding (Richmond 2011). Although all forensic organizations focus on exhuming and identifying victims, some have central provisions for supporting and training local practitioners (Bernardi & Fondebrider 2007; Drawdy & Katzmarzyk 2016), evident in the work of ICRC, EAAF and PHR in contexts like Cyprus. Finally, ICMP is the most affluent group, with an established capacity to deliver, so its selling point is its ability to make fast and effective identifications. Efforts to develop local ownership are more peripheral in its mandate. Essentially, although the forensic community *emerged from family acti-vism, its diffusion should be attributed to external opportunities,* such as normative shifts in international politics and competition over scarce resources, as these pushed them toward new types of investigations.

Technologies of truth are now a central tool of transitional justice. They have helped thousands of families globally to identify their loved ones. They have found objective incriminatory evidence, bringing perpe-trators to justice and facilitating the "justice" cascade. Forensic exhuma-tions have become a fundamental policy in victims' struggle to hold perpetrators accountable for clandestine human rights abuses, especially disappearances (Ferllini 2007; Haglund, Connor & Scott 2001). Paraphrasing Sikkink, there has been a "forensic truth cascade," with genetics playing a leading role in investigations of human rights abuses (Penchaszadeh 2015).[15]

To a significant extent, the global diffusion of these tools occurred simply because families never stopped looking for their missing relatives. Once again, institutional innovation was linked to the personal struggle of families. As a result, science now offers a credible way to provide hard evidence to challenge denial and empower victims.[16]

Institutions of Truth: Disappearances and Truth Commissions

As illustrated above, as a result of the clandestine nature of the crime of disappearances, uncovering the truth was the overarching priority in the mobilization of the families. Apart from technologies of truth, the innovative and persistent mobilization of the families of the disappeared paved the way for novel "institutions of truth," namely, truth commissions.

Over the past 35 years, truth commissions have become a central transitional justice mechanism in societies emerging from conflict and state repression and, as such, have received much academic attention (Hayner 2002; Wiebelhaus-Brahm 2010). Most analyses frame the first truth commissions as a "compromise" solution. National amnesty laws attached to negotiated transitions may have precluded the possibility of prosecuting perpetrators, but at the same time, significant popular pressure made some policy of dealing with the past inevitable, hence the appeal of the truth commission (Popkin & Roht-Arriaza 1995). This is true; despite the restrictive framework set by amnesties, the first truth commissions offered a novel political alternative somewhere between the two extremes of absolute impunity and human rights prosecutions. Yet this is only part of the story. Why did the mechanism not emerge at a different period, before (or after) the 1980s, in other countries with negotiated transitions? Why were the first truth commissions set up in Latin America?[17]

---

[15] See UN resolution 10/26 on Resolution 10/26. Forensic genetics and human rights, also available: http://ap.ohchr.org/documents/E/HRC/resolutions/A_HRC_RES_10_26.pdf, last accessed November 28, 2016.

[16] For a critical perspective on the role of forensic science in post-conflict settings, see Moon (2013).

[17] The first truth commission was established in Uganda in 1974, but most scholars challenge its legitimacy, as it was a "kangaroo truth commission" set up by the regime of Idi Amin.

To reply to these questions, let us use a counterfactual. Imagine the recent history of human rights if the practice of disappearances were absent. In this case, the most probable outcome would have been the absence of truth commissions. Between the late 1970s and 1980s, the common thread linking Latin American countries was that most were affected by disappearances as a result of a centralized form of state repression (McSherry 2002). The families of the missing were facing similar challenges, chief of which was the pressing need to find the whereabouts of hundreds or in some cases thousands of disappeared. Equally central was the need to challenge the "deniability" of the crime and prove disappearances were part of a broader policy of state repression. Families had to overcome obstacles set by amnesty laws, with extremely limited institutional, legal or political tools at their disposal.

As Chapter 3 explains, the primary objective of the Argentine CONADEP was to locate thousands of persons who were forcibly disappeared during the "dirty war" in Argentina (Hayner 1994). CONADEP, established in 1983,[18] filled an institutional gap. Its *raison d'etre* was to balance the need of relatives for truth with the inability to achieve justice amidst the constraints imposed by amnesty laws. For a number of relatives' associations and informed observers, CONADEP was an immoral trade-off of truth for impunity. Even so, it was a path-breaking institutional development. Since then, "institutions of truth" have been mushrooming around the world; their scope has expanded to address a number of issues related to violent repression, making them one of the most widely used mechanisms of transitional justice (Hirsch 2007).

Table 4.1 illustrates the historical (and causal) evolution of truth commissions as a policy of dealing with disappearances. The table includes all countries that set up truth commissions (or commissions of inquiry) to deal with the disappeared or missing.[19] In the horizontal column, countries appear according to their mandate (i.e. those with explicit references to the disappeared vs. those with a broader mandate, excluding the disappeared). On the vertical axis, a temporal distinction is made between commissions established before and after 1995. For most

[18] Law Decree No. 187/83, December 15, 1983.
[19] The construction of the table is based on the database included in the book and information on truth commissions' mandates found at the US Institute of Peace (USIP) Digital Collection, also accessible at: www.usip.org/publications/truth-commission-digital-collection. For the purposes of this table, I have included commissions of inquiry focusing on the disappeared (Nepal, Algeria, Chad, etc.).

Table 4.1 *Evolution of Truth Commissions*

	Explicit Reference to Enforced Disappearances	Broader Mandate
Period Preceding TRC (1974–1994)	Argentina (1983) Bolivia (1982) Chad (1990) Chile (1990) Honduras (1993)* Nepal (1990)* Sri Lanka (1994)* Uganda (1974) Uganda (1986) Uruguay (1985)	El Salvador (1992)
After TRC (1995–2009)	Algeria (2003)* Brazil (2011) Guatemala (1997) Morocco (2004) South Africa (1995)	Burundi (1995)* Democratic Republic of Congo (2003) Haiti (1995) Liberia (2006) Nigeria (1999) Paraguay (2004) Peru (2001) Rwanda (1999) Serbia (2002) Sierra Leone (2002) Timor (2002)

Source: US Institute of Peace Truth Commission Digital Collection.
The table includes those commissions which were set up, not their success in delivering.
* Commissions of inquiry for the disappeared.

scholars, the South African TRC set up in 1995 is a critical threshold for the global diffusion of the mechanism (Hayner 2000; Hirsch 2007; Wiebelhaus-Brahm 2010). An interesting finding is that in the first decade after the establishment of the first truth commission in Argentina, and definitely until the early 1990s, all truth commissions and commissions of inquiry had a very narrow mandate, tailored to document the crime of disappearances. It is not surprising that in this early period (1983–1995), almost all truth commissions were set up in Latin American countries, as this region was most heavily affected by the problem of disappearances. Even the design of these commissions reflects a nearly exclusive focus on the clandestine nature of the crime of disappearances. Although different truth commissions occasionally included other crimes, like torture or executions, in their scope of investigation, a common thread is a focus on enforced disappearances. For example, CONADEP invited forensic experts from the American AAAS to carry out exhumations to identify the disappeared and back the findings of the commission with forensic evidence (Joyce & Stover 1992). Similarly, the type of investigation adopted in this first historical phase was limited to confidential testimonies, in sharp contrast to the public hearings of the post-1995 period. Finally, in this initial phase, the narrow scope of truth commissions on the disappeared and the confidentiality of hearings reflect the objective of maintaining "negative peace," by which I mean the absence of violence or the prevention of violent democratic reversal (Galtung 1996). Most of these early fact-finding bodies were domestic commissions without external support, and this may explain their confined scope.

After the Salvadoran and South African commissions, however, the mechanism was reshaped to focus on broader human rights violations. These later commissions had more ambitious objectives, including establishing an authoritative account of the past to foster reconciliation.

In due course, the truth commission evolved into an all-encompassing mechanism of dealing with the past. No longer confined to post-authoritarian settings, it became a key element of peacebuilding in societies emerging from civil wars. Part of this broader change was the growing involvement of international organizations in the design of truth commissions, as for example, in the countries marked by an asterisk in the right box.

Simply stated, the emergence of truth commissions is historically and causally linked to the struggle of the families of the disappeared to put pressure on states to officially acknowledge a crime was committed in a systematic way. Needless to say, an ideational factor explaining the diffusion of truth commissions was the promotion of this tool by the growing "transitional justice" community (Hirsch 2007). However, without the existential need of the families to recover the remains and make their stories public, the elites' efforts would not have resonated so

Table 4.2 *A Dialectic Relationship: Truth Commissions and Exhumations (1981–2009)*[1]

	Truth Commissions With Exhumations	Truth Commissions Without Exhumations
1983–2009	Argentina (1983–1983) Chile (1990–1991) El Salvador (1992–1992) Guatemala (1997–1998) Haiti (1995–1995) Honduras (1993–1994) Paraguay (2004–2005) Peru (2001–2001) Serbia (2002–2002) Sierra Leone (2002–2002) South Africa (1995–1997) Timor (2002–2002)	Bolivia (1982)* Burundi (1995) Chad (1994) DR Congo (2003)* Liberia (2006) Nigeria (1999) Rwanda (1999)* Sri Lanka (1994) Uruguay (1985)*

Source of data on truth commissions: US Institute of Peace Truth Commission Digital Collection. Sources of data for exhumations: annual reports of EAAF, PHR, ICRC, ICMP and Forensic Program of the Human Rights Center at the University of California, Berkeley, and personal interviews with forensic experts.

The table excludes commissions of inquiry for specific human rights violations. It also includes those commissions which were set up; it does not indicate their success.

[1] The first date in parentheses is the date of the truth commission and the second is the date of exhumations, if applicable.

* Countries which carried out exhumations, but these were not explicitly linked to the mandate of the truth commission.

clearly, nor could such an outcome have been realized. Thus, the families' mobilization is responsible not only for the emergence of technologies of truth (i.e. forensic sciences) but also for the appearance of institutions of truth (i.e. truth commissions).

Table 4.2 highlights the *symbiotic relationship between the technologies and institutions of truth*, however. Truth commissions gained global currency partly because technologies of truth provided a scientific way to carry out demanding human rights investigations. Although truth commissions emerged out of the families' innovative mobilization, then, their global diffusion is explained by the availability and effective use of forensic instruments.

Most intriguingly, the right column tells an even more interesting story. Even among those countries that did not explicitly link exhumations to the mandate of the truth commission, most used forensic investigations, although at a different period after the transition, as for example, the cases marked with an asterisk on the right side of Table 4.2. Hence, the relationship between forensic tools and truth commissions works both ways: the global appeal of truth commissions legitimized further forensic investigations as a mainstream technology of truth. This lends credence to a core argument of the book, namely, that truth commissions and exhumations go hand in hand.

Conclusion

Despite the growing scholarly emphasis on normative and institutional aspects of transitional justice, little has been said about the impact of technologies on truth and accountability. By exploring the emergence and subsequent spread of the forensic epistemic community, the chapter sheds light on the critical contribution of science to transitional justice, peacebuilding and human rights. More importantly, it highlights the responsibility of the novel and persistent mobilization of the families of the disappeared for bringing new tools to transitional justice.

Technologies of truth have been critical for the success and global expansion of transitional justice policies, yet this has largely escaped critical notice. A striking example is their contribution to the "justice cascade." Kathryn Sikkink does excellent work enumerating the legal and normative processes leading to new accountability norms essential to the "justice cascade" but leaves out an important detail: for the first time in human history, science offers a credible way to use undisputable evidence from graves to convict culprits. It is impossible to fully grasp the "justice cascade" without acknowledging the "forensic cascade."

Of course, the availability of legal norms does not necessarily mean they will be used. For every successful case in which victims (and their families) have effectively deployed legal instruments, like Argentina or Chile, other countries have pursued ambitious legal avenues but failed. For example, Cyprus brought a case before the European Court of Human Rights (ECtHR) but failed to achieve a concrete outcome for decades.

Accountability is made possible when a legal case is supported by forensic incriminatory evidence. This is not a one-dimensional relationship: as illustrated above, the emergence of new norms and the broader normative shift created new opportunities for forensic techniques to gain global currency. The two processes, normative and technological, go hand in hand, creating new and unpredictable possibilities.

Finally, as illustrated in the analysis, although families' mobilization was critical to the *emergence* of the community, its *diffusion* should be attributed to external opportunities, including normative shifts in international politics and the competition of forensic groups over resources. The latter factor pushed groups to adopt distinctive agendas and expand to new areas of human rights investigations.

5

The "Missing" Tale of Human Rights

Only those problems that dramatically affect the daily life of human beings are worth studying. I still believe that it is the cluster of legal rules and institutions that may have a dramatic impact on the life and suffering of human beings that should constitute the main focus of our attention as scholars.

(Antonio Cassese, cited in Frulli 2014:808)

Introduction

The crime of forced disappearances dramatically affects the lives of thousands of families around the world. The crime is often deniable because the body cannot be found. And until quite recently, perpetrators could be shielded by amnesty laws after the fact. Worse yet, a legal and institutional vacuum often stymied the efforts of families to achieve accountability in the 1970s and 1980s. Laws covering the crime were simply non-existent.

This chapter explores how the families of the missing tackled the latter two problems, employing novel arguments, enlisting the aid of international organizations and ultimately helping to create a robust legal framework to address disappearances. It shows that relatives, guided by the logic of precedent setting, used innovative and effective legal strategies to trim national amnesty laws and gradually create a universal legal instrument. Drawing on interviews with protagonists and archival material, the chapter unpacks this fascinating story, hitherto "missing" from the human rights and transitional justice literatures.

Families and Their Influential Allies

As illustrated in the preceding chapters, for most families, the identification and return of the remains of their loved ones for the purpose of a decent burial was their most pressing need. As Chapter 4 notes, the development of technologies of truth helped thousands of Latin American families find and mourn their lost relatives. Yet this was simply the starting point. The availability of forensic evidence took the families a step farther in their journey. They also wanted accountability. Their ongoing efforts led to the overturning of amnesty laws to prosecute the offenders, leading, in turn, to another overlapping innovation, the development of a robust international legal framework for the disappeared.

In the 1970s and 1980s when a number of military dictatorships started disappearing dissidents in a systematic way, particularly in Latin America, relatives were operating in a legal vacuum. The crime of enforced disappearances was so novel that the legal framework of the time did not define it, let alone address it: "None of the normative instruments of the three bodies included a specific right not to be subject to enforced disappearance. The drafters of the respective texts, unsurprisingly, had not envisaged the rise and proliferation of this scourge" (Kyriakou 2014:18).[1] Stefanie Grant, Head of the Research Department of Amnesty International in this early critical period, remembers how the crime inhibited Amnesty International's work:

> Amnesty had to decide whether disappearances was a category that the organization would take up, if so, how should a disappearance be defined, and who were the disappeared. Then it had to decide what could be done. At a simplest level it was a question how you fitted this situation of absence into an organization whose work has been framed by individuals held in a named prison, or being tortured in a particular place. And that's methodologically straightforward because you have a person in this prison or detention center and you know where they are and your job is to get them out. But where the person is defined not by their presence in a prison camp or in a torture center but by their absence, it is much harder ... Amnesty International researchers were faced with a situation which was completely unfamiliar because the family was saying "this person was taken" or "we don't know where this person is" and that was the end of the trail, the government said this has nothing to do with us, this is a missing person.

> (Interview No.33)

Given the normative and legal vacuum, families had to invent new tools. And that is precisely what they did. With immense support from transnational human rights advocacy groups, they were instrumental in creating a legal framework which is now central in transitional justice and

---

[1] It is important to draw an analytical distinction between the "crime" of enforced disappearances and the "right not to be subject to enforced disappearance."

human rights debates, including key legal norms, such as the "right to know" the truth.

In their journey toward truth and accountability, the families were helped by influential transnational advocacy networks. For example, Anne Marie Clark highlights the critical role of Amnesty International (2010). Arguably one of the most authoritative theoretical accounts of how human rights norms emerged is offered by Keck and Sikkink (1998). In their account, a privileged role is reserved for transnational advocacy networks, including international and domestic non-governmental advocacy organizations (e.g. Amnesty International or Human Rights Watch), domestic social movements (e.g. victims' associations) and regional intergovernmental bodies (e.g. Inter-American Commission for Human Rights [IACHR]) (Keck & Sikkink 1998:9). A unique feature of these networks is their capacity to frame public debates – especially around sensitive questions of human rights – and in this way, to persuade political elites to take a preferred course of action. In their framing strategies, they often use "information politics"; as such, the role of forensic experts or fact-finding missions by leading human rights watchdogs is often critical (1998:16). Similarly, transnational advocacy networks have the capacity to frame debates by playing out symbols. This is a particularly important element of the mobilization of the families of the disappeared; pictures of mothers dressed in white scarves or powerful images from exhumations appearing in international media were very effective in convincing a global audience. Ethan Nadelmann aptly labels these groups "transnational moral entrepreneurs" and their activities "moral proselytization" (1990:482).

Moreover, "bridge figures" – or "political entrepreneurs" in Keck and Sikkink's terms – facilitated the struggle of the families by directly influencing the agenda of key organizations. For example, Jose Zalaquett, who had direct experience of the systematic use of disappearances in Chile, became Chair of Amnesty International, precisely when that specific crime was at the top of Amnesty's agenda (1979–1982). Wilder Tayler and Federico Andreu, both of whom played a role in drafting the 2007 International Convention for the Protection of All Persons from Enforced Disappearance (the Convention henceforth), previously worked in Amnesty International and International Commission of Jurists (ICoJ). Echoing the process which enabled the diffusion of the forensic epistemic community, most bridge figures had first-hand knowledge of enforced disappearances from their countries of origin. Their personal interactions and their redeployment into different influential human rights groups created a unique opportunity for them to set the policy agenda of important organizations.

The repertoire of mobilization evidenced by families and human rights advocacy groups was perfectly aligned as well. For example, Amnesty International adopted a "case-work" approach, framing its campaigns around stories of individual victims; this fit the scope of the families' mobilization perfectly. At the most fundamental level, their fact-finding activities provided documentation about the crime and, thus, influenced the decision-making of international human rights groups. During their national mobilizations, these associations and other umbrella organizations were very effective in gathering evidence to document patterns of human rights abuses. Early reports and documents published by international organizations such as the United Nations largely drew on material gathered by such groups. The documentation activity was critical in shaping the larger agenda on the problem of enforced disappearances, at a time when the clandestine nature of the crime constrained authoritative information gathering. For example, the systematic fact-finding activities of *Vicaria de Solidaridad*[2] in Chile were seminal to the landmark report of the United Nations on the fate of the disappeared (Amnesty International 1981:147–148). In short, the systematic documentation activities of the families and transnational advocacy groups, primarily Amnesty International, became the guiding compass for the United Nations and other intergovernmental organizations. To give only one example, the first human rights thematic mechanism to have a universal mandate, the UN Working Group on Enforced or Involuntary Disappearances (UNWGEID), set up in 1980, consulted closely and drew extensively on the experience of these groups, including Amnesty International, ICRC and ICoJ (Clark 2010:81).

It is worth noting that the precursor of UNWGEID was another groundbreaking venture. According to Thomas McCarthy, assistant to Theo Van Boven, the success of the ad hoc Working Group on the human rights situation in Chile in 1975 paved the way for the establishment of UNWGEID. The terms of reference of the Chilean working group, in turn, were shaped by the activities and needs of the victims of enforced disappearances. For example, the "urgency action procedure," namely initiatives to call the attention of states to individuals and save lives of alleged victims, traces its origins to the Chilean Working Group (Interview No.69). Similarly, the central procedure of UNWGEID, the

---

[2] The human rights organization of the Catholic Church in Chile.

processing of and reporting on individual cases of disappearances, epitomizes the traditional type of activity deployed by Amnesty International, documenting individual stories of those who disappeared in the 1970s and 1980s (Clark 2010). Theo Van Boven, Director of the UN Division of Human Rights (1977–1982), forerunner of the UN Human Rights Commission, who was the architect of UNWGEID, was among the first to realize the potentially critical role of victims in the United Nations. According to Thomas McCarthy, Van Boven saw "victims" entry into the United Nations as a force that could push for the realization of the ideas and proposals contained in speeches (Interview No.69). The UNWGEID was the first real opening of the UN system to victims' groups.

Another way through which the families, in concert with transnational human rights actors, contributed to the emergence of a strong legal framework is the development of *novel legal arguments in courts*, leading to fascinating *legal precedents*. National amnesty laws remained the main obstacle to prosecuting those responsible for the disappearance of their loved ones in much of the 1980s and 1990s. In addition to the long-term struggle to establish universally binding tools, analyzed below, families offered innovative arguments to circumvent the amnesty laws in regional and national courts; their persistence led to precedent-setting rulings, especially at the Inter-American Court of Human Rights (IACtHR). Subsequently, these rulings had significant impact on domestic trials and national law.

Leading the way was the 1988 *Velasquez Rodriquez* v. *Honduras* case, the first legally binding judgment of IACtHR on enforced disappearances (Kyriakou 2014:18).[3] The initial complaints were filled by an association of relatives' associations[4] and a leading human rights group, the *Comite para la Defensea de los Derechos Humanos en Honduras* (CODEH), in 1981 (Méndez & Vivanco 1990:530). The *Velasquez Rodriquez* case established some of the central ingredients of the contemporary international legal framework for disappearances. For example, the court found that the crime of disappearances creates a continuing legal obligation of the state to carry out an effective investigation into the conditions leading to the disappearances, to prosecute those responsible for the crime, to

---

[3] *Velasquez Rodriguez* v. *Honduras*, Judgment of July 29, 1988, IACtHR (Ser. C) No. 4 (1988).

[4] Two associations supporting the complaint were the *Comite de Familiares de Desaparecidos* (COFADEH) and the *Asociacion Centro-American de Familiares de Desaparecidos* (ACAFADE).

recover the truth about the disappearances and to offer reparation to the families (Kyriakou 2014; Méndez 2011:63).[5] Hence, by the late 1980s, certain regional legal bodies started to consider this systematic practice as a crime, setting the stage for the emergence of other legal norms in following years.

In general, IACtHR rulings had a wide reach, setting the tone for the action by national judges on enforced disappearances. Guided by "a sense of common enterprise" these judges gradually adopted and applied the external norms (McCrudden 2000). Ariel Dulitzky, an Argentine national and member of the UN Working Group, is adamant: "The judiciary was open, was receptive to the case law coming from the Inter-American system and that interaction gave judges new legitimacy ... the legitimacy of being part of this international community" (Interview No.34). By the late 2000s, the IACtHR provisions had become the cornerstone of the legal framework circumscribing the crime of disappearances. Over time, the jurisprudence of IACHR "proved to be extremely prolific, and paved the way for many interpretive break-throughs," including the "right to know the truth," innovative remedies and the standing of victims (Kyriakou 2014:20).

As noted, the relatives had more weapons in their arsenal. In their efforts to overcome amnesties, the major obstacle to truth recovery, they sought out and used original legal arguments. Their strategy was inge-nious and successful. In several Latin American countries, relatives managed to have the crime of disappearances excluded from amnesty provisions, while in some cases, their mobilization led to the annulment of amnesty laws entirely. For example, in Argentina, families convin-cingly argued the "disappearance of minors" should be excluded from the provisions of *Punto Final* law, thereby cutting back the scope of the amnesty law and setting the stage for its annulment in 2005 (Mallinder 2009). Similarly, in Chile, the families successfully framed the disap-peared as acts of kidnapping; in the absence of a body to prove the homicide, they argued the crime was ongoing.[6] More recently, the Chilean Supreme Court ruled amnesty law inapplicable in cases of dis-appearances (Lafontaine 2005).

---

[5] A similarly important ruling was case of *Barrios Altos* v. *Peru, Chumbipuma Aguirre and ors* v. *Peru*, Reparations and costs, IACHR Ser. C, No. 87, IHRL 1470, November 30, 2001, IACtHR. The court clearly said amnesty law was not applicable to the crime of enforced disappearances.

[6] See *Poblete Cordova*, Case No. 469–98, ruling of September 9, 1998, Supreme Court, para 11.

The Path to a Universal Instrument

Early on, the families were convinced that as a result of the unprece-dented nature of the crime of disappearances and the concomitant lack of codified comprehensive legal framework, any effort to comprehensively address the problem and effectively prosecute perpetrators would require the development of a universal instrument.[7] They deemed the recourse to rights in existing treaties insufficient to provide a comprehensive response to their needs. Despite some regional victories, primarily in Latin America, the long-term objective for families remained the adop-tion of a universally binding legal instrument. This came with the 2007 adoption of the International Convention for the Protection of All Persons from Enforced Disappearances (the Convention).

The process and the mobilization behind the 2007 Convention is fascinating. Wilder Tayler, Secretary General of the ICoJ and previously Policy Director of Human Rights Watch, was directly involved in its drafting, giving him real insight into the families' involvement: "Relatives had a tremendous degree of moral authority. So they became the engine of mobilization. They were the first ones to demand a universal conven-tion on disappearances" (Interview No.37). Olivier de Frouville, a member of the UN Working Group of Enforced or Involuntary Disappearances, agrees and is more specific: "From the beginning to the end ... the very idea of having international instruments dealing with enforced disappearances had come from associations of families of the disappeared in Latin America" (Frouville, forthcoming). In fact, the Latin American Federation of Families of Detained-Disappeared (FEDEFAM) led the initiatives for the adoption of a universal instru-ment; the group was later supported by other regional federations such as the Asian Federation against Involuntary Disappearances (AFAD).

At various critical junctures, certain "bridge figures" took center stage in the process, especially in preparing and drafting the new legal framework. Participation in colloquia, conferences and meetings on the topic of enforced disappearances consolidated their agenda and facilitated the emergence of a "network." The development of this network and the battle against impunity was given a boost by a broader policy shift in the United States, already evident by the late 1970s and set in motion by the Carter administration. In 1979, US State Department Assistant Secretary for

---

[7] It is worth noting that even a "universally binding treaty" binds only those states that have ratified it. Also, customary international law and peremptory norms of international law (*jus cogens*) are, in principle, universal.

Human Rights Particia Derian (a bridge figure in her own right) expressed a clear human rights agenda in which disappearances assumed a prominent position. In a Congress hearing, she stressed: "We consider the problem to be one of the most serious human rights issues confronting the world today necessitating attention and action not only by the US but by all members of the international community" (House of Representatives 1979:292).

Refugee and diaspora communities helped raise the issue in different European countries. There was a particular awareness of the problem in France, where a significant portion of the Argentine and Chilean political refugees fled in the 1970s. Some of them were lawyers with access to the French legal networks, and this helped draw attention to the issue. In any event, the first international colloquium on disappearances to discuss the prospect of a universal legal instrument was organized by the Human Rights Institute of the Paris Bar Association in Paris in 1981 (Scovazzi & Citroni 2007:255). Despite the French interest, in this early stage, regional non-governmental organizations (NGOs) and families continued to take the lead (Tayler 2001:65), especially in Latin America. For example, in 1982, FEDEFAM adopted a draft convention on disappearances; this became the founding document for a second international colloquium, this time organized by FEDEFAM in Colombia in 1986.

Largely as a result of the unrelenting pressure from the families, IACHR initiated a process to prepare a convention on disappearances, drawing on FEDEFAM's draft convention (Scovazzi & Citroni 2007:255). In 1988, IACHR presented a draft text which incorporated several path breaking innovations, most building on the landmark *Velazquez Rodriguez* case mentioned previously (Tayler 2001:67). Shortly thereafter, a meeting was set up by ICoJ in Geneva in 1988, with the participation of family associations, members of the UNWGEID and transnational human rights NGOs, in an attempt to improve the draft text which was then sent to the UN Commission for Human Rights for adoption. The final Declaration was adopted in 1992 without vote (Scovazzi & Citroni 2007:248; Tayler 2001:67).[8] Although it was not a treaty and not legally binding, the 1992 Declaration represented a decisive step, in more than simply symbolic terms. For the first time, an agreed-upon definition of the crime was adopted by an intergovernmental organization.

---

[8] UN Resolution 47/133, *Declaration on the Protection of All Persons from Enforced Disappearances*, A/RES/47/133, December 18, 1992.

In 1994, the Organization of American States (OAS) adopted the Inter-American Convention on Enforced Disappearance of Persons, the first legally binding instrument on enforced disappearances. The Convention recognized the practice of disappearances as a crime against humanity and reinforced the "continuous nature" of the offence (Scovazzi & Citroni 2007). Not surprisingly, the Latin American region, most heavily affected by the problem of disappeared persons, was the first to develop legally binding tools. In due course, these were diffused globally. In 1998, the Rome Statute of the International Criminal Court included the practice of enforced disappearances in the list of crimes against humanity (ibid.). Similarly, the European Court of Human Rights (ECtHR) throughout the 1990s and 2000s made a number of landmark rulings in which it recognized the continuous nature of the crime. In time, these became well-entrenched norms (Korff 2006:51–54).[9]

A major obstacle for the families in the 2000s was the reluctance of states to appreciate the value of and honor a universal convention. Federico Andreu, a Colombian national and a General Councel of ICoJ with direct involvement in the negotiations, says one way to convince international policymakers of the need for a new instrument was a request from an impartial and respected expert for an authoritative report shedding light on the gaps of the existing legal framework (Interview No.43). More specifically, in the 2000s, the UN Commission on Human Rights commissioned Manfred Nowak to carry out an independent investigation and publish a report on the existing legal framework on enforced disappearances (Scovazzi & Citroni 2007).[10] The report found that only a universally binding instrument would ensure that the statute of limitations would not apply to cases of enforced disappearances.[11] Again, the families were at work in the background; in an interview, Nowak claimed the "role of families in setting up this initiative was instrumental" (Interview No.42). Families requested globally known and respected figures to sign a petition on the need for such

---

[9] See *Kurt* v. *Turkey* (Application no. 2476/94), judgment of May 25, 1998; *Cyprus* v. *Turkey* (Application no. 25781/94), judgment of May 10, 2001, recognize the "right to know" the truth. On the continuous nature of the crime, see *Varnava and other* v. *Turkey* (Applications nos. 16064/90, 16065/90, 16066/90, 16068/90, 16069/90, 16070/90, 16071/90, 16072/90 and 16073/90), judgment of September 18, 2009. The duty of the state to exhume and identify the body and punish perpetrators is reaffirmed in *Bazorkina* v. *Russia* (Application no. 69481/01), judgment of July 7, 2006 (Article 117).

[10] E/CN.4/2002/71, January 8, 2002.

[11] UN Commission on Human Rights E/CN.4/2002/71, January 8, 2002, "Civil and Political Rights including Questions of Disappearances and Summary Executions," para 82.

a universal instrument. It was signed by hundreds of respected persons, including Adolfo Perez Esquivel, the Nobel Peace laureate (Interview No.43).

The groundswell of effort culminated in the adoption by the UN General Assembly of the Convention in 2007, the most authoritative and comprehensive instrument to date on the problem of the disappeared. Gabriella Citroni, a legal scholar who advocated for relatives' associations at that critical period, describes the negotiations leading to the Convention as a "Copernican revolution":

> It was conducted in a completely different way from other negotiations. The Chair Bernard Kessedjian, had a personal interest in enforced disappearances. He happened to know one of the Grandmothers of the Plaza de Mayo. One of the things he did during the negotiations on whether to go ahead for a binding treaty or not, was that every time he would give first the time to relatives who were present in Geneva and only afterwards to open the floor to States. This is unprecedented in international law. Usually we have states negotiating and at the end of it, when everything is agreed they open the floor to the civil society.
>
> (Interview No.45)

According to Ewad Plate, who advised families and participated in the process, families had the chance to "play the emotional card that made the difference. Relatives had the chance to tell their stories and half of the room was crying" (Interview No.36). Thus, human testimonies had a direct impact on convincing a reluctant delegation to support the initiative. Before the official adoption, in a highly symbolic gesture, the poem of the Uruguayan poet Mario Benedetti "*Desaparecidos*" was read at an emotionally charged moment – this too may have helped the cause.

Mary Aileen Diez-Bacalso, leader of the AFAD, shares a vivid story, illustrating how the repertoire of symbolic mobilization and the decision to share their life stories directly impacted certain provisions of the Convention:

> We decided to present our personal stories. For instance, in terms of the Article 24, Paragraph 7, on the new right established, that is the right of families of the disappeared to form associations. This was vehemently opposed by states. What I did was to share with the audience the story of Munir. Munir was our chairperson from Indonesia. He was with me in one of the first sessions of that drafting body. However, in that particular session when this matter was debated upon, he was no longer there because he was poisoned by arsenic in a flight from Jakarta to Amsterdam via Singapore. He was declared dead on arrival. He was

poisoned because of his human rights work. At that very session, I presented that his wife, Suciwati, received a box with a dead chicken and with a threat letter from the perpetrators saying that if she continued to find truth and justice for Munir, she would be likened to a dead chicken. After that intervention, no one on the floor anymore opposed that specific provision.

(Interview No.64)

In addition to learning how to play symbolic politics, the families had become skillful lobbyists in their own right by this point. To cite only one example, early in the 1990s the Dutch branch of Amnesty International set up a project entitled "Linking Solidarity" with the objective of organizing exchange meetings of families from different parts of the world. Those who attended not only found the meetings very useful but also requested help in capacity-building and lobbying techniques. Ewoud Plate, then Director of "Linking Solidarity," maintains learning how to lobby was pivotal in helping families convince reluctant members to adopt the Convention: "They spent every lunch break to talk to different delegations who were skeptical" (Interview No.36).

Manfred Nowak puts the two acquired skills together. In his view, "this mobilization and their suffering was instrumental" (Interview No.42) to the adoption of the particular wording of Article 22 of the Convention that recognizes families as direct victims of disappearances.

It is not going too far to see the Convention as a critical turning point. First, it recognizes the "continuous nature of the crime" (Article 8), thus rendering the crime not subject to statutes of limitations;[12] essentially, so long as the fate of the missing remains unknown, the offence is ongoing (Kyriakou 2012; McCrory 2007:553–554).[13] Second, it obliges states to investigate the conditions leading to the disappearance (Article 12(1)) and punish perpetrators (Article 6) (Vibhute 2008). Part and parcel of this provision is the inapplicability of amnesty laws and pardons to protect perpetrators (Scovazzi & Citroni 2007). Moreover, for the first time, the absolute rights of relatives "to know the truth" not subjected to any limitations or derogations are acknowledged (Article 24.2), while the

[12] This was recognized in a ruling on *Quinteros v. Uruguay* (Application no. 107/81), judgment on July 21, 1983, and in the following landmark *Velazquez Rodriguez v. Honduras* (Application no. 7920/86), judgment on July 29, 1988.

[13] A very interesting development is that when a state is recognized as responsible for enforced disappearances carried out even before the entry into force of a legally binding instrument, the state is still responsible because disappearance is an ongoing crime. This was verified in an ECtHR decision (*Janoviec and others v. Russia*, (Application nos. 55508/07 and 29520/09), judgment on October 21, 2013.

state has a duty to locate, respect and return the remains of people who have disappeared (Article 24.3) (Citroni & Scovazzi 2009; McCrory 2007). Finally, the Convention adopts a universal jurisdiction (Article 9), a mechanism to put pressure on states to punish perpetrators.

Some may question the extent to which the Convention constitutes a "critical" development. It is true that at the time of writing, only 43 states have ratified it. Its importance lies in its codification of what constitutes enforced disappearance; it also introduces obligations relating to the prevention and suppression of the offence and sets up an international monitoring mechanism (the 'Committee on Enforced Disappearances') to put pressure on states to address the crime. It represents the culmination of the mobilization of the relatives' associations and other NGOs and marks a turning point from preceding decades where only "soft law," resolutions and other non-binding texts were in place.[14] The requirement for "impartial and independent" investigation, the recognition of the role of NGOs/families' associations and the explicit introduction of the right of each victim to know the truth of the circumstances of the enforced disappearance (Article 24(2)) are all innovations introduced by the Convention, and all can be traced to the families.

The Families and the Evolution of the "Right to Truth"

In tandem with the robust legal framework, another way through which this mobilization has shaped contemporary transitional justice is the development of central international norms. One of the norms with growing appeal in debates of transitional justice is the "right to know" the truth. Historically, the "right to know" the truth can be traced to International Humanitarian Law and the rights of the families of missing persons in contexts of internal (or international) armed conflicts to find the whereabouts of their loved ones (Naqvi 2006:248–249).[15]

As indicated in previous chapters, the nature of the crime of disappearances traps families into a frozen grief and makes truth recovery imperative. The emergence of the right to truth as an undisputed norm is inextricably linked to the problem of disappearances, most notably the struggle of the relatives in Latin America to uncover the truth about their loved ones in the 1980s (IACHR 2014:7). As a recent IACHR report says,

---

[14] It should be noted that the International Committee of the Red Cross (ICRC) considers there is customary international law on disappearances.

[15] UN 2006 – E/CN.4/2006/91 – Study on the right to truth; Articles 32 and 33 of the 1977 Additional Protocol I to the Geneva Convention.

"Within the Inter-American System, the right to truth was initially linked to the phenomenon of forced disappearance" (2014:24).

Once again, the region most strongly affected by the crime was the most proactive in addressing it. As far back as 1977, IACHR had started issuing resolutions on disappearances.[16] In 1983, the General Assembly declared the crime "an affront to the conscience of the Hemisphere" (Tayler 2001:68). In one of its first reports, IACtHR is emphatic: "Family members of the victims are entitled to information as to what happened to their relatives" (IACHR 1985).[17] By 1985, IACHR had adopted a broad interpretation whereby the right to truth was not limited to the families but included the wider society:

> Every society has the inalienable right to know the truth about past events, as well as the motives and circumstances in which aberrant crimes came to be committed, in order to prevent repetition of such acts in the future. . . . [The Right to Truth] is a collective right which allows a society to gain access to information essential to the development of democratic system.[18]

In other words, a norm was gradually gaining currency, something clearly evidenced in the 1988 case *Velazquez Rodriquez* v. *Honduras*. As noted above, the court affirmed the relatives had the right to know the victims' fate and, if dead, the location of their remains. It was also acknowledged that as a form of redress, the state had an obligation to investigate the conditions under which disappearances took place (IACHR 2014:para 65). In a related note, as Ariel Dulitzky pointed out to me, IACtHR also adopted a very progressive interpretation of the Convention (Interview No.34).

Once again, the role of the families cannot be ignored. The right to truth has gained traction in law through their innovative repertoire of mobilization, especially in the Argentinian "truth trials." In the early 1990s, amnesty law precluded the possibility of prosecuting perpetrators

---

[16] AG/Res. 510 (X-O/80), AG/Res. 618 (XII-O/82), AG/Res. 666 (XIII-O/83) and AG/Res. 742 (XIV/O/84).

[17] Annual Report of the IACHR 1985-6, OEA/Ser.L./V/II/Doc.8 Rev1, 193.

[18] See IACHR 1958-6, AS Doc. No OEA/Ser.L/V/II.Doc8, rev.1, September 26, 1986, pp. 151 and 193; I/A Court H.R., Case of *Velásquez Rodríguez* v. *Honduras*. Judgment of July 29, 1988. Ser. C No. 4, para 181; Case of *Anzualdo Castro* v. *Peru*. Preliminary Objection, Merits, Reparations and Costs. Judgment of September 22, 2009. Ser. C, No. 202, para 118; Case of *Gomes Lund et al.* (*Guerrilha do Araguaia*) v. *Brazil*. Preliminary Objections, Merits, Reparations and Costs. Judgment of November 24, 2010. Ser. C, No. 219, para 201; Case of *Gelman* v. *Uruguay*. Merits and Reparations. Judgment of February 24, 2011. Ser. C, No. 221, para 243.

of the dirty war. Yet with the support of lawyers from the Center for Legal and Social Studies (CELS), the families managed to delink the investigation concerning disappearances from the prospect of indictment.[19] In essence, the court accepted the families' argument that irrespective of the duty to prosecute, the state had the obligation to investigate. This represents an acknowledgment of the rights of the families to know the truth. The Director of CELS explains the rationale for the strategy:

> The impossibility of pursuing authors of these crimes did not mean simply closure of any kind of judicial intervention ... the right of the relatives to know the final destiny of their loved ones and the right of the society to know in detail the methodology used by the military dictatorship to exterminate tens of thousands of Argentines. It was this need to know (in both its aspects, the personal right of the relatives and the collective right of the whole community) that was presented to the courts, pleading the "Right to Truth".
>
> (cited in Human Rights Watch 2001)

An intrinsic part of the right to know the truth is the right "to gain access to and obtain information."[20] Accordingly, truth recovery, access to information and transparency became the weapons used to attack the very clandestine nature of the crime (Garibian 2014). During the Argentinian truth trials, a critical mass of evidence was gathered, from both forensic and documentary investigations. Once the amnesty law was annulled, these findings became critical incriminatory evidence, leading to the reopening of hundreds of cases (EAAF 2007b:103). This supports a central argument of this book: simply stated, there is a sequence in the transitional justice process with forensic and truth recovery usually occurring first and accountability following.

In any event, the right to truth, one of the mainstays of transitional justice norms, emerged as a result of the innovative legal tactics of the families. Stefanie Grant, an informed observer of the evolution of these norms from the standpoint of the Head of Research Department of Amnesty International and the UN Office of the High Commissioner for Human Rights, captures the impact of the families:

---

[19] In this instance, families and legal advocates overlap, as one of the cases brought for examination was the (missing) daughter of the founder of CELS, Emilio Mignone.

[20] UN High Commissioner for Human Rights Resolution 2005/66, "Right to Truth," April 20, 2005, (E/CN.4/RES/2005/66). See also Article 13 of the IACtHR (2014:10, para 13).

> They (families) did something radical and creative, and of course [it] is an example of dynamic creative power of the human rights concept that as soon as you accept that a family has the right to know what happened to their loved ones, then certain obligations should follow.
>
> (Interview No.33)

Subsequently, the right to truth was diffused throughout a wider range of human rights violations, such as extrajudicial executions and torture, and has more recently been cited with respect to efforts to combat impunity, the rights of the Internally Displaced Persons (IDP) to know the fate of their relatives and other remedial actions for serious human rights violations.[21]

Although there is no explicit reference to the right to truth in any human rights treaty, it is a central concept in transitional justice debates. For example, a recent report by Special Rapporteur De Greiff unambiguously identifies the right to truth as a requisite ingredient of political transitions (United Nations 2015:para 18). The United Nations has also issued a number of resolutions on the missing and the right to truth since 1974.[22]

Coupled with the legal rulings on enforced disappearances, this suggests legal norms are dynamic processes, constructed by historical, transnational and ideation factors (Huneeus, Couso & Sieder 2010:9). Norms are not always imported from advanced liberal democracies; rather, local needs and historical experiences often shape legal and normative agendas on enforced disappearances in particular and on transitional justice more broadly. The landmark legal rulings of the IACtHR acknowledging the crime of enforced disappearances in the 1980s were critical both in "locking in" future rulings, as it became difficult for national judges to overlook from these legal precedents, but most importantly for setting the normative agenda globally.

Conclusion

The analysis in this chapter sheds light on the "missing" tale of human rights by describing how the families' attempts to achieve truth and

---

[21] UN Doc. A/HRC/5/7, June 7, 2007, para 81 and IACHR 2014: para 76, p. 37; UN Commission on Human Rights, The Guiding Principles on Internal Displacement, UN Doc. E/CN.4/1998/53/Add 21.

[22] General Assembly Resolution 3220 (XXIX), 33/173, 45/165 and 47/132). The General Assembly of the OAS has used the term "right to truth" in several resolutions. See, for example, AG/RES. 666 (XIII-0/83) of November 18, 1983, para 5, and AG/RES. 742 (XIV-0/84) of November 17, 1984, para 4.

accountability shaped contemporary transitional justice. Admittedly, as this and the preceding chapters made clear, the families were not alone. They drew upon and included within their mobilization certain influential allies, including transnational human rights groups and the epistemic community of forensic scientists discussed previously. Three central mechanisms of transitional justice, namely, truth commissions, the use of forensic sciences and a new legal vocabulary, owe a debt to this innovative mobilization.

These three mechanisms are not mutually exclusive but complement and reinforce each other. For example, without forensic evidence it would have been almost impossible to convict the guilty. In turn, the use of forensic sciences became important within the context of truth commissions because of the need to document the crime of disappearances. Finally, the emergence and diffusion of legal norms represents a long-term process dependent on evidentiary work undertaken in early stages after a transition by forensic teams and fact-finding (truth) commissions. In fact, the "missing" tale of human rights is one of incremental change, where each new step is an extension of a legal, forensic or documentary precedent.

Still, the passage of time alone fails to explain the astonishing outcomes. Some of the most heinous dictators/warlords have been convicted on charges related to the specific crime of the disappeared, not for other more visible and documented crimes such as extrajudicial executions. Legal outcomes are often the result of ongoing and persistent social and political struggles. This is no exception. By combining the three processes (truth commissions, exhumations and legal norms) and refusing to be deterred, the families set a "justice cascade" in motion. We tend to take scientific or normative developments for granted, but as my analysis suggests, in this case, we can look directly at the relatives for an explanation. This is the "missing" tale of human rights.

PART III

National Perspectives

6

Institutionalized Silences for the Missing in Lebanon

I lost hope. I pray for God to show me my son in my dreams. Sometimes I see him as a baby, others as a young man . . . I believe his is with his brother and father in heaven.

(Mother of a son missing since 1978 in Lebanon; Interview No.48)

If after 32 years we did not get the truth, we won't get it in a million years.

(Son of a man missing since 1983 in Lebanon; Interview No.49)

In November 1982, Wadad Halwani, a high school teacher whose husband went missing, made a radio call to all those who had a loved one being abducted during the Lebanese civil war, asking them to join her in a gathering; she was surprised when hundreds of families showed up (cited in Maalouf 2009). She found this surprising because at the height of the Lebanese civil war (1975–1990), most people were paralyzed by a deep-seated fear that reporting the problem to the police might have an adverse effect on the fate of their loved ones, if they were still in custody. Mrs. Halwani's husband was one of approximately 17,000 persons who went missing during the civil war and its violent aftermath (Jaquemet 2009). Despite the number of political and institutional obstacles set by the post-conflict realities, the families have deployed an active repertoire of mobilization over the past three decades. Yet as the excerpts from the interviews cited above illustrate, after more than 25 years, families are still in despair. They remain in limbo, unsure as to whether their lost ones are dead or alive, or if they are dead, where they are buried. Often they feel guilty for being unable to do something that would bring them back or find their whereabouts. According to a member of a support group who consults relatives, one father has "dreamt of his son asking him 'Father why aren't you searching for me?'" (Interview No.51).

The families have no reason to feel guilty, however. Responsibility (or blame) belongs elsewhere. Following the end of the war in 1990, the Ta'if Agreement, also known as the National Reconciliation Accord, set the stage for an amnesty law, which precluded the possibility of holding perpetrators accountable for massive human rights abuses. And while in the period following the transition a number of commissions of inquiry were set up to establish the truth about the disappeared, these were largely unsuccessful.

The Lebanese experience of the disappeared is interesting and instructive from the standpoint of transitional justice. First, the relevant literature reserves a special position for "success stories"; as such, Lebanon, a neglected story with limited mainstream transitional justice policies, can boost our understanding of the challenges faced by societies emerging from conflict in their pursuit of truth and justice. Second, addressing certain puzzles in Lebanon can help us assess the extent to which victims' mobilization affects transitional justice outcomes. For example, why, despite the persistent mobilization of the families over past decades, were they unable to overcome the "institutionalized silence" and enter a new era, with exhumations to identify the remains of their loved ones? Also as the international community was largely absent from the peacebuilding initiatives in Lebanon, it makes sense to use this case to probe how societies coming out from civil wars deal with sensitive questions of human rights in the absence of external actors – this remains the typical scenario in post-conflict settings globally, but looking at a different option will shed light on both scenarios.

Another puzzling feature of Lebanon is the passage of significant time not followed by any policy of addressing the past, making it a challenging test for proponents of "post-transitional justice," or delayed justice.[1] As the comparative experience of other post-conflict societies shows, at the early stages after transition, there are several and often insurmountable obstacles for truth recovery. Obviously, it was impossible for relatives to push for a policy to acknowledge their suffering in the early years after the end of the war, as the country was under de facto control of the Syrian regime (1990–2005). Yet as time passes, new opportunities generally emerge and these, in turn, allow transitional justice tools to be adopted. One obvious example is Cyprus (see Chapter 7). Years have gone by, with families continuing to mobilize, but nothing has happened in Lebanon; the prevailing "institutional silence" stymies post-transitional justice debates. It is interesting to examine why Lebanon remains so resistant.

The Lebanese experience is useful in the study of transitional justice for a third reason. As evident in the analysis of the database in Chapter 2,

---

[1] For more information on post-transitional justice, see Aguilar (2009) and Collins (2011).

Asia in general, and the Middle East in particular, has the highest rate of the use of amnesty laws to deal with the problem of disappearances. Given this overarching context, Lebanon can shed light on the dynamics of "institutionalized silence." In contrast to other countries in the region where conflicts are ongoing or the lack of democratization does not permit us to draw safe conclusions for transitional justice policies, Lebanon underwent a (negotiated) transition followed by an amnesty in the 1990s and, therefore, seems to have had a realistic possibility of addressing this issue. Moreover, as a result of the Arab Spring, a number of countries in the region are now in the midst of a transition; the Lebanese experience may suggest ways for these societies to deal more effectively with the missing.

The main objective in this chapter is to explain the persistence of "institutional silence." Why, despite the tireless mobilization of the families of the missing, did Lebanon not move into "forensic truth" recovery (i.e. humanitarian exhumations)? I argue that a combination of security, political and institutional constraints shaped an adverse political opportunity structure, which curtailed the families' mobilization prospects. The absence of a minimum level of security, coupled with feeble domestic institutions and the absence of international actors, made it almost impossible for families to create influential (domestic or inter-national) alliances to de-politicize debates around the missing. All these are prerequisites to overcome domestic veto players and set up a policy of exhumations. The Lebanese experience highlights the unique, often insurmountable, challenges families face in turning their mobilization into an effective transitional justice policy in post-conflict settings.

The chapter begins by setting the historical backdrop against which abductions became a key instrument of warfare over the past few decades in Lebanon, highlighting the unique trauma of the families. The section also explains how the large number of actors and paramilitary groups responsible for abductions complicated post-conflict efforts for truth recovery. To this end, I provide a typology of disappearances and discuss how the idiosyncratic nature of the violence has affected the relatives' demand for truth. I go on to discuss the persistence of the institutional silence. I challenge the view that amnesty law was the key obstacle to truth recovery; instead, I point to the institutional, political and security constraints preventing the effective mobilization of the families. I show that families had limited prospect of success, as the political opportu-nities available to them were simply absent. The continued presence of an embedded security apparatus even after the official termination of the conflict trimmed the minimum level of security necessary for setting up a policy of exhumations. Similarly, the weakening of domestic institutions, predominantly the judiciary, meant families could neither form domestic influential alliances (such as friendly lawyers or judges) nor utilize a growing set of relevant international legal norms to circumvent reluctant political elites. The lack of access to these opportunities explains families' inability to convert the mobilization into transitional justice outcomes. The final section is a bit more positive; in it, I explain how recent (post-2008) developments, predominantly the growing involvement of international actors, have helped the families take small but symbolically significant steps in their quest for truth and acknowledgment.

The Logic of Disappearances in Lebanon

The civil war took a heavy toll on Lebanese society. Approximately 144,000 were killed and 184,000 injured (Ghosn & Khoury 2011:381). One of the most traumatic – and definitely the most enduring – wounds of the civil war was the missing. Although accurate data are still unavailable, the number of missing according to the Lebanese government is approximately 17,415 (Amnesty International 1997:6; Maalouf 2009). As the vast majority (approximately 82 percent) were civilians, families were often afraid to report disappearances to the police (ICRC 2013). Therefore, the number may be even higher. A more recent study estimates the number of missing as 19,860, approximately 0.75 percent of the total population (cited in International Center for Transitional Justice [ICTJ] 2013:70).

Regardless of the precise figure, the widespread use of the practice deeply wounded the Lebanese society. In a 1983 survey, 21 percent of respondents said they had a relative or a family member who went missing and 30 percent had a close friend kidnapped (cited in Khalaf 2002:254). The ICRC branch in Lebanon conducted a survey in 2013; the very interesting findings clearly indicate enduring trauma. Although most victims went missing in the 1970s or early 1980s, it remains impossible for the relatives to reach emotional closure without some fundamental answers. Simply stated, they need to know what happened (ICRC 2013:11). The majority (over 70 percent) want to know the truth about the fate and whereabouts of their relatives (ibid. 18).

A unique feature of the Lebanese experience is that the civil war was a succession of interconnected wars involving domestic military actors, neighboring states and their local proxies, creating a complex set of conflicts (Makdisi & Richard 2005). Disappearances constituted a central feature of all waves of political violence, reaching a peak during the civil war but continuing afterwards. In addition, different groups have instrumentally used disappearances to achieve different strategic objectives at different periods during the conflict and afterwards as well. This has understandably influenced the demands and repertoire of mobilization. Thus, in the case of Lebanon, understanding the logic of the violence and creating a typology of disappearances are analytically valuable.

The central cleavages of the civil war in 1975 were the long-standing issue of power sharing between Christian and Muslim communities and the rising influence of Palestinian refugees (Makdisi & Richard 2005:62).[2] Radical Christian militants mobilized to protect the political status quo from both the Muslim community and the growing influence of the refugees. The opposing faction, composed mainly of Muslims and members of the political Left, was not only sympathetic to the struggle of the Palestinians but was striving to revise the power-sharing arrangement perceived to be outdated and unfair to the growing Muslim community. The traditional Christian/Maronite groups included the Kataeb and the Lebanese Forces, while the opposing group was composed of the Palestinian PLO, the Shi'a Amal party and the Druze-dominated progressive Socialist Party (ibid.). There were hundreds of minor militant groups; all told, there were 180 by 1984.

The military objective of all parties was to control the state and divide Lebanon along sectarian lines (Corm 1994:219; Ghosn & Khoury 2011: 381–382). To this end, abductions and disappearances were used to "cleanse" specific areas while controlling the population through terror (Corm 1994:221; Maalouf 2009). Both Christian and Muslim militias engaged in what came to be known as "bilateral physical liquidations" (Ghattas 2000). A significant number of disappearances took place in the first 2 years of the conflict (1975–1977) (Amnesty International 1997; see also Figure 6.1).[3]

---

[2] The roots of the political system in Lebanon were planted in the 1943 National Pact which reflected a power-sharing arrangement based on a 6:5 ratio of Christian to Muslim in public offices (Ghosn & Khoury 2011). By the 1970s, this ratio did not reflect the balance of the two communities; it became a bone of contention between pro status quo groups and groups struggling to revise it.

[3] The data presented above are from a survey conducted by the ICRC on a sample of 200 people; they sketch an indicative but not accurate picture of the distribution of disappearances.

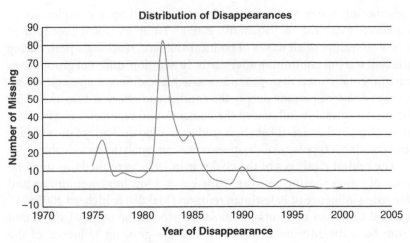

Figure 6.1 Disappeared in Lebanon

The type of warfare and the logic of disappearances changed in the early 1980s and continued in the 1990s with the military intervention of Israel and Syria. The massacre in the Palestinian refugee camps in Sabra and Shatila by Israeli forces and their local proxies triggered the intervention of Syria; soon the tool of disappearances resumed, becoming a conventional instrument of warfare in Lebanon. Between 1982 and 1984, the Lebanese army abducted over 3000 individuals and hundreds were transferred to detention camps in South Lebanon or to Israeli prisons (Amnesty International 1997:5–6). Throughout the war, hundreds of Palestinians and Lebanese Muslims or members of the political Left disappeared into Israeli detention, most significantly at the Center of Al Ansar in Southern Lebanon (ICTJ 2013); this lasted until the withdrawal of the Israeli army from Lebanon in 2000. This period is characterized by the strategic use of disappearances as a bargaining chip in exchange for the return of Israeli soldiers (alive or their remains) or intelligence. The ICRC facilitated several swaps that took place as late as 2008 (ICTJ 2013:77; Maalouf 2009). The fact that the Israeli forces instrumentally used the practice of disappearances was officially acknowledged by a decision of the Israeli Supreme Court; it officially sanctioned the political decision to continue the detention of ten Lebanese nationals held in Israeli prisons as leverage in the return of Israeli soldiers (Ben-Naftali & Gleichgevitch 2000). The vast majority of those who fall in the category of missing are presumed dead, however.

At the same time, the end of the war institutionalized Syrian domination of Lebanese politics. From 1990 until 2005, in tandem with previous
forms of disappearances which did not abate, a new pattern emerged;
massive waves of abductions of Lebanese were carried out by groups
controlled by Hezbollah, with victims transferred to Syrian prisons
(Maalouf 2009). Almost a decade after the official termination of the
war, human rights watchdogs continued to publish reports drawing the
attention of the international community to this growing trend (see
Amnesty International 1997; Human Rights Watch 1997).
Disappearances were used to extract information from civilians or militias held incommunicado for years, and the unique type of terror instilled
on the broader population meant more effective control of Lebanese
society (Human Rights Watch 1997:18). Lebanese security forces, controlled now by the Syrian regime, became a critical link in carrying out
disappearances (Lebanese Center for Human Rights 2008:19).
An interesting aspect of this wave of disappearances is the return of
a number of people considered missing from Syrian detention camps,
sometimes after a decade, rekindling the hope of thousands of relatives
(Lebanese Center for Human Rights 2008:19).

Families' Mobilization and Fragmentation

Against all odds, the families have continued to seek the truth. Yet they
have been unable to convert their mobilization into concrete outcomes.
From the standpoint of social movement literature, an important obstacle was the fragmentation of the movement for much of the past three
decades. The Lebanese experience deviates from the other conflicts discussed here, primarily because of the greater number of parties involved
in the conflict. In the absence of a single culprit, the relatives' associations
were fractionalized. Several groups formed, each with a different diag-
nosis of the problem and with its own priorities. Although in a highly
complex war as in Lebanon, it is difficult to create clear-cut typologies;
Table 6.1 roughly summarizes the main groups of families and their
distinct approaches.

A sizeable group of families, mostly Muslim, Palestinians and members of the political Left, have relatives who went missing within Lebanon
or who were transferred to Israel. Most are presumed dead, so the group's
main interest is the exhumation, identification and return or repatriation
of the remains. In 1982, relatives subscribing to this framing of the
problem established the Committee of the Families of the Kidnapped

Table 6.1 *Perpetrators and Victims' Groups in Lebanon*

Actors Responsible	Period and Logic of Disappearances	Place and Fate of Disappeared	Demands of Relatives	Primary Relatives' Association
Lebanese Paramilitaries	(1975–1990) Terror Control Homogenization	Missing presumed dead (Lebanon)	Exhumations	Committee of the Families of the Kidnapped and Disappeared in Lebanon (1982)
Syria and local proxies	(1990–2005) Collaborate Control	Detained/disappeared presumed alive (Syria)	Return alive Retributive justice	Support of the Lebanese in Detention and Exile (1989)
Israel and local proxies	(1980s–2000s) Bargaining chip	Missing presumed dead (Israel)	Repatriation of remains	Follow-Up Committee (1999)

and Disappeared in Lebanon (the Committee henceforth). The objective of this group is to put pressure on the government to implement a policy of exhumations that will acknowledge the truth about the whereabouts of their loved ones. The Committee is the most comprehensive and inclusive group and has remained open to relatives from other groups, to some extent.

A second group was created in 1990, after the intensification of the practice of disappearances by Syrian proxies in Lebanon. This group, mostly Christians, established the organization Support of the Lebanese in Detention and Exile (SOLIDE henceforth), and mobilized around returning relatives from Syrian detention camps. SOLIDE's framing of the problem significantly deviates from that of the Committee; the group believes most are being held incommunicado in Syria, and it demands their release and safe return to Lebanon. The credibility of this framing is substantiated by the fact that on several occasions, people have returned home alive after decades of detention. The mobilization of the group centers on attracting the attention of international actors, while the scope of their demands is focused on retributive justice for those responsible for the disappearances. A third smaller group, the Follow-Up Committee, has a more narrow focus, that is, to rebury those persons who went missing in Southern Lebanon or in Israel.

As the authorities/paramilitary groups responsible for the disappearances were different at different periods, families had to aim their mobilization strategies at a moving target. This naturally curtailed their effectiveness. As an activist with long-standing experience of civil society activities in Lebanon explains, coordination of different groups' mobilization was impossible because their objectives were so contradictory:

> The perpetrators were different and the solution is different. . . . Most of the members of the Committee have been kidnapped and most probably killed in Lebanon, whereas SOLIDE was requesting from the Syrian authorities to release the Lebanese detainees in Syria. So the strategy was a bit different.
>
> (Interview No.65)

For several years, this thwarted the prospect of concertation among victims' associations, as it was impossible for most families to sit at the same table as members of a group allegedly responsible for the abduction of someone they loved (Interview No.13). As a leading member of SOLIDE admitted, "one murderer at this group can be the hero of another group," voicing an element common to most post-conflict settings (Interview No.50). As illustrated below, it was only in the late 2000s or early 2010s that the two groups designed a joint agenda, and this can mostly be attributed to the good personal relationship of the two leading figures (ibid.).

This points to related obstacle to any grassroots truth recovery initiative. As a result of the sectarian division of society, coupled with the collapse of state institutions in the post-war period, many families of the missing found themselves in economic difficulties, as the vast majority of the missing were male and, thus, the family breadwinners. Influential political elites replaced the role of the state and provided financial assistance to victims of their own communities, but this created the long-term dependence of some families on groups who had often been involved in human rights abuses or abductions of members of other communities. This naturally stalled independent, grassroots truth recovery initiatives. The South African experience was similar. As I show in Chapter 8, most victims depended on government support to cope with economic hardship; this limited the potential for a truth recovery that might upset those in power. There are similar findings in other parts of the world where victims face economic and social inequalities (Aronson 2010; Lundy & McGovern 2008; Robins 2011).

This is not to a diminish the importance of the families' mobilization. Given the broader political instability and other external constraints, the mere fact that they continued their mobilization and kept the problem on the political agenda is worth noting. Since the 1980s, they have devised an innovative repertoire of mobilization to promote truth recovery. Mothers and female relatives more generally have taken the lead in most activities, based on the informed guess that the authorities will not suppress mothers, who are seen as non-contentious and non-threatening actors (Rowayheb & Ouaiss 2015:1012). Since the 1980s, they have staged strikes, demonstrations, sit-ins, road blockages – the very essence of contentious politics. These tactics recall those employed by the Latin American mothers, described in Chapter 3, but the outcomes in terms of truth recovery were radically different. In 1983, at the height of the Lebanese civil war, a petition was signed by hundreds of women/relatives, putting pressure on authorities to do something about the missing (Interview No.51). This culminated in the establishment of a fact-finding committee. Unfortunately, the committee – as several others to follow in the coming years – remained a dead letter, given the ongoing civil war and the reluctance of politicians to act.

In the period preceding the Syrian withdrawal (1990–2005), room for maneuvering was minimal. Nonetheless, the relatives' associations made numerous efforts to keep the chapter of the missing open, resisting the efforts of political elites to draw a line and leave the violent past in the past. As a result of this pressure, three commissions of inquiry were set up during the 2000s by different Lebanese cabinets.

The first commission of inquiry, established in 2000, was to investigate those who went missing during the civil war (1975–2000). The commission looked at approximately 2000 cases but soon concluded its operation by presuming all the missing to be dead (Ghosn & Khoury 2011:395). Although the short one-and-a-half-page report identified the existence of mass graves containing the remains of the missing, there was no follow-up process or any effort to unearth them (Byrns 2009). Nor did the report reveal any information about abductions carried out by Syria (Jaquemet 2009:73). Five months later, 54 of those considered "dead" returned alive from Syrian detention camps, throwing the credibility of the commission into question (Amnesty International 2011:5–7; Jaquemet 2009:73). The poor results are not surprising, given the situation. The commission was composed of members of the security forces, thus undermining the credibility and impartiality of the venture. Moreover, the design of the committee was flawed because it operated for a very short period of 6 months.

As a result of the vocal reaction of the relatives, a second commission was set up in 2001; it had a more restrictive mandate, namely to investigate the fate of those cases where reliable information suggested victims might be alive. The commission operated for 18 months, examining approximately 900 cases, but failed to issue a report or trace the whereabouts of any disappeared (ibid.). A third bi-lateral commission between Syria and Lebanon was set up after the Syrian withdrawal, but it remained a dead letter (Shadid 2006).

On the one hand, families remained vocal and publicly present throughout this period; on the other hand, however, this failed to lead the country forward to the necessary next step of truth recovery: the use of exhumations to achieve forensic truth.

Alternative Explanation: The Role of Amnesty

Although Lebanon was signatory to the 1948 UN Universal Declaration of Human Rights, the country has failed to accommodate even the most fundamental human rights of victims in the aftermath of the bloody civil war, such as returning bodies to relatives. This can be at least partially explained by the provision of amnesty to perpetrators. It is not uncommon for an amnesty law to follow a negotiated peace settlement, and the

Ta'if Agreement, which officially ended the 15-year civil war in Lebanon, was no exception. National reconciliation required some sort of concertation among political elites and warring factions, and the unqualified immunity of the perpetrators from prosecution for crimes committed during the war was intended to do precisely that (Ghosn & Khoury 2011:388). Accordingly, in August 1991, the Lebanese parliament passed an amnesty law (No. 84/91) covering crimes committed before the end of March 1991 (Wierda, Nassar & Maalouf 2007:1070).

The literature on post-war Lebanon agrees amnesty started an era of "state-sponsored" amnesia (Burgis-Kasthala 2013:501; Haugbolle 2010; Young 2000:421), confounding amnesty with amnesia and amnesia with silence. Certainly, the "amnesty has been the main transitional justice tool used since Lebanon's conflict-ridden independence" (Burgis-Kasthala 2013). As a result of the amnesty law, perpetrators of the most heinous crimes committed against civilians were safe from prosecution, creating a widespread feeling of impunity (Ghosn & Khoury 2011:288; Jaquemet 2009:74). At the same time, those who assassinated political or religious elites were not covered by amnesty; in other words, elite victims were more important than ordinary victims (Wierda, Nassar & Maalouf 2007:1070). Finally, neither a policy of forensic truth recovery nor a broader truth recovery mechanism to establish the facts surrounding disappearances was established.

Is this outcome the result of the amnesty law? Possibly. The problem amnesties pose to truth recovery for missing persons is twofold. First, amnesties deprive the relatives of access to legal instruments. Irrespective of the effectiveness of retributive mechanisms in addressing the needs of the families of the missing, legal tools often pave the way to reaching other objectives, such as convincing reluctant governments to proceed to exhumations even if for solely humanitarian purposes. Families with access to advanced legal tools and judicial institutions have better prospects of having their demands addressed; amnesty laws often block this option. Second, amnesty laws prevent truth recovery because they are designed to facilitate the smooth incorporation of those individuals (morally, politically and often physically) responsible for the disappearances into party politics. As the experience of other negotiated transitions shows, including Mozambique or post-Francoist Spain, parties representing the warring factions are equipped with the necessary institutional means to block inconvenient versions of truth from surfacing if these threaten to delegitimize the status quo (Kovras 2013; Manning 2002).

However, in the case of Lebanon, this is only partly true; attributing the persistence of silence to the amnesty law fails to explain why there was no truth recovery (or any legal action) for abductions not covered by the amnesty law. And as mentioned above, enforced disappearances continued well after the official termination of the civil war. Therefore, if the primary obstacle to truth recovery was the amnesty law, we might have expected to see a policy of truth recovery, or at least some lawsuits being lodged by relatives for the numerous cases of missing after 1990. The fact that a very limited number of lawsuits has come to court remains a puzzle, especially when we take into account that the families of the missing in other societies with blanket amnesties managed to create rifts in their amnesty laws, thus paving the way for truth recovery.

More importantly, it should be highlighted that the crime of enforced disappearances is not subject to statute of limitations (Article 1 of the Convention); therefore, there is ample room for legal maneuvering and truth recovery.[4] Finally, as a number of expert legal scholars argue, the duty to investigate (and provide some form of truth) does not necessitate the duty to prosecute, thereby delinking the prospect of truth recovery and exhumations from retributive justice (Freeman 2009; McEvoy & Mallinder 2012). In short, immunity does not necessarily mean silence. Amnesty certainly constitutes a significant obstacle but should not be considered the primary cause of the non-accommodation of the problem in Lebanon. As an informed observer with several years of advocacy work in the region stresses, "The amnesty law is not the cause; it is the symptom" (Interview No.13).

Consider the fate of some of the few individual lawsuits brought before national courts for cases not directly linked to the problem of the missing. Several decisions have deemed amnesty law irrelevant and prosecuted the perpetrators, but this has not led to any form of forensic/broader truth recovery. For example, Samir Geagea, leader of the Lebanese Forces and allegedly responsible for serious human rights violations during the civil war, was prosecuted for assassinating the leader of the National Liberal Party, Dany Chamoun, in 1994. As the crime of assassination(s) of political leaders is not covered by the amnesty law, he was brought to justice. Yet Amnesty International criticized the politicized nature of the trial, condemning Lebanon for the selective nature of the prosecution,

---

[4] According to Maalouf (2009), one clause in the amnesty law renders judicial procedures possible if "these crimes are repeated or uninterrupted" (Article 2.3.f), making disappearances applicable. Note that Lebanon has signed the Convention but not ratified it.

specifically, its targeting of those opposing Syrian intervention (Amnesty International 2011). This soured sectarian relations and definitely did not facilitate truth recovery for the violent past. Hence, even when amnesty law was out of the equation, it did not open the door for other forms of truth recovery to enter.

A similar example is the UN-backed Special Tribunal for Lebanon (STL), which was set up after the assassination of former Prime Minister Rafik Hariri in February 2005. The tribunal was based on the premise that "a court with international participation, could serve a symbolic and exemplary function to promote the rule of law domestically" (Sriram 2012:49). Despite the proactive international engagement safeguarding high standards of judicial accountability – where amnesty was not a concern – the tribunal failed to break the silence or promote account-ability. Instead, it further polarized sectarian politics, leading to the collapse of government and the return of violent street politics (Berti 2011:108).

In other words, amnesty is an important obstacle for truth recovery but in this case should not be considered the cause of silence or even the primary challenge to "forensic truth." Instead, it is an epiphenomenon, a symptom of broader problems of instability, the continued use of violence to resolve conflict and the limited consolidation of democratic institutions. The inability of families' mobilization to effectively push for a policy of exhumations should be attributed to the lack of access to institutional opportunities and influential (domestic and international) alliances, coupled with the absence of a certain minimum level of stability and security to unearth the contentious and divisive past.

Explaining Institutional Silence

Why did relatives' efforts to overcome silence and implement a policy of forensic truth not bear fruit in Lebanon, as it did in other countries with similar background conditions, like Cyprus? I point to three overlapping reasons. First, there was a lamentable absence of even a minimum level of security. In effect, the continued influence of an embedded security apparatus that was not demobilized after transition ruled out exhumations. Second, the passage of time was not followed by the democratization of central institutions, especially the judicial authorities who usually serve as a critical instrument in overcoming non-accommodating domestic actors. Third, the limited presence of interna-tional actors deprived families of influential international alliances and access to international normative instruments. The resulting volatility has led to the emergence of the derogatory term "Lebanization" in international politics (Knudsen 2005:1).

To begin with the first point, the absence of a minimum level of security and stability is critical to explain silence. In Lebanon, the relatives were deterred by fear. In fact, as an informed observer of Lebanese politics argues, the "society [is] paralyzed by fear" (Interview No.13). The pervasive fear can be broken down into two overlapping components: (1) talking about the past will result in the resumption of violence; (2) any demand for truth will endanger the safety of the missing, if they are still alive.

As mentioned previously, the Ta'if Accords did not take the necessary steps to dilute the power of those responsible for heinous human rights violations (Corm 1994:227). An embedded security apparatus (of militias and warlords) remained intact and even flourished after transition. As an informed observer remarks, the security apparatus is an "effective tool for the authoritarian control of the society" (Mrad 2011:11), curtailing the prospect of stabilization and the democratization of security forces (Corm 1994:216). An illustration of the uninterrupted reign of the embedded security apparatus in post-conflict Lebanon is the ongoing use of disappearances even after the end of the civil war. Talking about the missing in Lebanon is still taboo (Interview No.2). Many families fear for their loved ones or for their own personal safety (Human Rights Watch 1997:3–6).

There are sound reasons for this fear. Members of families' associations have often received death threats as a result of their involvement in these truth recovery initiatives (Rowayheb & Ouaiss 2015). As the ongoing abductions in post-conflict Lebanon illustrate, the security apparatus is both embedded and unchallenged. Engaging in the practice of disappearances presupposes the availability of infrastructures, logistics and some minimum level of authority structure that runs in tandem with state sovereignty. In fact, this is the major reason why Lebanon did not manage to move to the next level of truth recovery, in sharp contrast to countries that set up processes of forensic truth recovery and/or truth commissions and trials. This culture of fear is a key obstacle to truth recovery largely because it has prevented the broader society from supporting the families' quest for accountability. One of the distinguishing feature of most societies overcoming silence and climbing the ladder of truth is that the broader society has been a significant ally in putting pressure on domestic political elites to address the issue. In Lebanon, the recurrent waves of violence have made people wary about contentious policies, such as exhumations, delving into the divisive past.

A minimum level of security and stability is a sine qua non for exhumations for another more important reason. Identifying graves presupposes the creation of conditions of safety to convince perpetrators – most often the only eyewitnesses – to reveal contentious and potentially incriminatory information. These conditions were simply absent in post-1990 Lebanon. As a leading member of "ACT for the Disappeared," a local NGO, vividly explains, "If you open mass graves in Lebanon obviously it will point out the responsibility of one or another militia group. If you dig graves in the Christian part of Beirut it's a way of highlighting the responsibility of Christian militias" (Interview No.65). Digging up graves is an inherently contentious process, which explains the reluctance of paramilitary groups to allow exhumations 25 years after the end of the conflict.

An interview with Assaad Chaftari, a former senior intelligence officer of the Lebanese Forces, is an eye-opener. In 2000, he wrote an open letter in a national newspaper asking for forgiveness for his involvement in heinous crimes during the civil war. Since then he has been active in organizing an NGO "Fighters for Peace," which brings former combatants together to raise awareness about past violence. Although he has expressed his remorse for past actions, has dedicated his life to promoting reconciliation and has explicitly stressed he has information about the disappeared, he refrains from pointing to graves because of his fear of retribution at the hands of his own community (Rowayheb & Ouaiss 2015). He is explicit: "If a member of what was called 'Al-Mourabitoun' admitted that they had a prison, he will get killed the next day by his fellows." And he continues: "before having a national solution for this [i.e. disappeared], I am not ready to do anything. You can try to put pressure on me as much as you want, it's useless" (Interview No.50).

The absence of security as a preventive factor for eyewitnesses to come forward is confirmed by Hassana Jameleddine, a leading member of a consortium of 30 NGOs called "Wahdatouna Khalasouna" (Our Unity is Our Salvation) working to convince people to share information:

> The perpetrators got concerned about their security. So we told them that we can work on it and amend it until you get satisfied and feel secure. We do not want to threaten anyone. The most important thing for us is collecting the information because the perpetrators are ready to talk but not to a Lebanese party. They are afraid of revenge.

> (Interview No.51)

The continued presence of an embedded security regime has destabilized the state and created a deep-seated culture of fear, and this has been exacerbated by the continued proactive involvement of external actors, especially Syrian and Israeli proxies. In fact, the great number of actors involved in disappearances in Lebanon over the past three decades is another point of deviation from societies that have addressed the problem. Despite the end of war, since 1990, domestic politics has been shaped by external actors, especially Syria and its introduction of a period called "Pax Syriana." In 1991, Lebanon and Syria signed the treaty of Brotherhood, Cooperation and Coordination, setting the terms for Syrian control of the country (ICTJ 2013:77). As a result, state institutions such as the judiciary and the army were in the iron grip of Syria until the withdrawal of Syrian forces in 2005. For example, from 1995 until 2005, pro-Syrian forces handpicked the senior military security chiefs, and the military was transformed into a patronage network tasked with accommodating political interests (El-Hokayem & McGovern 2008:12). The embedded security apparatus has remained intact and powerful, so much so that the UN Fact-Finding Mission investigating the assassination of Prime Minister Hariri, concluded the Lebanese security services and Syrian military intelligence were involved in the assassination (Mrad 2011:11).

Amidst this climate of terror, intelligence services were unable to deter human rights violations and, worse yet, even facilitated the flow of abductees to detention centers in Syria (ICTJ 2013). Throughout the late 1990s and early 2000s, Syria released a number of the detained (considered missing), some after their death, reinforcing the climate of fear (Lebanese Center for Human Rights 2008:19–25). Israel and its local proxies were also strategically deploying disappearances as a means of furthering their political interests. It is not surprising, then, that the relatives were so extremely cautious in raising the issue of the missing (Interview No.30). Although 17,000 is the official number of the missing, the number of relatives participating in families' associations is considerably lower (Interview No.30). Other pro-truth-seeking groups, such as lawyers or the press, have also been deterred from talking about the problem (Human Rights Watch 1997:21). In short, the embedded security apparatus weakened and often destabilized the state while it also prevented perpetrators from talking and families from airing their experiences (Interview No.2). Those with the courage to speak out were often treated as reckless individuals who endangered the fragile peace and stability.

It is quite common in the immediate aftermath of a negotiated transition for silence to dominate public discourse. In the long term, however, the gradual process of democratic consolidation strengthens democratic institutions; this, in turn, provides the necessary instruments to domestic truth seekers to address the problem, even with a significant delay (Kovras 2013). Yes, the Lebanese civil society in general and the relatives of the disappeared in particular have been proactive (Barak 2007:58; Yakinthou 2015), and yes, they have mobilized to seize all available opportunities. Unfortunately, however, they have had negligible impact because the tools at their disposal have been limited.

The implementation of a policy of forensic truth (i.e. exhumations) presupposes the democratization of domestic institutions that provide domestic truth seekers institutional channels to express their needs. International experience shows that relatives often deploy legal instruments to put pressure on non-accommodative actors, such as former warlords and dictators, to at least concede to the opening of mass graves. Yet in Lebanon, the problem remains highly politicized two decades after the official transition to democracy, and the judiciary has not reached a minimum level of independence.

An interesting question, though, is why the relatives, individually, did not seek recourse to legal tools to demand the forensic truth; the comparative experience of other post-conflict societies shows that legal instruments have been very effective in putting pressure on non-accommodative political elites to open graves. Since the 1980s only approximately ten families have brought their cases to the court (ICTJ 2013:11). Apart from the obvious factor of widespread fear, another equally important explanation is distrust of the judiciary, the second factor noted in the introduction to this section. A son in search of his father for more than 32 years who prefers to remain anonymous maintains: "I won't get any results because the Lebanese parties will not be held accountable. It is a fact that in Lebanon you cannot hold anyone accountable" (Interview No.49). There are clear examples of this. The few lawsuits launched by relatives were either ruled inadmissible by the court or met with a disappointing decision (Lebanese Center for Human Rights 2008:10). In effect, although families made an attempt to invoke the legal argument used by families in Chile, Argentina or Cyprus to trim amnesty law, framing abductions as ongoing crimes, it did not work in Lebanon.

The example of Nacouzi Hashisho is intriguing; she lodged a lawsuit against three individuals who allegedly participated in the abduction of her husband, Muhieddine Hashisho. In 2013, after almost 23 years of delay, the Criminal Court of South Lebanon issued its ruling, concluding there was insufficient evidence against the suspects (Interview No.10). In another lawsuit lodged in 2001 for a person who went missing in 1982, the court found the lawsuit admissible – essentially overcoming the amnesty law – and found the defendant guilty. In its ruling the court acknowledges the crime of enforced disappearance is not covered by the amnesty law; Article 2.3.f indicates the "amnesty is null and void for the perpetrators of the crimes mentioned in this article if those crimes are replicated or ongoing."[5] Yet the sentence was only three years in prison (Jaquemet 2009:88).

The politicization of the Lebanese judiciary is instrumentally deployed by political elites to curtail the freedoms of their opponents, with judges appointed arbitrarily (Mrad 2011). Although the objective of democratic institutions is to set a standardized set of rules to regulate social life and conflict resolution (Robinson & Acemoglou 2012), the judiciary in Lebanon is dependent, politicized and opaque. As Chapters 3 and 9 show in the context of Argentina and Chile, respectively, the common thread linking the remarkable mobilization and effectiveness of the relatives in acknowledging truth was the presence of influential allies in courts, including lawyers who carried out a systematic struggle to erode the scope of amnesty law. This entails some minimum level of democratization of central institutions, a process still pending in Lebanon; even lawyers sympathetic to the cause of relatives are afraid to support some of these cases. A leading figure of SOLIDE describes the problem: "The lawyers, the bar association and the judges are also afraid to raise this issue because most lawyers (associations) belong to political groups so if one group would like to raise this issue, two or three other groups will not accept it. So they put it aside and they don't work on it." For these reasons, he says Lebanon is "a country of compromise and you have to compromise Justice. I would say the first victim in Lebanon is Justice" (Interview No.50). In short, some very significant institutional channels to overcome domestic obstacles to truth seeking were absent in Lebanon. As a result, families were unable to depoliticize debates around sensitive human rights issues.

As noted at the beginning of the section, isolation from international institutions is a final constraint in the mobilization of Lebanese families of the missing. Since the 1980s, there has been limited involvement by

---

[5] Article 2.3.f of Law 84 August 26,1991. *Ratiba Dib Fares* v. *Hussein Muhammad Hatoum*, Judgment of December 13, 2001, the Criminal Tribunal of Mount Lebanon.

international organizations/actors in peacebuilding activities in Lebanon. The literature shows that when faced with non-accommodative domestic political elites or other insurmountable obstacles, domestic groups often direct their claims to influential international allies who keep the issue on the agenda of international organizations, raise awareness and create a "boomerang effect" (Risse & Sikkink 1999). External influences often catalyze domestic change when domestic institutional channels are blocked. Yet that opportunity was not available to Lebanese families of the missing.

Taken together, these factors have sharply decreased the ability of families to get around reluctant domestic political elites and challenge the institutional silence. Debates about the missing have remained politicized, leaving families of the missing expressing a deep-seated despair. Nevertheless, their goal remains simple and unchanged: "We only care to know the fate of our kids. If they are dead, give us a piece of bones so that we can bury them our way and as per our religious rituals" (Interview No.48).

Recent Developments: A Silver Lining?

Despite the generally gloomy tone of the preceding pages, two important developments have recently facilitated significant steps forward. The first is internationalization; since the late 2000s, mobilization has been characterized by growing cooperation with international actors. The second is alliances between family groups. After the withdrawal of the Syrian forces, they have gradually managed to overcome their internal divisions and set out common objectives, such as the demand for humanitarian exhumations. Within this changing landscape, and in an effort to depoliticize the problem, 17 NGOs prioritized the problem of the missing. This effort, along with good personal relationships between a handful of leading members of the main family associations (Interview No.2), culminated in a 2012 Decree to establish a committee on the issue (Maalouf & Maalouf 2015).

Given the commentary in the previous section of the chapter, a pivotal move was the formation of influential international alliances. The strategic decision to internationalize their cause has facilitated truth seeking in a number of societies globally, including Cyprus and Chile. Learning from other countries facing similar challenges was an important impetus behind the change in Lebanon. An informed observer who participated in the process explains:

Instead of just lobbying and claiming the "right to know," the two committees started to look at what happened in other countries' experiences. We have been to a lot of conferences, we have visited other countries to improve our knowledge of what would be the solution on the problem of the missing. The issue of the missing is also technical, it's not merely an issue of political will, you have to locate the graves, exhume the remains and identify them. ... The civil society was not prepared at the time, we didn't know. So our focus was developing our expertise, while continuing lobbying.

(Interview No.65)

The movement to internationalize led to a recent breakthrough: the establishment of an ICRC mission with an enriched mandate. Traditionally, the ICRC, guided by the principle of "humanitarian diplomacy," has avoided politicization and worked in parallel with both national government and family groups. Yet as a member of the ICRC delegation in Lebanon who preferred to remain anonymous explained, the passage of time and the aging of most relatives, coupled with a perception that the Lebanese authorities were part of the problem, motivated the ICRC to devise a proactive agenda (Interview No.11). A decision was made to circumvent the state and work directly with the families. Following the example of other countries, the ICRC set up a concrete policy to facilitate future exhumations including taking DNA samples from relatives, developing a genetic database (post- and ante-mortem data) and locating mass graves (Amnesty International 2011:10; Maalouf 2009). In a related decision, in 2011, the ICRC decided to compile the list of the missing in Lebanon since 1975. Several years before, in 2008, the ICRC had facilitated the return of the remains of 185 abducted by Israeli proxies in exchange for the return of two coffins by Hezbollah to Israel.

The participation of international actors in exhumations is important. Exhumations are contentious and often transcend the capacity of post-conflict societies. For example, a British journalist (Ale Collet) abducted in Beirut in 1985 was exhumed in 2009, but the remains of another body found at the scene were not identified because of the lack of a forensic infrastructure or a genetic database against which to match the sample (Maalouf & Maalouf 2015:198).

In the post-2005 period, another important shift has been the re-framing of families' demands for exhumations by adopting the language of international human rights and accountability. Similarly, several international think-tanks have found an opportunity to create an active truth-seeking agenda in Lebanon, most notably the ICTJ. With the support of the ICTJ, by 2009, two motions had been submitted, one demanding the Lebanese state re-affirm the "right to know" and the other seeking "compensation" because the findings of previous commissions had not been disclosed (Interview No.10; Maalouf 2009). Interestingly, the ICTJ and Fridrich Steiftung Institute sponsor trips for families to visit other post-conflict countries facing similar challenges and learn lessons. According to a leading member of "ACT for the Disappeared" who participated in some of these visits, the Bosnian experience was particularly instructive in re-framing the quest to protect the graves as part of the "right to know" the truth (Interview No.65).

The use of a human rights vocabulary and universal legal instruments led to a breakthrough. A 2012 draft law prepared by relatives and influential partners set the stage for the establishment of an independent commission of inquiry mandated to carry out exhumations (Al-Hasan 2012; Dhumi Ëres 2011). The law largely drew on the Bosnian and Iraqi framework; central provisions included preparing the list of missing and the protection of gravesites as part of families' right to know the truth. Finally, a number of events, roundtables and archival initiatives appeared with the primary objective of resisting the silence (Yakinthou 2015).

Most importantly, these efforts culminated in a landmark ruling. In March 2014, the Lebanese State Council annulled a previous cabinet decision banning access to the final report based on the inalienable "right to know" the truth (Yakinthou 2015). It is one of the few instances when a Lebanese court "speaks" the language of international human rights. As it turned out, the commission had not carried out any serious investigations and had been understandably reluctant to publicize this fact. A member of the "Legal Agenda," an NGO spearheading the initiative, maintains: "This is when I discovered that it is a dossier of a half box for approximately 3000 missing and that practically no investigation was made. This is when I understood why the government was afraid to deliver this dossier because there was no investigation" (Interview No.52).

The efficacy of international alliances cannot be denied. In the Lebanese case, they have helped families re-frame their demands in human rights and humanitarian terms, sending some early signals of the gradual depoliticization of debates about the missing. Where this will lead has yet to be determined, however, and optimism ought to remain cautious.

Conclusion

One of the key findings of the analysis of Lebanon is that the *form of violence* responsible for the creation of the problem of the missing largely *determines the type of truth recovery* a society will pursue after transition. The challenges and the dilemmas faced by post-conflict societies trying to address the problem of the missing are greater than those encountered by post-authoritarian societies. The weakness of state institutions, the feeble infrastructure and the priority of boosting economic recovery and accommodating the demands of survivors of the conflict often become major obstacles to a more comprehensive form of truth recovery. This is particularly relevant in the aftermath of negotiated transitions, which are often based on mutual silence, as the experience of Lebanon clearly illustrates. In contrast, in post-authoritarian settings state institutions may be weakened but usually they are not annihilated. For example, even during the reign of Pinochet in Chile, the judiciary was still operating (albeit within an extremely confined space), thereby providing an opportunity for relatives to bring their cases to court. Although none of these lawsuits was effective at the early stages after the transition, the strategy was instrumental in keeping an official record of the crimes, a useful precedent in subsequent truth recovery initiatives, such as the truth commission. Finally, in the aftermath of state repression, relatives have more institutional tools available, including the media; they also have better economic prospects and access to political parties to introduce their demands into the political agenda.

The study of Lebanon is instructive, precisely because it sheds light on the scope and magnitude of challenges that families have to face and overcome in post-conflict settings. It shows that despite insistent and ongoing mobilization, the weak democratic institutions, the absence of international influential allies and the lack of a minimal level of security have curtailed the efforts of the families to overcome *institutional silence*. In essence, the political opportunities that could have facilitated domestic truth seekers to promote their agenda were quite simply absent.

As the previous pages argue, the absence of a minimum level of stability and security is essential for any step toward "forensic truth." The ongoing instability after the end of the conflict in Lebanon has meant perpetrators and eyewitnesses remain extremely reluctant to reveal information because they fear revenge. The comparative experience of other post-conflict societies shows that convincing eyewitnesses to reveal contentious and incriminatory evidence requires not only stability but also some provision of immunity from future prosecution or anonymity. Similarly, the continued reign of the embedded security apparatus, epitomized by the continued waves of disappearances even after the conflict, has terrorized the broader population. While in other societies facing similar challenges the society itself and certain influential allies (i.e. lawyers, activists, journalists and priests) were critical in promoting the families' cause, in Lebanon, they were reluctant to do so openly.

The transition in Lebanon was not followed by the democratization of state institutions, another clue to the failure of the families. Social movement theory suggests access to independent institutions is a critical opportunity, with the potential to add specific problems to the political agenda. The weakening of the state institutions in Lebanon has precluded the use of institutional channels. Especially salient is the politicization of the judiciary; in effect, a tool that helped families in other societies overcome the politicized framing of sensitive questions of human rights was simply absent.

Finally, and probably most importantly, the limited presence of international actors after the transition meant the loss of an influential ally. Research has shown that the deadlock created by a combination of domestic veto, players reluctant to address the past, weak domestic institutions and the politicization of debates around sensitive questions of human rights can be broken by international actors. As Chapter 3 shows, the Argentine quest for acknowledgment was facilitated by transnational human rights groups who helped families add the issue onto the agenda of international organizations; this had a boomerang effect that pushed domestic elites to adopt a more flexible position. The families in Lebanon did not have the same level of international attention, and definitely not the same type of transnational normative instruments at their disposal, such as access to international courts (i.e. IACHR or ECHR).

As these are not uncommon challenges in post-conflict settings, the study of Lebanon can greatly benefit our understanding of the quest for justice and acknowledgment. The literature of transitional justice prefers "success stories" where transitional justice has been implemented with a relative degree of success. Yet this excludes countries with limited transitional justice instruments, and their study is surely equally imperative. For example, Lebanon can help explain why certain international norms fail to resonate in certain countries.

However, there may still be some hope for Lebanon. In the post-2008 period, the influx of international advocacy groups has led to some change and a small number of tactical victories, such as the landmark 2014 court ruling acknowledging the "right to know" the truth. The domestication of international norms, coupled with lessons from other societies, may lead Lebanon to gradually end the silence and set up a policy of "forensic truth." Although as the book argues, this is often a very slow process, Wadad Halwani, the founder and leader of the Committee introduced at the opening of the chapter, is optimistic: "With no doubt this ruling will give the Committee a strong incentive to continue its search, giving us the legal right to ask the Lebanese government and all who are held responsible for the disappearance of many Lebanese to tell them the truth about what happened to their loved ones" (cited in Rowayheb & Ouaiss 2015:2023). After all these years, she may soon be able to exhume and identify the remains of her beloved husband.

7

Cyprus

The Bright Side of a Frozen Conflict

Most accounts of the Cyprus conflict frame it as a story of "missed opportunities," intransigence and intractability; it is not a coincidence that the conflict has remained frozen for almost four decades.[1] Against this backdrop, the management of the problem of missing persons stands out – one of the few bright spots, it highlights how answering sensitive questions of human rights can be transformed into bi-lateral cooperation and mutual trust.

Cyprus is unique among the cases discussed here. It remains de facto a partitioned island, and despite proactive international efforts to reach a political settlement, the conflict has remained frozen since 1974, making it one of the most intractable conflicts globally (Heraclides 2011; Joseph 1997; Loizides 2016; Yakinthou 2008). Despite the absence of a political settlement, however, the country has crossed the threshold of "forensic" truth through a policy that enables the exhumation and identification of the bodies of those who went missing from both communities in the conflict.

When compared to Lebanon, examined in Chapter 6, Cyprus offers a glimmer of hope. Comparing the experiences of Cyprus and Lebanon makes sense; their respective conflicts have similar background conditions as well as comparable time lags and challenges in uncovering the truth about the missing. For example, the last wave of violence in Cyprus in the summer of 1974 closely corresponded to the start of the Lebanese civil war in 1975. Both societies had to deal with similar problems well before dealing with the violent past became a normative imperative in international politics (in the 1990s). Most importantly, a constitutive element of both conflicts was the intervention of external actors, in the case of Cyprus, the invasion/peace operation[2] of Turkey, and in Lebanon,

---

[1] At the time of writing in early 2016, negotiations for a peace settlement were ongoing, but the conflict remained unresolved.

[2] The term used by the two communities differs, and it highlights the different approaches to the past. In Greek Cypriot discourse, it is perceived as an illegal "invasion" breaching the sovereignty of the RoC, while Turkish Cypriots frame it as a "peace operation" undertaken

the forceful intervention of Israel and Syria and their local proxies. Oddly, however, these critical cases have received little attention in the literature on transitional justice.

Another common element is inertia. As the preceding chapter shows, Lebanon has been unable to make any progress in dealing with the problem of the disappeared. Similarly, in Cyprus, a bi-communal Committee for Missing Persons (CMP), established in 1981, remained inoperative for more than 25 years. Yet unlike Lebanon, Cyprus has shaken off its inertia. By the late 2000s, the CMP had become a successful bi-communal project (Kovras 2012). Between 2006 and early 2016, it exhumed 1192 victims and identified 737 (CMP 2016). This development has enabled thousands of families from both communities to bury their loved ones, after decades of distress and uncertainty. Moreover, the structure of the CMP is exceptional, as the entire project has been carried out predominantly by Greek-Cypriot and Turkish-Cypriot experts (forensic archaeologists, geneticists, etc.), bolstering local ownership.[3] Finding the forensic truth has empowered a vibrant bi-communal group of relatives to use the problem of the missing as a symbol of rapprochement and reconciliation. For all these reasons, the UN Secretary General describes it as "a model of successful cooperation between the Greek Cypriot and the Turkish Cypriot communities" (Loizides 2016:8) and a model to be exported to other societies emerging from the conflict. As the chapter shows, though, CMP's success is not unproblematic; the humanitarian nature of exhumations has created moral and legal tensions.

The chapter raises and addresses a number of questions. First, how did Cyprus overcome institutionalized silence and enter the stage of forensic truth by enforcing a policy of humanitarian exhumations? To comprehensively address this question, it is important to break it down into two interrelated questions. Why, despite the availability of political opportunities, were families trapped in institutionalized silence for almost 30 years? What changed to catalyze the impressive transformation of CMP?

by Turkey to protect Turkish-Cypriot citizens of the Republic against the atrocities that could have followed the violent assumption of power by Greek and Greek-Cypriot nationalists.

[3] Argentine Forensic Anthropology Team (EAAF) contributed to the training of the local groups of forensic and genetic experts. Since 2012, ICMP has been responsible for extracting and matching DNA from bone samples. Both key forensic groups, the role of whom was examined in Chapter 4, have participated in exhumation in Cyprus.

The next section provides a short but comprehensive historical explanation of the phenomenon of the missing in Cyprus. Then, it describes the repertoire of mobilization of families over the past four decades, exploring why despite skillful deployment of political, financial and legal opportunities they were unable to break the institutionalized silence for over 30 years. It suggests new opportunities facilitated the emergence of a new bi-communal group of relatives which actively supported exhumations and explains the transformation of the CMP by looking at the changing positions of all major players, including the Republic of Cyprus and Turkey, and discussing the power of international norms. The following section evaluates the virtues and vices of the Cypriot model of (forensic) truth recovery and notes the tensions between the immunity clauses – deemed necessary for exhumations – and the duty of the state to carry out an effective investigation and punish perpetrators. The final part of the chapter puts the Cypriot experience into a comparative context, examining to what extent forensic truth is effective in dealing with the missing in post-conflict settings more generally.

The Problem of the Missing in Cyprus

As early as the 1940s, when the island was under British rule, the two dominant communities, Greek and Turkish Cypriots, had adopted divergent views about the future of the island. Greek Cypriots mobilized around the demand for *enosis* or union with mainland Greece, a quest which after 1955 was taken up by the paramilitary anti-colonialist *Ethniki Organosis Kyprion Agoniston* (EOKA) movement. Turkish Cypriots, alarmed by the prospect of being annexed by Greece, supported *Taksim* or the partition of the island (Ker-Lindsay 2011). The London–Zurich Agreements (1960) officially declared the establishment of an independent state, the Republic of Cyprus (RoC henceforth), based on a power-sharing settlement. However, the two communities never fully endorsed the legitimacy of the new state; it was perceived to be an interim venture that could set the stage for the fulfillment of the overarching political objectives of the two communities.

The power-sharing scheme was short lived, followed by two periods of extensive violence, during which approximately 2000 persons went missing from both communities.[4] Between 1963 and 1967, Greek-

---

[4] According to the official figures provided by the CMP there are 1508 Greek-Cypriot and 493 Turkish-Cypriot missing persons.

Cypriot extremist paramilitary groups carried out a number of atrocities, including the abduction of Turkish Cypriots; after being executed, their bodies were thrown into common graves in an effort to instill terror and to control Turkish-Cypriot villages (Patrick 1976). While most of those missing during this period are Turkish Cypriots, there are approximately 40 cases of Greek Cypriots (Kovras & Loizides 2011). As a result of the violence, Turkish Cypriots withdrew to enclaves controlled by Turkish-Cypriot paramilitary groups, while Turkish-Cypriot officials removed themselves from all posts in the public sector, government and parliament. This ended the short period of consociation and set the stage for the division of the island.

The second period of violence was characterized by the intervention of external actors. The short-lived coup against the President of the RoC, orchestrated by the Greek military junta in Athens in the summer of 1974, was immediately followed by the Turkish invasion, allegedly to protect Turkish Cypriots from potential atrocities. The result of the Turkish invasion in human suffering was colossal, with about 6000 dead, thousands of refugees and internally displaced, and approximately 1500 missing. In sharp contrast to the first period when targets were civilians taken from their homes, in the second period, the majority of the missing were executed during military operations, usually by paramilitary groups who were settling old scores, often with the support of Turkish officers (Yakinthou 2008).

In the following decades, the missing became the most sensitive aspect of the Cyprus problem. Given the small population of the island, the problem directly affected a significant part of the Cypriot society. In a recent survey, more than a 20 percent of the respondents claimed that a close family member went missing during the two periods of violence (Stefanovic, Loizides & Psaltis 2016). Although the communities adopted different positions, for both, the missing was, and still is, a highly symbolic issue. Understanding the official framing deployed by the communities can give us a better grasp of their official negotiating line on the Cyprus problem. As Paul Sant Cassia shows, Turkish Cypriots refer to their missing as *sehitler* (martyrs), dead in the effort to protect the community from Greek-Cypriot aggression. The official framing is not necessarily endorsed by all relatives but was officially imposed by political elites to indicate that the problem of the missing, as well as the Cyprus problem more generally, was de facto resolved (Sant Cassia 2006). Meanwhile, the Greek-Cypriot political elites refer to their missing as *agnooumenoi* (unaccounted for), indicating the ongoing nature of the problem and, more broadly, the Cyprus conflict (ibid.). Part and parcel of this framing is the fact that even now, some Greek Cypriots believe some missing might still be alive in secret detention centers in Turkey.[5] For them, a moral framework was fractured by the illegitimate intervention of an external actor, and only that actor (Turkey) can establish the truth. This framing complies with the broader discourse of victimhood that characterizes the post-1974 official framing of the Cyprus problem (Papadakis 1993).

Mobilization of Families (1974–2004)

The families of the missing in Cyprus were both active and resourceful in their mobilization[6] but were trapped in institutionalized silence for decades, much like the families in Lebanon today. The lack of any outcome to their mobilization is especially intriguing when we consider the favorable political opportunity structure. The mobilization lasted for years, it had the full and unconditional support of the state, Cypriot society embraced the families' cause and the relatives deployed a very successful legal strategy at the European Court of Human Rights (ECtHR) putting pressure on Turkey to cooperate. These conditions tick most boxes for effective mobilization proffered by contentious politics literature (Kriesi 1995a; Tarrow & Tilly 2007). On top of this, the families mobilized in a stable, safe and free political context with access to democratic institutional channels to express their discontent as evident by the accession of Cyprus to the European Union in 2004. Still, these conditions were not sufficient to help the families move to forensic truth. This section goes on to explain all the things that were right about the Cypriot mobilization before suggesting reasons for its failure.

The mobilization was proactive and had a diverse repertoire, including protests, rallies and making powerful domestic political alliances. It also had a strong international flavor, as they lobbied international actors and

---

[5] For a representative example, see Kasimatis (1997).

[6] This section of the chapter focuses on the mobilization of the Greek-Cypriot families of the missing, largely excluding the Turkish-Cypriot families from the analysis. There are two reasons for this decision. First, until 2003, the northern part of the island was controlled by the Turkish army and an authoritative Turkish-Cypriot leadership, precluding any realistic possibility for the families to mobilize in the public sphere. I focus on the (Greek-Cypriot) group of families who had more opportunities to mobilize and overcome the institutionalized silence. Second, the language skills and the level of access to central actors and policy makers in the south convinced me to focus on the repertoire of mobilization in the RoC for this period (1974–2004).

deployed available legal instruments, taking their cases to the ECtHR, for example. In several ways, their repertoire of mobilization echoes that of the Argentine relatives, but the outcomes differ.

Just days after the cessation of hostilities in the summer of 1974, the families carrying photos of their missing children and relatives gathered at the checkpoints dividing the island to ask released prisoners whether they had seen their loved ones. As years passed, the mothers continued to gather at the border with photos of their children, now dressed in black with black headscarves echoing *Las Madres* in Argentina; in the Greek-Orthodox culture, the black headscarf is a symbol of grief (Danforth & Tsiaras 1982), while the image of mothers looking for their children transcends cultures. The main objective of these annual rallies at the checkpoints/buffer zone controlled by the United Nations was first and foremost to keep the issue on the political agenda. In parallel, these rallies put pressure on the international community to convince Turkey to reveal information about the whereabouts of their loved ones, last seen alive in the northern part of the island, now under Turkish occupation.

Apart from rallies, shortly after the Turkish invasion, Greek-Cypriot families set up an official relatives' association, the Pan-Cyprian Organization of Parent and Relatives of Undeclared Prisoners and Missing Persons (the Organization henceforth).[7] Few victims' groups in Europe had so much political influence on national politicians or have received so much attention both domestically and internationally. This was facilitated by the proactive support of the Cypriot diaspora, especially in the United Kingdom. The leadership of the Organization was very skillful in playing along with political elites' framing of the problem of the missing as the symbol highlighting the ongoing victimhood and suffering of the Greek-Cypriot people. Given this, the Organization became a powerful and highly regarded group in Greek-Cypriot society. Its leader explains: "We are a group which puts pressure on the government, but the government is at the same time the biggest advocate, so we put pressure on them to continue to support us" (Interview No.66).

Over the past 30 years, relatives of the missing have received a wide range of benefits, including pensions, positive discrimination in employment, property tax exceptions, to name only a few. The state has reserved several privileges for the relatives; roads, parks, squares and even

---

[7] There is an interesting gender aspect in the hierarchy of the official association of the families of the missing in Cyprus. Although mothers have been the main actors in the protest activities, the organization is led by men: originally a priest and then a brother of a missing person.

a museum are dedicated to the missing (Sant Cassia 2005:157). Parliament passes annual resolutions on the problem of the missing, praising the constructive role of the Organization, while families are always invited to important meetings on issues related to the negotiations of the Cyprus problem.

Apart from making political alliances, the families have deployed a resourceful legal strategy. As explained by an experienced lawyer who prepared the legal cases of a number of families, by the 1990s, it was clear to the majority of the relatives of the missing that political pressure alone would not suffice to convince Turkey to reveal information, so they used the "instrument of the weak against the powerful," in other words, the law (Interview No.67). Several families brought their cases against Turkey to the ECtHR; in this effort, they had the abundant but implicit (material and legal) support of the state. As discussed below, this culminated in a number of landmark ECtHR rulings on the problem of the missing. The most important one was in 2001; it acknowledged that Turkey had violated Article 2 (right to life) of the European Convention of Human Rights, and Turkish authorities failed to carry out an "effective investigation into the whereabouts of the fate of Greek-Cypriot missing persons" as the victims were last seen under Turkish custody (cited in Hoffmeister 2002).[8] Most significantly, the court recognized the continuous nature of the crime. As explained below, a number of ECtHR rulings were critical in convincing Turkey to support (or at least tolerate) a policy of exhumations.

Despite the innovative and influential repertoire of mobilization, coupled with the favorable political opportunities, the families were trapped in institutionalized silence for more than two decades. This is not surprising, as they faced several apparently insurmountable obstacles. First, Turkey's uncompromising stance left little room for maneuvering. The official Turkish position was that all Greek-Cypriot missing should be considered dead, either executed by other Greek-Cypriot paramilitary during the short-lived coup or killed in the battlefield in the summer of 1974. Therefore, Turkey had no information about their whereabouts. Essentially, there was no viable policy without Turkey's cooperation.

Second, the problem was politicized both by Greek-Cypriot authorities and the Organization. In effect, the issue of the missing was inextricably

---

[8] *Fourth Interstate Application* v. *Turkey* (Application no. 25781/94), judgment of May 20, 2001, para 136.

linked to the political negotiations; therefore, any solution was conditional on progress at the negotiating table (Loizides 2016). A comprehensive examination of party manifestos, parliamentary speeches and laws on the subject matter reveals that the problem was never seen outside the context of the Cyprus conflict (Kovras & Loizides 2011). The leadership of the Organization contributed to the politicization of the problem by endorsing the official view that their group symbolized the national suffering of Greek Cypriots – the only "real" victims on the island. This confrontational stance alienated many families. It excluded Turkish-Cypriot families of the missing as well as Greek-Cypriot relatives who felt the leadership of the Organization had hijacked the issue to play politics (Drousiotis 2000).

This is important, as it precluded any efforts to frame the problem as a purely humanitarian issue. As the Organization became stronger and accumulated political capital, the leadership developed its own agenda, which, at times, contravened the humanitarian needs of the families. The relatives' association had acquired significant symbolic capital in Greek-Cypriot society by encapsulating the victimhood of the community, and they used this capital to influence politics (Drousiotis 2000). For example, when informed about the government's decision to proceed to unilateral exhumations in Greek-Cypriot cemeteries to clarify the whereabouts of several missing persons in the mid-1990s, the leaders of the victims dragged their feet. They were convinced exhumations would strengthen the official Turkish position that all missing were dead, especially if some were buried within the RoC, and eventually exculpate Turkey (Kovras & Loizides 2011). The relatives' fierce reaction, coupled with resistance from other conservative clusters in the Ministry of Foreign Affairs (MFA) loyal to the policy of linkage, significantly delayed the implementation of the policy (Interview No.25). This is not an uncommon reaction to exhumations. International experience shows that families may resist exhumations for a number of reasons; they may be afraid of challenging authority or they may fear exhumations will prove their loved ones are dead or will curtail the calls for justice (Rosenblatt 2015). In any case, the government stepped back, and the policy was not implemented until 1999.

In their official politicization of the problem, Greek-Cypriot authorities used a humanitarian problem to play the blame game with/against Turkey. A senior politician and member of the parliamentary committee on the missing acknowledges: "For us [Greek-Cypriot politicians] it was a major issue and as such there was an element of political exploitation"

(Interview No.68). This, of course, lessened the prospects of Turkish cooperation. The RoC also carved out a proactive agenda naming and shaming Turkey for its non-accommodative role in the missing in international forums, including the United Nations and the European Union.

New Actors Representing the Families (2004–)

A significant number of the families of the missing felt they were not represented by the Greek-Cypriot-dominated Organization and, thus, remained silent for decades. The Organization largely excluded Turkish-Cypriot victims, while Greek-Cypriot families felt the leaders had hijacked the problem to promote an official/national political agenda that did not necessarily meet their needs.

New opportunities became available in the early 2000s, allowing the emergence of a new and vocal bi-communal group of relatives and a broader civil society that demanded the truth about the violent past. The first new opportunity was the opening of the checkpoints in 2003. Bi-communal activities quickly blossomed (Hadjipavlou 2007). After nearly 30 years of prohibited communication, human rights groups found natural allies on the other side of the divide. The timing was perfect; mobilization on the upcoming referenda on a solution (Annan Plan) to the Cyprus conflict in 2004 offered an ideal platform for bi-communal activities, and the missing became a rallying cry for previously excluded truth-seeking actors. The mobilization was particularly important for Turkish Cypriots, as it allowed them to break the long silence imposed on them by the Turkish-Cypriot leadership (Kovras & Loizides 2011).

As the leader of the initiative reveals, they made a conscious decision to highlight their suffering to challenge the official agenda of the Organization, as it precluded certain policy outcomes, like exhumations:

> In the first few years we had realized that interpersonal bonds have been developed among relatives, so we needed to come forward and speak out instead of leaving the nationalists to use our problem to further their own interests ... because nobody has experienced what we [relatives] have gone through.
>
> (Interview No.31)

The group adopted a more inclusive repertoire of mobilization in an effort to build bridges with their natural allies, the families of Turkish-Cypriot missing. Before this time, any collaboration with the "other" side, particularly on a sensitive issue linked to the Cyprus conflict, would have been impossible and seen as a betrayal. A well-informed Greek-Cypriot journalist puts it bluntly: "Until 1990s even talking about Turkish Cypriot missing was a betrayal" (Interview No.25). It is worth noting that the new initiative comprises a younger generation, the children of the missing, and they had different needs and perspectives than their parents.

Briefly stated, their mobilization aimed at promoting an alternative view of the violent past by drawing on shared experiences of grief, distress and motherhood across the divide (Kovras 2012). The original repertoire had a strong grassroots flavor, including school visits, raising awareness through media and organizing public events in different districts on the island. Interestingly, interviews with members of this initiative suggest not all agree on the next step: some prioritize the prosecution of perpetrators, while others just want an apology. However, they all endorse this plurality of transitional justice preferences (Interview Nos.21 and 26).

The group has had key allies who ensure their activities appear in the public discourse. Investigative journalists from both sides of the divide, Sevgul Uludag and Andreas Parashos, have published detailed stories of disappearances, most often based on revelations of eyewitnesses or even perpetrators from their own communities. Initially, this endeavor was very risky; one of them received death threats and both were heavily criticized (Interview No.24). Yet the thirst for information about this silenced chapter of the past, along with the need of some perpetrators/eyewitnesses to share their experiences as they were growing older, made this wave of truth recovery process unstoppable. Parashos echoes this demand for truth when he says: "If we do not speak the truth, if we do not tell the stories we know, if we do not say the real stories about the relatives we will not have peace on this island" (Interview No.22).

Despite the significance of the mobilization of the families, it is important not to mistake the causal chain. The mobilization of the bi-communal group of families greatly facilitated the leap from silence to forensic truth, but it did not cause it. As argued below, the families' mobilization in the mid- and late-2000s was critical to create a more inclusive forum and to legitimize and protect the policy of exhumations, but this obviously means a policy of exhumations was already in place. The long-dormant CMP was reinvigorated just months after the peace referenda in 2004, but it was based on long-term policy processes, the seeds of which were planted several years before, as evident in the unilateral exhumations carried out by the Cypriot government in 1999

(Loizides 2016). So, the causal chain that enabled Cyprus to move to forensic truth was set in motion with broader policy changes that had little to do with the mobilization of the families. These included the removal of veto players from the Turkish-Cypriot leadership, the revised Turkish foreign policy toward Europe and ideational shifts within the MFA in the RoC.

In essence, forensic truth legitimized the activities of the bi-communal group; by offering concrete scientific evidence, exhumations legitimized previously excluded voices. For example, in the period preceding the resumption of the CMP, most Greek Cypriots were not even aware of the existence of Turkish-Cypriot missing persons. Even former President Tassos Papadopoulos denied it in an interview (cited in Charalambous 2004). Hence, one of the biggest achievements of the passage to a level of forensic truth was that it "narrowed the number of permissible lies" in public discourse (Ignatieff 1998). In their place, new and more legitimate discourses emerged, democratizing the debates about the past – the essence of truth recovery (Breen-Smyth 2007).

CMP: The Story of an Effective Transformation

The question that inevitably emerges is how, despite the obstacles discussed above, could the CMP be transformed from a long-inoperative body into an influential humanitarian platform? To fully account for the impressive transformation, it is important to address a unilateral policy shift in the RoC (Kovras 2014). By the mid-1990s, a small group of policy makers in the MFA had realized that the policy of linking this specific human rights problem to the waxing and waning of political negotiations for the resolution of the Cyprus problem had failed to bear fruit. As a senior policy maker in the MFA indicated, although this strategy secured political gains – evident in the repeated rulings of the ECtHR convicting Turkey for breaching the fundamental human rights of the relatives – it failed to produce any tangible solution to the problem of the disappeared (Interview No.29). Twenty years after the cessation of hostilities, relatives had no conclusive answers about the whereabouts of their loved ones and the official policy guaranteed that the only possible solution was linked to the solution of the broader Cyprus problem.

With the prospect of EU accession in the 1990s for the RoC, pending human rights issues had to be resolved. A small group of policy makers and bureaucrats managed to convince political leaders of the need to implement a novel policy on the missing (Interview Nos.22 and 28) based on two fundamental tenets: (1) the need to decouple the solution of the issue from political negotiations for the solution of the Cyprus problem and (2) the need to handle the cases of the missing citizens of the Republic (both Greek Cypriot and Turkish Cypriot) transparently. Both signified points of departure from past policy and opened the door for humanitarian exhumations.

As explained above, there was valid information that a number of persons on the list of missing were, in fact, dead as a result of the Turkish invasion and had hurriedly been buried in a Greek-Cypriot cemetery (Paroutis 1999; Theodoulou 2009). One of the leading figures of the group of policy makers in the MFA revealed that one of his personal reasons for engaging in the effort to change the policy was the fact that a family friend considered missing for almost 20 years was buried in a cemetery within the jurisdiction of the RoC, and he felt obliged to help the family reach closure (Interview No.28).

Although a decision was made as early as 1995 to proceed to unilateral exhumations in the Greek-Cypriot cemetery, the policy was delayed until 1999 as a result of the vocal resistance of the leaders of the official Organization of relatives, described above. Informed observers have since commented that to neutralize potential reactions and implement the policy, the team had to "leak" information to the press (Interview No.22). The 1999 exhumations in the Greek-Cypriot cemetery represented a landmark occasion. Of the 55 persons exhumed, 24 had been missing for more than two decades. It was also the first time that the RoC had officially apologized to its citizens for its negligence (Alitheia 1999; Anastasiou 2008:149) in not honoring the grief of the relatives.

Unilateral exhumations were a small part of a broader policy change, however. In 2000, a decision was made to prepare an authoritative list with explicit information on the status and number of disappeared. In most post-traumatic societies, the "politics of measurement" is a constitutive part of the struggle for truth (Brysk 1994). Cyprus is no exception. Since 1974, both communities had inflated the number of the disappeared to become political symbols.[9] Hence, even when there was valid information that specific cases included on the list were not missing but dead, other cases were retrospectively added in an effort to maintain

---

[9] According to the CMP, 1493 Greek Cypriots and 502 Turkish Cypriots are missing. These numbers deviate from the narratives of the communities (Greek Cypriots claim 1619 and Turkish Cypriots 803).

the "sacred" number intact (Sant Cassia 2005:51). Part of the problem was that the list of the missing remained a classified document, and therefore, only a handful of officials had access to it. As a journalist who followed the developments explains, the objectives of the revised policy included publicizing the list, bringing transparency into the process and receiving public information that would potentially lead to the resolution of some of the cases (Interview No.22).

Compiling and publicizing the lists of the missing and dead as a result of the Turkish invasion and determining the number of casualties of the short period of violence during the coup in July 1974 were key components of the policy of transparency. A fundamental position of the Turkish-Cypriot leadership was that all missing were dead, victims of the intra-communal violence during the coup; therefore, it was expected that Turkey would approve of this unilateral step (Parashos 2009). Moreover, a specific provision specified 126 families would be told their relatives should be considered dead (in light of the new information) and would be provided with social–legal support relevant to this change of status.

The most important illustration of the shift in policy was that for the first time the Turkish-Cypriot relatives were included. A decision was made to create a databank with genetic samples from both Greek-Cypriot and Turkish-Cypriot families. One of the designers of the policy says it was essential to be prepared when a more comprehensive policy of exhumations and identification of the missing was set in place in the future (Interview No.27). The strategy worked, especially after 2003, when the opening of the checkpoints enabled hundreds of Turkish-Cypriot families to give genetic samples. More importantly, the RoC explicitly acknowledged the existence of Turkish-Cypriot missing persons. Previously, any reference to Turkish-Cypriot missing would have implied responsibility and, therefore, was downplayed. Yet in 2003, the official list of Turkish-Cypriot missing persons was published in the Gazette of the RoC (House of Representatives nos. 3418 and 3713). That was the first official document acknowledging the atrocities committed against Turkish Cypriots.

The striking and unilateral *volte face* of the RoC was based on a careful and long-term policy design that included previously excluded actors and required an excellent grasp of developments in societies facing similar dilemmas. I had privileged access to confidential memos prepared for the MFA of the RoC; it was evident that as early as the mid-1990s, the Ministry was familiar with the use of DNA identification and the protocols followed by Clyde Snow and Eric Stover in Argentina. Clearly paying close attention to developments in international forensic science, the RoC carried out the first Cypriot exhumations when the International Commission on Missing Persons (ICMP) was set up in Bosnia, just as the use of forensic identification of human remains was becoming accepted worldwide.

However, by itself, the government's unilateral shift cannot explain the transformation of the CMP or the delinkage of the missing from the political negotiations. Also crucial were the ECtHR's consecutive landmark rulings on the Cypriot missing; simply stated, these rulings transformed the normative framework within which Turkey acted. For several decades, Turkey dragged its feet over the missing. To overcome Turkey's non-accommodation, individual relatives of Greek-Cypriot missing and the RoC brought cases before the ECtHR. The first precedent-setting ruling in May 2001[10] found Turkey responsible for violation of Article 2 of the European Convention, referring to the right to life. The court held that Turkey had failed to carry out an "effective investigation into the whereabouts and the fate of Greek-Cypriot missing persons who disappeared in life-threatening circumstances" (Hoffmeister 2002: para 136). The same ruling found Turkey had breached Article 5 of the Convention, referring to the right to liberty and security; despite credible evidence that a number of missing were last seen in Turkish custody, the country failed to carry out an effective investigation (para 150). Similarly, the ruling noted that the treatment of the relatives of the missing was "inhuman or degrading," breaching Article 3 of the Convention (para 158). Finally, it acknowledged the ongoing nature of the crime. The crime of enforced disappearances is not subject to a statute of limitations; thus, the country concerned is required to carry out an investigation, even after decades. The court did not accept Turkey's long-standing argument that the missing should be presumed dead. In later rulings, the court reaffirmed these findings and created a solid legal precedent.[11]

The rulings were followed by consecutive resolutions of the Committee of Ministers condemning Turkey for its non-compromising stance. Although not officially precluding Turkey's EU accession, these

[10] *Fourth Inter-State Application of the Republic of Cyprus* v. *Turkey* (Application no. 25781/94), ruling of May 10, 2001.

[11] This duty is reaffirmed in the latest decision of the ECHR in the case of *Varnava and Others* v. *Turkey* (Applications nos. 16064/90, 16065/90, 16066/90, 16068/90, 16069/90, 16070/90, 16071/90, 16072/90 and 16073/90), decision January 10, 2008.

resolutions tested Turkey's progress in human rights by asking the country to establish an independent fact-finding commission to mount a serious investigation of the missing (Council of Europe 2003). In several subsequent resolutions, the Council maintained the CMP's limited mandate did not ensure an effective investigation, thereby challenging another traditional argument proffered by Turkey (Council of Europe 2004, 2005).

These resolutions backed up the court's decisions and put political pressure on Turkey to improve its poor record of compliance with international human rights norms, a clear prerequisite of EU accession. Turkey had to make at least some gestures of good will. The least painful scenario was to allow the resumption of the CMP.

As the previous paragraph hints, Turkey's change should be put in the broader context of its trajectory to EU accession and the concomitant tectonic changes in domestic politics. For 20 years, Turkey's official position on the Cyprus problem was that it was resolved in the summer of 1974 with the partition of the island (Heraclides 2011). This uncompromising position left little room for negotiations on a political settlement, let alone truth recovery for the missing. However, a growing number of citizens and political elites were disillusioned by the continued presence of the military in national politics and the performance of the economy in the mid-1990s (Grigoriadis 2009). Therefore, a sizable segment of the Turkish society perceived the path to the European Union as the only viable route to stability, development and democratic consolidation. The emergence of the Justice and Development Party (AKP henceforth), with its strong EU orientation, at least in the first years after its first election, became the driving force of reform in the early 2000s. Performance in democratic governance, human rights and independence of the judiciary were the biggest obstacles to EU accession (Müftüler Baç 2005). Between 1999 and 2004, one of the most sensitive periods for the problem of the missing in Cyprus, the AKP government made significant efforts to improve the image of Turkey, establishing, for example, the General Secretariat for the European Union to work in close collaboration with the Prime Minister (Grigoriadis 2009:80; Müftüler Baç 2005).

Changes in Turkey had always affected domestic politics in the Turkish-Cypriot community, but on this occasion, they became the catalyst for truth recovery. The adoption of a pro-solution agenda by Turkey was followed by the active support of local Turkish-Cypriot actors. A moderate leader of the left, Mehmet Ali Talat, came to power in 2003, a year before the final negotiations for a UN-brokered peace plan (the ill-fated Annan plan). Rauf Denktas, the unquestioned Turkish-Cypriot leader, identified by his rejectionist approach to a potential reunification of the island, was ousted from leadership in the 2003 elections, and an important obstacle was removed.

The removal of long-standing obstacles to truth recovery, combined with external pressure for compliance with international norms and the emergence of previously silenced bi-communal truth-seeking actors, culminated in the policy of exhumations and the resumption of the CMP. Despite the rejection of the peace settlement in the 2004 referenda, the grassroots mobilization around forensic truth had already taken on a life of its own. In fact, this forensic bi-communal project functioned after the failure of the peace negotiations.

Crossing the Threshold of Forensic Truth

The CMP was established in 1981, under the aegis of the United Nations (1981). Purely humanitarian in scope, it was composed of one non-political representative from each community and a Chair directly appointed by the UN Secretary General from a pool of inter-national experts of the International Committee of the Red Cross (ICRC). The exclusive aim of the committee was to establish the where-abouts of the missing persons from the two waves of violence (1963–1974).

The terms of reference and the mandate are revelatory of the restrictive framework within which the CMP was to function. For example, as a purely humanitarian body, the CMP could not "attribute responsibility for the death of any missing or make any findings as to the cause of death."[12] The other two founding principles were "confidentiality" of information circulated in the CMP and "consensus" in decision-making.[13] I should point out that the CMP was established in 1981, well before the normative shift in international politics and the emphasis on human rights' norms. It would be extremely difficult for a present-day UN operation to include these provisions in its peacebuilding initiatives,

---

[12] The terms of reference and mandate of the CMP can be found on its website (para 11): www.cmp-cyprus.org/about-the-cmp/terms-of-reference-and-mandate/.
[13] Paragraphs 3 and 9 of CMP's mandate.

as they contradict fundamental tenets of human rights and international justice.

As the preceding discussion has indicated, for several decades, the CMP remained inoperative. The non-cooperative position of the Turkish-Cypriot leadership noted above, coupled with its restrictive mandate, nullified any serious attempts to make the project work. An important initiative to revise the CMP appeared in 1997; on July 31, the leaders of the two Cypriot communities, Rauf Denktas and Glafkos Clerides, reached a landmark agreement, marking the first effort to decouple the solution of the missing from political negotiations and to endorse a purely humanitarian approach. They agreed that all available information about burial sides would be circulated and thoroughly investigated to facilitate identification. For the first time, a Turkish-Cypriot leader signed an official document agreeing to exhumations in the northern part of the island. Although he did not follow through on the agreement, we cannot disregard it, as it set an important precedent, and when new opportunities arose in 2004, the agreement was already in place.

Despite the promising start, CMP did not dig up a single body in more than 20 years. Of course, in the aftermath of the rejection of the peace plan, bi-communal relations reached a nadir – not an ideal time to deal with human rights issues. And with the passage of time and the deaths of critical eyewitnesses, not to mention relatives, identification became increasingly problematic. Nonetheless, a few months after the rejection of the Annan plan in 2004, the Turkish-Cypriot leader sent a letter to the UN Secretary General asking for his assistance in resuming the activities of the CMP. Since then, the CMP has become the most successful bi-communal project on the island, helping thousands of families find and bury their lost loved ones. Paradoxically, the same restrictive mandate that paralyzed the CMP for 23 years became the catalyst for its transformation; its insulation from political interference and confidentiality ultimately led to its success.

The Cypriot CMP is unquestionably one of the most successful bodies of humanitarian exhumations among societies emerging from conflict, especially when we consider the absence of a political settlement, the partition of the island and the decades-long deadlock in the management of the missing.

In the period 2006–2016, it unearthed 1192 victims of two waves of violence; 737 have been identified and returned to their families (CMP 2016). Of these, 553 are Greek Cypriots and 184 Turkish Cypriots;

unsurprisingly, this is a proportional representation of the total number of the missing of the two communities. In other words, an element of reciprocity steers the process. Moreover, a substantial number of victims have been exhumed and will soon be identified, sketching a bright future for the CMP. People now trust the viability of the venture, making them more likely to speak out and point to other clandestine gravesites. The fact that the remains of more than a thousand missing have been exhumed within 10 years is impressive, making the Cypriot CMP a much more effective platform for identification of human remains than the much-celebrated South African truth commission, or even the Chilean commission, under far less advantageous conditions.

Apart from the sheer number of exhumations, it is important to highlight the high quality of the identification process. The use of DNA identification of human remains minimizes the risk of misidentifications, a frequent problem in post-conflict settings. In Chile and South Africa, for example, some exhumations were recklessly carried out, destroying vital evidence that led to the misidentification of the victims; relatives were often asked to return bodies for a second identification, a process which retraumatized them, especially when they were left with no body to mourn (Robben 2014; Rousseau 2009). In the CMP, however, the anthropological team updates families on the forensic process and answers their questions, facilitating proper identification.

As noted above, the need for confidentiality and consensus and the insulation from political negotiations that initially hindered the CMP later became the secret of its transformation. One critical innovation was a directive from the RoC Attorney General, saying any person providing critical information to the CMP would not be legally or politically liable nor would such information be used against those responsible for the disappearances (Solomonidou 2010). Immunity from prosecution has convinced perpetrators to come forward and encouraged eyewitnesses to share vital information about burial sites (Interview No.27). As members of the CMP have revealed, this process of information sharing has gradually led the committee members to develop personal ties of trust, ensuring high quality of work and confidentiality (Interview Nos.23 and 27). Cooperation has ranged from the top level of the commissioners to the lowest ranking bi-communal teams of forensic scientists carrying out the excavations. The CMP carries high symbolic capital, as it proves "digging" up the past can become the basis for bi-communal cooperation. And the fact that domestic actors lead the process has given a sense of local ownership.

In short, the CMP has become an effective confidence-building measure, something long needed on the divided island.

Forensic Truth: Moral and Legal Tensions

On the negative side of the equation, the success of the CMP should be measured against its delimited conception of truth. Legal accountability is precluded, and more disturbingly, forensic scientists are not allowed to inform the families about the cause of death. Hence, after decades of ambiguous loss, relatives receive only a small coffin with the remains; they are not allowed to ask the questions that unavoidably emerge. Was the death painful? Was she/he executed? Who gave the information to the CMP and could the same person be the perpetrator? The CMP has been repeatedly criticized for the "immoral" trade-off between forensic truth and immunity/confidentiality for perpetrators/eyewitnesses. Even the commissioners have been highly critical of an arrangement that denies families the right to a fuller version of truth or justice (Interview No.27). In fact, it could be argued that the relatives are denied their right to seek legal redress. Paradoxically, this restriction sheds light on an alternative reading of the families' experiences of humanitarian exhumations, a story of solidarity, empathy and compassion.

In the international legal framework, the state has a duty to carry out an effective investigation into the circumstances of the disappearance of the missing and the relatives have a right to know the truth (Scovazzi & Citroni 2007). The state also has the duty of punishing those responsible. The CMP's current mandate, structure and terms of reference prohibit relatives from exercising their rights; as mentioned above, this has been clear in the rulings of the ECtHR and resolutions of the Council of Europe discrediting CMP as a mechanism of effective investigation. Part and parcel of the right to know the truth is the "right to gain access to and obtain information."[14] As such, any family has the non-derogable right to lodge a lawsuit demanding free access to the information and evidence gathered by the CMP which led to the location of the grave as well as to the forensic evidence from the graves. As Achilleas Demetriades, a prominent Cypriot human rights lawyer and pro-truth seeking campaigner, clarifies, "I see no legal impediment in a civil action to summon in a civil case the relevant records of the CMP" (Interview

---

[14] UN High Commissioner for Human Rights Resolution 2005/66, "Right to Truth," April 20, 2005.

No. 70). In such cases, the families could access information to get a full picture or initiate a criminal case. As illustrated by their repeated applications to the ECtHR, Cypriot families are familiar with the use of legal instruments to promote their rights. Surprisingly, they have not played this card. Why not?

If a family decides to initiate a process of legal accountability, this will immediately affect the progress of the CMP. Eyewitnesses will be reluctant to provide incriminatory evidence that may lead to their own prosecution, the process of exhumations will stop and thousands of families desperately looking for the remains of their loved ones will be forced to keep waiting. So far, this has not happened because of a subtle, but robust, sense of solidarity and respect for the need of families to bury their dead. An implicit hierarchy of priorities has been established, whereby all relatives seem to prioritize the need of other families to get the remains back over their own right to justice. This incredible gesture of compassion transcends the divide and gives families from the "other" community the right to mourn their victims.

The fact that any measure of legal accountability would paralyze the work of the CMP is evident. The Turkish-Cypriot member of the CMP, Plümer Küçük, put it bluntly: "This project is working because grass-roots people are giving us information and if we start dealing with punishment, these people are not going to give us any more information. It is not time to do it [criminal investigations] now" (Interview No.23). Past experience supports this view. For example, in 2009, a former Turkish soldier publicly revealed that during the Turkish invasion in 1974, he had engaged in atrocities; a wave of protests ensued, with people calling for him to be held accountable. Although this was not directly related to the missing, for a few weeks, the flow of information to the CMP stopped, with eyewitnesses fearful of providing information that might have legal repercussions. This indicates how sensitive and fragile the whole process is.

Having said that, it is almost certain that once most bodies are exhumed and identified, a new stage of broader truth recovery which could possibly include retributive justice will emerge. This will have a very solid basis, including forensic findings and testimonies of eye-witnesses. In addition, the two communities are already familiar with the use of international legal tools and will increasingly call on them as time goes on. Their present refusal to take advantage of these tools is not a story of failure; rather, this is a story of impressive solidarity across the divide amidst the least likely conditions of a frozen conflict.

An interesting lesson deriving from the study of the transformation of the CMP is the moral and legal tension inherent in forensic truth. On the one hand, all available empirical evidence suggests one of the most important legal rights and human needs of the families is the return of the remains, so they may end their ambiguous loss and start the mourning process, even after several decades. On the other hand, as illustrated above, this is often based on a policy of immunity that precludes some families from exercising their rights "to know" the truth about the broader conditions behind the disappearances and causes the state to fail in its duty to prosecute perpetrators. This raises a number of complex moral and legal issues. For example, what happens when two duties appear to be in conflict (i.e. right to get the remains vs. duty to prosecute)? When a transitional society is split, with some demanding justice and families simply wanting the remains, who should decide? This is a core moral and legal debate in transitional justice. The literature is divided between those arguing for a legalist/principled view (i.e. duty to prosecute) and those taking a consequentialist view and claiming actions with possible negative repercussions (i.e. prosecutions) should be avoided. Still, the families may be less divided on this issue, and the study of their management of forensic findings could benefit our understanding of the sequencing in transitional justice politics.

Families and victim groups in general are strategic in their mobilization. Although families in Cyprus have skillfully used legal arguments in their mobilization, and although forensic findings could make the legal case for a prosecution more appealing and plausible, not one of the 737 families who have identified their loved ones has initiated such a process. As explained above, the success of the CMP is based on the incentives offered to eyewitnesses to come forward. If a handful of families use the forensic findings from the graves to initiate a criminal investigation, the process would stop, leaving thousands of families without a dead body to mourn. There is most likely some element of utilitarianism in their thinking, however: while prosecutions could stop exhumations, which are central to the needs of most families, justice could follow at a later stage.

Cyprus in Comparative Perspective

Despite the absence of a political settlement and the decades-long de facto partition of the island, the two Cypriot communities have worked together to solve a sensitive issue. The experience of Cyprus is exceptional when compared to most cases of frozen or ongoing conflicts, like Lebanon, Abkhazia, Chechnya and Pakistan, making the CMP a model accommodation that might be emulated by other societies facing similar dilemmas (Jaquemet 2009; Kovras 2012).

One of the most interesting findings of this book is that although Cyprus and Lebanon have faced comparable challenges, the former has proceeded to forensic truth recovery and the latter has not. Two variables are pivotal: the impact of international influences and democratic consolidation in Cyprus, both absent in Lebanon. A distinctive feature of the Cypriot experience is the access to international instruments, both legal and political; this considerably facilitated the efforts of the families. It is important to remember that the presence of these tools alone does not always guarantee success; despite similar or even better access to external influences in Northern Ireland, the problem of the missing is only partially resolved (McDonald 2007). In a best-case scenario, external influences can empower the struggle of domestic actors. For example, the prospect of EU accession impacted the priorities of both Cyprus and Turkey, subtly legitimizing the small team of policy makers to change the policy and delink it from political negotiations. Finally, the application of an international legal framework has the potential to depoliticize issues, thus facilitating the quest for forensic exhumations.

Another variable helping Cyprus cross this minimal threshold is the level of democratic consolidation and the concomitant demobilization and/or incorporation of perpetrators into party politics. In the aftermath of the Turkish invasion, the RoC built strong democratic institutions (Ker-Lindsay 2011; Ker-Lindsay & Faustman 2008). Despite intense politicization and a predominant discourse that precluded comprehensive truth seeking, domestic actors had access to key instruments that encouraged their demand for truth. For example, the independence of the judiciary, security from persecution, free circulation of information in media and a competitive political party system all created favorable political opportunities for domestic truth seekers/relatives, something absent in Lebanon and other comparable cases like Kashmir or Chechnya.

All these are preconditions for any post-conflict society to exit institutional silence and enter an era of humanitarian exhumations. I mentioned Northern Ireland above. During the conflict in Northern Ireland, also known as the "Troubles" (1972–1999), 16 persons went missing as a result of intra-communal violence within the Republican community (Dempster 2016). The kidnapping of community members (often labeled informants) was instrumentally used by Republican para-military groups to intimidate and control their own community (McDonald 2007; Interview No.9).

Interestingly, relatives in Northern Ireland seem to have had a favorable opportunity structure to address the problem. The peace agreement was followed by the establishment of a specific mechanism to deal with the problem of the disappeared. Following the Good Friday Agreement, which put an official end to violence and paved the way for a consociational settlement, an Independent Commission for the Location of Victims' Remains (ICLVR) was set up to deal with the problem.[15] The ICLVR is based on a formula similar to the CMP, offering "carrots" to perpetrators/eyewitnesses to persuade them to come forward with information. The 1999 Northern Ireland Act (Location of Victims' Remains) establishing the ICLVR is based on confidentiality; the information obtained through this procedure is inadmissible in criminal procedures, and the sole objective of forensic exhumations is to identify and return bodies without determining the cause of death (Dempster 2016).

Obviously, the small number of disappearances should have made it easier to exhume and identify these persons. But 15 years after the establishment of the ICLVR, only 12 of the 16 cases have been resolved, leaving four families in pain and distress. The experience of Northern Ireland illustrates the significance of confidentiality in processing sensitive information related to the missing. Boston College organized a research project focusing on the oral history of the Troubles, and a number of former members of paramilitary groups were interviewed. Although there was an explicit agreement that transcripts would be published only after their death, a court in the United States ordered the tapes be handed over to Police Service Northern Ireland for further investigation. This directly affected the handling of the disappeared. One of the 16 disappeared persons during the Troubles, Mrs. Jean McConville, was framed by the IRA as an alleged informer and forcibly abducted and killed in 1972 by the same group; the "Boston tapes" contained contentious information about her disappearance (Dalby 2014). The findings of the "Boston tapes" served as evidentiary basis in a Belfast court decision to reject the application for bail of one of the alleged perpetrators of the crime (Young 2014). Apart from being used as a legal instrument, the public exposure of sensitive testimonies of

---

[15] Northern Ireland (Location of Victims' Remains) Act 1999, April 27, 1999.

perpetrators heavily politicized debates about the disappeared and affected the progress of the ICLVR.

In sharp contrast to Cyprus, where the relatives (especially Greek Cypriots) brought their cases to the ECtHR, in Northern Ireland, relatives have never used legal tools, although they have a similar domestic legal framework and access to the ECtHR. For one thing, as paramilitary groups/non-state agents are allegedly responsible for these disappearances, the legal path is difficult, if not futile. The international factor is often critical not only in creating concrete outcomes but also in putting pressure on parties responsible. In Northern Ireland, however, although main Republican political parties, such as Sinn Fein, support the workings of the ICLVR, they cannot effectively pressure a small group of dissidents with a monopoly on information about burial sites.

The obstacles societies and relatives confront in their quest for truth recovery in contexts of ethnic/sectarian violence are daunting, to say the least. First, in even the most successful peace processes, perpetrators (or parties representing them) are integrated into party politics, giving them a vested interest in, and more institutional power to perpetuate, "institutionalized silence." It is hardly surprising that some of the most effective transitions are based on negotiated agreements that preclude truth recovery about the contentious past. Second, in the wake of ethnic/sectarian conflict, societies often have to deal with other urgent priorities, and they have limited economic resources or infrastructures to support truth recovery. It is only when international bodies assume the leading role in a transition that abundant economic support and international expertise enable the setting up of a mechanism of truth recovery. Third, in most cases, more than one party is involved in disappearances; the perpetrators are often low-ranking officers or paramilitary leaders who are following their superiors' orders. This is significant, as it becomes difficult to assign moral responsibility. In addition, perpetrators in post-conflict settings have a monopoly on information about gravesites, and any process of narrow truth depends on their contribution. Of course, this can become an opportunity for humanitarian exhumations if a policy based on immunity from prosecution, confidentiality and anonymity is properly designed. In short, the Cypriot formula can realistically be exported to other countries with frozen conflicts.

A similar example comes from Colombia, a country greatly affected by the problem of the disappeared. Despite a robust regional and international legal framework, according to an online database (National Institute of Forensic Sciences), approximately 50,000 persons have disappeared, with 7500 persons missing in 2012 alone (De Rivaz 2013). The practice of disappearances is now a constitutive element of the efforts of paramilitary groups to gain and maintain control (United Nations 2010).

Against this backdrop of continued violence and disappearances, in 2005, President Uribe and the leader of the United Self-Defense forces of Colombia (AUC) negotiated a deal leading to the enactment of the Peace and Justice Law.[16] A main provision was the demobilization of combatants; in exchange for reduced sentences (maximum 8 years), they were to decommission their weapons and make full disclosure of their crimes. Although the main objective was to induce combatants to demobilize, it was also designed to address the issue of the disappeared, as perpetrators were given incentives to reveal information about the location of graves. This caused a wave of exhumations, far exceeding any previous effort (García, Pérez-Sales & Fernández-Liria 2010:58). For example, according to the annual report of the Inter-American Commission for Human Rights on Colombia, by 2011, approximately 26,026 perpetrators had disclosed information leading to 3378 exhumations of 4185 corpses, of whom almost 1600 had been identified and returned to their families (IACHR 2011:para 88). More recent estimates increase the number to 5322 exhumations (De Rivaz 2013; Latin American Herald Tribune 2014).

This increased flow of information has led to institutional innovations, including the passage of several laws focusing on victims[17] and the creation of an internationally renowned team of forensic anthropologists (Sperling, Klieman & Ap 2008). With the financial support of the United States, along with expertise of the International Criminal Investigative Training Assistance Program, Colombia has now developed expertise in the identification of human remains. Exhumations are carried out by the Exhumations Sub-unit of the Unit of Justice and Peace, while the Human Rights Unit processes information coming from demobilized combatants.[18]

Most human rights watchdogs, including Human Rights Watch and the International Center for Transitional Justice (ICTJ), have criticized this law as an attempt to "legalize impunity" (Human Rights Watch 2008). However, when we consider the conditions of open conflict, the

---

[16] Law No. 975/2005, *Ley de Justicia y Paz*, July 25, 2005.
[17] See, for example, Law 1448/2011 *Ley de Victimas y de Restitución de Tierra*, June 2011.
[18] The Exhumations subunit was set up by State prosecutor's resolution 0–3891/2006.

decades-long practice of disappearances and the previous inability to cope with the problem, it seems that at the very least, the 2005 law gave some dignity back to thousands of families. It is also important to remember that forensic truth is a stage within a broader process of truth recovery. Colombia is located in a region with an advanced legal toolkit on enforced disappearances; therefore, when conditions are right, a new wave of broader truth recovery will probably emerge, even though with some delay.

That said, the value of forensic truth recovery cannot be underestimated. It provides much-needed closure to relatives, especially in cases like Lebanon, Abkhazia or even Kashmir. The international sponsorship of programs of forensic truth has the potential to make a more direct impact on families than costly international tribunals. Apart from helping individual families find their loved ones, it can act as a confidence-building measure in the larger society, becoming the basis for other common ventures among former enemies and reducing the risk that relatives will believe they have an ethnic/religious monopoly on suffering.

Finally, it is important to keep in mind that the international community can help a society take the first step by offering resources, infrastructure and expertise, and this may well lead to humanitarian exhumations. But subsequent steps toward truth recovery can (and should) be taken only when a society decides to do so. For truth recovery to be effective, international institutions should be ready to adapt to domestic demands, not simply to impose predetermined solutions. Cyprus is a case in point.

Conclusion

The study of Cyprus offers three important lessons for transitional justice. First, it confirms the value of a longitudinal approach to study transitional justice processes. By extending the boundaries of transitional justice to include the decades following the official transition (or cessation of hostilities), it provides a more dynamic picture of how societies may revisit or even challenge transitional settlements. A salient case in point is the impressive transformation of the moribund CMP into a mechanism of truth recovery.

Second, the study of Cyprus highlights the pitfalls of truth recovery in post-conflict settings, particularly if international actors are not present in designing transitional justice. Despite more favorable conditions and opportunities than in most societies emerging from conflict, the best the families of the missing in Cyprus could hope for was breaking the institutionalized silence and setting up a policy of humanitarian exhumations. Obviously, any demand for setting up a truth commission or prosecuting perpetrators was out of the question. As Cyprus illustrates, the conditions that keep post-conflict societies locked in institutional silence include the politicization of humanitarian issues and the fragmentation of victims' groups along national or sectarian lines.

Third, in post-authoritarian settings families' mobilization and the use of political opportunities are crucial if they are to cross the threshold of forensic truth, but in post-conflict settings, the role of the families is marginal. The conditions explaining why Cyprus was able to advance toward forensic truth have little to do with the mobilization of the families. Having relative security and stability for 30 years made it easier for perpetrators/eyewitnesses to reveal contentious information in Cyprus than in other countries with turbulent or unstable transitions, like Lebanon. Based on an exclusively humanitarian and depoliticized approach, the transformation of the CMP was made possible by three important incentives provided to the eyewitnesses/perpetrators: immunity from prosecution, confidentiality of information and anonymity.

Finally, the exploration of the families' mobilization both in Cyprus and in Lebanon challenges the view of victims' groups as homogenous. Different groups adopt different repertoires of mobilization, reflecting their divergent needs, and they often create their own political agendas. The study of families' mobilization is critical in revising the naive presentation of victims as idealist groups united by a single cause; an examination of Cyprus clearly indicates that victims' associations can use their symbolic capital to advance their personal agendas, promote their political and material interests or even play party politics, and these are often at odds with the needs of a significant part of the families.

8

Truth Commissions and the Missing

South Africa's "Unfinished Business"

> My family and I have not rested since we learnt that my sister went missing.
> We know the most terrible things about what she suffered. But we don't know
> how she died, and where her body is today. We have spent three decades
> looking for Nokuthula. . . . Until we find her remains, or get an answer about
> what really happened to her we remain trapped in the past.
>
> (Nkadimeng 2013)

Advocates of the South African Truth and Reconciliation Committee
(TRC henceforth) highlight the catalytic use of recovering the truth
about the violent past to achieve reconciliation; as the saying goes, "revealing is healing."[1] As indicated in Chapter 4, the TRC's mandate, structure
and investigative activities marked a point of departure from other historic
truth commissions, reflecting a broader normative turn in peacebuilding.

Since TRC, instead of simply seeking the absence of violence
("negative peace"), fostering reconciliation among former enemies has
become a Grail quest of truth commissions (Brewer 2010; Lambourne
2000), with the documentation of past human rights violations a central
feature. Their mandate has shifted from simply recovering bodies to
establishing authoritative truths about the violent past.
As documenting past human rights violations became instrumental in
repairing relations broken by violence, so too the scope of investigation
evolved: from seeking anonymous confidential testimonies, commissions
moved to holding public hearings and naming offenders in their final
reports (Freeman 2006:24). One of the most important innovations was
the shift of attention from accommodating victims' need for forensic

---

[1] Here I use Mark Freeman's definition of a truth commission as an "ad hoc, autonomous,
and victim-centered commission of inquiry set up in and authorized by a state for the
primary purposes of investigating and reporting on the principal causes and consequences
of broad and relatively recent patterns of severe violence or repression that occurred in the
state during determinate periods of abusive rule or conflict and making recommendations
for their redress and further prevention" (2006:18).

truth to "restoring" relations between perpetrators and victims (Breen-Smyth 2007; Leebaw 2011). Public hearings were considered – at least by the early scholarship on truth commissions – to facilitate psychological healing and foster a culture of human rights (Gibson 2004; Minow 1999, 2002). By turning in this direction, truth commissions have been transformed into healing mechanisms mandated not merely to deal with victims' needs but also to transform the broader society.

Yet Thembi Nkadimeng's experience is radically different. After 33 years, she is still looking for the remains of her sister, Nokuthula Simelane, who went missing in 1983 allegedly at the hands of agents of the apartheid regime. Despite the passage of more than three decades, Ms. Nkadimeng remains in limbo. She explains, "My father went to his grave without knowing what happened to Nokuthula. My mother, now sick and old, fear that she will die without knowing; without burying Nokuthula's remains with the dignity she deserves" (Nkadimeng 2013). It is impossible for her to forgive or reconcile with the perpetrators of the disappearance of her sister without having the remains back first. She is also frustrated by the fact that the state has never prosecuted those responsible: "It deprived me and my family of closure and our right to dignity" (ibid.).

Nkadimeng's story highlights the tension between the declared restorative goals of the TRC and the more pressing humanitarian needs of specific victims' groups, in this case the effort of the families to find and identify their loved ones and offer them a dignified burial. On the one hand, the TRC has acquired global visibility as the textbook case of transitional justice, one that highlights the transformative role of truth, forgiveness and reconciliation (see Boraine 2000; Graybill 2002). It is hardly surprising that the TRC captured the hearts and minds mainly of international policymakers, academics and activists in transitional justice in the late 1990s and throughout the 2000s. On the other hand, the global visibility of the TRC stands in stark contrast to the "invisibility" of the problem of the missing in South Africa. The need of the families to uncover the truth has been sidelined not only by the TRC's activities but also by the broader academic literature on South African transitional justice policies.[2]

Revisiting the TRC from the perspective of the missing makes sense for several reasons.[3] First, the purported objectives (and strengths of the

---

[2] For notable exceptions, see Aronson (2010) and Rousseau (2015).

[3] As explained in Chapter 1, I acknowledge the legal distinction between "missing" and "disappeared," but to help enable the reader follow the argumentation, I use the terms "the

TRC) were twofold: to identify the truth about the violent past was deemed pivotal for reconciling a divided society, while also bringing victims center stage in the truth recovery processes to address their needs. Both are essential for the families of the missing, much more relevant in their case than with most other victim groups. For example, recovering the remains is an alternative form of "forensic" truth recovery that may enable families to take a step away from ambiguous loss and start the mourning process (Boss 2006; Robins 2011). Second, in contrast to other countries with disappearances where families' mobilization was a visible element of the transition, in South Africa the families of the missing remain largely invisible despite their institutional role in the TRC. Most importantly, the TRC's scope of investigation included the problem of the "abducted" in its mandate,[4] with a follow-up policy of exhumations designed shortly thereafter.

The theoretical framework proffered here hypothesizes that those countries coupling exhumations with truth commissions have a better chance of using incriminatory evidence to prosecute perpetrators. Yet, to this day in South Africa, there have been very few convictions of perpetrators responsible for disappearances.[5] As such, South Africa is an intriguing outlier. Understanding why certain societies, such as South Africa, do not take the step toward retributive justice, despite apparently facing fewer constraints than other countries, could help us refine the theoretical framework. Similarly, as truth commissions were historically intended to deal specifically with the crime of disappearances, assessing the (in)effectiveness of the most renowned commission, the TRC, in dealing with missing persons is instructive.

For all these reasons, I deploy the interesting experience of the South African TRC, as the "most crucial" case (Eckstein 1975; George & Bennett 2005; Gerring 2004). It was the first to make amnesty conditional on "full disclosure" of truth about human rights violations, and it paid particular attention to the healing function of truth (Freeman 2006; Hayner 2011; Wiebelhaus-Brahm 2010). Given all this, the TRC seems the most "likely case" to be effective in meeting its declared objectives (Eckstein 1975), and therefore merits critical attention. In addition, in

missing" as the noun denoting the people and "disappearances" as the noun denoting what happened to them and "disappear" or "go missing" as the verb.

[4] Report Vol. I, Chapter 4, Subsection 4b.

[5] According to Transitional Justice Collaborative database, there is only one such case (Dancy et al. 2014). Eugene de Kock was charged and convicted in 1996 on several charges, including kidnapping.

contrast to most recent commissions where the intervention of the
international community largely determines the outcome, the South
African experience is purely a domestic one, making it a challenging
case to test the utility of the proffered theoretical framework. Last but by
no means least, the time lag permits safer conclusions than more recent
cases. Early literature treat the South African TRC as a "success story"
(Gibson 2004; Minow 1999), and it remains one of the most influential
commissions (Hirsch 2007). Yet as illustrated below, a more critical
scholarship focusing on the weaknesses of the TRC has emerged (see
Chapman & Ball 2001; Leebaw 2011; Moon 2008; Ross 2003; Wilson
2001).

The chapter raises and addresses three interrelated questions. First,
what made it possible for South Africa to set up a truth commission and
move to the "broader" level of truth recovery for the missing? Despite an
amnesty provision, South Africa mandated a truth commission to investigate the fate of the missing (among other crimes), coupling this with
a policy of exhumations. Understanding the context is pivotal if we want
to answer this question.

Second, the chapter asks probably the most important question. How
effective was the TRC in addressing the needs of the relatives of the
missing, particularly in learning the truth? To answer, I use two criteria.
The first is a very narrow yet relevant indicator, namely, the number of
identified victims. Although it should be acknowledged that victims have
diverse needs, accessing all available empirical evidence to identify the
remains is the most pressing one (Boss 2006; ICRC 2013). Similarly, it is
a state's legal obligation to locate, identify and return remains to the
relatives (Convention, Article 24.3), so it serves as a crude measure of
how effectively the TRC performed "forensic" truth recovery. A second
criterion is the extent to which the TRC carried out an "effective investigation" into the conditions leading to the disappearances. This reflects
the essence of "broader" truth recovery and overlaps with the right of the
families to "know."

Third, the chapter inquires into the puzzling absence of retributive
justice.[6] The families have refrained from utilizing forensic incriminatory
evidence from the graves and other documentation from the truth

---

[6] Obviously the "negotiated" nature of the transition precluded any human right prosecutions, at least in the early stage after the transition. All cases examined in this book
experienced a negotiated transition, however, and in some cases, with time, perpetrators
were charged and convicted. In fact, as explained below, families in South Africa had
opportunities to move in this direction but did not capitalize on them.

commission to bring their cases to court. Further, amnesty was conditional on full confession of crimes at the TRC, so for a number of cases, litigation was an option. Why, then, despite apparently favorable conditions, did South Africa not take the final step and prosecute culprits?

In what follows, I provide a brief historical context for the disappearances during apartheid. I continue by addressing the first question: the conditions that enabled South Africa to set up the TRC and move to the next level of "broader" truth recovery. Admittedly, South Africa was able to overcome the obstacles set by a negotiated transition (i.e. amnesty) and establish a truth commission, while other societies, such as Northern Ireland and Lebanon, did not. The next section explores the ways the TRC failed to establish "forensic truth," as it identified only 89 of the approximately 2000 missing. It was equally ineffective in investigating the conditions leading to the disappearances. I then raise the central puzzle of this chapter: why, despite favorable conditions, South African families did not pursue the issue in court?

In what follows, I argue that apart from the obvious reason that the specific crime was not so widespread to catalyze a powerful families' movement, the most significant explanation lies in the absence of institutional, political and material opportunities. This should be linked to the unique nature of the transition in South Africa, moving away from a long institutionalized racist regime deviating from other countries where dictatorships were shorter or longer intervals within otherwise democratic states. As such, transition marked a particular challenge both for victims and political parties. As I argue below, the ANC had minimal incentives to take the retributive path, as the political winner of the transition had no incentive to facilitate retributive justice, especially as its own members might be fingered. Besides, the ANC had created a hegemonic framing of the missing as "heroes" of the liberation struggle. This may have enhanced ANC's image, but it implicitly deprived some families of the ownership of the bodies of their loved ones. This, coupled with families' continued dependence on political elites to address pressing material and social problems, ruled out any challenge of the country's most powerful political party.

The Problem of the Missing in South Africa

Although gross human rights violations associated with the apartheid regime (1960–1994) are widely documented, relatively little is known about the problem of the missing. The majority of human rights violations occurred in the late 1980s and early 1990s (TRC Report 2003). In the late 1980s, the regime intensified its repression by deploying extrajudicial means to instill terror in the activists and guerrillas (EAAF 2006). According to a 2010 study by the Khulumani, a human rights group, more than half of the total number of those deemed missing disappeared in the 1980s (53 percent) and about one third disappeared in the 1990s (31 percent) (Khulumani 2010). It is estimated that in these two decades alone approximately 15,000–25,000 persons were killed (Guelke 1999:45). According to Jay Aronson, an expert on the post-conflict and post-disaster identification of victims, although disappearances were not a systematic tool of the apartheid regime – definitely used less routinely than torture or detention – disappearances "were used to scare people" and deter them from joining liberation movements (Interview No.15).

Against this backdrop, hundreds of activists died in extrajudicial operations or in secret detention and were buried in common graves. Interestingly, the bodies were not always buried in secrecy. Nicky Rousseau describes this process:

> These [dead] bodies were assigned to a police domain. Photographed, fingerprinted, and transported to a police mortuary, the corpse would be recorded in a mortuary register as "unknown black male" or "unknown terrorist" and a state pathologist or state appointed district surgeon would conduct a post-mortem examination. In many instances, even where identity had been established these "unknown" bodies were not released to the care of families, but buried in local cemeteries by private under-takers recorded by the state to bury indigent or unclaimed bodies.

(2015:177)

This highlights the logic of disappearances – there must be a high level of coordination among different sectors of the repressive state, infrastructural support and other material resources to hide bodies. Although one might assume such institutionalized violence would leave a paper trail that would make future identifications easier, this was not the case in South Africa. The majority of the victims were buried as "unknown paupers," inhibiting later identification.

In the early 1990s, incidents of violence and enforced disappearances increased as a result of the intra-civilian strife that erupted between armed groups, primarily MK (uMKhonto we Sizwe), the armed wing of the African National Congress (ANC) and the Inkatha Freedom Party (IFP) (Berat & Shain 1995). Approximately three-quarters of the casualties during the four final years of apartheid resulted from conflicts within black communities, fueled covertly by the state (Fullard & Rousseau 2001:69). The element of ethnicity was equally important, as the IFP, composed mostly of Zulu nationalists, was cautious of the growing influence of the Xhosa-dominated ANC (Backer 2004:81). During this period of inter-organizational conflict, approximately 15,000 persons were killed, with many remaining unaccounted for (Rousseau 2009:363). It is worth noting the regional variations in the distribution of the missing, as security forces used different modes of repression in different parts of the country. For example, in Port Elizabeth, perpetrators used to burn the dead bodies, while in Natal, the commonest practice was the use of explosives to destroy incriminatory evidence (Rousseau 2009:362).

Although it remains a subject of debate, the number of the missing in South Africa ranges from 477, the official figure established by the TRC, to approximately 2000, according to certain human rights organizations (Aronson 2012; Sarkin 2015); this point is discussed in greater detail below.

The multiple sources of violence created different categories of missing persons. For example, some were "disappeared" by state authorities. Others went "missing" in inter-civilian conflicts or under other circumstances and remain unaccounted for. In the section documenting the problem of the missing, the TRC Report recognizes three broad groups (Aronson 2012). The first is composed of persons abducted by members of the security forces or armed groups, often tortured and subsequently buried in common graves. The second contains those who went missing either in efforts to flee South Africa or in detention camps controlled by liberation groups in the neighboring countries, such as Tanzania (Aronson 2010:265). A third group comprises South Africans who went missing during periods of inter-civilian conflict or who were killed in armed combat (Missing in Action) in the civil strife between ANC and IFP and remain unaccounted for (ibid.). As explained above, identification was impossible, most often for practical reasons; for example, the victims might have been burned to death or the mortuaries may have been overloaded and bodies were hurriedly buried. Similarly, problems of positive identification posed, for example, by fake IDs, left a number of families in limbo; in such cases, although there was valid information on the death of a loved one, the remains were never recovered (EAAF 2006). According to the Task Team responsible for exhumations in South Africa, each of these three groups accounts for one-third of the total amount of the missing (Interview No.63).

The experience of South Africa of both "disappeared" and "missing" challenges the utility of legal definitions of victims in contexts of complex political violence: it is often irrelevant and/or impossible to determine whether victims disappeared at the hands of security agents during state repression or went missing in internal strife. Yet from the perspective of the families, the challenges to the quest for truth and acknowledgment are identical regardless of the circumstances.

Establishing the TRC and Broader Truth

The South African experience confirms that the type of violence under consideration is critical in shaping the boundaries of transitional justice policies. Despite emerging from a long racist/repressive regime and an intense internal conflict, the types of challenges for truth recovery in South Africa cannot be compared to those of post-conflict societies that did not cross the threshold of broader truth and set up a truth commission. The transition in post-authoritarian settings usually offers more institutional opportunities for victims' groups and their families to add their demands to the political agenda. For example, the return of electoral politics means political parties can represent victims and legitimize their voices in the public domain. As evident in the work of the first commissions in Latin America, truth commissions are often political balancing mechanisms spearheaded by politicians. They promise to address victims' needs by establishing the truth, without necessarily putting perpetrators on trial. This makes it important to trace the process leading to the establishment of a truth commission.

In South Africa, the period of violence in the late 1980s coincided with the intensification of negotiations among political elites to reach a deal on a peaceful transition to democracy. All parties involved subtly or overtly acknowledged that any transition was conditional on two apparently conflicting factors: amnesty for past violence and some form of acknowledgment of the suffering of non-white South Africans. Immunity was deemed necessary to appease members of security forces engaged in the vast majority of the violations of human rights during the regime.[7] But the ANC, as the dominant party representing the black community and

---

[7] Any post-1994 agreement would avoid excluding whites for a more practical reason; their skills were needed in the economy.

the party paying the heaviest toll in human lives, stressed the importance of an institution that would acknowledge their persecution.

The TRC was also influenced by a number of domestic fact-finding commissions set up to investigate the violence in the period preceding the transition. For example, in 1992, the Goldstone Commission[8] was mandated to document acts of violence by police, the South African Defence Force (SADF) and KwaZulu police. A powerful incentive for perpetrators to participate in the venture was the offer of amnesty in exchange for "full disclosure" of crimes (Backer 2004:82). The Goldstone Commission was quite successful, managing to discredit prevalent myths, while showing that the state (i.e. the "third force") was partly responsible for fueling intra-civilian political violence in the period preceding democratic transition. The amnesty formula was so pivotal in the success of the commission that Richard Goldstone proposed the use of a blanket amnesty to facilitate the working of the TRC. While this was emphatically rejected by the ANC (Berat & Shain 1995:176), the TRC did adopt the "amnesty for full disclosure" formula.

Two commissions set up by the ANC to investigate alleged incidents of intra-party violence within the detention camps, especially Tanzania (Hayner 1994:623), also influenced the decision to set up the TRC. At the time, the ANC was the only non-governmental entity to create independent fact-finding commissions to address human rights violations committed by its own members, with a mandate that included the missing (Boraine 2000:11). The ANC's 1992 Commission of Inquiry into Complaints by Former African Congress Prisoners and Detainees (Asmal 2000:11) was set up so that the ANC could "cleanse" itself of those who had committed crimes. The ensuing report included cases of missing persons in camps in exile, thus paving the way for a follow-up commission to investigate the missing and other forms of human rights violations committed by the ANC (Berat & Shain 1995:179). Obviously, these and similar endeavors would have been impossible in contexts of civil war/internal conflicts. This highlights how the nature of violence and the balance of power in South Africa created space for experimentation with mini-transitional justice mechanisms even before the official transition.

This early familiarization with the use of commissions made it easier for the ANC to incorporate the TRC into the transitional justice design.

---

[8] This is formally known as the "Commission of Inquiry Regarding the Prevention of Public Violence and Intimidation."

The TRC was the means chosen by the ANC to implement the provisions of the transitional constitution of 1994, based on amnesty (Guelke 2000:303). The ANC's decision to set up the commission created political tensions, as both the National Party (NP) and the IFP had reservations (ibid.). As Bronwyn Leebaw shows in her seminal study, the TRC was shaped by influential groups of intellectuals within the ANC. Legal scholars emphasized the importance of shedding light on structural and institutional causes of violence, rather than seeking individual legal accountability. At the same time, members of healing professions, including psychologists and theologians, lobbied for a "restorative form of justice" (Leebaw 2011:67–70). Building on the traditional African principle of "Ubuntu" (humanity), many argued that the overarching objective should be the restoration of social relations fractured by violence, not narrow (Western) retributive justice (De Ycaza & Schabas 2011; Leebaw 2011).

As a result, the TRC significantly deviated from previous commissions. First, it was designed to advance psychological healing by providing factual information about victims to their families, an important issue, especially for the relatives of the missing. In turn, it was hoped that accurate information would "restore" the fractured dignity of victims. Second, documenting the full picture of past human rights violations was deemed to have a cathartic effect on the public, ultimately becoming a stepping stone to national unity and reconciliation. Third, while it granted amnesty to perpetrators, this was conditional on the full disclosure of truth. Fourth, the TRC was tasked with publishing a report pinpointing the causes of human rights violations from 1960 to 1994; it was asked to make recommendations to strengthen institutions and prevent the reoccurrence of physical and structural violence in the future.

A fifth point of departure from past commissions was its fortified investigative powers; in principle, at least, the TRC was better suited to address the problem of the missing. The commission was composed of three committees: the Human Rights Committee, the Amnesty Committee and the Reparations and Rehabilitation Committee (Wiebelhaus-Brahm 2010). The Amnesty Committee had unprecedented powers, including subpoenaing perpetrators and issuing individual amnesties conditional upon full disclosure of crimes of a political nature, a clear deviation from the use of blanket amnesties in past truth commissions (Hayner 2011:209). Sixth, unlike previous commissions, the TRC featured public hearings, instead of confidential testimonies (Backer 2004:101; Quinn & Freeman 2003:1121). The impact of public hearings was magnified by the intense media coverage. A final unprecedented practice purportedly essential to healing was that victims were allowed to participate in the hearings and make their stories public (Backer 2004:101). Perhaps a clearer illustration that the TRC marked a turning point in truth commissions globally is the more elaborate conceptualization of "truth" it was tasked to "uncover." In its mandate, it acknowledged four types of truth: factual, personal, healing and social (see Chapman & Ball 2001). While early truth commissions focused on "factual truth" by determining the whereabouts of the disappeared, the other three were explicitly introduced by the TRC.

The TRC had significant resources too; a budget of $18 million per year was allocated for its activities, a considerably higher amount than previous truth commissions, including the Chilean ($1 million) and the Salvadoran ($2.5 million) (Torrens 1999). To sum up, according to Priscilla Hayner, the TRC "provided the most complex and sophisticated mandate for any truth commission to date, with carefully balanced powers and an extensive investigator reach" (2011:27).

Forensic Truth: The "Unfinished Business" of the TRC

Still, more than 20 years after the establishment of the TRC, hundreds of families are struggling to uncover the remains of their loved ones and to start the mourning process. A mother explains, "I am still looking for his bones returned ... How would you reconcile if you do not have bones? If I do not get my child's bones I would not forgive" (cited in Urbsaitis 2009:157). Although not the most pressing issue during the transition, the problem of missing persons was included in the TRC's mandate. The National Unity and Reconciliation Act of 1995 included politically motivated "abductions" in its scope of investigation.[9] The TRC was tasked to "establish the identity of victims in such violations, their fate or present whereabouts and the nature and the extent of the harm suffered by such victims."[10] To reach this objective, it was armed with three mechanisms. Under Section 29, it had the power to subpoena those with information about abductions. In addition, the amnesty hearings offered a forum where information about missing South Africans was

---

[9] Although by the time the TRC was established – in 1995 – the term "disappearance" was already used in legal and political discourse, the National Unity and Reconciliation Act referred to "abductions," thus indicating minimal familiarization with transitional justice debates in Latin America.

[10] Report Vol. I, Chapter 4, Subsection 4b.

solicited (Article 40). The early truth commissions of the 1980s were designed to extract factual information about burial sites critical for the recovery of bodies and the identification of individual missing persons. Third, as explained below, exhumations became a de facto mechanism of the TRC.

Exactly how effective was TRC's effort to uncover forensic truth? Although in theory it was designed to document the truth about the conditions leading to the deaths of the missing, in practice it was flawed. The first important drawback of the TRC in the management of the missing was the restrictive definition of the missing, which left hundreds of missing out of its investigative scope (Interview No.1). Originally, the TRC received approximately 1500 testimonies, but it accepted only 477 (TRC Report 2003). Although human rights organizations cite approximately 2000 cases of missing persons (Africa News 2005; Aronson 2010; Nolen 2007), the definition adopted by the TRC excluded all those cases that were not "politically motivated" and thereby not heroic (Aronson 2010:271). Needless to say, the definition of "victim" in post-conflict settings and its measurement are always political and hotly contested. What is remarkable in the case of the TRC is that the definition was so restrictive as to exclude the majority of the missing from its mandate. Moreover, the politicization of the definition led to overrepresentation of ANC victims in those 447 cases. Admittedly, the party had more casualties, but party members were advised to testify at the TRC, as it was easier for them to prove their political affiliation and convince the commissioners of the "political nature" of crimes (Aronson 2012:296).

Probably the most obvious failure of the TRC was the quality of exhumations and identification of human remains. According to all available information, a number of exhumations ordered by the TRC in the 1990s were inadequately performed. In the absence of a specific protocol, authorities tasked with exhuming graves employed different mechanisms in different regions of the country leading to a significant number of misidentifications. An internal audit carried out by the TRC shows only 60 percent of exhumations were accurate (2003:560). According to Madeleine Fullard, the leader of the Missing Persons Task Team (MPTT henceforth), the team currently in charge of exhumations, the TRC exhumed 50 victims, 20 of whom were misidentified (Interview No.63). A number of remains could not be positively identified as a result of the absence of conclusive evidence; this problem could have been resolved if DNA testing was used (TRC Report 2003:532). According to Fullard, the mid-1990s represent a transition period for forensic sciences;

at the time, DNA was not used as a mainstream identification tool (Interview No.63). As a result of the misidentifications, a number of families were re-traumatized, as they had to return the body. Added to this, the process of exhumations led to the destruction of invaluable forensic material, thereby inhibiting future efforts to deal with the problem (Interview No.15).

The key explanation of the failure of the TRC to identify more victims is the flawed design of the amnesty hearings. Simply put, the TRC offered too many "carrots" to perpetrators, without the concomitant use of "sticks" in cases of "non-full" disclosure. This became an insurmountable obstacle. Those who decided to participate could tell a story that would increase their possibility of being granted an amnesty without being forced to reveal crucial facts, such as burial sites. The final report acknowledges that a number of perpetrators provided the commission with information about gravesites and enabled it to carry out a small number of exhumations (TRC Report 2003). But at the same time, it stresses "even where most factors pointed to the probability of the missing being dead, it was not possible to make a finding to this effect in the absence of conclusive proof," namely, a dead body (TRC Report 2003:532).

In essence, in the absence of a follow-up mechanism to undertake exhumations, it was impossible to confirm the validity of the information provided by perpetrators. On many occasions, this left relatives worse off. Participation in the public hearing exposed them to horrific details about the suffering of their loved ones, without being given information to end their ongoing suffering, namely, the burial sites of their loved ones. In addition, they saw perpetrators being granted amnesty, freeing them of future criminal accountability. All these contributed to the perpetuation of their suffering.[11] The TRC has admitted this; in discussing the case of Moss Morudu, the report stresses that "although the amnesty hearing provided the family with new information, the Amnesty Committee was in the end unable to establish the exact fate of Moss Morudu. And so the quest of the Morudu family continues" (TRC 2003: para 11). A mother explains her sorrow:

> It is difficult because to whom are you going to reconcile because you do not even know the perpetrator. I saw them only once at the amnesty hearings. And since then, I have never seen them. I attended the hearing in

---

[11] Several studies suggest participation in the truth commission was often harmful for victims (Brouneus 2008:59). For an excellent review of the impact of the truth-telling processes, see Mendeloff (2009).

1996 on the 1st of November. I have never seen them again. They said
nothing. To whom am I going to reconcile?

(cited in Urbsaitis 2009:155)

This raises a related issue. By design, the TRC was tasked to "sacrifice" the
demand for justice by the few (i.e. victims) to the needs of the broader
society to learn the truth about the past (Graybill 2002). Yet in the case of
the missing, the design of the TRC inhibited society's efforts to recover
the full truth. Restoring fractured social relations depends on perpetrators' testimony that could lead to the identification of the victims.
The failure of the TRC to safeguard a meaningful "truth for amnesty"
procedure, putting pressure on perpetrators to supply credible forensic
evidence, destroyed any prospect of restoring victim–perpetrator relations. Flatly put, the TRC failed. The final report of the TRC makes a stark
admission of failure: "The resolution of these disappearance cases is
perhaps the most significant piece of unfinished business for the commission" (2003:532).

To be fair, all truth commissions operate within a restrictive time
frame, and it is impossible to identify every single case. This is particularly relevant for those commissions with broader mandates. As the
experience of Chile, Argentina or Guatemala shows, some of the most
successful truth commissions have established follow-up mechanisms
(either another commission or a forensic panel) to deal specifically with
the disappeared. And, in fact, the TRC offered recommendations for the
logical "next steps," including the establishment of a follow-up commission to deal with the "unfinished business" of the missing. In 2005, several
years after the conclusion of the TRC, a new mechanism was established,
the MPTT, under the auspices of the National Prosecution Authority.
The MPTT managed to incorporate a number of the TRC's suggestions,
largely as a result of the painstaking effort of its leader, Madeleine Fullard.
It introduced DNA analysis and institutionalized collaboration with one
of the most prestigious forensic anthropologists' group, the Argentine
Forensic Anthropology Team (EAAF), thereby marking a turning point
in the approach to unearthing human remains in South Africa (EAAF
2006). Exhumations carried out by the MPTT have attracted significant
media attention, and it is frequently framed as "CSI South Africa" (Africa
News 2007; Dugan 2011; Kubheka 2013).

Between 2005 and early 2016, the MPTT unearthed 101 missing
persons and identified 89 (Interview No.63). Again, the number of
identified missing is relatively small, and the MPTT should not be

considered a success story. As an extension of the TRC, it also reflects some of its design flaws. For example, the team is mandated to look only at the list of missing established by the TRC; by so doing, it excludes most of the missing (De Kock 2013). In addition, the MPTT remains politicized; the majority of the exhumed bodies are MK/ANC members[12] and exhumations are framed as paying homage to "freedom fighters," or "unsung heroes" (Africa News 2013). Even worse, the majority of the families have yet to identify the remains of their relatives, despite the availability of "factual" information stemming from the TRC's hearings.

The cases of the TRC and the MPTT shed light on one of the most counterintuitive findings of the book. Paradoxically, setting up an effective policy of humanitarian exhumations, that is with the primary goal of identifying the remains of the victims without necessarily leading to prosecutions, is often more difficult in the aftermath of state repression transitions rather than in post-conflict settings. As opposed to mass graves in post-civil war countries, where exhumations can be carried out directly by forensic experts, in contexts like South Africa, identifying individual graves depends on information offered by perpetrators who are the only eyewitnesses of the clandestine crime. This is confirmed by Madeleine Fullard, leader of the MPTT. To this she adds:

> We can essentially do nothing in certain cases without some assistance from the perpetrators ... Our challenge now is that three quarters of the security forces are already dead. Within three to five years will all be dead. What do we do now? Now we are trying to find some mechanism to approach them to make disclosure about these activities.

Incentives need to be offered to the perpetrators to come forward and share information about burial sites. The immunity provision could be an important carrot, but as the case of the TRC shows, the design of the amnesty is critical. Incentivizing perpetrators to provide details on clandestine and potentially self-incriminating activities requires anonymity and confidentiality. This is confirmed by the experience of the MPTT. According to Fullard:

> I would say that in a third of the cases we have uncovered bodies we have done so because of the amnesty process, because we got information that they took that person to that place and they blew that person up or they

---

[12] It should be noted this is not because of pressure from the ANC or bias in the system, but the result of the availability of information.

burned the body. We would never, ever have found those bodies without
that information.

(Interview No.63)

This points to a perhaps inevitable tension between the high visibility of
the TRC and the contentious nature of truth related to the missing and
the concomitant need for discreet forums to share forensic truth without
supplying incriminatory evidence (*corpus delicti*). Adrian Guelke highlights this tension, arguing that "the more popular the mechanism of
a truth commission process the more likely it is that ... it will help to
ensure that much of the truth is never known" (2007:365). Exhumations
and identification of victims' remains are, by default, challenging tasks,
and the design of modern truth commissions may paradoxically inhibit
exhumations, even if they are intended exclusively for humanitarian
purposes.

TRC and Effective Investigation

As mentioned above, the report of the TRC labels the problem of the
missing "unfinished business." It unearthed and identified less than one-
fifth of the victims and excluded from its scope of investigation
a significant number of missing who did not fit its narrow mandate.
This is not a very promising start to our investigation, but it is time to
turn to the next question. How effective was the TRC in investigating the
political and institutional conditions that led to the disappearances in the
first place? The TRC undoubtedly made a huge contribution to delegitimizing dominant myths. As mainstream media did not cover incidents of
human rights violations during apartheid, for a sizeable segment of the
white population this was the first time they had heard about mass
atrocities being carried out in a systematic way by the state.

As illustrated above, the TRC was given special powers, most notably,
its "special investigative hearings" and its amnesty granting process. Both
were designed to offer a powerful incentive to perpetrators to reveal the
"full truth" about their crimes. Yet in the restorative model adopted by
the TRC, there is an *instrumental approach to truth*, whereby a testimony
is a means to achieve a higher end, in this case reconciliation. Instead of
establishing an authoritative version of (factual) truth, the TRC looked
for a master narrative that would facilitate reconciliation between victims
and perpetrators. So long as the objective was to reconcile a nation
divided by violence, the driving force of the TRC became the "narrative

truth," delinked from "factual" truth (Wilson 2001); I will return to this point below. Unfortunately, this instrumental approach to human rights inhibited an effective investigation of the causes, the nature and the extent of disappearances in South Africa.

An obvious problem of the TRC was that the "public" hearings made perpetrators reluctant to participate or discouraged those who testified from revealing the more sensitive aspects of their misdeeds. Such knowledge was crucial to shed light on the political and structural conditions behind the disappearances, including the chain of command or the racist culture. Otherwise, it became difficult to explain the "logic of disappearances" in that particular historical period (TRC Report 2003:515). As Jeremy Sarkin says, "applicants limited their revelations to what they believed was in the public domain or was likely to emerge after further investigations" (Sarkin 2004). In the end, only 80 persons applied for amnesty for political crimes related to the missing (TRC Report 2003:522). Essentially, the design guaranteed a non-effective investigation.

One of the most interesting aspects of the TRC and the South African model of the management of the missing was the instrumental use of human rights as a means of reaching political goals (Wilson 2001). The transition was preceded by excessive violence, and political elites sought to protect the fragile transition from experiencing a similarly violent backlash. Truth recovery was instrumentally used to provide an account that would comfort victims but at the same time would not challenge perpetrators – a typical story of negotiated transition without accountability. This meant there was a need to establish a widely acceptable and non-contentious truth. This clearly limited the prospect of effective investigation for the missing; as an informed participant explained, although there was a "need to catalogue the crimes of both sides, it never intended to do forensic investigation for every case"; rather, the objective was to equalize blame and, in this sense, the hearings helped build a representative sample (Interview No.15).

In fact, TRC made a conscious effort to present an image of equal suffering throughout the nation, evoking a broader "healing discourse" (Moon 2008). But Bronwyn Leebaw, for one, strongly criticizes the TRC for depoliticizing debates about the causes of past violence (2011). With respect to the missing, the picture is even more complex, as the problem was used as a political instrument. For one thing, the definition was restricted to the victims of political violence, and only those relatives who could prove affiliation with a political party were eligible for reparations. In a similar vein, the rationale for the investigation of cases was often the level of "political" usefulness. A number of migrants from neighboring countries went missing, but this aspect of human rights violations was excluded, deemed incompatible with the political master narrative. Equally, although there were cases where perpetrators' testimony could have revealed critical evidence, key witnesses were not invited out of political expediency (Quinn & Freeman 2003:1126).

It is clear that by the time the TRC was concluding its activities, the goal of documenting human rights violations had succumbed to the overarching objective of reconciliation (Quinn & Freeman 2003:1126). Effective investigation was sidelined, as forensic evidence had the potential to unearth inconvenient truths that might preclude or at least slow down reconciliation. Leebaw is right to argue the "TRC's investigations functioned to legitimate transitional compromises, . . . a process that would largely avoid, rather than examine, the historical and political context of apartheid" (2011:60).

The instrumental use of the missing drew on the widespread, politicized discourse of heroic suffering. A brief look at the media coverage of the time, as well as more recent coverage of exhumations, reveals a presentation of the missing as "heroes" of a liberation struggle. It is interesting that even a forensic scientist working in the MPTT, when asked in an interview about her motivation to get involved, argued it was a moral obligation to honor those heroes who "died fighting for the freedom we enjoy today" (Lakha 2012:16). Usually, in post-traumatic societies, forensic scientists present their work as restoring human rights and the dignity of victims – a neutral, humanitarian discourse, not a politicized one (Rosenblatt 2015). In the issue of the missing, the TRC transformed apartheid "terrorists" into "victims of state terror" and ultimately into "heroes of liberation" (Rousseau 2009:351). In this binary framing of politicized deaths (heroes vs. repressors) (Fullard & Rousseau 2001:69), there is no space for nuances or unaffiliated victims. The drama of the missing is dominated by stories of heroism, often fueled by the political interests of the ANC. In effect, "because nonpolitical civilian cases do not generate the same kind of political capital for the ANC-led government," they are left unattended, leaving an instrumental, politicized approach to dominate public debates on the missing (Fullard & Rousseau 2001:69).

The politicized selection criteria mentioned above meant the TRC and the MPTT focused on ANC-affiliated victims, a clear selection bias (Interview No.15). It is hardly surprising that the media cover a very specific subset of the missing – the politically oriented (Interview No.1). In fact, angry relatives frequently demand "collective (social and public) recognition not just of their victimhood but also of their sacrifice for the freedom of all South Africans, primarily through acknowledgment of the missing as military heroes by the state" (Aronson 2010:273). This picture sharply deviates from the framing used by other relatives in other countries around the world, namely, "individualized" human rights to truth. Arguably, this instrumental and politicized framing prevented a comprehensive investigation by the TRC and the MPTT. Critical questions, such as who gave the orders and why specific individuals were selected over others, were never asked or answered.

The Puzzling Absence of Retributive Justice

South Africa is one of the few countries where perpetrators were not convicted,[13] although its truth commission was coupled with exhumations. This is odd, particularly because the families in South Africa apparently had opportunities to push for retributive justice similar to those of families in other post-authoritarian societies who brought their cases to court, for example, Chile and Argentina. Obviously, this does not reflect a normative assumption or a moral judgment; nor is it a perception that criminal accountability is more valuable or beneficial for families than other forms of acknowledgment. Yet, it leaves us wondering. Why, despite the availability of opportunities that led families in other countries to indict culprits, did South Africa take a different route?

In sharp contrast to other societies where blanket amnesties posed a significant hurdle to holding perpetrators accountable for their crimes, in South Africa, the amnesty was individualized and conditional on the "full disclosure" of truth. According to the TRC's final report, however, only a very small percentage, approximately 12 percent of the applicants, finally received amnesty (Backer 2004:102). We might therefore expect relatives in South Africa to have fewer obstacles to initiating a legal process of truth recovery. Yet only a handful challenged the amnesty at an early stage of the transition period. In a well-known example, the

---

[13] There is only a handful of known cases, such as the highly visible trial of Eugene de Kock in 1996; he was found guilty on several charges, including kidnapping, and was given two life sentences and 212 years imprisonment (Smith 2015). De Kock was the leader of a death squad responsible for some of the most heinous crimes during apartheid and was known as the "prime evil."

relatives of Steve Biko challenged its constitutionality. Despite their efforts, the Constitutional Court found "reparations as satisfactory substitute for the rights of individuals to seek redress in criminal and civil courts" (Backer 2004:102; Biko 2000:195).

We might also expect that so long as "full disclosure" was the legal precondition for amnesty, cases where forensic evidence contradicted the validity of the testimony would result in the amnesty being overturned for the individual in question. A number of exhumations carried out by the MPTT in the 2000s revealed a pattern of amnesties granted based on mistaken testimonies. For example, in the "Pebco three" case in Eastern Cape,[14] the perpetrators testified before the TRC that they burned the bodies and threw the "ashes" in a nearby river to destroy incriminating evidence. More than a decade after their testimony, forensic evidence from exhumations contradicted their original statement, as parts of the victims' bodies were found in a nearby septic tank (Gurney & Johnson 2008; Nolen 2007). This forensic evidence could have served as a legal basis to overturn the amnesty, yet this did not happen. Similarly, the MPTT mandate to exhume graves and identify remains is overseen by the National Prosecutorial Authority (NPA henceforth); therefore, one might well expect forensic evidence to be used in building criminal cases against perpetrators. This is not the case. Finally, since the transition, the ANC has dominated the electoral politics of South Africa. As the party representing the vast majority of victims, one would expect it to be a powerful ally supporting victims' call for justice. As illustrated below, this has yet to happen.

One might argue that a deep-seated distrust of judicial authorities prevents families from using this tool. For long stretches of time, and definitely throughout apartheid, courts were the institutionalized tools of repression and racial discrimination against non-white communities (Abel 2015). In fact, this explanation accounts for the original decision of the ANC and certain leading intellectuals to abstain from using prosecutions during the transition (Leebaw 2011:64). Yet, in other countries with comparable challenges and long authoritarian regimes, like Chile (1973–1990), that was not an obstacle; it did not prevent families from bringing cases to court. Besides, even if this explanation was valid for the first period after transition, it fails to account for the lack of cases

---

[14] Pebco, Port Elizabeth Black Civic Organization refers to the abduction of Champion Galela, Qaqaquli Godolozi and Sipho Hashe, the three black activists, by members of the repressive regime in 1985.

in court today, more than 20 years later. As indicated below, certain structural flaws from the apartheid era remain intact and there is ongoing distrust of judicial authorities;[15] still even this cannot explain why so few families have stepped up.

An alternative explanation points to the constraints to mobilization encountered by the families. The number of the missing is quite small, ranging from 500 to 2000, making it difficult for families to mobilize around a cause. This may explain the lack of visibility of disappearances during or after transition, like rallies or other forms of protest, but it is largely unrelated to the judicial front, precisely because criminal prosecutions focus on individual cases. As such, why even a few families did not follow the judicial path is mystifying.

Simply stated, the main obstacle preventing families from bringing their cases to court is a political one. More specifically, apart from the obvious restrictive framework set by the negotiated transition, the ANC is reluctant to open a Pandora's box of criminal justice, as such a move has the potential to shed light on notorious and potentially incriminatory activities of its own members during apartheid. In transitions in Latin America, perpetrators were isolated in the ranks of the military, and the gradual democratization of state institutions created more opportunities for victims to seek justice. In contrast, in South Africa, the liberation movement – led by the ANC – was partly responsible for a number of victims (both killed and missing). The ANC, as the political winner of the transition, had minimal incentives to facilitate trials shedding unwelcome light on leading members. For example, Winnie Mandela, the ex-wife of President Mandela and currently an influential MP, allegedly played a leading role in the kidnapping of two ANC members missing for more than 25 years. Their bodies were only recently uncovered (Tay 2013).

Political interference is most evident in a handful of cases where relatives attempted to bring their case to court, like the struggle of the family of Nokuthula Simelane explored at the beginning of the chapter. Because she was an MK operative, she was kidnapped by security agents in 1983; her remains have never been recovered. Her case was reviewed by the TRC, and although the perpetrators received amnesty for torture

---

[15] Weak prosecutorial power was evident in the early years after transition. Along with others in the military, Magnus Malan, a former Minister of Defense, was charged with murdering 13 individuals. The case was brought by the Investigation Task Unit of the TRC; it resulted in his acquittal, mostly because of the failure of the prosecution (Varney & Sarkin 1997).

and kidnapping, in their testimony they did not admit murdering her. The specific case is crucial because the TRC handed it over to the NPA's "Priority Crimes Litigation Unit" (PCLU) for further investigation. The PCLU was set up to deal with international crimes covered by the ICC, as well as to build criminal cases stemming from the TRC's findings. In theory, such cases should have a more realistic chance of a successful prosecution. Yet since 2003, there has been no follow-up development. Moreover, in 2005, the government granted amnesties and pardons to those involved who were not amnestied during the TRC.

The family has engaged in a long-term battle to uncover the truth and prosecute the culprits. They have even sued the government for granting amnesties to perpetrators as a violation of international law and the national constitution (Sarkin 2015:29). In the absence of a criminal prosecution and the continued inertia of the authorities, the family filed an inquest at the High Court in May 2015.[16] The family, supported by the Khulumani group, a human rights movement, submitted documents showing political interference had precluded meaningful criminal prosecution. The former head of the PCLU admitted in an affidavit that he was removed from his place largely because he had built cases and carried out investigations that could have led to the prosecution of ANC members (Sarkin 2015:31).[17] Fearing the head of the PCLU would launch criminal cases against ANC members for crimes committed before 1994, cabinet ministers vetoed any prosecution of cases handed over by the TRC.[18] Marjorie Jobson, the leader of the Khulumani group, says: "It reveals that the people who lead this country are so complicit in some of these murders themselves they do not want this to come out in public. It is a terrible, shameful chapter of our history, but it is not fair on the families. To save their political careers they refuse to do what the families need" (Interview No.62).

In addition to its direct political interference, the ANC "hijacked" issues of victimhood in the post-1990s period in South Africa, framing individual victims as "heroes" of the liberation struggle, thereby

---

[16] *Thembisile Phumelele Nkadimeng* vs. *National Director of Public Prosecutions*, May 20, 2015, High Court of South Africa, Pretoria.

[17] See a supporting affidavit provided by Anton Ackermann, former NPDD, in *Thembisile Phumelele Nkadimeng* vs. *National Director of Public Prosecutions*, May 20, 2015, High Court of South Africa, Pretoria, pp. 217–235.

[18] See supporting affidavit provided by Vusi Pikoli, former NPDD, in *Thembisile Phumelele Nkadimeng* vs. *National Director of Public Prosecutions*, May 20, 2015, High Court of South Africa, Pretoria, pp. 170–216.

depriving families of a more personal form of memory and mourning. The transition from apartheid marked a radical departure from a racist state to a democratic one. For most leading figures in the ANC, however, the transition was not merely to democracy; it was also a form of nation building (Wilson 2001). To facilitate this process, victimhood, especially visually salient forms of victimhood, like the missing (exhumations, bones) were instrumentally used as the "bodies of the new nation" as Rousseau aptly puts it (2015:177). The strategic decision of the TRC to focus only on a subset of the total who disappeared, that is, "politically motivated" abductions, is another illustration of the instrumental approach – in fact, only one of the 477 cases of the missing reviewed by the TRC was not officially a guerilla (Rousseau 2015).

Similarly, the first exhumations in the late 1990s were highly politicized. Nelson Mandela was present, the coffins were draped with ANC flags and veterans sang freedom songs. This ceremony has become an ongoing ritual taking place in "freedom park," a location with obvious political significance (Rousseau 2015). ANC local committees take the lead in organizing burials, part of their claim to ownership of the "missing heroes" (Aronson 2010).

These and other stories suggest the ANC has created a hegemonic framing around the missing and dead. The missing (and other victims) are members of an imagined community of heroes who served the ANC and liberated the country. They are treated as soldiers fallen in the line of duty, not as victims. Those families who do not subscribe to this discourse simply cannot challenge it. Nor can they honor their more intimate, personal need to mourn and remember their lost ones as individuals. Most importantly, this instrumental and heroic approach excludes any discussion about the legal rights of the families or the duties of the state. Of course, a number of families are very proud to have their relatives buried with honors. But this does not diminish the families' loss of independence.

The politicized framing goes a long way to explain the lack of trials. First, the framing of the missing as heroes of the liberation struggle implicitly deprives families of the status of victims. While in post-authoritarian Chile, those who disappeared were victims of a moral harm caused by a ruthless military regime, in South Africa they had the moral privilege of sacrificing their lives for liberation. Within this delimited framing, it becomes impossible for families to initiate judicial procedures that would challenge the ANC's central post-transitional discourse. As Adelaide Dlamini, a mother who lost her child, puts it

"They [ANC] lied to me, because our people [were] for ANC [but] they don't care for us" (cited in Urbsaitis 2009:157). The leader of Khulumani is even more critical: "The only people this government will look after is only those who received military training and carried weapons. These are the only victims they consider legitimate, so when those people disappeared, these are the people they prioritize and try to exhume ... that political (discourse) suits the ANC and all other activist are just neglected" (Interview No.62).

Second, the ANC has no incentive to proceed to trials. It is the undisputed political winner of the transition, and trials are used by the weak to challenge injustice. An informed observer who participated in the TRC but who prefers to remain anonymous maintains: "Why should they [ANC] do anything that would threaten that power? They are the gigantic electoral winners in South Africa and anything they can do to sustain that transition they would do" (Interview No.14).

As suggested elsewhere in the book, to understand why a country advances to a broader truth and, more precisely, to retributive justice, we need to shift our attention to the families and their effectiveness in deploying (or creating new) opportunities to overcome legal and political obstacles. These opportunities include access to the political system, influential domestic and international alliances, novel legal arguments, etc.

Still, this *requires agency, namely, an actor that understand itself as independent with an independent political voice and demand.* Although opportunities are necessary, opportunities alone are insufficient to catalyze change – the deployment of the tools requires the agency of the families. The above-mentioned political obstacles trimmed the opportunities of families to mobilize in an independent way around this problem. An informed observed who prefers to remain anonymous says:

> There is no organized missing persons movement in South Africa, unlike other places, so you don't get large demonstrations, you'll never have a mass protest or thousands of people show up on the doorstep of parliament.
>
> (Interview No.15).

In my search of media, I found only one such gathering; it was on the International Day of the Disappeared in late August 2005 in the Vlakplaas and it occurred a decade after the establishment of the TRC (Africa News 2005). The restrictive framework has precluded the creation of independent human rights groups, which otherwise might support the families' struggle for truth. An exception is the Khulumani group, whose name means "Speak Out." Although this group is also politicized, it is one of the few with the declared objective of promoting justice, and it has about 20,000 members. In early 2016, it launched an initiative titled "Justice Heals" highlighting justice as a fundamental need of victims (April 19, 2016). Its leader, Marjorie Jobson, claims the group has offered practical advice to help families prepare the paperwork necessary to add new cases to the list of missing, names excluded from the TRC investigation (Interview No.62). They are now also supporting litigation, and cases are going to court. Yet the prospects of success in the court are curtailed by both the insurmountable political obstacles and the limited resources available to Khulumani.

Although the transition marked a change in the balance of political power, with the black community now represented politically, this was not accompanied by a similar transition in economic and structural relations. As John Brewer quite rightly notes, the "political peace" was not followed by "social peace." He underlines, "While Black South Africans now control the state, they do not share in the country's economic wealth to any greater degree" (Brewer 2010:38). In effect, the structural and material inequalities have not been addressed 20 years after the transition (Seekings & Nattrass 2008). As research shows, families in such contexts may prioritize material needs over punitive justice, and of course, they frequently cannot afford the expenses of a criminal trial (Robins 2013). According to a recent study by the Khulumani group, the most pressing needs of the families of the missing in South Africa are material, including employment (71 percent), housing (22 percent) and skills training (17 percent) (Khulumani 2010). In practical terms, this means families may depend on ANC support for survival; being close to the party or declaring their relatives to have been resistance fighters will secure them both much needed benefits and state support.[19] As an interviewee reveals, "Most victims' communities were very loyal to the ANC ... There are some groups ... but they are very few and very weak. Most of them are connected to the ANC so when

[19] For example, the state offers "special pensions" to the victims of the liberation struggle, but the conditions to secure them are challenging and politicized, including proving at least a 5-year membership in a group (Aronson 2010:276). In this way, the ANC incentivizes victims to conform to the dominant framing. Compensation is not provided for victims but for "military operatives."

it made the deal everybody had to go along with it and they stick"
(Interview No.14).

The mobilization of families in Latin America was helped by the fact
that the primary targets of disappearances were middle-class members of
professional organizations, labor unions, lawyers, etc. The institutional
support of professional unions during and after transition was critical for
families' movements, with free legal advice, for example, or practical help
in bringing cases to court. In contrast, the apartheid victims were framed
as operatives of resistance movements and, therefore, the search for the
truth depended on the support of political parties. As the political
transition precluded certain transitional justice alternatives, it became
impossible for families to issue a challenge.

Conclusion

The study of the missing in South Africa teaches us important lessons in
transitional justice. For one thing, it identifies a paradox. Truth commissions historically emerged to deal with disappearances, but for the TRC,
arguably the most renowned such commission, this task remains "unfinished business." The mandate and the structure of contemporary truth
commissions focus on airing past wrongdoing in public. This is all well
and good, but it may prevent culprits from pointing to graves, and this is
often the most realistic way for families to find their loved ones.
The TRC's public hearings and media attention may have been important
in raising awareness or even promoting reconciliation at the societal
level, but they had an adverse impact on establishing forensic truth.
In its present form, then, the mechanism invented to deal with the
missing may be the least useful mechanism to address the pressing
(humanitarian) need of the families for identification.

The experience of the TRC sheds light on the interesting interplay
between amnesty, truth and justice. Although amnesties could serve an
important role in getting the guilty on board and facilitating forensic
truth recovery by leading to humanitarian exhumations, if not properly
designed, they could not only fail to accommodate the humanitarian
needs of the families but also deprive them of their legal rights. In other
words, the design of amnesties is critical to forensic truth recovery and
determines what future steps will be taken toward retributive justice.

The examination of the TRC also suggests political opportunities are
merely tools. Alone they are insufficient to catalyze any change; they
require agency. The South African experience reveals the interesting

dynamics of party politics in extending or resisting transitional justice settlements in the long run. It shows how dominant political parties can "hijack" the politics of victimhood, delimiting the array of available transitional justice policies and precluding other options, in this case retributive justice. Jelena Subotic (2009) finds a similar pattern in the Balkans – an interesting point deserving more attention. Probably the most interesting aspect of the South African experience, also evident in the case of Lebanon, is that the influence of the political parties or other influential patrons is more important in contexts where the transition is not followed by "social peace" and where structural injustices continue after transition.

9

Poetic Justice

The Chilean Desaparecidos

A paradox circumscribes transitional justice debates in Chile. During his long reign (1973–1990), General Augusto Pinochet designed, ordered and excelled in heinous human rights violations, including torture, extrajudicial executions and rape. However, one of the crimes that led to his indictment, the disappearance of thousands of Chileans, was the one for which during the transition it was the least possible to be held accountable. An amnesty law protected the military, and the fragile balance of power was definitely not conducive for governmental initiatives on sensitive questions of human rights. Most importantly, the "disappearance" of over a thousand Chileans left no *corpus delicti* (body of evidence) to prove the crime in the first place. In the end, however, the persistent efforts of the families of the missing challenged the silence, and Pinochet and a number of military officers were held accountable, many specifically for the crime of enforced disappearance. Renowned Chilean novelist and playwright Ariel Dorfman encapsulates this turn as "poetic justice":

> It is particularly marvelous, then, that it should be precisely those missing and supposedly dead bodies that have come back to haunt Pinochet, turning into the instrument of what might well be his punishment and that of his accomplices. To get off the hook, Pinochet will now have to prove that he killed – or ordered the assassination – of the prisoners; he would have to disinter them from their anonymous graves, drag them out of the rivers and seas from where they were cast. Then and only then could his amnesty be applied to him ... Poetic Justice indeed.
>
> (Dorfman 2000:31)

In essence, the Chilean experience highlights the "boomerang" effect of the crime of enforced disappearances. Although the primary reason for its deployment by warlords and dictators is to minimize the prospect of future accountability, it is the crime that comes back to haunt them.

208

Worse yet, they are brought down by a group that as shown in preceding chapters should have been helpless – the families of the victims. In countries around the world, the relatives refuse to remain silent; they build influential alliances and design innovative mobilization strategies to create opportunities for successful truth recovery. This is the story of one such group – the Chilean families of *Desaparecidos* who resisted silence and denial to hold powerful perpetrators accountable.

The challenging case of Chile enhances our understanding of transitional justice debates in several ways. First, it is important to remember that when compared to other societies in the region that dealt with the problem of the disappeared, such as Argentina, Chile had a more fragile transition (De Brito 2003:181). In Argentina, the defeat of the military junta over the Malvinas/Falkland islands led to its deligitimization, but in Chile, the military continued to be seen as a legitimate and powerful actor by a significant proportion of Chilean society (Huneeus, Couso & Sieder 2010). Pinochet stayed in power for 17 years, far exceeding the short-term junta in Argentina, and the relative success of his economic policy made him quite popular among specific segments of the society (De Brito 2001). His removal from power came as a result of a very narrow defeat (54.6 percent) in a referendum in 1989, a figure indicative of his ongoing popularity.

The negotiated nature of the Chilean transition set up several obstacles to truth recovery for human rights abuses, including an amnesty law that protected members of the *ancien regime* from accountability; Pinochet retained his position as the Commander in Chief of the Army, for example, and the archives of the secret police (Central Nacional de Informaciones, CNI) were destroyed covering up even atrocities carried out by the previous secret police (Dirección de Inteligencia Nacional, DINA) responsible for 90 percent of disappearances (Wilde 1999:480; Zalaquett 1991). In addition, the judiciary played an important institutional role by facilitating Pinochet's authoritarian policies (Hilbink 2007), curtailing popular trust in and access to one of the key instruments of acknowledging the truth about state repression.

In this chapter, I describe the logic of disappearances in Chile and take a look at the families' mobilization to uncover the truth about their loved ones. As I go on to show, truth recovery in Chile followed a gradualist logic of "peeling the onion"; in early stages, constrained by the realities of the fragile transition, transitional justice mechanisms were geared primarily toward the recovery of forensic truth. As time passed and bodies were not exhumed, families used new institutional opportunities to peel another layer, entering the stage of retributive justice.[1] Interestingly, the families seemed to gain strength from the failure of the country's truth commission to find the whereabouts of their loved ones and its follow-up mechanisms. Given all this, the Chilean experience becomes an instructive test of transitional justice policies, specifically in addressing the problem of the disappeared.

The Logic of Disappearances

The military dictatorships in the Southern Cone of Latin America in the 1960s and 1970s shared the common objective of eliminating sources of clandestine left-wing subversion; hence the high level of covert cooperation among different regimes in the region (De Brito 2001:119). As the seminal research of Tony Robben on Argentina shows, the tool of disappearance was best suited to instill terror in the broader population, erode social trust and ensure obedience (Robben 2005a:270). The deployment of the crime as a tool of suppression emerged partly as a result of learning from the experience of other societies in the area. On the one hand, keeping secretly detained individuals alive after they had been forced to reveal sensitive information made little sense, while on the other hand, openly killing enemies could backfire and create symbols of resistance. Here, Bolivia's management of the death of Ernesto Che Guevara was an instructive lesson for dictators in the region. In any event, kidnapping enemies was deemed a cost-effective tool allowing the military regime in Chile to extract information and guarantee submission of the population through terror, while the absence of a body made it almost impossible to hold state agents accountable. Accordingly, the Chilean regime "disappeared" approximately 1200 of its citizens.

Despite the setting up of a number of official bodies tasked to provide an authoritative account of the disappeared, the precise figure remains unknown. The final report of the truth commission published in the early 1990s indicates that 979 of 2396 cases of human rights violations are disappearances, while a follow-up commission with exclusive focus on the disappeared added another 123 (UNWGEID 2013:para 7).[2] In 2009 (Valech

---

[1] It should be noted that relatives engaged with the criminal justice system from the very beginning, but as explained below there was not a realistic prospect of a successful legal strategy of prosecuting those responsible in the early years after the transition.

[2] The picture becomes more complicated when we consider the estimated number of disappeared gathered by unofficial, yet consistent, fact-finding bodies, such as the human rights branch of the Catholic Church (*Vicaria*).

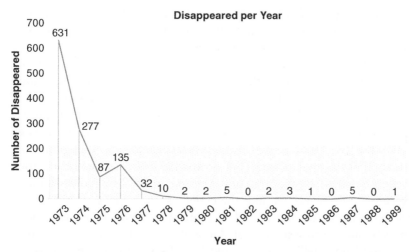

Figure 9.1 Disappeared in Chile

Commission II), eight more cases were included, raising the number to 1110 (UNWGEID 2013:para 12). Yet this categorization probably underestimates the number of persons who went missing. Approximately 3216 people were executed and 1200 are recognized as "disappeared" (Robben 2014:340). Yet, the majority of those "executed" remain unaccounted for; therefore, in legal terms, they are missing too. In fact, this separation between "executed" and "disappeared" to some extent was self-imposed by the relatives in the 1970s and it is not based on an authoritative account.

Understanding the "politics of measurement" can shed light on our understanding of how authoritative accounts of truth create hierarchies of victims' groups, silencing some (Brysk 1994; Lawther 2014). For example, as will be shown below, following this official categorization, two major associations of relatives of victims have formed in Chile: one focuses exclusively on the detained-disappeared and another on the politically executed, although, in reality, families in both categories share similar dilemmas, challenges and objectives.

It is worth examining the chronological distribution of disappearances to get a better grasp of the logic of violence in Chile. Using data from the official Truth Commission (Rettig Commission), Figure 9.1 clearly illustrates the patterns of violence although probably underestimates the total number of the disappeared. The vast majority of disappearances (95 percent) occurred between 1973 and 1976. After 1978, the practice abates; this should be partly attributed to the success in instilling terror on the

Chilean society as well as to the international reactions to the excessive use of disappearances, not only in Chile but also in Argentina, with mounting external pressure to stop (Shelton 1980).

Broadly defined, there are two periods of disappearances. The first wave took place right after the coup in September 1973 and lasted until late 1974. In this period, the secret police (DINA) targeted militants of the Revolutionary Left Movement (MIR, Movimiento de Izquierda Revolucionaria) in an effort to eradicate leftist resistance. It is estimated that in the first 3 months, 631 persons disappeared, accounting for more than half of the total missing (Ballesteros 1995:48). Hence, the majority, though not all, of disappeared of the period are MIR militants who were executed; DINA agents hid their bodies to remove incriminatory evidence. In the second period of repression (1975–1978), disappearances became a more sophisticated tool of terror; the selection of victims was based on intelligence gathered by DINA while the extraction of information was facilitated by the setting up of clandestine detention centers (Ensalaco 2000:83). During this period, repression was directed at a broader circle of students, workers and sympathizers with socialist and communist ideas (ibid.).

Peeling the Onion I: Early Mobilization and Forensic Truth

In 1997, Ariel Dorfman wrote a moving article comparing the experience of contemporary Chile to Homer's Iliad. After repeatedly abusing the dead body of Hector, Achilles finds the human decency to give Hector's body to his father Priam, so that he may properly mourn his loss. Dorfman draws parallels with Pinochet, arguing:

> There is one man in the world who, like Achilles, could render the dead into the living ... He [Pinochet] has the power to order his subordinates to investigate their own misdeeds, search their records, reveal where the bodies of the disappeared lie ... He is the only man alive who could force the Chilean army, an institution that fervently believes in hierarchy and obedience, to discover the truth.
>
> (September 17, 1997: 17)

Dorfman's extract is important. It shows that until the late 1990s, recovering forensic truth was a pressing demand in Chilean society. Viviana Díaz, the daughter of the leader of the Communist party who disappeared during the dictatorship, explains this lingering existential need for the truth: "We always hoped that even if we wouldn't find him alive we wanted to find what was left of him, his remains" (Interview No.54). To be able to mourn, families are known to visit the cemetery of Santiago and leave flowers on crosses bearing "N.N" (unknown), although they do not know who lies beneath (Robben 2015).

The intensity and the type of the crime affected thousands of families and set the stage for a persistent struggle to recover their loved ones. It did not just set the stage, however; the trauma actually became a catalyst for mobilization. Evelyn Gahona, whose father disappeared when she was a child, explains: "[W]hen you are 7 and someone tells you your father is in prison, you tend to think he must have done something bad. But I came to understand that that wasn't the case and then you start on this road of always looking for the truth; truth and justice" (Interview No.57).

As early as 1974, the first official organization of relatives, the Association of Relatives of Detained-Disappeared (*Agrupación de Familiares de Detenidos Desaparecidos* [AFDD]) was set up; even now it remains one of the most active human rights groups in Chile. AFDD's repertoire of mobilization was innovative. The main purpose was to use family values and accentuate the role of mothers, while deconstructing Pinochet's self-portrayal as custodian of the family and the country (Thomas 2011). The repertoire of mobilization included protesting women carrying photos of their relatives on their chests, accompanied by a question *"Donde Estan?"* (Where are they?). This became a global symbol of their suffering. Their repertoire included public events like the *Cuecas* (traditional Chilean dance) organized by the *Conjunto Folclor* group; Cuecas is a traditional dance for partners and was used by AFDD members to symbolically highlight the absence of the natural partner in dance and in life (AFDD 1997; Thomas 2011: 177). Another form of protest was a campaign of hunger strikes, *Nuestra Vida Por La Verdad* (our life for the truth), coupled with religious services for the disappeared to raise domestic and international awareness on the issue.

As Díaz remembers it, in the early years, a key objective was to convince both a domestic and an international audience that disappearances were taking place and to challenge the official deniability of the crime:

> In 1977 it was the first hunger strike [by relatives] in the headquarters of CEPAL.[3] Well, that made the news around the world because it was the relatives of the disappeared on the strike … So we had to convince our

---

[3] Comisión Económica para América Latina (ECLAC, according to its English acronym) can be considered an international organization, part of the United Nations. This explains why the AFDD used this building considered diplomatic territory.

own fellow Chileans that we were facing this new kind of repressive practice, not just arresting your political opponents, but disappearing them without a trace. That first strike in CEPAL managed to get international assistance and attention, because from the CEPAL [building] we could send out cables about what was really going on in the country. And we got solidarity messages back.

(Interview No.57)

Part of the early mobilization of AFDD focused on establishing a record of disappearances. First, the Vicaría (the human rights branch of the Catholic Church) remained the closest ally of the group; in fact, AFDD was set up at the suggestion of Vicaría and within it. A group of lawyers within the Vicaría kept a rigorous record of disappearances. As explained later in the analysis, the paper trail provided useful evidence that facilitated future truth-seeking initiatives, including the truth commission. Overall, this was a long, yet effective, struggle to recover the truth about the disappeared.[4]

As indicated above, during the Chilean repression, the vibrant mobilization of relatives of the disappeared and other human rights organizations attracted international media attention and mobilized transnational advocacy networks (Collins 2006; Ropp & Sikkink 1999). As most domestic institutional channels were blocked, the support of external actors was required to keep domestic struggles for truth recovery alive; it turned Chile into a global point of reference for truth recovery. Even during the dictatorship, the Catholic Church gathered concrete data, and evidence of human rights abuses was transferred to international bodies, influencing their policies toward Chile. For example, in 1975 the UN Working Group of Human Rights established a fact-finding mission to Chile (Kyriakou 2012:33). Its follow-up report encapsulated the many human rights violations in Chile and became one of the first official documents to discuss the "ongoing nature of the crime" of disappearances (ibid.). The members of the Chilean relatives' associations were also core members of FEDEFAM (*La Federación Latinoamericana de Asociaciones de Familiares de Detenidos-Desaparecidos*), the regional association in Latin America, and they actively advocated for the adoption of the global Convention against disappearances (described in detail in Chapter 5). Viviana Díaz was in charge of the international relations of FEDEFAM for 4 years (Interview No.54).

---

[4] The original aim of the group was to release them and, more generally, protect them from executions. That explains why they used the habeas corpus writ. Although they were not effective in this original aim, they were very effective in documenting cases of disappearances.

Given their tenacity, it is not surprising that Chilean families became role models for other human rights groups in the region (Ropp & Sikkink 1999:180). We should also remember that the practice of disappearances started in Chile in 1973, well before Argentina (1976). Therefore, Chilean families had to navigate the uncharted waters of human rights mobilization strategies. In fact, some now common inclusions in the repertoire of mobilization adopted by relatives' associations globally, such as weekly street protests or the recourse to transnational advocacy networks to uncover the truth, were pioneered in Chile, not exclusively in Argentina as most assume. Chile produced the "strongest and most consistent human rights culture" in Latin America (De Brito 2003:183). Even amidst military repression, relatives formed alliances with influential partners, including the Catholic Church, lawyers, international human rights networks and think-tanks.

Transition and Truth Commission

During the transition, more opportunities became available for an official truth recovery process to address the problem of the disappeared. As the families of the missing represented the most significant victims' group in the country and one of the most visible globally, the resumption of party politics opened a window of opportunity to push for policies of acknowledgment.

The first elected President of Chile after transition, Patricio Aylwin (1990–1994) was the leader of the *Concertación* – a coalition of left-wing parties – who in principle supported victims' demands for finding their loved ones. On the one hand, his policy of dealing with the past was pragmatic, geared toward reconciliation with the military and identification of the remains of *desaparecidos*. On the other hand, although the prosecution of perpetrators was hindered by the amnesty law, the investigation of the whereabouts of the disappeared and the conditions under which human rights abuses took place was not only feasible but also desirable (De Brito 2001). Accordingly, in 1990, a Truth and Reconciliation Commission (TRC) was tasked with preparing a report documenting human rights violations, gathering information about the whereabouts of the disappeared and recommending reparations for victims (Aguilar 2002:415).[5] The report of the TRC (also known as the Rettig Commission, named after its chairman Raul Rettig) sought to

[5] Decreto Supremo 255, April 25, 1990.

create an authoritative account of human rights abuses. This was pivotal in a number of ways. First, it created an official narrative, making it impossible for the military to deny that disappearances constituted a systematic tool of terror. Second, it raised awareness among the broader citizenry. Third, it acknowledged the suffering of the relatives. Fourth, files of the background investigation were made available to the courts to investigate cases of disappearances, irrespective of the amnesty law (Ensalaco 2000:214).

As the disappeared seemed to represent one of his most pressing problems, President Aylwin proposed specific initiatives to find them (Aguilar 2002:415). He proposed a law offering incentives to perpetrators, including anonymity and confidentiality, to pinpoint burial sites; the information gathered would then be assigned to 15 investigative judges (*ministros en visita*) (De Brito 2003:186; Ensalaco 2000:233). But after vocal reactions from the political right, socialists and most human rights organizations, including the AFDD, the proposal was never implemented. So the first major attempt failed.

The commission had limited investigative powers and a restricted period of work (9 months), and these two factors inhibited its efforts to locate graves. In addition, there were several design flaws, most importantly, the limited powers of the commission in naming perpetrators. It was also stripped of subpoena powers (Collins 2011:74). As the leader of the AFDD maintained, "The report did not help us very much with respect to the clarification of the fate suffered by our family members, and to this day, we are in the same situation as before" (cited in Ensalaco 2000:231). As a result of its flaws, the Rettig report recommended the establishment of a follow-up body to focus exclusively on the problem of the disappeared.

The follow-up mechanism, the National Corporation for Reparations and Reconciliation (CNRR), was set up in 1992 and was mandated to uncover the forensic truth by taking all necessary measures to find the location of the disappeared.[6] The work of the CNRR was based on evidence collected during the Rettig Commission and founded on the "inalienable right" of relatives to find their loved ones. The CNRR's systematic work contributed to the inclusion of a number of cases previously excluded from the official list of the Rettig Commission. This follow-up mechanism was very effective in providing reparations to relatives, including a monthly pension (140,000 pesos), medical care,

---

[6] Act No. 19.123, January 11, 1995.

exemption of the children of the disappeared from military service, and educational support (Aguilar 2009; Collins 2011:75).

The third systematic effort to carry out exhumations and identify victims was undertaken during the presidency of Frei in 1999, shortly after Pinochet's arrest in London in 1998. It took the form of a 'Roundtable', with religious leaders, members of the army, former politicians, lawyers and other intellectuals invited to participate. Then, under President Ricardo Lagos in 2000, the recovery of the victims' remains became the top priority. Lagos' strategy largely reflected Aylwin's early proposal, offering a 6-month period for eyewitnesses or perpetrators to come forward with credible information in exchange for a reduced sentence (Aguilar 2002; Roht-Arriaza 2005:95). As a result of the Roundtable, the military provided a list with details on the fate of 200 disappeared, even admitting to throwing 151 of them into open waters (Robben 2015:68). Although it was the first time the military officially acknowledged its commission of the crime, breaking almost three decades of silence and denial, the quality of the information offered was so poor and, at times erroneous, that relatives were disillusioned (Bakiner 2010; Collins 2010). In a number of cases when bodies were supposedly thrown into the sea, the bodies were located in common graves (Collins 2010). So this third attempt failed too.

The common theme in the quest for forensic truth until the early 2000s was the expectation that the truth commission and the follow-up mechanisms would lead to the exhumation and identification of bodies. Chile seemed to have good prospects of finding the disappeared. In addition, as Latin America had acquired significant "forensic capital," Chile's efforts to identify its disappeared should have come to fruition (EAAF 2007a). For example, as early as 1998, the Argentine Forensic Anthropology Team (EAAF) was invited to Chile to create a databank of genetic material from relatives (EAAF 1998, 2007a). In short, things seemed promising.

Yet the fate of the disappeared remains one of the flawed aspects of (post-)transitional justice in Chile. The number who have been exhumed, identified and returned to their families is low. As of late 2013, only 129 persons on the list of the disappeared had been identified (Jarroud 2012; UDP 2013:30)[7] and only 282 persons, presumed either

---

[7] The figures are taken from the official site of the MLS: www.sml.cl/sml/, last accessed: February 2, 2014. The UN Working Group says 142 disappeared have been identified so far (UNWGEID 2013:para 17). In any case, the figure remains minimal.

detained-disappeared or politically executed had been identified (UNWGEID 2013:para17). The disappeared totaled approximately 1200 persons and about 3000 were executed, so fewer than 10 percent of the victims have been identified two decades after the transition.[8] The slow pace of exhumations should partly be attributed to the priority of political elites in the *concertación* government to foster reconciliation with – in reality, not provoking – the military. They emphasized memorialization practices rather than exhumations. The latter had the potential to reveal incriminatory evidence, that would urge the incumbent to use them in courts of law; yet that was a particularly problematic threat in the still fragile period of transition in the 1990s (Robben 2015:68).

The quality of identification was often flawed as well, making many relatives leery of forensic exhumations. The exhumation and identification processes were overseen by the state (García, Pérez-Sales & Fernández-Liria 2010:56) through the Medical Legal Service (MLS henceforth) (Aguilar 2009:520), and only in the early 2000s was a DNA test included in the protocol of the MLS (Egan 2002). This led to a number of misidentifications of bodies recovered early after transition. A well-known example is Plot 29 (Patio 29), an exhumation carried out in 1991 in the general cemetery of Santiago where approximately 135 bodies were disinterred, identified and returned to the families (Ferrándiz & Robben 2015:18). However, after genetic samples from relatives were tested by a UK-based lab, it was discovered that 96 were wrongly identified (García, Pérez-Sales & Fernández-Liria 2010:58; Jarroud 2012; Wilde 1999:485). Hence, after 20 years of effort, relatives were re-traumatized and left with no body to mourn (Interview No.56). Quite understandably, this created strong mistrust of the MLS in particular, and of the quest for forensic truth in general (Bustamante & Ruderer 2009; EAAF 2007a; Zanocco 2002). Indicatively, although an effort was made to create a databank, fewer than 400 people had given blood samples halfway through the first decade of the new millennium (Nelsen 2009).

For almost 15 years, the process stopped, resuming only after Pinochet's death in 2006 (Robben 2014). With the arrival of the Bachelet presidency (2006–2010) and the radical restructuring of the MLS since 2007, it has gradually regained credibility, but the pace of identifications has remained extremely slow. Further, as time passes, both

---

[8] It should be highlighted that although "executed" and "disappeared" are distinct social and legal categories in Chile, some of the most fundamental challenges faced by the families of both groups are common, including the need to find and identify the remains of those who were executed.

perpetrators and victims are getting older and their numbers are dwindling.

To be sure, identification although the most pressing, is only one of the needs of the families, and Chile has fared much better on other fronts. For example, the state has carved out an innovative and comprehensive policy of reparations to victims. In fact, the UN Working Group on Enforced or Involuntary Disappearances comments, "Chile is perhaps the country that has granted the highest level of financial reparation to victims of enforced disappearance ... and counseling support for relatives in relation to identification and return of remains of victims" (UNWGEID 2013:para 44). The CNRR designed a policy offering significant financial benefits, as well as psychological and social support to the relatives recognized by the Commission; these benefits are channeled through the Program of Compensation and Comprehensive Health-Care (ibid.). Psychological counseling is state sponsored and comprehensive, preparing relatives for exhumations and continuing after the identification of the remains (Aguilar 2009; García, Pérez-Sales & Fernández-Liria 2010:56).

Explaining the Ineffectiveness of Forensic Truth

What accounts for the minimal progress in exhumations, especially as the conditions looked so promising? After all, the policy was designed to uncover forensic truth, perpetrators were offered rewards for information, relatives maintained persistent pressure and regional expertise in identifying bodies was readily available. Two possibilities come immediately to mind. First, the practice of "destructive exhumations," or the relocation of remains, inhibited efforts at identification. Second, exhumations were linked with the truth commissions, a structural flaw preventing the type of investigation that would lead to graves.

The first possibility is the phenomenon of "destructive exhumations" (Ferrándiz & Robben 2015:18). The Chilean transition took place after the respective transitions in Brazil and Argentina, so drawing parallels with neighboring countries was inevitable. At time of the transition, the Chilean military was well aware of truth recovery for the disappeared in Argentina, including truth trials, exhumations of graves and efforts to prosecute the military; this regional experience naturally shaped their own position. Early Chilean exhumations showed that some bodies were taken from the locations where they had originally been buried and transferred elsewhere (Collins 2011:79). In most cases, the remains were air dropped into the sea or reburied in mountainous areas of the country (Bustamante & Ruderer 2009:63; Ferrándiz & Robben 2015). The orchestrated effort of the military to conceal incriminatory evidence from graves severely affected the process of identification not only because some bodies were never found but also because families often could only recover specific parts of the body, precluding proper mourning for their loss (García, Pérez-Sales & Fernández-Liria 2010:57). Diego Cabezas, a grandson of a *desaparecido* and a leading member of a regional initiative, shares a revealing story. He says a person/soldier who participated in one of these operations confessed the following:

> They (military) told him (the soldier) to recover the bodies, take them away, that it was an order from Pinochet, to remove the bodies from all the places where they had been buried secretly. In this case, to go and dig them up, with the Air Force people and throw them into the sea from there ... and then they took them (victims) away again in 1978.

> (Interview No.56)

According to available information, there were two main periods of destructive reburials. The first occurred in 1978, right after the enactment of the self-amnesty and the dissolution of DINA, which signified the end of the most severe repression. A second period of reburials took place in 1989, around the time of the transition (Franklin 1999; Robben 2014). As an informed observer says, for the first wave of re-interment, "the circle of people who know gets smaller because people now in power do not know" the actions of DINA (Interview No.7). The passage of time and ensuing changes in the structure of the military made it impossible to trace the whereabouts of those reburied in 1978. Meanwhile, members of the second group remain reluctant to participate in any truth recovery mechanism because they fear charges of illegal reburial. Although they were simply following the orders of their superiors, they are more likely to be prosecuted than the perpetrators of the original crime, as these latter persons are protected by amnesty. To get around this problem, investigative police often attempt to cut deals offering immunity to low-ranking officers.

This raises an interesting paradox. As explained below, in 1998 a court ruling excluded the crime of disappearances from amnesty law. Since that point, we might expect perpetrators to have been more willing to indicate burial sites so they could be charged with homicide – instead of kidnapping – and thus be protected by amnesty (Collins 2010:125). Some people did provide information after 1998, but agents of the regime had already removed and reburied the bodies. In addition, another law included leniency provisions for cases brought to court after 2007. Hence, the benefits of remaining silent outweighed the risks of revealing incriminatory information that could potentially lead to prosecution. For all these reasons, the military remained reluctant to share information. Even those willing to participate had no knowledge of the location of graves after the wave of reburials by the military. The circle of people with useful information about graves is getting smaller as well, and people are understandably suspicious of the military; in a recent study, 62.5 percent of respondents said they believe the armed forces know where the bodies are buried but do not want to hand over information (UDP 2009).

A second and more important reason relates to the use of truth commissions as guiding mechanisms for collecting information that will lead to forensic exhumations. Although most commissions, particularly in the region, were historically set up to deal with the specific problem of disappearances, their design makes them inappropriate to carry out effective forensic investigation – as the experience of South Africa also illustrates (see Chapter 8).

For one thing, truth commissions are political instruments and therefore reflect the balance of power; this, in turn, shapes their investigative powers. Fearing the military, the early governments after the Chilean transition opted for a conciliatory approach, seeing truth recovery as a means to reconciliation. Hence, although financial benefits were given to the relatives, the state invested little effort in forensic truth. For almost 15 years, the exhumations stopped entirely (Robben 2014). There was no forensic investigation to confirm the findings of the TRC or its follow-up mechanisms. Roberto D'Orival, an active member of various groups working to uncover the truth about the disappeared, explains:

> In the Roundtable a huge chunk of false testimonies are included and it was through judicial investigations that they were later proven false. In the Roundtable there was talk about Fuerte Arteaga[9] as a place where there had been burials here and there. But after forensic investigations which found nothing [that was discredited].
>
> (Interview No.61)

According to Luis Fonderbrider, a leading forensic expert of EAAF with significant international experience, the government recalcitrance is not surprising: "Usually the interest of the politicians for truth recovery after

---

[9] This is currently a training military facility. It used to be a military base where bodies of some of the disappeared were buried and hidden.

a truth commission goes down. So the only people fighting for this are the human rights activists and the families" (Interview No.8).

For another thing, structural flaws in the design of the committees prevented the recovery of forensic truth. Simply stated, too many people were involved. The Roundtable included members of the judiciary, the Catholic Church, the military, lawyers and human rights organizations. However, as the experiences of Northern Ireland and Cyprus indicate, most bodies tasked to carry out humanitarian exhumations require the creation of an informal and subtle context that will facilitate exchange of information on clandestine and criminal activities. This is usually achieved by engaging a small number of actors and providing direct access to individuals. But the Roundtable engaged myriad diverse actors and was designed to extract information from the military as an institution, instead of providing direct incentives to individual perpetrators to come forward.

Added to this, the close participation of relatives in bodies tasked to extract sensitive information can curtail the prospects of forensic exhumation. For example, according to a forensic expert with international experience, an ingredient in the effectiveness of the Cypriot CMP was that the relatives had limited access and had to accept government's decisions. In contrast, in contexts like Chile where the families acquire power and develop a strong human rights discourse, the potential for a purely humanitarian body based on confidentiality, secrecy and immunity is limited. To be sure, this is not a normative argument. After all, the transitional justice design always reflects preferences of the relatives and the balance of power. If the prospect of holding perpetrators accountable is more attractive, and the relatives have power and legitimacy, as in Chile, the prospect of uncovering the forensic truth is curtailed.

Similarly, the flawed incentive structure for perpetrators to come forward and share information is part and parcel of all commissions of inquiry. Even relatives are convinced that the military is crucial to unlock this process: "If the Army talked – they know where the disappeared are, they know whether there are bodies or not: the army, detectives, police, the navy, air force, they know, somebody knows ... there are pacts of silence" (Interview No.60). To break this silence, the right "carrots" must be offered to the perpetrators. Although the original strategy was to give immunity in exchange for information about the whereabouts of the disappeared, this was never properly implemented in the first decade of the transition. During the Roundtable, a similar policy was enforced, yet it was too little, too late. The mandate of the Roundtable was restrictive, especially the 6-month operation period. And by the time the Roundtable was set up, Chile had already entered its second period of (post-)transitional justice, dominated by retributive approaches to its past, as explained below. Therefore, a policy of incentives to perpetrators in the form of immunity was discredited. It was thought to run counter to the main objective of punitive justice then dominating Chilean politics, and the military, conscious of the growing number of prosecutions in neighboring countries, remained reluctant to share incriminatory evidence that would later be used against them.

Although the objective of the CNRR was to carry out humanitarian exhumations, to identify the remains without necessarily prosecuting the culprits, its work was subtly linked to criminal investigations, because legal action was required to proceed to exhumations (Collins 2010:7). As the state was responsible for exhumations, and MLS was working under the aegis of the Ministry of Justice, the role of the judiciary was pivotal. For example, only judges could order exhumations, and these could take place only under their supervision (Aguilar 2009:520; Varas & Leiva 2012). This implied the objective of forensic truth recovery was not limited to identifying remains (unlike the CMP in Cyprus and its purely humanitarian approach) but was designed to determine the cause of death and name the perpetrators (UNWGEID 2013:para 17). The central role of judges created a judiciary-driven approach to forensic truth, partly explaining the reluctance of the military to share evidence. The subtle linkage of forensic truth to criminal-type investigation is usually achieved at the expense of the former, especially in contexts like Chile where the military retains its legitimacy. In the end, it becomes extremely difficult to challenge the pact of silence. This has created a practical problem, as explained by a leading member of a relatives' association:

> For the judges it is extremely difficult to have a break in a case without the help of one of the culprits, and we need to know that truth. Because when we speak of truth, what is said in the investigations is only a part of the truth, but perpetrators have the other part . . . And the biggest difficulty we have in knowing the final destination of the victims relies in the hands of the armed forces, which have acted like one organization when it comes to hiding the truth with these pacts of silence.
>
> (Interview No.35)

Taking all these factors into account, it is hardly surprising that most families were disappointed by the truth commissions, often described as a "farce" (Interview Nos.58 and 35). Their despair with the lack of investigation and the absence of identification of their loved ones convinced them of the need to take the next step to retributive justice on their own. A relative explains it this way: "I don't think we'll ever know the truth . . . since we don't have the truth, we want the justice system to act in that area. I mean we are not going to rest, we are going to continue insisting on truth, that people uncover certain things" (Interview No.56). As such, in parallel with (or as a result of the lack of progress on) the forensic front, families decided to peel another layer in the truth recovery process, this time entering the retributive stage.

Peeling the Onion II: Retributive Justice

The experience of Chile confirms two of the central hypotheses of the book. First, if the passage of time is followed by the democratization of state institutions, families have more chances of taking the judicial path. Second, societies that pursue exhumations and also set up a truth commissions have a better chance of taking the final step toward retributive justice. The Chilean experience shows that the retributive stage of truth recovery largely depends on families' ability to use the available institutional opportunities to bring their cases to court.

This section explains how the mobilization of the Chilean families helped make the amnesty law inapplicable to the crime of enforced disappearances and brought a growing number of perpetrators to justice. During the repression and shortly after transition, international actors and local allies (NGOs and lawyers) helped keep the issue on the political agenda and collected valuable evidence. As time passed, the democratization of key institutions offered new opportunities, especially the availability of influential domestic allies. Similarly, evidence collected in previous waves of truth recovery strengthened the prosecutions. The families took advantage of these and other opportunities to bring perpetrators to justice.

Today, Chile has comprehensive screening of past human rights violations, especially for the disappeared. By 2013, almost 75 percent of the cases were under judicial investigation (UNWGEID 2013:para 26). More than 771 individual perpetrators have been tried and most convicted for human rights violations since 2000 (ibid.).[10] It is estimated that between

---

[10] Still not all of them are in prison; most have benefited from leniency provisions serving non-custodial sentences (Act Nos. 18.2161 and 20.603.2).

1998 and 2013, approximately 868 persons were investigated, charged and/or sentenced (UDP 2013:19). To appreciate how Chile reached this stage, it is important to ask how families deployed the institutional opportunities available to them.

The gradual democratization of the armed forces was essential. Despite ongoing reluctance to share information, the military withdrew into its barracks, creating the conditions for the gradual democratization of public debates, a prerequisite of truth recovery. Even when a growing number of officers were convicted, the threat of a military coup remained minimal. As Bakiner shows, especially after Pinochet's arrest, the military was gradually transformed, even assuming institutional responsibility for some crimes (Bakiner 2010:51). The withdrawal of an institutional veto player from politics gave domestic truth seekers a unique opportunity.

However, the most significant boost in the quest of families for justice was the democratization of the judiciary. As mentioned above, in the early years after the transition, trust in the judiciary was minimal, given its role during the dictatorship (Hilbink 2007). Although relatives and their lawyers made consistent efforts to bring their cases before the court, judges were reluctant to grant an application for a writ of habeas corpus, and thousands of cases were dismissed (Collins 2010). As a result of the growing mistrust, coupled with the amnesty law protecting perpetrators, relatives had no real hope of retributive justice in the early days after transition. Exacerbating the situation, the government considered the judicial approach was both perilous and politically unhelpful (Wilde 1999).

Still, the second period of truth recovery for the disappeared in Chile began with two developments on the judicial front in 1998. Although by late 1998 the prospect of extraditing Pinochet from the United Kingdom to Spain was making headlines in international media, in September 1998, the Chilean Supreme Court had issued a landmark ruling whereby cases of disappearances where remains had not been recovered should be considered ongoing crimes. This interpretation means that kidnappers were not protected by amnesty law and the crime of disappearances was not subject to a statute of limitations (Collins 2011:83; Requa 2012: 84).[11] The ruling also said the state had a duty to investigate the conditions leading to disappearances (Correa & Foxcroft 2013:78, paras 9–10). The ruling was a game changer, because before the amnesty law could be applied, the perpetrator needed to be

---

[11] *Poblete Cordova*, Case No. 469–98, ruling of September 9, 1998, Supreme Court, para 11.

identified and the crime had to properly defined (Collins 2010:122). An effective investigation became a precondition of granting amnesty, a point of departure from previous blanket amnesty to all cases related to human rights violations. The decision clearly illustrated the supremacy of international law over a national amnesty law (ibid.). In any event, the judgment trimmed the amnesty law and offered an unprecedented opportunity to domestic truth seekers. Immediately following the decision, judges started reopening cases of enforced disappearance (Aguilar 2009:523).

At the same time, Spanish investigative judge Baltazar Garzon petitioned UK authorities to arrest and extradite General Pinochet to Spain. All charges were related to the disappearance (or extrajudicial execution) of Spanish citizens and priests in Chile (Roht-Arriaza 2009:104). The prospect of extraditing the Chilean general initiated a chain of reactions both nationally and internationally, creating the so-called "Pinochet effect" (Roht-Arriaza 2005). The "Pinochet effect" reinvigorated "post-transitional justice" in Chile (Collins 2011) and activated debates about the silenced Francoist past in Spain, leading to a wave of exhumations of the disappeared of the Spanish civil war (Aguilar 2009; Araguete-Toribio 2015; Kovras 2013). Interestingly, the problem of the disappeared was central in all charges against the Chilean dictator – an important way to circumvent amnesty and bring a key perpetrator to justice.

The democratization of the judiciary helps to explain the emergence of this new opportunity for the families (see Collins 2010). The example of Judge Guzman, who ruled in the landmark Poblete-Cordoba case in 1998, is illustrative. Although he was a conservative judge during the reign of Pinochet, he became an influential seeker of accountability following the transition (Rohter 2006). This can be attributed to the emergence of a new generation of judges and to the growing independence of the judiciary from the executive – an indication of democratic consolidation. A member of a regional team of relatives in Paine, a district outside Santiago with the highest per capita disappearances, is adamant about the catalytic role of the judge in a case he was involved in, to the extent they hanged a picture of the judge in their premises: "Hector Solis Montiel [the judge] took it on. That's the judge you can see in this photo here, and he's the one that really made inroads into the case" (Interview No.56). In short, the high quality of democratic institutions provided a more advantageous political opportunity structure for relatives to push for exhumation and a new law for the recovery of historical memory. A similar process explains the influential role of Judge Baltazar Garzon in paving the way for post-transitional justice in Spain. Garzon, also known as the Spanish "super-judge," investigated cases of disappeared victims of the Spanish civil war (1936–1939).

The role of the judiciary in Chile is particularly important for two reasons. First, Chile has a strong legalistic tradition, which means court rulings shape political outcomes. Second, in the Chilean judicial system, an investigation opens only after a relative files a complaint. In this context, selecting the right case and creating influential alliances in court are crucial for success. The families in Chile were very strategic. Roberto D'Orival, who has participated in some of the cases brought by families, maintains:

> Chilean justice does not undertake criminal investigations except if complaints are made against identifiable individuals. So we launched a case for the investigation of Operation Colombo.[12] That was mainly in the hands of Judge Guzman and later on by the judges who replaced him. . . . I think this has been a real even if modest achievement, that we have been able to start up these investigations.
>
> (Interview No.61)

Probably the most influential allies have been the lawyers who have supported families in bringing their cases to court and developed novel legal arguments to plead before the judges. The Chilean families have been particularly "fortunate" because many of the victims were middle-class members of professional organizations. Solidarity was strong even during the dictatorship, and it never stopped. Even during repression, hundreds of lawyers representing families of disappeared brought their cases to court. As Viviana Diaz remembers, "The Vicaria,[13] the Chilean Human Rights Commission, CODEPU[14] and other organizations gave legal assistance and practical help free of charge" (Interview No.54). The lawyer representing the Poblete family in the landmark of 1998 case that deemed amnesty law inapplicable for the disappeared, Sergio Concha, was an ex-Vicaria lawyer. He continued to work on the case after the death of the last living relative, as a matter of conscience (Collins 2015).

---

[12] This refers to the operation of the military to cover up the disappearance of 119 MIR militants.
[13] Human rights office of the Catholic Church in Chile.
[14] Two human rights organizations during the dictatorship.

Although none of the cases was won, a legal record was created, leaving a paper trail for others to follow (Collins 2010:101). Paradoxically, the hierarchical structure of the violence was useful in a similar way. In sharp contrast to the Argentine semi-autonomous military cells, disappearances in Chile were top bottom, structured and systematic (Robben 2015:66) and, thus, left records. The authoritative archive of the Vicaria, the human rights office of the Catholic Church, was another invaluable source of evidence in the reopened cases (EAAF 2007a:4). With the support of a network of lawyers, families gradually devised legal strategies that maximized the possibilities. Diego Cabezas represents the grandchildren of the disappeared. He says the grandchildren have not launched charges yet "because if at any point it should happen that the case started due to the complaints by the widows and children get rejected, they wouldn't be able to lodge a new complaint for the same case. So then the grandchildren could step in" (Interview No.56). This not only illustrates the families' high degree of familiarity with legal language but also shows that families are strategic. Like any other social movement, their main objective is to increase the potential for success.

More recently, another institutional opportunity became available to the families in the form of state support for their legal cases. As explained above, the human rights Program of the Ministry of Interior (CNRR) was originally restricted to uncovering the remains.[15] In the mid-2000s, though, its mandate was transformed to cover legal and social support to families included in the Roundtable report. Gradually, it became the key mechanism of investigating cases of disappearances and prosecuting culprits, fully funded by the state (Interview No.55). It became "colonized" by ex-Vicaria lawyers, who were previously independent of and critical to the state (Collins 2015). This is crucial, because lawyers in the program have very close ties with investigators and critical actors in the justice system (Collins 2015). This enhances the likelihood of success. In addition, lawyers working on early cases of disappearances during repression built up a certain amount of "legal capital," and this has been helpful in developing a network of influential actors within the judicial system (Collins 2010:116).

Furthermore, it should be highlighted that early truth-seeking ventures, such as the Rettig Commission, created opportunities for subsequent legal efforts to investigate disappearances. After two waves of truth commissions and a Roundtable, a large body of empirical

---

[15] Decreto Supremo 1005, April 25, 1997.

evidence was available. Even though it was unable to find the forensic truth, the Roundtable forwarded evidence to the Supreme Court; in this type of gradualist approach, forensic truth paves the way for broader truth and vice versa. These particular cases advanced rapidly because the Human Rights Investigative Brigade, a branch of the Investigative Police, actively contributed (Collins 2011:89) by carrying out thorough interviews and establishing a network of key eyewitnesses.

Developments in forensic truth continued to cause new breakthroughs on the judicial front, and the reopening of old cases led to new landmark decisions. In 2004, the Supreme Court ruled relatives had the "just and legitimate right to know the whereabouts of those who have been detained,"[16] thus confirming that the crime of disappearance is continuous and outside the scope of amnesty (Lafontaine 2005; Requa 2012). In 2006, the Inter-American Court of Human Rights ruled amnesty was incompatible with the "right to truth," central in the Inter-American Convention of Human Rights; this ruling triggered a new and heated debate on the possibility of overturning the amnesty law. Also in 2006, the court took a more comprehensive approach to human rights protection, by declaring the crime was of international character while acknowledging the right of relatives to an effective remedy (Requa 2012). In light of the new developments, since 2010, approximately 2000 criminal complaints have been registered, and several investigative judges are now designated to investigate 1400 cases of disappearances or executions (UDP 2013:8–9).

When we look back, we see how effective Chilean relatives were in overcoming legal and political obstacles, including opening rifts in the amnesty law, creating alliances and putting pressure on the government to keep the issue of the disappeared on the agenda. Every step was a precedent and strategically used to maximize position. Until the late 1990s, the only realistic objective for relatives was finding the location of the disappeared (forensic truth), but by the early 2000s, perpetrators were held accountable and more authoritative accounts of the fate of the disappeared were available.

Judging the Trials

The quest for broader truth recovery was effective for three key reasons. First, as illustrated above, even during dictatorship, the record keeping

---

[16] *Miguel Angel Sandoval* case, Supreme Court, Case No. 517–04, November 17, 2004, para 18.

was a key to later truth recovery. Second, in Chile there were several waves of truth, creating a spiral effect. The setting up of the CNRR followed the Rettig Commission, while the judiciary's trimming of the amnesty law, coupled with previous fact-finding mechanisms, painted an accurate picture of the human rights violations during authoritarianism. This was pivotal in delegitimizing the military's denial that heinous human rights were part of the repertoire of the dictatorship. Third, the fact that the judiciary drove truth recovery processes after 2000 facilitated the detailed reconstruction of the conditions under which kidnappings took place, a prerequisite of effective investigation. The contribution of the judiciary was essential in holding perpetrators accountable and in acknowledging that a moral framework had been fractured (Nesiah 2002:826). Equally important was the fact that according to the families, the quality of exhumations and the identification process improved since the judiciary took over (Interview No.56).

Despite the Chilean entry into the retributive stage of truth recovery, there is a downside. Retributive justice is a time-consuming enterprise with slow progress. Even today, only 29 judges are struggling to deal with 1400 cases (UDP 2013:9). Timing is also a constitutive element of justice; after more than 25 years, the thirst for justice is waning. Most of the cases were reopened only after 1998, and they remain open. Third, despite Chile's impressive struggle against impunity, the amnesty law remains intact for cases other than disappearances, causing tensions with regional bodies, such as the Inter-American Commission for Human Rights.

On a more practical level, in the absence of a body to bury, for many families, trials are of secondary importance. The daughter of a disappeared person highlights the fine line between criminal trials and justice: "Well, the Association [AFDD] was always focused on trials, punishment, truth and justice. There is no denying that there have been trials, but I don't feel as though there has been justice" (Interview No.57). In the absence of conclusive evidence about the remains of their loved ones, the experience of appearing before the courts takes a heavy emotional toll on families:

> It's a terrible thing. And in those days [of trial] we used to go to the court hearings, but you had to try and keep yourself together in front of the defense lawyers, but then you got home and it was terrible, because in the end we hadn't managed it, we weren't going to find him. And then it became clear that they'd thrown him into the sea. ... that was terrible, because I always hope to find him.

> (Interview No.54)

In essence, families are exposed to disturbing revelations about their loved ones, but still have no body to mourn.

Finally, and most importantly, the judicial approach may have been very effective in setting out the facts, but to some extent it has inhibited exhumations. Retributive justice is designed to focus on individual accountability and bring perpetrators to justice; therefore, the logic of secrecy, anonymous information and immunity practiced by Chile is incompatible with the logic of retributive justice. The majority of Chileans (58 percent) believe trials only "serve to intensify hatred among Chileans" (UDP 2009). In short, the domination of the judiciary has inhibited alternative forms of truth recovery.

Conclusion

The study of Chile offers three important lessons for the study of transitional justice. First, it shows truth recovery is a long-term process best described as "peeling an onion." Limiting analysis to the period of the transition or its immediate aftermath is like taking a snapshot which does not capture the dynamic state of the subject. For example, in the early mid-1990s, an analysis of the state of truth recovery in Chile would have been grim and would have seen limited prospects for holding perpetrators accountable. The study of Chile highlights an important question of (post-)transitional justice, namely, why (and how) societies revisit transitional settlements after decades of delay. More specifically, the experience of Chile confirms a key hypothesis of the book: countries whose transition is followed by the democratization of key institutions have more realistic chances of circumventing amnesties and proceeding to the retributive stage of truth recovery. A number of countries, ranging from Spain to Brazil, have started to revise certain violent chapters of the past after significant deferral.

Second, as noted above, truth recovery is a time-consuming yet non-linear process. In some cases, forensic evidence from graves paves the way for human rights prosecutions (Argentina and Guatemala), while in others, it is the failure of humanitarian exhumations (Chile) that makes relatives more determined to take their case to court. In Chile, the families' refusal to quit led to broader truth recovery. Although the type of crime seems to be the key to winning legal and political battles, these battles are fought gradually and are won in the long term. For example, Chile was originally limited to fact-finding mechanisms (Rettig Commission, CNRR, Valech); justice was not on the table.

Despite yielding minimal results, however, the compilation of documentary and forensic evidence opened a new period of truth recovery dominated by judicial decisions. The evidence presented in legal cases and the landmark rulings reinvigorated forensic truth and boosted initiatives to investigate the past. As Chile shows, there is a constant dialogue between various mechanisms of transitional justice. Together, they gradually uncover the truth; this is the logic of "peeling the onion." Argentina followed a similar route: CONADEP focused on the disappeared, and the gathered forensic evidence was used in courts, leading to landmark legal decisions which first circumvented and then annulled the amnesty law.

Third, the study of Chile reflects the tension between forensic and retributive approaches, illustrated in the previous chapters. One thing the Chilean experience tells us is that offering incentives to perpetrators does not always work. The design and the timing of the incentives are crucial. For example, the recommendation of President Aylwin to offer impunity, anonymity and confidentiality in exchange for information was only implemented in 2000 during the Roundtable and then it was too late. Courts had already tried military officers, and any promise of immunity had lost credibility. But this strategy was successful in Argentina where the military were on the defensive. What does this tell us? Simply stated, in cases where the military retains power, there is a need for a more rigorous design of humanitarian exhumations to provide guarantees of immunity to eyewitnesses. They must be convinced that the findings from graves will not be used as evidence against them. To circumvent "pacts of silence" made by a powerful institutional actor, like the Chilean army, incentives should target individual eyewitnesses rather than the institution itself.

10

Conclusions

Five Lessons for Transitional Justice

Lesson 1: The Boomerang Effect of Disappearances

When Franco (Spain), Pinochet (Chile), Karadzic (Bosnia-Herzegovina), Ríos Montt (Guatemala) or Videla (Argentina) were disappearing their enemies, they could not possibly have imagined this was the crime that would come back to haunt them. But it did. Perpetrators generally use the crime to deny the existence of their enemies and to control the broader population through fear. They think they can avoid accountability by eliminating the bodies of evidence (*corpus delicti*). Yet in countries around the world, families of the missing and the disappeared have fought to make their stories heard, irrespective of the risks to their own security. They have disobeyed the orders of the military and defied powerful warlords. The *Madres* and *Abuelas* of Plaza de Mayo in Argentina staged weekly protests at the height of the dictatorship. Some Mothers and Grandmothers were murdered or went missing themselves, but this did not affect the mobilization. The same occurred in Chile, Lebanon, Cyprus and other contexts. As a result of the relentless efforts of the families, most of the above leaders have been indicted and/ or convicted on charges related to the systematic abduction of their enemies.

The courageous efforts by relatives, especially in Latin America, comprise the "missing" part of our now well-known contemporary "justice cascade." Kathryn Sikkink ably describes the emergence and diffusion of accountability norms, and rightly highlights the role of transnational allies in internationalizing their struggle. But it does not fully appreciate the unique nature of the crime of disappearances or the agency of the relatives. Accountability and calls for justice require the *construction of a victim* in need of repair. That was a key normative contribution of the mobilization of the families of the disappeared to contemporary debates in human rights. Before

1970s, the dead, abducted, executed, tortured and raped were commonly considered "casualties" or even "martyrs," in ethnic conflict settings, but definitely not "victims." For example, although previously considered "casualties" of a period of "collective madness," those who went missing in the Spanish civil war have recently been re-framed as "victims," and truth recovery has finally begun after many long years (Aguilar 2002; Kovras 2014).

It is not an overstatement to claim that the relatives of the missing and disappeared have shaped contemporary human rights norms and transitional justice institutions and practices. Everyone will agree that truth commissions have become a mainstream transitional justice instrument. The literature has rightly framed them as a compromise solution, particularly in negotiated transitions, deployed by political elites to draw a line with the past without prosecuting wrongdoers. Yet without the specific crime of disappearances and the families' refusal to quit looking for the bodies, we may not have had truth commissions at all. A study of the mandates of the first commissions (1980s to early 1990s) indicates that almost all fact-finding bodies set up in this period were geared toward documenting the crime of disappearances and finding the whereabouts of the missing (Chapter 4). And this can be attributed to the families' ability to keep the issue central on the political agenda.

Families' mobilization has been innovative, persistent and international. Despite the clandestine nature of the crime and the obstacles set by amnesty laws, relatives have found ways to circumvent and erode (or even annul) amnesty laws, as illustrated by the experience of Chile and Argentina. This has contributed to the development of a new and robust international legal framework that renders the crime not subject to statutes of limitations and strips perpetrators of any immunity provisions, while offering innovative tools to truth seekers. Again, the families can take much of the credit.

The disappeared and the missing now represent the rallying cry of those who challenge protracted silences in countries with entrenched cultures of denial. The recent waves of delayed or post-transitional justice in Spain or Brazil are framed around disappearances, not least because the families built on and used the symbolic capital they had accumulated over decades. All in all the grassroots and transnational mobilization of the families of the disappeared is the "missing" tale of contemporary human rights.

Lesson 2: The Forensic Cascade

The introduction of new scientific tools has been a lynchpin in the efforts of societies to reconstruct their violent past, with the epistemic community of forensic experts profoundly influencing the course of contemporary transitional justice. The *raison d'etre* of transitional justice is to use a range of policies to deal with the legacy of past violence, in an effort to address victims' needs and in this way to consolidate peace and democracy. It is impossible to explain this shift without noting the unique tools offered by forensic technologies.

Exhumations are able to address the most pressing humanitarian needs of thousands of victims (in this case, the families) to identify their loved ones and bury them according to religious and cultural rituals that facilitate healing. Interestingly, although an obvious way to "unearth" the past, exhumations have never been considered a distinct policy by mainstream transitional justice literature. When we add forensic sciences to the discovery of the bodies, we have a fascinating story, typically neglected in favor of scholarship that emphasizes the disproportionate influence of lawyers, therapists and religious leaders as professionals who have influenced transitional justice discourses and practices. This underrates the astonishing impact of forensic sciences, now used in more than 35 post-conflict countries.

The technologies of truth and justice were critical for the success and global expansion of other transitional justice policies. A number of restorative or retributive practices would not have been possible in the absence of forensic tools. The most striking example is its contribution to the "justice cascade." Kathryn Sikkink does excellent work in shedding light on political, legal and normative processes that led to the emergence of new accountability norms, yet fails to explore the obvious: for the first time in human history, science offers a credible way to use indisputable incriminatory evidence from graves to secure the conviction of the guilty in a court of law. This is pivotal in explaining not only the outcome, namely that a growing number of culprits end up in jail, but also the original decision to set up trials. In the past, in the absence of these instruments, it was extremely difficult for political leaders to initiate criminal proceedings, as without concrete evidence they ran the risk of destabilizing fragile transitional processes. After all, the only worse policy than no trials is a bad trial. For all these reasons, the availability of these forensic tools makes the deployment of trials a more appealing tool for political leaders in times of transition.

It is impossible to fully grasp the justice cascade without acknowledging the forensic cascade. The availability of legal norms does not necessarily mean they will be used or will have a concrete outcome. For every successful case in which the victims have effectively deployed these legal instruments to prosecute perpetrators, such as Argentina or Chile, there are other countries, such as Cyprus, that pursued ambitious legal avenues, such as bringing cases to the European Court of Human Rights (ECtHR), and failed to get anywhere for decades. It is only when a legal case is supported by forensic incriminatory evidence that accountability become more possible.

In short, technologies of truth and justice have been crucial to the success of the justice cascade. This is not to argue that it is a one-dimensional relationship: as illustrated in the preceding chapters, the emergence of new norms and the broader normative shift in international politics created new opportunities for forensic techniques to gain global currency. In effect, the two processes, normative and technological, go hand in hand, each opening up new and unpredictable avenues for the other.

But why, despite the availability of these forensic tools, have different countries used them in different ways? As illustrated in Chapter 4, although in the early phase, the forensic community was homogenously used to address a very specific human rights problem in Latin America, its global diffusion was facilitated by its adaptation to the needs of individual countries emerging from conflict or sponsoring international organizations. In essence, forensic investigations created new possibilities for addressing the past. For example, in contexts of negotiated transitions or frozen conflicts with legacies of clandestine crimes, forensic sciences offered political leaders the opportunity to delink humanitarian exhumations from criminal procedures. In Cyprus, Northern Ireland, Georgia or Colombia, these humanitarian exhumations have helped thousands of families reach closure, without leading to prosecutions, at least for the moment. Most often a legal provision enables the decoupling of these two distinct processes, offering incentives (i.e. immunity, confidentiality, anonymity) to eyewitnesses and perpetrators to share information that could lead to exhumations. At the same time, other countries have used forensic evidence to trim amnesty laws and bring perpetrators to justice, as in Argentina, Guatemala or Rwanda. This retributive agenda has been particularly influential since major international organizations such as the United Nations, ad hoc international criminal tribunals and the ICC have started to deploy technologies of justice.

This is critical for the study of transitional justice, as it helps us to approach the "peace vs. justice" debate from a novel perspective. The study of the technologies of truth and justice enables us to see complex moral and legal tensions between the rights of the relatives, the legal duties of the state and the pragmatic constraints set by realities in post-conflict/post-authoritarian settings. Scholars have long debated whether societies should prioritize peace and stability, even if it means the creation of amnesty laws that preclude dealing with the past (Cobban 2006; Vinjamuri & Snyder 2004) or holding perpetrators of past human rights violations accountable (Kim 2012; Sikkink 2011). The underlying assumption is the existence of a trade-off between justice initiatives and efforts to consolidate peace in fragile transitions. Yet the introduction of forensic tools offered post-conflict societies novel ways to eschew this dilemma by delinking the "right" of the families "to know" from the "duty" of the state "to prosecute," for specific crimes like the disappeared. By exhuming victims of violence purely for humanitarian reasons, a growing number of societies are addressing the "rights" of the victims to know part of the truth without necessarily prosecuting the guilty.

Although this humanitarian phase in the transitional justice process may last a long time, especially in fragile transitions, this does not necessarily mean the end of the process. If we consider some of the landmark cases, such as Guatemala or Argentina, once societies have gathered a critical mass of (forensic and other) incriminatory evidence, they may enter a second stage of broader truth recovery leading to prosecutions and convictions. As Snyder and Vinjamuri argue, "Justice does not lead; it follows" (2004:6).

Forensic sciences have greatly facilitated the ability of political leaders to temporally and thematically delink specific issues from broader transitional justice architecture: they can address some of the most pressing needs of the victims without derailing the transitional process while simultaneously keeping retributive approaches for the future open. That said, a caveat is in order: although forensic tools emerged as a radical "weapon of the weak" Mothers and Grandmothers to uncover the truth, they have become a tool controlled by the most powerful to legitimize particular preferences of political elites (i.e. truth, justice, reconciliation).

Lesson 3: Expanding the Temporal and Conceptual Scope of Transitional Justice

There is a need to broaden the conceptual and temporal boundaries of the study of transitional justice. Although the *raison d'etre* of transitional justice is to restore social relations fractured by violence, most analyses treat different victims' groups as a homogenous unit ("the victims") with uniform transitional justice preferences.[1] This is evident by the common focus on a restricted set of generic transitional justice tools, including but not limited to truth commissions, trials, reparations, vetting policies or rewriting history textbooks implicitly understood to be applicable or relevant to all victims. As suggested above, this has created a paradox: influential and widely used policies of dealing with particular groups of victims, such as exhumations to unearth the disappeared, are not even considered transitional justice policies. In other words, the restrictive conceptual boundaries have constrained our efforts to develop theories that reflect and explain real policy outcomes. A lesson this book under-lines is that our quest to theorize could benefit from a disaggregated view of human rights, explaining and assessing transitional justice policies tailored to address specific crimes and groups of victims.

Similarly, we need to expand the temporal scope of transitional justice, moving beyond the mainstream static approach which focuses on periods of transition or their immediate aftermath. As a growing number of countries have started to renegotiate their transitional justice settlements, we need more dynamic theories that are able to capture not only why an outcome occurred but also how and when it occurred. Longitudinal approaches focusing on the repertoire of mobilization of grassroots truth-seeking actors – in this case, the families of the disappeared – could prove fruitful. Exploring the opportunities that enable families to revisit transitional settlements in certain countries and the obstacles that trap others in silence could paint a more dynamic picture, one that accounts for continuities and ruptures in truth recovery.

As a first step in this direction, the preceding analysis has suggested the use of a phase-based theoretical framework to explain the timing and sequence of transitional justice policies dealing with the disappeared and missing in post-conflict settings. As discussed in Chapter 2, the most significant obstacles to truth recovery in the

---

[1] Recently, a growing critical scholarship has challenged this view (see, for example, Lundy & McGovern 2008; McEvoy & McGregor 2008; Robins 2013).

early phases after a negotiated transition are amnesty laws and political elites' priorities in maintaining security and stability. To overcome this early phase of institutionalized silence, most families prioritize a forensic form of truth by exhuming and identifying victims. This allows relatives to end years of ambiguity and to begin to mourn. In the presence of amnesties, however, a society's ability to cross to this forensic phase of truth depends on a minimum level of security and stability, as well as incentives to convince perpetrators to come forward with valid information on burial sites. These incentives may include immunity from prosecution, anonymity and confidentiality. The forensic stage is often the end of the truth recovery process for countries emerging from intrastate conflicts (civil wars) with negotiated transitions and the absence of international organizations to lead the transition.

Most post-authoritarian societies that link exhumations to truth commissions open a new chapter of broader truth recovery. Broader truth refers to a more comprehensive official process of documenting past crimes and may include trials and/or truth commissions. These correspond to the legal duties to prosecute those responsible and to carry out an effective investigation, respectively. In countries where the passage of time is followed by the democratization of institutions, new opportunities become available for a criminal investigation of the conditions behind the initial disappearances. Forensic evidence from the graves, coupled with the documentation of patterns of abuses by truth commissions, greatly facilitates the struggle of the families for retributive justice.

Obviously, I am not making a clear-cut distinction between these three levels of truth. Instead, one of the benefits of the phase-based argument is that it is dynamically geared to explain when and how the families' struggle takes (or fails to take) extra steps up the ladder of truth recovery. What I have referred to as the repertoire of mobilization is pivotal in determining whether families reach a broader stage of truth recovery or remain at forensic truth – if, indeed, they get that far. An effective repertoire will include the successful deployment of domestic and international legal tools, the formation of influential alliances and the addition of the issue of the missing to the political agenda. However, consolidating the minimum level of security required to create the conditions for perpetrators to point to gravesites and, thus, to get from institutionalized silence to forensic truth is determined by the conditions of the transition, something the families cannot control.

Lesson 4: Types of Violence and the Study of Transitional Justice

One of the key findings of the analysis is that the form of violence responsible for the creation of the problem of the missing largely determines the type of truth recovery a society will follow after transition. In other words, the nature of the violence/conflict shapes the boundaries within which actors design policies of dealing with the past.

In the absence of external actors to drive transitional justice policies, it is almost impossible for the families of the missing to cross to the broader level of truth in post-conflict settings. The logic of abductions in the context of intrastate conflicts ranges from instilling terror to cleansing specific areas of the "other." Violent legacies are transferred to the following generations, as illustrated by the recent efforts of the grandchildren of the disappeared of the Spanish civil war to uncover the remains of their families. This deviates from the logic of disappearances in times of state repression, where the tool is used by a clearly identifiable group within the society, namely the military. Such operations are often confined to a particular period, typically in the aftermath of a military coup. For example, in Chile and Argentina, despite the high numbers of disappearances, the practice was almost terminated in the third or fourth year of the regime.

In post-authoritarian settings, although the trauma for families remains the same, the return of electoral politics offers new opportunities to the families. Political parties often accommodate the requests of the most visible and vocal victims' groups, setting up institutional mechanisms like truth commissions to reap electoral benefits. Of course, the experiences of South Africa and Chile show political parties may hijack or distort the original petitions of the victims. Nonetheless, the return of competitive party politics offers a unique opportunity not available to families in post-conflict settings. Any meaningful peace process requires the inclusion of former paramilitary groups; accordingly, most negotiated transitions are followed by the incorporation of perpetrators into political parties. Hence, political parties could be seen as potential spoilers; any effort to prosecute the offenders would likely derail the peace process. Not surprisingly, political elites in post-conflict settings are usually guided by realist considerations, prioritizing the minimization of violence ("negative peace") and stability.

In dealing with the disappeared, the dilemmas and the challenges of post-conflict societies are generally greater than those of post-authoritarian societies. The weakness of democratic institutions, the deficient infrastructures and the priority of strengthening economic recovery and accommodating the demands of survivors often prove to be insurmountable obstacles to broader truth recovery. This is particularly relevant in the aftermath of negotiated transitions, commonly based on institutionalized silence and amnesty laws. Although state institutions may be weakened during an autocratic regime, they are usually not totally annihilated. For example, during the height of the repression in Chile, the judicial authorities were still operational (albeit with an extremely restricted scope), thus creating an opportunity for relatives to record their cases in court. Although none of the lawsuits lodged during the dictatorship was effective, this strategy created an official paper trail supporting later truth recovery initiatives, such as the truth commission and the reopening of criminal cases in the 2000s.

Fully accounting for the nature of violence can also shed analytical light on popular theoretical perspectives. Different scholars have built their theories studying different types of political violence. On the one hand, "realist" scholars focusing on the distribution of political power in determining transitional justice outcomes have designed their theories based on the study of societies emerging from civil wars; it is hardly surprising, then, that they prioritize the role of amnesty laws, stability, security, the role of spoilers/perpetrators and elite agreements in peace settlements. As illustrated in the preceding chapters, these insights are analytically relevant in explaining truth recovery in post-conflict settings, helping to explain Lebanon's entrapment in institutionalized silence or the humanitarian logic of forensic truth in Cyprus.

On the other hand, "idealist" scholars, usually more optimistic about transitional justice outcomes, seek to account for the justice cascade and the diffusion of human rights prosecutions. Accordingly, they explore the experience of societies emerging from authoritarian rule, including the most celebrated cases in Latin America. This scholarship is best placed to shed light on the dynamics that enable certain countries to enter the broader stage of truth recovery. By emphasizing the transformative role of the transnational advocacy networks and the impact of external normative influences, they augment our understanding of the conditions that enable victims' groups to overcome amnesty laws and bring perpetrators to justice.

In effect, the two strands shed light on two different, yet interesting, aspects of transitional justice. An awareness of their analytical strengths and limitations is important, however, as certain insights are more relevant in some cases than others. To overcome the dialogue of the deaf, we must acknowledge these fine differences and incorporate the strengths of each approach.

Lesson 5: Moral and Legal Tensions in Transitional Justice

For the most part, the literature has taken a simplistic approach to the complex ethical, political and legal dilemmas faced by transitional societies, especially those related to human rights. But when we turn to a comparative study of societies dealing with the problem of the missing, we see complex moral and legal tensions between the rights of the relatives, the legal duties of the state and the pragmatic constraints set by realities in post-transitional settings.

Consider, for example, the right to reparation and the legal obligation of the state to punish perpetrators. According to the UN's "Basic Principles and Guidelines" (Mallinder 2008:179–180) and the 2007 Convention (Article 24, paras 2–4), the relatives of the disappeared have the right to reparation, creating an obligation by the state to "take all appropriate measures to search for, locate and release disappeared persons and, in the event of death, to locate, respect and return their remains" (Article 24.3). As illustrated above, forensic exhumations in post-conflict settings require some form of assistance from eyewitnesses/ perpetrators, usually conditional upon immunity, anonymity and confidentiality. However, immunity contravenes the fundamental duty of the state to prosecute perpetrators of the crime (Article 6), while confidentiality of information often contradicts the state's duty to carry out an effective investigation (Article 3).

This tension between the "logic of principles" and the "logic of consequences" permeates all societies investigated here (Vinjamuri & Snyder 2004). Some have prioritized the deontological supremacy of the law, while others have been more pragmatic, compromising legal principles to achieve more tangible humanitarian outcomes. For example, the CMP in Cyprus has prioritized forensic truth, but this has been achieved at the expense of the duty to prosecute and carry out an effective investigation. In Chile, the whole process (guided by the judiciary) has prioritized the punishment of perpetrators; yet this breakthrough has been achieved at the expense of forensic truth, as out of the approximately 3000 families of the disappeared and executed, only 282 have buried their loved ones.

But who has the right to decide? Transitional justice preferences of the broader society may be radically different from (or even contradict) the demands of victims for truth and justice. In such circumstances, whose demand should be the guiding compass? The relatives' right to truth or society's demand for stability? Obviously, in established democracies, the legal duties of the states would be non-negotiable, but this is often not the case in post-conflict societies. In Uruguay, for example, an amnesty law has been backed by popular vote in two referendums, denying the right of relatives to see justice (Lessa 2012). Under these circumstances, should the consequentialist/democratic principle or the deontological duty to uphold fundamental human rights be the priority?

Most interestingly, if there is a disagreement within victims' groups as to the preferred transitional justice mechanism, then who is responsible for shaping the policy to deal with the problem? Equally, if relatives prioritize their right to forensic truth which often requires some form of immunity for perpetrators, should the state abstain from implementing the law (duty to "prosecute" and "investigate")? Or should the state fulfill its duties, even if it means perpetrators are discouraged from sharing information, humanitarian exhumations are halted and families are deprived of their "right to know"? A similar dilemma emerged in Colombia in the aftermath of the implementation of the Justice and Peace law in 2005. This institutionalized exchange of reduced sentences for information leading to gravesites has helped almost 3000 families mourn their relatives. But it has triggered heated comments from human rights watchdogs who argue the law institutionalizes impunity. Although a very useful tool in the relatives' struggle for truth, the law's inflexibility in dealing with such delicate moral and political dilemmas makes it an unsophisticated instrument and, at times, an obstacle to truth recovery.

There is also a broader meta-theoretical question. How should scholars studying transitions approach these dilemmas? At the moment, there is an implicit miscommunication between legal scholars who take the individual (rights) as their primary unit of analysis and social scientists who are interested in the broader societal level. The gulf between the individual and the societal is well entrenched in the literature. This might explain the absence of a comprehensive analytical toolkit to address some of these tensions.

Yet the most challenging moral and political dilemmas emerge at the margins of law. For example, the CMP in Cyprus tells a fascinating story of solidarity among victims, one that transcends ethnic cleavages and political debacles. The subtle consensus of the Greek-Cypriot and Turkish-Cypriot families of the missing who have buried their relatives to abstain from using forensic evidence in their quest for truth and justice is revealing. This is particularly relevant for those families who have already identified their loved ones, and as such do not depend on the testimony of the perpetrators anymore. Yet, the need of the remaining families still looking for their relatives to bury and properly mourn their loved ones is prioritized over their own individual legal right to seek legal redress or right to "know the truth," such as learning the conditions leading to the deaths of their relatives. Yet this is not necessarily the end. Although at this stage they choose not to play the legal card, when the time is ripe they may do so. They are familiar with legal instruments, as evident in their previous battles at the European Court of Human Rights, so when the cycle of forensic truth is over and the families bury their loved ones, they may gather the critical mass of incriminatory evidence from graves and take the legal path. As explained throughout the book, families are strategic actors and choose their fights carefully. Timing and sequence are crucial to transitional justice outcomes.

LIST OF INTERVIEWS

Interview No.	Participant's status	Date
1	Academic and activist from South Africa	February 19, 2014 (Telephone Interview)
2	Researcher with expertise in post-conflict Cyprus and Lebanon	February 11, 2014 (Telephone Interview)
3	Researcher investigating transitional justice in Northern Ireland	February 10, 2014 (Belfast, Northern Ireland)
4	Forensic scientist with international experience in post-conflict settings	May 15, 2015 (Skype Interview)
5	Legal scholar with expertise in Chilean politics	February 13, 2014 (Belfast, Northern Ireland)
6	Anthropologist exploring exhumations in Latin America	January 17, 2014 (Telephone Interview)
7	Academic with significant experience in the study of transitional justice in Chile	January 27, 2014 (Belfast, Northern Ireland)
8	Forensic scientist founding member of EAAF	January 24, 2014 (Telephone Interview)
9	Researcher investigating the disappeared in Northern Ireland	March 3, 2014 (Belfast, Northern Ireland)
10	Founder of "ACT for the Disappeared" in Lebanon	December 11, 2013 (Telephone Interview)
11	Humanitarian practitioner representative of ICRC in Lebanon	November 5, 2013 (Telephone Interview)

(cont.)

Interview No.	Participant's status	Date
12	Academic with expertise in political violence in Latin America	October 31, 2013 (Telephone Interview)
13	Humanitarian practitioner with expertise in Lebanese politics	October 25, 2010 (Telephone Interview)
14	Researcher with significant international experience in human rights investigations and truth commissions	June 3, 2013 (Telephone Interview)
15	Academic expert on the application of forensic tools in human rights investigations	May 20, 2013 (Telephone Interview)
16	Academic expert in South African politics	May 17, 2013 (Telephone Interview)
17	Academic and forensic scientist with significant international experience in post-conflict societies	May 2, 2013 (Telephone Interview)
18	Director general of the ICMP	April 25, 2013 (Telephone Interview)
19	Legal scholar and former member of UNWEID	April 19, 2013 (Telephone Interview)
20	Former member of UNWEID and expert on South African politics	February 13, 2013 (Telephone Interview)
21	Turkish-Cypriot Academic and activist	July 26, 2008 (Nicosia, Cyprus)
22	Greek-Cypriot investigative journalist and member of bi-communal committee of relatives of missing in Cyprus	July 17, 2008 (Nicosia, Cyprus)
23	Turkish-Cypriot member of the CMP	July 16, 2008 (Nicosia, Cyprus)
24	Turkish-Cypriot investigative journalist and member of	July 30, 2008 (Nicosia, Cyprus)

(*cont.*)

Interview No.	Participant's status	Date
	bi-communal committee of relatives of missing in Cyprus	
25	Greek-Cypriot journalist	February 10, 2009 (Nicosia, Cyprus)
26	Greek-Cypriot relative of missing	February 7, 2009 (Nicosia, Cyprus)
27	Greek-Cypriot former member of the CMP	June 21, 2010 (Telephone Interview)
28	Greek-Cypriot diplomat	July 20, 2010 (Telephone Interview)
29	Greek-Cypriot retired diplomat	April 18, 2013 (Princeton, USA)
30	Lebanese activist	November 14, 2013 (Telephone Interview)
31	Greek-Cypriot member of bi-communal group of relatives	February 11, 2009 (Nicosia, Cyprus)
32	Academic expert on human rights groups' mobilization	February 18, 2015 (Skype Interview)
33	Human Rights advisor former director of research of Amnesty International and UN Office of the High Commissioner for Human Rights	January 19, 2015 (London, UK)
34	Academic and member of UNWGEID	February 2, 2015 (Skype Interview)
35	Argentinean geneticist and activist	February 2, 2015 (Skype Interview)
36	Human rights consultant	May 29, 2015 (Skype Interview)
37	Deputy secretary-general of the ICJ	February 25, 2015 (Skype Interview)
38	Policy director of the ICMP	February 23, 2015 (Strasbourg, France)

(cont.)

Interview No.	Participant's status	Date
39	Academic with expertise on forensic sciences and human rights	February 20, 2015 (Skype Interview)
40	Academic working on victims groups in Latin America	February 18, 2015 (Skype Interview)
41	Academic with expertise on forensic sciences and human rights	February 12, 2015 (Skype Interview)
42	Human rights lawyer UN special rapporteur on terror	June 11, 2015 (Skype Interview)
43	Human rights lawyer general counsel ICJ	May 20, 2015 (Skype Interview)
44	Leader of the Association for the Recovery of Historical Memory (ARMH)	March 20, 2009 (Madrid, Spain)
45	Academic human rights advocate of families of the disappeared	May 19, 2015 (Skype Interview)
46	Academic and forensic anthropologist	February 26, 2015 (Skype Interview)
47	Leader of the Asian Federation against Involuntary Disappearances (AFAD)	June 4, 2015 (Skype Interview)
48	Lebanese Mother of a missing son	March 17, 2016 (Beirut, Lebanon)
49	Lebanese Daughter of a father abducted	March 19, 2016 (Beirut, Lebanon)
50	Senior intelligence official of the Christian militia Lebanese forces	April 26, 2016 (Beirut, Lebanon)
51	Leader of Wahdatouna Khalasouna association	April 8, 2016 (Beirut, Lebanon)
52	Human rights lawyer member of "Legal Agenda" organization	March 17, 2016 (Beirut, Lebanon)
53	Coordinator of the Centre of Investigation and Promotion of Human Rights in Temuco,	April 18, 2016 (Temuco, Chile)

(cont.)

Interview No.	Participant's status	Date
	former political prisoner, former exile	
54	Daughter of the abducted leader of the Chilean Communist Party	April 5, 2016 (Santiago, Chile)
55	Member of the Agrupación de Familiares de Detenidos Desaparecidos and member of the Comité de Ética contra la Tortura, brother of a victim of political execution	April 6, 2016 (Temuco, Chile)
56	Grandson of a disappeared and leader of Paine memorial organization	March 31, 2016 (Paine, Chile)
57	Chilean Relative of disappeared and member of family organizations	April 20, 2016 (Santiago, Chile)
58	Member of Londres 38 Memorial Committee	April 29, 2016 (Santiago, Chile)
59	Chilean Sister of disappeared	March 9, 2016 (Temuco, Chile)
60	Head of the social work team at the Ministry of the Interior's Human Rights Program	April 29, 2016 (Santiago, Chile)
61	Chilean Brother of a detained-disappeared member of the 119 Collective and Londres 38 Memorial Committee	March 30, 2016 (Santiago, Chile)
62	Leader of Khulumani Group	May 3, 2016 (Skype Interview)
63	Leader of the Missing Persons Task Team	May 5, 2016 (Skype Interview
64	Member of the Asian Federation against Involuntary Disappearances (AFAD)	June 4, 2015 (Skype Interview)
65	Activist member of "ACT for the Disappeared"	February 12, 2016 (Skype Interview)

(*cont.*)

Interview No.	Participant's status	Date
66	Leading member of the Greek-Cypriot association of relatives of missing	July 3, 2008 (Nicosia, Cyprus)
67	Human rights lawyer	July 16, 2008 (Nicosia, Cyprus)
68	Greek-Cypriot MP member of the parliamentary committee on missing persons	July 15, 2008 (Nicosia, Cyprus)
69	Member of the ad hoc Working Group on the human rights situation in Chile in 1975	September 12, 2016 (Skype Interview)
70	Cypriot lawyer and human rights activist	October 18, 2016 (Telephone Interview)

BIBLIOGRAPHY

Abel, R. (2015). *Politics by Other Means: Law in the Struggle against Apartheid, 1980-1994.* London: Routledge.

Adler, E. & Haas, P. M. (1992). "Conclusion: Epistemic Communities, World Order, and the Creation of a Reflective Research Program," *International Organization,* 46(1), 367-390.

AFDD (1997). "*20 años de historia de la Agrupación de Familiares de Detenidos Desaparecidos de Chile. Un camino de imágenes ... que revelan y se rebelan contra una historia no contada,*" Santiago: Chile.

Africa News (2005). " 'Vlakplaas Victims' Relatives Gather to Mark 'Day of the Disappeared'," *Africa News,* September 1, 2005.

Africa News (2007). "South Africa: Final Rest for Struggle Victims Identified in Graves," *Africa News,* May 10, 2007.

Africa News (2013). "Dignity for 12 Families," *Africa News,* March 25, 2013.

Aguilar, M. (2002). "The Disappeared and the Mesa de Diálogo in Chile 1999-2001: Searching for Those Who Never Grew Old," *Bulletin of Latin American Research,* 21(3), 413-424.

Aguilar, P. (2008). "Transitional or Post-Transitional Justice? Recent Developments in the Spanish Case," *South European Society and Politics,* 13 (4), 417-433.

Aguilar, P. (2009). "The Timing and the Scope of Reparation, Truth and Justice Measures: A Comparison of the Spanish, Argentinian and Chilean Cases," in *Building a Future on Peace and Justice.* Ambos, K., Large, J. & Wierda, M. (Eds.), Berlin: Springer Berlin Heidelberg, pp.503-529.

Akhavan, P. (2005). "The Lord's Resistance Army Case: Uganda's Submission of the First State Referral to the International Criminal Court," *The American Journal of International Law,* 99(2), 403-421.

Al-Hasan, J. (2012). "Decree for Missing Persons Nearly Finalized, Justice Minister Says," *The Daily Star,* August 30, 2012.

Alfonsín, R. (1993). "'Never Again' in Argentina," *Journal of Democracy,* 4(1), 15-19.

Alitheia (1999). "*Ταπεινά συγγνώμη ζήτησε χθές η Πολιτεία απο τους συγγνείς νεκρών,*" November 7, p.1.

Amnesty International (1977). *Report of an Amnesty International Mission to Argentina*. London: Amnesty International.

Amnesty International (1997). "Lebanon: Human Rights Developments and Violations," Index Number: MDE 18/019/1997, October 8, 1997, also available at: www.amnesty.org/en/library/info/MDE18/019/1997/en (last accessed: January 10, 2014).

Amnesty International (2011). *Lebanon: Never Forgotten: Lebanon's Missing People*, Index Number MDE 18/001/2011, April 14, 2011, also available at: www.amnesty.org/en/library/info/MDE18/001/2011 (last accessed: January 9, 2014).

Anastasiou, H. (2008). *The Broken Olive Branch. Nationalism, Ethnic Conflict and the Quest for Peace in Cyprus*. Syracuse: Syracuse University Press.

Andreas, P. & Greenhill, K. (2011). "Introduction: The Politics of Numbers," in *Sex, Drugs, and Body Counts: The Politics of Numbers in Global Crime and Conflict*. Andreas, P. & Greenhill, K. (Eds.), Ithaca: Cornell University Press, pp.1–22.

Araguete-Toribio, Z. (2015). "Negotiating Identity: Reburial and Commemoration of the Civil War Dead in Southwestern Spain." *Human Remains and Violence: An Interdisciplinary Journal*, 1(2), 5–20.

Arditti, R. (1999). *Searching for Life: The Grandmothers of the Plaza de Mayo and the Disappeared Children of Argentina*. San Francisco: University of California Press.

Arditti, R. (2002). "The Grandmothers of the Plaza de Mayo and the Struggle against Impunity in Argentina," *Meridians*, 3(1), 19–41.

Aronson, J. (2010). "The Strengths and Limitations of South Africa's Search for Apartheid-Era Missing Persons," *The International Journal of Transitional Justice*, 5, 262–281.

Aronson, J. (2012). "Humanitarian DNA Identification in Post-Apartheid South Africa," in *Genetics and the Unsettled Past*. Wailoo, K., Nelson, A. & Lee, C. (Eds.), New Jersey: Rutgers University Press, pp.295–312.

Arthur, P. (2009). "How 'Transitions' Reshaped Human Rights: A Conceptual History of Transitional Justice," *Human Rights Quarterly*, 31(2), 321–367.

Asmal, K. (2000). "Truth, Reconciliation and Justice: The South African Experience in Perspective," *The Modern Law Review*, 63(1), 1–24.

Autesserre, S. (2010). *The Trouble with the Congo: Local Violence and the Failure of International Peacebuilding*. Cambridge: Cambridge University Press.

Backer, D. (2004). *The Human Face of Justice. Victims' Responses to South African Truth and Reconciliation Process*, Unpublished PhD thesis, University of Michigan.

Backer, D. (2009). "Cross-national Comparative Analysis," in *Assessing the Impact of Transitional Justice: Challenges for Empirical Research*. Van der Merwe, H., Baxter, V. & Chapman, A. (Eds.), Washington: United States Institute of Peace Press, pp.23–90.

Baines, E. (2010). "Spirits and Social Reconstruction after Mass Violence: Rethinking Transitional Justice," *African Affairs*, 109(436), 409–430.

Bakiner, O. (2010). "From Denial to Reluctant Dialogue: The Chilean Military's Confrontation with Human Rights (1990–2006)," *International Journal of Transitional Justice*, 4(1), 47–66.

Ballesteros, E. P. (1995). *La memoria y el olvido: detenidos desaparecidos en Chile*. Santiago: Ediciones Orígenes.

Barak, O. (2007). " 'Don't Mention the War?' The Politics of Remembrance and Forgetfulness in Postwar Lebanon," *Middle East Journal*, 61(1), 49–70.

Beissinger, M. R. (2002). *Nationalist Mobilization and the Collapse of the Soviet State*. Cambridge: Cambridge University Press.

Bell, C. (2008). *On the Law of Peace: Peace Agreements and the Lex Pacificatoria*. Oxford: Oxford University Press.

Ben-Naftali, O. & Gleichgevitch, S. (2000). "Missing in Legal Action: Lebanese Hostages in Israel," *Harvard International Law Journal*, 41(1), 185–252.

Benford, R. (1993). "Frame Disputes within the Nuclear Disarmament Movement," *Social Forces*, 71(3), 677–701.

Benford, R. (1997). "An Insider's Critique of the Social Movement Framing Perspective," *Sociological Inquiry*, 67(4), 409–430.

Benford, R. & Snow, D. (2000). "Framing Processes and Social Movements: An Overview and Assessment," *Annual Review of Sociology*, 26, 611–639.

Berat, L. & Shain, Y. (1995). "Retribution or Truth-Telling in South Africa? Legacies of the Transitional Phase," *Law and Social Inquiry*, 20(1), 163–189.

Bermeo, N. (1992). "Democracy and the Lessons of Dictatorship," *Comparative Politics*, 273–291.

Bernardi, P. & Fondebrider, L. (2007). "Forensic Archaeology and the Scientific Documentation of Human Rights Violations: An Argentinian Example from the Early 1980s," in *Forensic Archaeology and Human Rights Violations*. Ferllini, R. (Ed.), Springfield: Charles C Thomas Publisher, pp.205–232.

Berti, B. (2011). "Peace vs. Justice in Lebanon: The Domestic and Regional Implications of the UN Special Tribunal," *Strategic Assessment*, 13(4), 101–111.

Biazzini, N. (2013). "El Tribunal Oral Federal 5 de Capital Federal juzga a 66 imputados," *Infojus Noticias*, November 20, 2013, also available at: http://info jusnoticias.gov.ar/nacionales/no-hay-palabras-para-el-dolor-por-la-desaparicion-de-mis-padres-2333.html (last accessed: March 19, 2015).

Biggar, N. (Ed.) (2003). *Burying the Past: Making Peace and Doing Justice after Civil Conflict*. Washington: Georgetown University Press.

Biko, N. (2000). "Amnesty and Denial," in *Looking Back Reaching Forward. Reflections on the TRC of South Africa*. Villa-Vicencio, C. & Verwoerd, W. (Eds.), London: Zed Books, pp.193–198.

Binford, L. (1996). *The El Mozote Massacre: Anthropology and Human Rights*. Tucson: University of Arizona Press.

Blaauw, M. & Lähteenmäki, V. (2002). "Denial and Silence or Acknowledgment and Disclosure," International Review of the Red Cross, 84(848), 767–784.

Blau, S. & Skinner, M. (2005). "The Use of Forensic Archaeology in the Investigation of Human Rights Abuse: Unearthing the Past in East Timor," The International Journal of Human Rights, 9(4), 449–463.

Bonner, M. (2005). "Defining Rights in Democratization: The Argentine Government and Human Rights Organizations, 1983–2003," Latin American Politics and Society, 47(4), 55–76.

Boraine, A. (2000). A Country Unmasked inside South Africa's Truth and Reconciliation Commission. Oxford: Oxford University Press.

Bosco, F. (2004). "Human Rights Politics and Scaled Performances of Memory: Conflicts among the Madres de Plaza de Mayo in Argentina," Social & Cultural Geography, 5(3), 381–402.

Bosco, F. (2006). "The Madres de Plaza de Mayo and Three Decades of Human Rights' Activism: Embeddedness, Emotions, and Social Movements," Annals of the Association of American Geographers, 96(2), 342–365.

Boss, P. (2006). Loss, Trauma, and Resilience. Therapeutic Work with Ambiguous Loss. New York: W.W. Norton & Company.

Boss, P. G. (2002). "Ambiguous Loss: Working with Families of the Missing," Family Process, 41(1), 14.

Bouris, E. (2007). Complex Political Victims. Virginia: Kumarian Press.

Breen-Smyth, M. (2007). Truth Recovery and Justice after Conflict: Managing Violent Pasts. London: Routledge.

Brewer, J. D. (2010). Peace Processes: A Sociological Approach. Cambridge: Polity.

Brouneus, K. (2008). "Truth-Telling as Talking Cure? Insecurity and Retraumatization in the Rwandan Gacaca Courts," Security Dialogue, 39, 55–76.

Brysk, A. (1994). "The Politics of Measurement: The Contested Count of the Disappeared in Argentina," Human Rights Quarterly, 16(4), 676–692.

Brysk, A. (2013). Speaking Rights to Power: Constructing Political Will. Oxford University Press.

Buergenthal, T. (1994). "United Nations Truth Commission for El Salvador," The Vanderbilt Journal of Transnational Law, 27, 497.

Burgis-Kasthala, M. (2013). "Defining Justice during Transition? International and Domestic Contestations over the Special Tribunal for Lebanon," International Journal of Transitional Justice, 7, 497–517.

Bustamante, J. & Ruderer, S. (2009). Patio 29. Tras la Cruz de Fierro. Santiago: Ocholibros Editores.

Byrns, K. (2009). "Protestors Demand Right to Know Fate of Missing Relatives," The Daily Star, May 14, 2009.

Cardenas, S. (2010). Conflict and Compliance: State Responses to International Human Rights Pressure. Philadelphia: University of Pennsylvania Press.

Castro, J. L. G., Beristain, C. M. & Rovira, D. P. (2000). "Rituals, Social Sharing, Silence, Emotions and Collective Memory Claims in the Case of the Guatemalan Genocide," *Psicothema*, 12(1), 117–130.

Chapman, A. R. & Ball, P. (2001). "The Truth of Truth Commissions: Comparative Lessons from Haiti, South Africa, and Guatemala," *Human Rights Quarterly*, 23 (1), 1–43.

Charalambous, L. (2004). "Does the President Have Memory Problems?" *Cyprus Mail*, September 12, 2004.

Cingranelli, D. & Richards, D. (1999). "Respect for Human Rights after the End of the Cold War," *Journal of Peace Research*, 36(5), 511–534.

Cingranelli, D., Richards, D. & Clay, C. (2014). "The CIRI Human Rights Dataset," Version, 2014.04.14, available at: www.humanrightsdata.com (last accessed: July 3, 2016).

Citroni, G. & Scovazzi, T. (2009). "Recent Developments in International Law to Combat Enforced Disappearances," *Revista Internacional de Direito e Cidadania*, 3, 89–111.

Clark, A. M. (2010). *Diplomacy of Conscience: Amnesty International and Changing Human Rights Norms*. Princeton: Princeton University Press.

Clark, A. M. & Sikkink, K. (2013). "Information Effects and Human Rights Data: Is the Good News about Increased Human Rights Information Bad News for Human Rights Measures?" *Human Rights Quarterly*, 35(3), 539–568.

CMP, Committee on Missing Persons (2016). Fact Sheet, November 2016, also available at: www.cmp-cyprus.org/nqcontent.cfm?a_id=1 (last accessed: November 28, 2016).

Cobban, H. (2006). "International Courts," *Foreign Policy*, 153, 22–28.

Coelho-Filho, P. (2012). "Truth Commission in Brazil: Individualizing Amnesty, Revealing the Truth," *The Yale Review of International Studies*, also available at: http://yris.yira.org/essays/440 (last accessed: November 28, 2016).

Collier, D. (1993). "The Comparative Method," in *Political Science: The State of Discipline II*. Finifter, A. (Ed.), Washington: American Political Science Association.

Collier, D. & Mahoney, J. (1996). "Insights and Pitfalls: Selection Bias in Qualitative Research," *World Politics*, 49(01), 56–91.

Collins, C. (2006). "Grounding Global Justice: International Networks and Domestic Human Rights Accountability in Chile and El Salvador," *Journal of Latin American Studies*, 38(04), 711–738.

Collins, C. (2010). "Human Rights Trials in Chile during and after the 'Pinochet Years'," *International Journal of Transitional Justice*, 4(1), 67–86.

Collins, C. (2011). *Post-transitional Justice: Human Rights Trials in Chile and El Salvador*. Philadelphia: Penn State Press.

Collins, C. (2015). *Lawyers and Transition in Chile*. Policy Brief: Lawyers, Conflict and Transition Project, March 2015, Queen's University, Belfast, also available at: http://lawyersconflictandtransition.org/themainevent/wp-content/uploads/2014/07/lawyers-and-transition-in-chile-march-2015.pdf (last accessed: July 6, 2016).

Collins, C., Balardini, L. & Burt, J. M. (2012). "Mapping Perpetrator Prosecutions in Latin America," *International Journal of Transitional Justice*, 7(1), 8–28.

Congram, D. (2013). "Deposition and Dispersal of Human Remains as a Result of Criminal Acts: Homo Sapiens Sapiens as a Taphonomic Agent," in *Manual of Forensic Taphonomy*. Pokines, J. & Symes, S. (Eds.), New York: CRC Press, pp.249–285.

Congram, D. & Sterenberg, J. (2009). "Grave Challenges in Iraq," in *Handbook of Forensic Anthropology and Archeology*. Blau, S. & Ubelaker, D. (Eds.), New York: Routledge, pp.441–453.

Cordner, S. & McKelvie, H. (2002). "Developing Standards in International Forensic Work to Identify Missing Persons," *Revue Internationale de la Croix-Rouge/International Review of the Red Cross*, 84(848), 867–884.

Corm, G. (1994). "The War System: Militia Hegemony and Reestablishment of the State," in *Peace for Lebanon? From War to Reconstruction*. Collings, D. (Ed.), Boulder: Lynne Rienner, pp.215–230.

Correa, P. & Foxcroft, D. (2013). "The On-going Case: Getting Around Amnesty Laws by Seeking Justice for the Disappeared. O contorno da lei da anistia na busca de justiça: uma comparação das abordagens no Brasil e no Chile sobre os desaparecidos," *Relações Internacionais no Mundo Atual*, 1(17), 74–84.

Council of Europe (2003). Committee of Ministers of the Council of Europe, CM/inf(2003a)14, November 26, 2003.

Council of Europe (2004). Committee of Ministers of the Council of Europe, Interim Report DH(2004)4/1, November 26, 2004.

Council of Europe (2005). Committee of Ministers of the Council of Europe, Interim Resolution ResDH, "Concerning the Judgment of the European Court of Human Rights of 10 May 2001 in the Case of Cyprus against Turkey," June 7, 2005.

Crenzel, E. (2008). "Argentina's National Commission on the Disappearance of Persons: Contributions to Transitional Justice," *International Journal of Transitional Justice*, 2(2), 173–191.

Crenzel, E. (2011). "Between the Voices of the State and the Human Rights Movement: Never Again and the Memories of the Disappeared in Argentina," *Journal of Social History*, 44(4), 1063–1076.

Crettol, M. & De La Rosa, A. M. (2006). "The Missing and Transitional Justice: The Right to Know and the Fight against Impunity," *International Review of the Red Cross*, 88(862), 355–362.

Crossland, Z. (2009). "Of Clues and Signs: The Dead Body and Its Evidential Traces," *American Anthropologist*, 111(1), 69–80.

Crossland, Z. (2013). "Evidential Regimes of Forensic Archaeology". *Annual Review of Anthropology*, 42, 121–137.

Dalby, D. (2014). "No Bail for Former I.R.A. Member Charged in '72 Killing'," *New York Times*, March 22, 2014, also available at: www.nytimes.com/2014/03/23/world/europe/no-bail-for-former-ira-member-charged-in-72-killing.html?_r=0 (last accessed: November 28, 2016).

Dancy, G., Francesca, L., Bridget, M., Leigh, A. P., Gabriel, P. & Kathryn, S. (2014). "The Transitional Justice Research Collaborative: Bridging the Qualitative-Quantitative Divide With New Data," also available at: www.transitionaljusticedata.com (last accessed: July 3, 2016).

Dancy, G., Kim, H. & Wiebelhaus-Brahm, E. (2010). "The Turn to Truth: Trends in Truth Commission Experimentation," *Journal of Human Rights*, 9(1), 45–64.

Danforth, L. M. & Tsiaras, A. (1982). *The Death Rituals of Rural Greece*. Princeton: Princeton University Press.

Davies, T. (2014). *NGOs: A New History of Transnational Civil Society*. Oxford: Oxford University Press.

De Brito, A. (2001). "Truth, Justice, Memory and Democratization in the Southern Cone," in *The Politics of Memory. Transitional Justice in Democratizing Societies*. De Brito, A., Aguilar, P. & Gonzalez-Enriquez, C. (Eds.), Oxford: Oxford University Press, pp.119–160.

De Brito, A. (2003). "Passion, Constraint, Law and Fortuna. The Human Rights Challenge to Chilean Democracy," in *Burying the Past. Making Peace and Doing Justice after Civil Conflict*. Biggar, N. (Ed.), Washington: Georgetown University Press, pp.177–208.

De Kock, R. (2013). "I Want My Hasbund's Remains so I Can Die in Peace," *The Herald*, May 8, 2013.

De Rivaz, C. (2013). "Over 5000 Bodies Exhumed in Colombia since 2007," *Colombia Reports*, also available at: http://colombiareports.co/5000-bodies-exhumed-colombia-last-6-years/ (last accessed: November 28, 2016).

De Ycaza, C. & Schabas, W. (2011). "'Transitional Justice and the African Experience', Forum: Transitional Justice: The Quest for Theory to Inform Policy," *International Studies Review*, 13(1), 564–570.

Dempster, L. (2016). "The Republican Movement, 'Disappearing' and Framing the Past in Northern Ireland," *International Journal of Transitional Justice*, 20(2), 250–271.

Dhumi Ëres, M. (2011). "Investigate Civil War Missing: Amnesty," *The Daily Star*, April 15, 2011.

Diana, T. (1997). *Disappearing Acts: Spectacles of Gender and Nationalism in Argentina's "Dirty War."* Durham: Duke University Press.

Dorfman, A. (1997). "Last Chance for Redemption in Chile," *The Guardian*, September 17, 1997, p.17.

Dorfman, A. (2000). "The General is Hoist on His Own Petard: Victory against Impunity for the Chilean Dictator Belongs to the Disappeared and their Families," *Observer*, December 3, 2000, p.31.

Drawdy, S. & Katzmarzyk, C. (2016) "The Missing Files: The Experience of the International Committee of the Red Cross," in *Missing Persons: Multidisciplinary Perspective on the Disappeared*. Congram, D. (Ed.), Toronto: Canadian Scholar's Press.

Drousiotis, M. (2000). *1,619 Ενοχές – Τα λαθη, τα Ψέμματα και οι Σκοπιμότητες*. Nicosia: Alfadi.

Druliolle, V. (2013). "HIJOS and the Spectacular Denunciation of Impunity: The Struggle for Memory, Truth, and Justice and the (re-) Construction of Democracy in Argentina," *Journal of Human Rights*, 12(2), 259–276.

Dugan, E. (2011). "CSI South Africa: Apartheid's Last Murder Mystery," *Independent*, January 16, 2011.

EAAF (1998). "Chile: A Mission to Assist the Identification Unit of the Chilean Medical Legal Institute Establish a Bank of Blood Samples from Relatives of Disappeared Chilean Citizens," Argentine Forensic Anthropology Team Annual Report, p.19, also available at: http://eaaf.typepad.com/cr_chile/ (last accessed: April 13, 2015).

EAAF (2006). "South Africa: Annual Country Report," Argentine Forensic Anthropology Team, also available at: http://eaaf.typepad.com/cr_south_africa/ (last accessed: April 13, 2015).

EAAF (2007a). "Chile," Argentine Forensic Anthropology Team Annual Report, pp.1–17, also available at: http://eaaf.typepad.com/cr_chile/ (last accessed: April 13, 2015).

EAAF (2007b). "Annual Report," Special Section the Right to Truth, pp.102–109, also available at: http://eaaf.typepad.com/annual_report_2007/ (last accessed: April 13, 2015).

Eckstein, H. (1975). "Case Study and Theory in Political Science," in *Handbook of Political Science*. Greenstein, F. & Polsby, N. (Eds.), Vol. 7, Reading, MA: Addison-Wesley, pp. 79–128.

Edkins, J. (2011). *Missing: Persons and Politics*. Ithaca: Cornell University Press.

Egan, L. (2002). "DNA Helps Chileans Put Names to Long-lost Bodies," *Reuters News Agency*, February 27, 2002, p.10.

El-Hokayem, E. & McGovern, E. (2008). *Towards a More Secure and Stable Lebanon: Prospects for Security Sector Reform*. Washington: The Henry L. Stimson Center, also available at: www.stimson.org (last accessed: January 9, 2014).

Elkin, M. (2008). "María Barragán Succeeds in Getting Adoptive Parents Jailed," *The Times*, April 5, 2008, www.thetimes.co.uk/tto/news/world/americas/arti cle1997182.ece. (last accessed: November 28, 2016).

Elster, J. (2004). *Closing the Books: Transitional Justice in Historical Perspective.* Cambridge: Cambridge University Press.

Ensalaco, M. (2000). *Chile under Pinochet: Recovering the Truth.* Philadelphia: University of Pennsylvania Press.

Fearon, J. & Laitin, D. (2003). "Ethnicity, Insurgency, and Civil War," *American Political Science Review,* 97(01), 75–90.

Femenía, N. & Gil, C. (1987). "Argentina's Mothers of Plaza de Mayo: The Mourning Process from Junta to Democracy," *Feminist Studies,* 13(1), 9–18.

Ferllini, R. (2007). *Forensic Archaeology and Human Rights Violations.* Springfield: Charles C Thomas Publisher.

Ferrándiz, F. (2009). "Fosas comunes, paisajes del terror," *Revista de Dialectología y Tradiciones populares,* 64(1), 61–94.

Ferrándiz, F. & Robben, A. (2015). "Introduction: The Ethnography of Exhumations," *Necropolitics. Mass Graves and Exhumations in the Age of Human Rights.* Ferrándiz, F. & Robben, A. (Eds.), Philadelphia: University of Pennsylvania Press, pp.1–40.

Finnemore, M. (1993). "International Organizations as Teachers of Norms: The United Nations Educational, Scientific, and Cultural Organization and Science Policy," *International Organization,* 47(04), 565–597.

Fisher, J. (1989). *Mothers of the Disappeared.* Boston: South End Press.

Fondebrider, L. (2002). "Reflections on the Scientific Documentation of Human Rights Violations," *International Review of the Red Cross,* 84(848), 885–891.

Forsythe, D. (2011). "Human Rights and Mass Atrocities: Revisiting Transitional Justice," *International Studies Review,* 13(1), 85–95.

Frankl, V. E. (1985). *Man's Search for Meaning.* New York: Simon and Schuster.

Franklin, J. (1999). "Chilean Lawyers Using New Human Rights Strategy," *The Globe and Mail,* August 12, 1999.

Freeman, M. (2006). *Truth Commissions and Procedural Fairness.* Cambridge: Cambridge University Press.

Freeman, M. (2009). *Necessary Evils: Amnesties and the Search for Justice.* Cambridge: Cambridge University Press.

Frouville, O. (forthcoming 2017). "The Committee on Enforced Disappearances," in *The United Nations and Human Rights: A Critical Appraisal.* Alston, N. & Megret, F. (Eds.), 2nd edition, Oxford: Oxford University Press.

Frulli, M. (2014). "Nino Cassese and the Early Stages in the Fight against Enforced Disappearances," *Journal of International Criminal Justice,* 12(4), 805–808.

Fullard, M. & Rousseau, N. (2001). "Truth-telling, Identities, and Power in South Africa and Guatemala," in *Identities in Transition Challenges for Transitional Justice in Divided Societies.* Arthur, P. (Ed.), New York: Cambridge University Press, pp.54–86.

Galtung, J. (1996). *Peace by Peaceful Means: Peace and Conflict, Development and Civilization.* London: Sage.

Gamson, W. & Meyer, D. (1996). "Framing Political Opportunity," in *Comparative Perspectives on Social Movements. Political Opportunities, Mobilizing Structures and Cultural Framing.* McAdam, D., McCarthy, J. & Zald, M. (Eds.), Cambridge: Cambridge University Press, pp.259–270.

García, S., Pérez-Sales, P. & Fernández-Liria, A. (2010). "Exhumation Processes in Fourteen Countries in Latin America," *Journal for Social Action in Counseling and Psychology,* 2(2), 48.

Garibian, S. (2014). "Ghosts Also Die Resisting Disappearance through the 'Right to the Truth' and the Juicios por la Verdad in Argentina." *Journal of International Criminal Justice,* 12(3), 515–538.

Gates, S., Binningsbo, H. & Lie, T. (2007). "Post-conflict Justice and Sustainable Peace," *World Bank Policy Research Working Paper* (4191).

Geddes, B., Wright, J. & Frantz, E. (2014). "Autocratic Breakdown and Regime Transitions: A New Data Set," *Perspectives on Politics,* 12(02), 313–331.

George, A. & Bennett, A. (2005). *Case Studies and Theory Development in the Social Sciences.* Cambridge: MIT Press.

Gerring, J. (2004). "What Is a Case Study and What Is It Good for?" *American Political Science Review,* 98(2), 341–354.

Gerring, J. & Seawright, J. (2007). "Techniques for Choosing Cases," in *Case Study Research: Principles and Practices.* Gerring, J. (Ed.), Cambridge: Cambridge University Press, pp.86–150.

Ghattas, F. (2000). "Lebanese Government Declares 17,000 War Missing Dead," *Associated Press,* July 26, 2007.

Ghosn, F. & Khoury, A. (2011). "Lebanon after the Civil War: Peace or the Illusion of Peace?" *The Middle East Journal,* 65(3), 381–397.

Gibson, J. (2004). *Overcoming Apartheid. Can Truth Reconcile a Divided Nation?* New York: Russell Sage Foundation.

Gibson, J. (2006). "The Contributions of Truth to Reconciliation: Lessons from South Africa," *Journal of Conflict Resolution,* 50(3), 409–432.

Goffman, E. (1974). *Frame Analysis: An Essay on the Organization of the Experience.* New York: Harper Colophon.

Goni, U. (2014). "Argentina's Campaigning Grandmother Finds Grandson Born to Death Camp Mother," *The Guardian,* August 6, 2014, also available at: www.theguardian.com/world/2014/aug/06/argentinian-grandmothers-find-son-of-woman-murdered-under-dictatorship (last accessed: March 19, 2015).

Graybill, L. (2002). *Truth and Reconciliation in South Africa. Miracle or Model?* Boulder, London: Lynne Rienner Publishers.

Gready, P. & Robins, S. (2014). "From Transitional to Transformative Justice: A New Agenda for Practice," *International Journal of Transitional Justice,* 8(3), 339–361.

Grenfell, D. (2015). "Of Time and History: The Dead of War, Memory and the National Imaginary in Timor-Leste," *Communication, Politics & Culture*, 48 (3), 16.

Grigoriadis, I. (2009). *The Trials of Europeanization. Turkish Political Culture and the European Union*. Basingstoke: Palgrave.

Guelke, A. (1999). *South Africa in Transition. The Misunderstood Miracle*. London: I.B. Tauris.

Guelke, A. (2000). "South Africa's Morality Tale for Our Time." *Review of International Studies*, 26(2), 303–309.

Guelke, A. (2007). "Commentary: Truth, Reconciliation and Political Accommodation," *Irish Political Studies*, 22(3), 363–366.

Guest, I. (1990). *Behind the Disappearances: Argentina's Dirty War against Human Rights and the United Nations*. Philadelphia: University of Pennsylvania Press.

Gurney, K. & Johnson, S. (2008). "Digging Up Dirt: A Forensic Team is Tracking Down South Africa's Disappeared – and Reopening Some Very Cold Cases," *Newsweek*, 151(15).

Haas, P. M. (1989). "Do Regimes Matter? Epistemic Communities and Mediterranean Pollution Control," *International Organization*, 43(03), 377–403.

Haas, P. M. (1992). "Introduction: Epistemic Communities and International Policy Coordination," *International Organization*, 46(01), 1–35.

Hadjipavlou, M. (2007). "The 'Crossings' as Part of Citizens' Reconciliation Efforts in Cyprus?" *Innovation*, 20(1), 53–73.

Hafner-Burton, E. & Ron, J. (2009). "Seeing Double," *World Politics*, 61(02), 360–401.

Haglund, W. (2001). "Archaeology and Forensic Death Investigations," *Historical Archaeology*, 35(1), 26–34.

Haglund, W., Connor, M. & Douglas, S. (2001). "The Archaeology of Contemporary Mass Graves," *Historical Archaeology*, 35(1), 57–69.

Hanson, I. (2008). "Forensic Archaeology: Approaches to International Investigations," in *Forensic Approaches to Death, Disaster and Abuse*. Oxenham, M. (Ed.), Bowen Hills: Australian Academic Press, pp.17–28.

Haugbolle, S. (2010). *War and Memory in Lebanon*. Cambridge: Cambridge University Press.

Hayner, P. (1994). "Fifteen Truth Commissions – 1974 to 1994: A Comparative Study," *Human Rights Quarterly*, 16(4), 597–655.

Hayner, P. (2002). *Unspeakable Truths. Facing the Challenges of Truth Commissions*. London: Routledge.

Hayner, P. (2011). *Unspeakable Truths: Transitional Justice and the Challenge of Truth Commissions*, 2nd edition. New York: Routledge.

Heraclides, A. (2011). "The Cyprus Gordian Knot: An Intractable Ethnic Conflict," *Nationalism and Ethnic Politics*, 17(2), 117–139.

Herrera, Y. M. & Kapur, D. (2007). "Improving Data Quality: Actors, Incentives, and Capabilities," *Political Analysis*, 15(4), 365–386.

Hilbink, L. (2007). *Judges beyond Politics in Democracy and Dictatorship: Lessons from Chile*. Cambridge: Cambridge University Press.

Hirsch, M. (2007). "Agents of Truth and Justice: Truth Commissions and the Transitional Justice Epistemic Community," in *Rethinking Ethical Foreign Policy: Pitfalls, Possibilities and Paradoxes*. Chandler, D. & Heins, V. (Eds.), London: Routledge, pp.184–205.

Hirsch, M. (2009). *And the Truth Shall Make You Free: The International Norm of Truth-seeking*. Doctoral dissertation, Tel Aviv University.

Hoffmeister, F. (2002). "Cyprus v. Turkey App. No. 25781/94," *The American Journal of International Law*, 96(2), 445–452.

House of Representatives (1979) "Human Rights and the Phenomenon of Disappearances: Hearings before the Subcommittee on International Organizations of the Committee on Foreign Affairs," House of Representatives, Ninety-sixth Congress, first session, September 20, 25, and October 18, 1979.

Human Rights Watch (1997). "Syria/Lebanon an Alliance Beyond the Law. Enforced Disappearances in Lebanon," May 1997 vol. 9, no. 3, also available at: www.hrw.org/node/24483/section/1 (last accessed: January 10, 2014).

Human Rights Watch (2001). "Reluctant Partner: The Argentine Government's Failure to Back Trials of Human Rights Violators," Special Report, December 2001, also available at: www.hrw.org/reports/2001/12/12/reluctant-partner (last accessed: April 13, 2015).

Human Rights Watch (2008). "Breaking the Grip? Obstacles to Justice for Paramilitary Mafias in Colombia," October 2008, also available at: www.hrw.org/reports/2008/10/16/breaking-grip-0 (last accessed: November 28, 2016).

Human Rights Watch (2013). "Lebanon: Tit-for-tat Border Kidnappings: Civilians Describe Experiences; Meager Government Response," also available at: www.hrw.org/news/2013/05/02/lebanon-tit-tat-border-kidnappings (last accessed: January 10, 2014).

Huneeus, A., Couso, J. & Sieder, R. (2010). "Cultures of Legality: Judicialization and Political Activism in Latin America," *Studies in Law and Society*, Cambridge: Cambridge University Press, June, pp.3–24.

Huntington, S. (1993). *The Third Wave: Democratization in the Late Twentieth Century*, Vol. 4. Oklahoma: University of Oklahoma Press.

ICMP (2014). *Bosnia and Herzegovina. Missing Persons Form the Armed Conflicts of the 1990s: A Stocktaking*. Sarajevo: International Commission on Missing Persons.

ICRC (2003). "ICRC Report: The Missing and their families," Geneva, International Committee of the Red Cross, also available at: www.icrc.org/eng/assets/files/other/icrc_themissing_012003_en_10.pdf (last accessed: December 8, 2016).

ICRC (2009). "Missing People, DNA Analysis and Identification of Human Remains. A Guide to Best Practice in Armed Conflicts and Other Situations of Armed Violence, Second Edition 2009," Geneva, also available at: www.icrc.org/en/publica tion/4010-missing-people-dna-analysis-and-identification-human-remains-guide-best-practice (last accessed: July 5, 2016).

ICRC (2013). "The Families of People Missing in Connection with the Armed Conflict That Have Occurred in Lebanon Since 1975. An Assessment of Their Needs," June 2013, also available at: www.icrc.org/eng/resources/documents/report/06-20-lebanon-missing.htm (last accessed: January 10, 2013).

Ignatieff, M. (1998). *The Warrior's Honor: Ethnic War and the Modern Conscience.* New York: Holt Paperbacks.

Interamerican Commission on Human Rights (IACHR) (1985). *Annual Report of the IACHR 1985–6,* OEA/er.L./V/II/Doc8, 193.

Interamerican Commission on Human Rights (IACHR) (2011). "Annual Report of the Inter-American Commission on Human Rights in Colombia," also available at: www.oas.org/en/iachr/docs/annual/2011/toc.asp (last accessed: November 24, 2016).

International Commission on Human Rights (IACHR) (2014). *The Right to Truth in the Americas,* OEA/Ser.L/V/II.152, 13 August 2014.

International Center for Transitional Justice (2013). "Lebanon's Legacy of Political Violence. A Mapping of Serious Violations of International Human Rights and Humanitarian Law in Lebanon, 1975–2008," September 2013, also available at: http://ictj.org/publication/lebanon-legacy-political-violence (last accessed: January 10, 2014).

Jaquemet, I. (2009). "Fighting Amnesia: Ways to Uncover the Truth about Lebanon's Missing," *International Journal of Transitional Justice,* 1, 69–90.

Jarroud, M. (2012). "Families of 'Disappeared' and Forensic Institute on Good Terms Again," *Inter Press Service,* September 4, 2012, also available at: www .ipsnews.net/2012/09/families-of-disappeared-and-forensic-institute-on-good-terms-again/ (last accessed: November 28, 2016).

Jelin, E. (1994). "The Politics of Memory: The Human Rights Movements and the Construction of Democracy in Argentina," *Latin American Perspectives,* 21(2), 38–58.

Joseph, J. (1997). *Cyprus: Ethnic Conflict and International Politics: From Independence to the Threshold of the European Union.* New York: St. Martin's Press.

Joyce, C. & Stover, E. (1992). *Witnesses from the Grave: The Stories Bones Tell.* London: Little, Brown, 45–53.

Juhl, K. (2005). *The Contribution by (Forensic) Archaeologists to Human Rights Investigations of Mass Graves.* Stavanger, Norway: Museum of Archaeology.

Juliá, S. (1999). "De 'guerra contra el invasor' a 'guerra fratricida.' " *Víctimas de la guerra civil,* pp.11–54.

Kalyvas, S. (2006). *The Logic of Violence in Civil War*. Cambridge Studies in Comparative Politics, Cambridge: Cambridge University Press.

Kaminski, M., Nalepa, M. & O'Neill, B. (2006). "Normative and Strategic Aspects of Transitional Justice," *Journal of Conflict Resolution*, 50(3), 295–302.

Kasimatis, P. (1997). *Αγνοούμενοι – Άκρως απόρρητο – Τα δεκατρία περιστέρια*, Athens: Livanis.

Keck, M. & Sikkink, K. (1998). "Activists beyond Borders," *Advocacy Networks in International Politics*. Vol. 6, Ithaca: Cornell University Press.

Kelman, H. (1999). "Building a Sustainable Peace: The Limits of Pragmatism in the Israeli-Palestinian Negotiations," *Peace and Conflict: Journal of Political Psychology*, 5(2), 101–115.

Ker-Lindsay, J. (2011). *The Cyprus Problem: What Everyone Needs to Know*. Oxford: Oxford University Press.

Ker-Lindsay, J. & Hubert, F. (2008). *The Government and Politics of Cyprus*. Oxford: Peter Lang.

Khalaf, S. (2002). *Civil and Uncivil Violence in Lebanon: A History of the Internationalization of Communal Conflict*. New York: Columbia University Press.

Khulumani (2010). Khulumani Apartheid Reparation Database: Report on Cases of the Disappeared, July 31, 2010, Johannesburg, also available at: www.khulumani.net/ (last accessed: July 6, 2016).

Kim, H. J. (2012). "Structural Determinants of Human Rights Prosecutions after Democratic Transition," *Journal of Peace Research*, 49(2), 305–320.

Kim, H. J. & Sikkink, K. (2010). "Explaining the Deterrence Effect of Human Rights. Prosecutions for Transitional Countries," *International Studies Quarterly*, 54(4), 939–963.

Klandermans, B. (1997). *The Social Psychology of Protest*. Oxford: Blackwell.

Knudsen, A. (2005). *Precarious Peacebuilding: Post-war Lebanon, 1990–2005*, Chr. Michelsen Institute, CMI Working Paper n. 12, also available at: http://hdl.handle.net/10202/103 (last accessed: January 9, 2014).

Korff, D. (2006). "The Right to Life: A Guide to the Implementation of Article 2 of the European Convention on Human Rights," *Council of Europe-Human Rights Handbook*, 8, also available at: https://papers.ssrn.com/sol3/papers.cfm?abstract_id=1288555 (last accessed: November 28, 2016).

Kovras, I. (2012). "De-linkage Processes and Grassroots Movements in Transitional Justice," *Cooperation and Conflict*, 47(1), 88–105.

Kovras, I. (2013) "Explaining Prolonged Silences in Transitional Justice: The Disappeared in Cyprus and Spain," *Comparative Political Studies*, 46, 730–756.

Kovras, I. (2014). *Truth Recovery and Transitional Justice: Deferring Human Rights*. London: Routledge.

Kovras, I. & Loizides, N. (2011). "Delaying Truth Recovery for Missing Persons," *Nations and Nationalism*, 17(3), 520–539.

Krause, W. C. (2004). "The Role and Example of Chilean and Argentinian Mothers in Democratisation," *Development in Practice*, 14(3), 366–380.

Kriesi, H. (1995a). "The Political Opportunity Structure of New Social Movements: Its Impact on their Mobilization," in *The Politics of Social Protest: Comparative Perspectives on States and Social Movements*. Jenkins, G. & Klandermans, B. (Eds.), Minneapolis: University of Minnesota Press, pp.167–198.

Kriesi, H. (1995b). *New Social Movements in Western Europe: A Comparative Analysis*, Vol. 5. Minneapolis: University of Minnesota Press.

Kubheka, A. (2013). "Closure as MK Operative Is Exhumed," *Daily News*, April 10, 2013, p.2.

Kyriakou, N. (2012). *An Affront to the Conscience of Humanity: Enforced Disappearance in International Human Rights Law*. Doctoral dissertation, European University Institute.

Kyriakou, N. (2014). "An Affront to the Conscience of Humanity: Enforced Disappearances in the Case Law of the Inter-American Court of Human Rights," *Interamerican and European Human Rights Journal*, 4(1), 17–38.

Lacina, B., Gleditsch, P. & Russett, B. (2006). "The Declining Risk of Death in Battle," *International Studies Quarterly*, 50(3), 673–680.

Lafontaine, F. (2005). "No Amnesty or Statute of Limitation for Enforced Disappearances: The Sandoval Case before the Supreme Court of Chile," *Journal of International Criminal Justice*, 3, 467.

Lakha, K. (2012). "A Day in the Life of the MPTT," *Quest*, 8, 16–17.

Lambourne, W. (2000). "Post-Conflict Peacebuilding," *Security Dialogue*, 31, 357.

Landsman, S. (1997). "Alternative Responses to Serious Human Rights Abuses: Of Prosecutions and Truth Commissions," *Law and Contemporary Problems*, 59 (4), 81–92.

Landman, T. & Carvalho, E. (2009). *Measuring Human Rights*. New York: Routledge.

Lange, M. (2011). *Educations in Ethnic Violence: Identity, Educational Bubbles, and Resource Mobilization*. Cambridge: Cambridge University Press.

Laqueur, T. W. (2015). *The Work of the Dead: A Cultural History of Mortal Remains*. Princeton: Princeton University Press.

Latin American Herald Tribune (2014). "More Than 3,000 Militia Victims Exhumed in Colombia," *Latin American Herald Tribune*, February 7, 2014, also available at: www.laht.com/article.asp?CategoryId=12393&ArticleId=356810 (last accessed: November 28, 2016).

Lawther, C. (2014). *Truth, Denial and Transition: Northern Ireland and the Contested Past*. Transitional Justice Series, London: Routledge.

Lebanese Center for Human Rights. (2008). "Report: Lebanon Enforced Disappearances and Incommunicado Detentions," Beirut, February 21, 2008, also available at: www.solida.org (last accessed: January 10, 2014).

Lederach, J. P. (2005). *The Moral Imagination: The Art and Soul of Building Peace*, Vol. 3. New York: Oxford University Press.

Leebaw, B. (2011). *Judging State-Sponsored Violence, Imagining Political Change*. Cambridge: Cambridge University Press.

Lessa, F. (2012). "Barriers to Justice: The Ley de Caducidad and Impunity in Uruguay," in *Amnesty in the Age of Human Rights Accountability. Comparative and International Perspectives*. Lessa Franscesca & Payne Leigh (Eds.), Cambridge: Cambridge University Press, pp. 123–151.

Lieberman, E. (2005). "Nested Analysis as a Mixed-Method Strategy for Comparative Research," *American Political Science Review*, 99(03), 435–452.

Lieberman, E. (2010). "Bridging the Qualitative-Quantitative Divide: Best Practices in the Development of Historically Oriented Replication Databases," *Annual Review of Political Science*, 13, 37–59.

Linz, J. & Stepan, A. (1996). *Problems of Democratic Transition and Consolidation: Southern Europe, South America, and Post-communist Europe*. Baltimore: Johns Hopkins University Press.

Lobar, S. L., Youngblut, J. M. & Brooten, D. (2006). "Cross-cultural Beliefs, Ceremonies, and Rituals Surrounding Death of a Loved One," *Pediatric Nursing*, 32(1), 44.

Loizides, N. (2016). *Designing Peace: Cyprus and Institutional Innovations in Divided Societies*. Philadelphia: University of Pennsylvania Press.

London, A. J., Parker, L. S. & Aronson, J. D. (2013). "DNA Identification after Conflict or Disaster," *Science*, 341(6151), 1178–1179.

Lundy, P. & McGovern, M. (2008). "Whose Justice? Rethinking Transitional Justice from the Bottom Up," *Journal of Law and Society*, 35(2), 265–292.

Lutz, E. & Reiger, C. (2009). *Prosecuting Heads of State*. Cambridge: Cambridge University Press.

Lutz, E. & Sikkink, K. (2001). "Justice Cascade: The Evolution and Impact of Foreign Human Rights Trials in Latin America," *The Chicago Journal of International Law*, 2, 1.

Maalouf, L. (2009). "Enforced Disappearances in Lebanon: A Nation's Unyielding Legacy," Report prepared for the ACT for the Disappeared, Beirut, July 2009, also available at: www.actforthedisappeared.com/reports-articles-press.php (last accessed: January 10, 2014).

Maalouf, L. & Maalouf, R. C. (2015). "Forensic Archaeology in Lebanon. Forensic Archaeology: A Global Perspective," in *Forensic Archaeology: A Global Perspective*. Márquez-Grant, N. & Janaway, R. (Eds.), New Jersey: John Wiley & Sons, pp.293–299.

Mahoney, J. (2004). "Comparative-Historical Methodology," *Annual Review of Sociology*, 30, 81–101.

Mahoney, J. (2000). "Path Dependence in Historical Sociology," *Theory and Society*, 29(4), 507–548.

Mai'a K, D. C. (2013). "Rethinking Epistemic Communities Twenty Years Later," *Review of International Studies*, 39(01), 137–160.

Makdisi, S. & Richard, S. (2005). "The Lebanese Civil War, 1975–1990," *Understanding Civil War Evidence and Analysis, Vol. 2: Europe, Central Asia and Other Regions.* Collier Paul and Sambanis Nicholas (Eds.), Washington: World Bank Publications, pp.59–86.

Malin, A. (1994). "Mother Who Won't Disappear," *Human Rights Quarterly*, 16(1), 187–213.

Mallinder, L. (2008). *Amnesty, Human Rights and Political Transitions: Bridging the Peace and Justice Divide.* London: Hart Publishing.

Mallinder, L. (2009). "The Ongoing Quest for Truth and Justice: Enacting and Annulling Argentina's Amnesty Laws," also available at SSRN 1531759. http://papers.ssrn.com/sol3/papers.cfm?abstract_id=1531759 (Last accessed: November 28, 2016).

Mallinder, L. & O'Rourke, C. (2016). "Databases of Transitional Justice Mechanisms and Contexts: Comparing Research Purposes and Design," *International Journal of Transitional Justice*, 10(3), 492–512.

Manning, C. (2002). "Conflict Management and Elite Habituation in Postwar Democracy: The Case of Mozambique," *Comparative Politics*, 35(1), 63–84.

Mansfield, E. & Snyder, J. (2005). *Electing to Fight.* Cambridge, MA: MIT Press.

Martin, J., van Wijk, C., Hans-Arendse, C. & Makhaba, L. (2013). "Missing in Action: The Significance of Bodies in African Bereavement Rituals," *Psychology in Society*, 44, 42–63.

McAdam, D. (1999). *Political Process and the Development of Black Insurgency, 1930–1970.* Chicago: University of Chicago Press.

McAdam, D., Tarrow, S. & Tilly, C. (2001). *Dynamics of Contention.* Cambridge: Cambridge University Press.

McAdam, D., Tarrow, S. & Tilly, C. (2009). "Comparative Perspectives on Contentious Politics," *Comparative Politics: Rationality, Culture, and Structure.* Lichbach, M. & Zuckerman, A. (Eds.), Cambridge: Cambridge University Press, pp.260–290.

McCormick, J. & Mitchell, N. (1997). "Human Rights Violations, Umbrella Concepts, and Empirical Analysis," *World Politics*, 49(04), 510–525.

McCrory, S. (2007). "The International Convention for the Protection of All Persons from Enforced Disappearance," *Human Rights Law Review*, 7(3), 545–566.

McCrudden, C. (2000). "Common Law of Human Rights? Transnational Judicial Conversations on Constitutional Rights," *Oxford Journal of Legal Studies*, 20(4), 499–532.

McDonald, H. (2007). "Churches Plea to IRA over 'Disappeared'," *The Observer*, January 7.

McEvoy, K. & McGregor, L. (Eds.) (2008). *Transitional Justice from Below: Grassroots Activism and the Struggle for Change.* London: Bloomsbury Publishing.

McEvoy, K. & Mallinder, L. (2012). "Amnesties in Transition: Punishment, Restoration, and the Governance of Mercy," *Journal of Law and Society,* 39(3), 410–440.

McNally, R. J. (2003). "Psychological Mechanisms in Acute Response to Trauma," *Biological Psychiatry,* 53(9), 779–788.

McSherry, P. (2002). "Tracking the Origins of a State Terror Network: Operation Condor," *Latin American Perspectives,* 29(1), 38–60.

Mecellem, J. G. (2016). "Human Rights Trials in an Era of Democratic Stagnation: The Case of Turkey." *Law & Social Inquiry* (early view: Doi: 10.1111/lsi.12260).

Meguerditchian, V. (2012). "Relatives of Missing Propose Draft Law," *The Daily Star,* February 25, 2012.

Mendeloff, D. (2009). "Trauma and Vengeance: Assessing the Psychological and Emotional Effects of Post-Conflict Justice," *Human Rights Quarterly,* 31(3), 592–623.

Méndez, J. (2001). "National Reconciliation, Transnational Justice, and the International Criminal Court," *Ethics and International Affairs,* 15(1), 25–44.

Méndez, J. (2011). *Taking a Stand. The Evolution of Human Rights.* Basingstoke: Palgrave.

Méndez, J. & Vivanco, J. (1990). "Disappearances and the Inter-American Court: Reflections on a Litigation Experience," *Hamline Law Review,* 13, 507.

Meyer, D. (2004). "Protest and Political Opportunities," *Annual Review of Sociology,* 30, 125–145.

Minow, M. (1999). *Between Vengeance and Forgiveness: Facing History after Genocide and Mass Violence.* London: New Beacon.

Minow, M. (2002). "Breaking the Cycles of Hatred," in *Breaking the Cycles of Hatred: Memory, Law and Repair.* Minow, M. (Ed.), Princeton: Princeton University Press, pp.16–75.

Moon, C. (2008). *Narrating Political Reconciliation: South Africa's Truth and Reconciliation Commission.* Maryland: Lexington Books.

Moon, C. (2013). "Interpreters of the Dead Forensic Knowledge, Human Remains and the Politics of the Past," *Social & Legal Studies,* 22(2), 149–169.

Moon, C. (2016) "Forensic Humanitarianism and the Human Rights of the Dead," *International Social Science Journal.* Doi: 10.1111/issj.12071, also available at:http:// onlinelibrary.wiley.com/doi/10.1111/issj.12071/full (last accessed: Novemebr 28, 2016).

Moreno, F. (1999). "La represión en la posguerra," in *Víctimas de la guerra civil.* Juliá, Santos, Solé, Josep M., Vilarroya, Joan & Casanova, Franc y Julián (Eds.), Madrid: Temas de hoy, pp.277–406.

Moyn, S. (2010). *The Last Utopia*. Cambridge: Harvard University Press.

Mrad, E. (2011). "Some Legal and Political Factors Affecting the Civil Society and Democratization in Lebanon," *International Journal of Civil Society Law*, IX (II), 1–25.

Müftüler-Baç, M. (2005). "Turkey's Political Reforms and the Impact of the European Union," *South European Society and Politics*, 10(1), 17–31.

Munck, G. L. & Verkuilen, J. (2002). "Conceptualizing and Measuring Democracy Evaluating Alternative Indices," *Comparative Political Studies*, 35 (1), 5–34.

Nadelmann, E. (1990). "Global Prohibition Regimes: The Evolution of Norms in International Society," *International Organization*, 44(04), 479–526.

Naqvi, Y. (2006). "The Right to the Truth in International Law: Fact or Fiction?" *International Review of the Red Cross*, 88(862), 245–273.

Navarro, M. (1989). "The Personal is Political: Las Madres de Plaza de Mayo," *Power and Popular Protest: Latin American Social Movements*, Susan, Eckstein (Ed.), Berkeley: University of California Press, pp.241–258.

Nelsen, A. (2009). "Chile Compiles DNA to Identify Remains of 'Disappeared'," *Reuters*, November 2, 2009.

Nesiah, V. (2002). "Overcoming Tensions between Family and Judicial Procedures," *Revue Internationale de la Croix-Rouge/International Review of the Red Cross*, 84(848), 823–844.

Nettelfield, L. J. (2010). *Courting Democracy in Bosnia and Herzegovina*. Cambridge: Cambridge University Press.

Nettelfield, L. J. & Wagner, S. (2013). *Srebrenica in the Aftermath of Genocide*. Cambridge: Cambridge University Press.

Newman, E. (2002). " 'Transitional Justice': The Impact of Transnational Norms and the UN," in *Recovering from Civil Conflict: Reconciliation, Peace and Development*, Newman, E. & Schnl, A. (Eds.), London: Frank Cass, pp.31–52.

Newman, E. (2004). "The 'New Wars' Debate: A Historical Perspective Is Needed," *Security Dialogue*, 35(2), 173–189.

Nkadimeng, T. (2013) "My Sister's Heart," December 26, 2013, news24.com, available at: www.news24.com/Archives/City-Press/My-sisters-heart-20150430 (last accessed: July 6, 2016).

Nolen, S. (2007). "What's Bred in the Bones," *The Globe and Mail*, October 20, 2007, p.F1.

Nosiglia, J. (2007). *Botín de guerra*. Buenos Aires: Cooperativa Tierra Fértil.

Ocampo, L. (1999). "Beyond Punishment: Justice in the Wake of Massive Crimes in Argentina," *Journal of International Affairs*, 52(2), 669.

O'Donnel, G., Schmitter, P. & Whitehead, L. (1986). *Transitions from Authoritarian Rule*, Vols. I–IV. Baltimore: Johns Hopkins University Press.

Olsen, T., Payne, L. & Reiter, A. (2010). "The Justice Balance: When Transitional Justice Improves Human Rights and Democracy," *Human Rights Quarterly*, 32 (4), 980–1007.

Orentlicher, D. (1991). "Settling Accounts: The Duty to Prosecute Human Rights Violations of a Prior Regime," *Yale Law Journal*, 100(8), 2537–2615.

Osiel, M. (1986). "The Making of Human Rights Policy in Argentina: The Impact of Ideas and Interests on a Legal Conflict," *Journal of Latin American Studies*, 18 (01), 135–180.

Papadakis, Y. (1993). "The Politics of Memory and Forgetting," *Journal of Mediterranean Studies*, 3(1), 139–154.

Parashos, A. (2009). "Μάρτυρας Δολοφονίας Αιχμαλώτων', Καθημερινή," August 11, 2009, p.3.

Paroutis, S. (1999). "Υπόθεση Αγνοουμενων:Ανοίγουν οι Τάφοι των «Αγνώστων»," Πολίτης, June 3, 1999, p.5.

Patrick, R. (1976). *Political Geography and the Cyprus Conflict. 1963–1971*. Waterloo: Department of Geography, University of Waterloo.

Paul, A. (2010). *Katyn: Stalin's Massacre and the Triumph of Truth*. DeKalb: Northern Illinois University Press.

Penchaszadeh, V. (2011). "Forced Disappearance and Suppression of Identity of Children in Argentina: Experiences in Genetic Identification," in *Racial Identities, Genetic Ancestry, and Health in South America: Argentina, Brazil, Colombia, and Uruguay*. Gibbon, S., Santos, R. & Monica, Sans. New York: Palgrave Macmillan, pp.213–243.

Penchaszadeh, V. (2015). "Ethical, Legal and Social Issues in Restoring Genetic Identity after Forced Disappearance and Suppression of Identity in Argentina," *Journal of Community Genetics*, 6(3), 1–7.

Pérez-Sales, P., Durán-Pérez, T. & Herzfeld, R. B. (2000). "Long-term Psychosocial Consequences in First-degree Relatives of People Detained-Disappeared or Executed for Political Reasons in Chile. A Study in Mapuce and Non-Mapuce Persons," *Psicothema*, 12(Suplemento), 109–116.

Pierson, P. (2000). "Increasing Returns, Path Dependence, and the Study of Politics," *American Political Science Review*, 94(02), 251–267.

Pierson, P. (2004). *Politics in Time: History, Institutions, and Social Analysis*. Princeton: Princeton University Press.

Poe, S., Carey, S. & Vazquez, T. (2001). "How are these Pictures Different? A Quantitative Comparison of the US State Department and Amnesty International Human Rights Reports, 1976–1995," *Human Rights Quarterly*, 23(3), 650–677.

Popkin, M. & Roht-Arriaza, N. (1995). "Truth as Justice: Investigatory Commissions in Latin America," *Law & Social Inquiry*, 20(1)(Winter), 79–116.

Quinn, J. (2007). "Social Reconstruction in Uganda: The Role of Customary Mechanisms in Transitional Justice," *Human Rights Review*, 8(4), 389–407.

Quinn, J. & Freeman, M. (2003). "Lessons Learned: Practical Lessons Gleaned from Inside the Truth Commissions of Guatemala and South Africa," *Human Rights Quarterly*, 25(4), 1117–1149.

Quirk, G. J. & Casco, L. (1994). "Stress Disorders of Families of the Disappeared: A Controlled Study in Honduras," *Social Science & Medicine*, 39(12), 1675–1679.

Ramos, H., Ron, J. & Thoms, O. (2007). "Shaping the Northern Media's Human Rights Coverage, 1986–2000," *Journal of Peace Research*, 44(4), 385–406.

Requa, M. (2012). "A Human Rights Triumph? Dictatorship-Era Crimes and the Chilean Supreme Court," *Human Rights Law Review*, 12(1), 79–106.

Richmond, O. (2011). *Liberal Peace Transitions: Between Statebuilding and Peacebuilding*. Edinburgh: Edinburgh University Press.

Risse, T. & Sikkink, K. (1999). "The Socialization of International Human Rights Norms into Domestic Practices: An Introduction," in *The Power of Human Rights: International Norms and Domestic Change*. Risse, T., Ropp, S. & Sikkink, K. (Eds.), Cambridge: Cambridge University Press, pp.1–38.

Robben, A. (2000). "State Terror in the Netherworld: Disappearance and Reburial in Argentina," in *Death Squad: The Anthropology of State Terror*. Sluka, J. (Ed.), Philadelphia: University of Pennsylvania Press.

Robben, A. (2005a). *Political Violence and Trauma in Argentina*. Philadelphia: University of Pennsylvania Press.

Robben, A. (2005b). "How Traumatized Societies Remember: The Aftermath of Argentina's Dirty War," *Cultural Critique*, 59(1), 120–164.

Robben, A. (2014). "Massive Violent Death and Contested National Mourning in Post-Authoritarian Chile and Argentina: A Sociocultural Application of the Dual Process Model," *Death Studies*, 38(5), 335–345.

Robben, A. (2015) "Exhumations, Territoriality, and Necropolitics in Chile and Argentina," in *Necropolitics. Mass Graves and Exhumations in the Age of Human Rights*. Ferrándiz, F. & Robben, A. (Eds.), Philadelphia: University of Pennsylvania Press, pp. 53–75.

Robins, S. (2011). "Towards Victim-centred Transitional Justice: Understanding the Needs of Families of the Disappeared in Post-conflict Nepal," *International Journal of Transitional Justice*, 5(1), 75–98.

Robins, S. (2013). *Families of the Missing. A Test for Contemporary Approaches to Transitional Justice*. New York: Routledge.

Robinson, J. & Acemoglou, D. (2012). *Why Nations Fail: The Origins of Power, Prosperity, and Poverty*. New York: Crown Business.

Roht-Arriaza, N. (2005). *The Pinochet Effect: Transnational Justice in the Age of Human Rights*. Philadelphia: University of Pennsylvania Press.

Roht-Arriaza, N. (2009). "The Multiple Prosecutions of Augusto Pinochet," in *Prosecuting Heads of State*. Lutz, E. & Reiger, C. (Eds.), Cambridge: Cambridge University Press, pp.77–94.

Roht-Arriaza, N. & Mariezcurrena, J. (2006). *Transitional Justice in the Twenty-First Century: Beyond Truth versus Justice.* Cambridge: Cambridge University Press.

Rohter, L. (2006). "Shinning a Light into the Abyss of Chile's Dictatorship," *New York Times*, February 25, 2006, p.4.

Ron, J. (1997). "Varying Methods of State Violence," *International Organization*, 51(02), 275–300.

Ron, J., Ramos, H. & Rodgers, K. (2005). "Transnational Information Politics: NGO Human Rights Reporting, 1986–2000," *International Studies Quarterly*, 49 (3), 557–588.

Ropp, S. & Sikkink, K. (1999) "International Norms and Domestic Politics in Chile and Guatemala," in *The Power of Human Rights: International Norms and Domestic Change.* Risse, T., Ropp, S. & Sikkink, K. (Eds.), Cambridge: Cambridge University Press, pp.172–204.

Rosenblatt, A. (2015). *Last Rights: Forensic Science, Human Rights, and the Politics of Mass Graves.* California: Stanford University Press.

Ross, F. C. (2003). *Bearing Witness: Women and the Truth and Reconciliation Commission in South Africa.* Virginia: Pluto Press.

Rousseau, N. (2009). "The Farm, the River and the Picnic Spot: Topographies of Terror," *African Studies*, 68(3), 351–369.

Rousseau, N. (2015). "Identification, Politics, Disciplines: Missing Persons and Colonial Skeletons in South Africa," in *Human Remains and Identification: Mass Violence, Genocide and the "Forensic Turn."* Anstett, É. & Dreyfus, J. M. (Eds.), Oxford University Press, pp.175–202.

Rowayheb, M. G. & Ouaiss, M. (2015). "The Committee of the Parents of the Missing and Disappeared: 30 Years of Struggle and Protest," *Middle Eastern Studies*, 51(6), 1010–1026.

Salama, C. (1992). *Tumbas anónimas: informe sobre la identificación de restos de víctimas de la represión ilegal.* Buenos Aires: Equipo Argentino de Anthropologia Forense, Catalogos Editora.

Sandal, N. (2011). "Religious Actors as Epistemic Communities in Conflict Transformation: The Cases of South Africa and Northern Ireland," *Review of International Studies*, 37(3), 929–949.

Sanford, V. (2003). *Buried Secrets: Truth and Human Rights in Guatemala.* Basingstoke: Palgrave Macmillan.

Sant Cassia, P. (2005). *Bodies of Evidence. Burial, Memory and the Recovery of Missing Persons in Cyprus.* Oxford: Berghahn Books.

Sant Cassia, P. (2006). "Guarding Each Other's Dead, Mourning One's Own: The Problem of Missing Persons and Missing Pasts in Cyprus," *South European, Society & Politics*, 11(1), 111–128.

Sarkin, J. (2004). *Carrots and Sticks: The TRC and the South African Amnesty Process.* Cambridge: Intersentia.

Sarkin, J. (2015). "Dealing with Enforced Disappearances in South Africa (With a Focus on the Nokuthula Simelane Case) and Around the World. The Need to Ensure Progress on the Rights to Truth, Justice and Reparations in Practice," *Speculum Juris Volume*, 29(PART 1), 20–48.

Scovazzi, T. & Citroni, G. (2007). *The Struggle against Enforced Disappearance and the 2007 UN Convention*. Leiden: Martinus Nihoff Publishers.

Seekings, J. & Nattrass, N. (2008). *Class, Race, and Inequality in South Africa*. New Haven: Yale University Press.

Sewell, W. (1996). "Three Temporalities: Toward an Eventful Sociology," in *The Historic Turn in the Human Sciences*. McDonald, T. J. (Ed.), Anne Arbor: University of Michigan Press, pp.245–280.

Shadid, A. (2006). "Mothers Press Issues of War That Lebanese Want to Forget; Loved Ones Still Missing From Years of Conflict," *Washington Post Foreign Service*, A Section; A01, January 21, 2006.

Shelton, D. (1980). "International Enforcement of Human Rights: Effectiveness and Alternatives," *Proceedings of the Annual Meeting of American Society of International Law*, 74(April 17–19, April 1980), 6–16.

Sikkink, K. (2004). *Mixed Signals, US Human Rights Policy and Latin America*. Ithaca: Cornell University Press.

Sikkink, K. (2008). "From Pariah State to Global Protagonist: Argentina and the Struggle for International Human Rights," *Latin America Politics and Society*, 50 (1), 1–29.

Sikkink, K. (2011). *The Justice Cascade: How Human Rights Prosecutions Are Changing World Politics* (The Norton Series in World Politics). London: WW Norton & Company.

Sikkink, K. & Walling, C. (2007). "The Impact of Human Rights Trials in Latin America," *Journal of Peace Research*, 44(4), 427–445.

Skaar, E. (2011). *Judicial Independence and Human Rights in Latin America: Violations, Politics, and Prosecution*. Berlin: Springer.

Skinner, M. (2007). "Hapless in Afghanistan: Forensic Archaeology in a Political Maelstrom," in *Forensic Archaeology and Human Rights Violations*. Ferllini, R. (Ed.), Springfield: Charles C Thomas Publisher, pp.233–265.

Smith, D. (2015). "South African Death Squad Leader Eugene de Kock to be Freed from Jail," *The Guardian*, January 30, 2015.

Snow, C. & Bihurriet, M. J. (1992). "An Epidemiology of Homicide: Ningún Nombre Burials in the Province of Buenos Aires from 1970 to 1984," *Human Rights and Statistics: Getting the Record Straight*. Philadelphia: University of Pennsylvania press, pp.328–363.

Snow, C. C., Stover, E. & Hannibal, K. (1989). "Scientists as Detectives-Investigating Human-Rights," *Technology Review*, 92(2), 42.

Snow, D. A. & Benford, R. D. (1992). "Master Frames and Cycles of Protest," in *Frontiers in Social Movement Theory*, Morris, A. D. (Ed.), New Haven: Yale University Press, pp.133–155.

Snow, D. A., Rochford, Jr, E. B., Worden, S. K. & Benford, R. D. (1986). "Frame Alignment Processes, Micromobilization, and Movement Participation," *American Sociological Review*, 51(4), 464–481.

Solomonidou, A. (2010). "Ξενοφών Καλλής: Ποτέ Ξανά Αγνοούμενοι – Ποτέ Ξανά Πόλεμος," *Fileleftheros*, August 29, 2010, p.10.

Sperling, L., Klieman, G. & Ap, L. (2008). "Political Changes Influence Forensic Science in Colombia," *Forensic Magazine*, August 1, 2008, also available at: www.forensicmag.com/articles/2008/08/political-changes-influence-forensic-science-colombia#.Uv3zMvZvBtk (last accessed: November 28, 2016).

Sriram, L. (2012). "The Special Tribunal for Lebanon, Promoting Justice or Prolonging Conflict?" *Conciliation Resources*, also available at: www.c-r.org/accord-article/special-tribunal-lebanon (last accessed: January 9, 2014).

Sriram, C. L. (2004). *Confronting Past Human Rights Violations: Justice vs. Peace in Times of Transition*. London: Frank Cass.

Stefanovic, D., Loizides, N., & Psaltis, C. (2016). "Attitudes of Victims towards Transitional Justice: The Case of Cyprus," Conference paper, "Referendums and Peace Processes," October 26 & 27, 2016, Nicosia, Cyprus.

Stover, E. (1985). "Scientists Aid Search for Argentina's 'Desaparecidos'," *Science*, 230(4721), 56–57.

Stover, E. & Shigekane, R. (2004). "Exhumation of Mass Graves: Balancing Legal and Humanitarian Needs," in *My Neighbor, My Enemy: Justice and Community in the Aftermath of Mass Atrocity*. Stover, E. & Weinstein, H. M. (Eds.), Cambridge: Cambridge University Press, pp.85–104.

Stover, E., Sissons, M., Pham, P. & Vinck, P. (2008). "Justice on Hold: Accountability and Social Reconstruction in Iraq," *International Review of the Red Cross*, 90(869), 5–28.

Subotic, J. (2009). *Hijacked Justice: Dealing with the Past in the Balkans*. Ithaca: Cornell University Press.

Tarrow, S. (1998). *Power in Movement. Social Movements and Contentious Politics*, 2nd edition. Cambridge: Cambridge University Press.

Tarrow, S. & Tilly, C. (2007). "Contentious Politics and Social Movements," *The Oxford Handbook of Comparative Politics*. Oxford: Oxford University Press, pp.435–460.

Tay, N. (2013). "Bodies Exhumed in ANC 'Murder' Case Linked to Winnie Mandela," *Independent*, March12, 2013.

Tayler, W. (2001). "Background to the Elaboration of the Draft International Convention on the Protection of All Persons from Forced Disappearance," *Review-International Commission of Jurists*, 62, 63–72.

Thelen, K. (2000). "Timing and Temporality in the Analysis of Institutional Evolution and Change," *Studies in American Political Development*, 14(01), 101–108.

Theodoulou, G. (2009). "Ανοίγουν οι γνωστοί ομαδικοί τάφοι αγνώστων," *Αλήθεια*, February 2, 2009, p.13.

Thomas, G. (2011). *Contesting Legitimacy in Chile: Familial Ideals, Citizenship, and Political Struggle 1970–1990*. Philadelphia: University of Pennsylvania Press.

Thoms, O., James, R. & Roland, P. (2010). "State-level Effects of Transitional Justice: What Do We Know?" *International Journal of Transitional Justice*, 4 (3), 329–354.

Tidball-Binz, M. (2006). "Forensic Investigations into the Missing," in *Forensic Anthropology and Medicine*. Schmitt, A., Cunha, E. & Pinheiro, J., New York: Humana Press, pp.383–407.

Tilly, C. (1984). *Big Structures, Large Processes, Huge Comparisons*. New York: Russell Sage Foundation.

Tilly, C. (1995). *Popular Contention in Great Britain, 1758–1834*. London: Routledge.

Torrens, J. (1999). "The Many Faces of Amnesty," *America*, July 17–24, 181(2), 12–17.

TRC Report. (2003). *Truth and Reconciliation Commission of South Africa Report*, released on March 21, 2003, also available at: www.info.gov.za/otherdocs/2003/trc/ (last accessed: November 28, 2016).

Tremlett, G. (2008). "Spanish Judge Orders Poet García Lorca's Grave to be Opened," *The Guardian*, October 16, 2008, also available at: www.theguardian.com/world/2008/oct/16/lorca-grave-spain (last accessed: November 28, 2016).

UDP (2009). "Perceptions of Human Rights in the National Public Opinion Survey," Santiago Chile: University Diego Portales, also available at: www.icso.cl/observatorio-derechos-humanos/ (last accessed: November 28, 2016).

UDP (2013). "Truth, Justice and Memory for Dictatorship-Era Human Rights Violations, 40 Years after the Military Coup," Annual Report of the Center for Human Rights of the University Diego Portales, also available at: www.icso.cl/observatorio-derechos-humanos/ (last accessed: November 28, 2016).

UNFICYP (2007). "The UN in Cyprus: An Inter-communal Survey of Public Opinion by UNFICYP," available at: www.unficyp.org/nqcontent.cfm?a_id=1324 (last accessed: September 20, 2011).

United Nations (1981). "General Assembly Resolution," A/RES/34/164, December 16, 1981.

United Nations (2006). "Rule of Law Tools for Post-conflict States: Truth Commissions," HR/PUB/06/1, also available at: www.ohchr.org/Documents/Publications/RuleoflawTruthCommissionsen.pdf (last accessed: November 28, 2016).

United Nations (2010). "Report of the UN High Commissioner for Human Rights on the Situation of Human Rights in Colombia," A/HRC/13/72, March 4, 2010.

United Nations (2015). "Report of the Special Rapporteur on the Promotion of Truth, Justice, Reparation and Guarantees of Non-Recurrence, Pablo de Greiff," A/.HRC/30/42, September 7, 2015.

UNWGEID (2013). "Report of the Working Group on Enforced or Involuntary Disappearances: Mission to Chile," A/HRC/22/45, January 29, 2013.

Urbsaitis, B. M. (2009). *Wounded Healers & Reconciliation Fatigue: The Search for Social Justice & Sustainable Development in South Africa.* VDM: Verlag.

Vallejo-Nájera, J. A. (1937). *Eugenesia de la Hispanidad y Regeneración de la Raza.* Madrid: Editorial Española.

Varas, C. G. & Leiva, M. I. (2012). "Managing Commingled Remains from Mass Graves: Considerations, Implications and Recommendations from a Human Rights Case in Chile," *Forensic Science International,* 219(1), 19–24.

Varney, H. & Sarkin, J. (1997). "Failing to Pierce the Hit Squad Veil: An Analysis of the Malan Trial," *South African Journal of Criminal Justice,* 10, 141–161.

Verbitsky, H. (2005). *Confessions of an Argentine Dirty Warrior: A Firsthand Account of Atrocity.* New York: The New Press.

Vibhute, K. (2008). "The 2007 International Convention against Enforced Disappearance: Some Reflections," *Mizan Law Review,* 2(2), 281–310.

Vinjamuri, L. (2010). "Deterrence, Democracy, and the Pursuit of International Justice," *Ethics & International Affairs,* 24(2), 191–211.

Vinjamuri, L. & Snyder, J. (2004). "Advocacy and Scholarship in the Study of International War Crime Tribunals and Transitional Justice," *Annual Review of Political Science,* 7, 345–362.

Wagner, S. (2008). *To Know Where He Lies: DNA Technology and the Search for Srebrenica's Missing.* Oakland: University of California Press.

Wagner, S. & Kešetović, R. (2016). "Absent Bodies, Absent Knowledge: Forensic Work of Identifying Srebrenica's Missing and the Social Experiences of Families," *Missing Persons: Multidisciplinary Perspectives on the Disappeared.* Congram, D. (Ed.), Toronto: Canadian Scholars' Press, pp. 42–60.

Walsh, F. (2007). "Traumatic Loss and Major Disasters: Strengthening Family and Community Resilience," *Family Process,* 46(2), 207–227.

Wiebelhaus-Brahm, E. (2010). *Truth Commissions and Transitional Societies. The Impact on Human Rights and Democracy.* New York: Routledge.

Wierda, M., Nassar, H. & Maalouf, L. (2007). "Early Reflections on Local Perceptions, Legitimacy and Legacy of the Special Tribunal for Lebanon," *Journal of International Criminal Justice,* 5, 1065–1081.

Wilde, A. (1999). "Irruptions of Memory: Expressive Politics in Chile's Transition to Democracy," *Journal of Latin American Studies,* 31, 473–500.

Wilson, R. (2001). *The Politics of Truth and Reconciliation in South Africa: Legitimizing the Post-Apartheid State.* Cambridge: Cambridge University Press.

Wood, R. M. & Mark, G. (2010). "The Political Terror Scale (PTS): A Re-introduction and a Comparison to CIRI," *Human Rights Quarterly*, 32 (2), 367–400.

Yakinthou, C. (2008). "The Quiet Deflation of Den Xehno? Changes in the Greek–Cypriot Communal Narrative on the Missing Persons in Cyprus," *Cyprus Review*, 20(1), 15–33.

Yakinthou, C. (2015). "Living with the Shadows of the Past the Impact of Disappearance on Wives of the Missing in Lebanon," International Center for Transitional Justice, March 2015.

Young, M. (2000). "The Sneer of Memory: Lebanon's Disappeared and Postwar Culture," *Middle East Report*, 217, 42–45.

Young, D. (2014). "Jean McConville Murder Arrest Based on Boston Tape," *Irish Independent*, March 22, 2014, also available at: www.independent.ie/irish-news /jean-mcconville-murder-arrest-based-on-boston-tape-30116713.html   (last accessed: November 28, 2016).

Zalaquett, J. (1991). "Balancing Ethical Imperatives and Political Constraints: The Dilemma of New Democracies Confronting Past Human Rights Violations," *Hastings Law Journal*, 43, 1425–1438.

Zalaquett, J. (1990). "Confronting Human Rights Violations Committed by Former Governments: Applicable Principles and Political Constraints," *Hamline Law. Review*, 13, 623.

Zanocco, G. (2002). " 'Concealed' Report Emerges on Victims' Remains," *Inter-Press Service*, August 22, 2002.

INDEX

AAAS. *See* American Association for the Advancement of Sciences
abductions, 45, 79, 116, 191. *See also* disappearances
accountability, 4, 30–31, 84. *See also* justice cascade; retributive justice
  in Argentina, 74
  CMP and, 172–174
  EAAF and, 96, 98
  families of disappeared and, 111–126
  ICMP and, 103
  mobilization of families and, 12–13
  technologies of truth and, 109–110
ACT for the disappeared, 144, 150
Adler, Emanuel, 93, 94
AFAD. *See* Asian Federation against Involuntary Disappearances in Chile
AFASD, 82
AFDD. *See* Association of Relatives of Detained-Disappeared
African National Congress (ANC), 188–189
  commissions of inquiry and, 189
  disappearances and, 186–187
  restorative justice and, 200–204
  retributive justice and, 185
  TRC and, 189–190, 198
  victimhood and, 202–204, 207
AKP. *See* Justice and Development Party
ALAF. *See* Latin American Forensic Anthropology Association
Alfonsín, Raúl, 70–71, 73
Ali Talat, Mehmet, 169
Alliende, Salvador, 1
American Association for the Advancement of Sciences (AAAS), 72, 95–96, 107

Amin, Idi, 104
amnesty, 11
  in Argentina, 77, 78–80, 83, 116
  in Chile, 12, 116, 225–226
  disappearances and, 115, 116
  institutionalized silence, 131
  in Lebanon, 56, 129–130, 139–142
  retributive justice and, 206
  in South Africa, 188–189, 199–200
  transitional justice and, 3–4, 29, 31–32, 40
  TRC and, 190, 193
  truth commissions and, 104
  truth recovery and, 41, 42, 140, 206, 238–239
Amnesty International, 26, 113, 121
  Argentina and, 69
  disappearances and, 21, 22, 25, 88, 89, 112
  documentation by, 114
  Lebanon and, 141–142
ANC. *See* African National Congress
Andreu, Federico, 113, 119
Antigone, 82, 88
Antokoletz, María Adela, 75
Apartheid, 1, 185–186
APDH. *See* Permanent Assembly for Human Rights
Argentina. *See also* Due Obedience Law; Grandmothers; Mothers; Mothers and Grandmothers; *Punto Final* (Full Stop) law
  accountability in, 74
  amnesty in, 77, 78–80, 83, 116
  Amnesty International and, 69
  Chile and, 209
  democratization and, 70–71
  disappearances in, 46, 61–62, 64–65, 66, 69, 210

IACHR and, 69–70
judiciary in, 146
mobilization of families in, 61–77
right to truth and, 79, 81
Sikkink on, 81
timing and, 63, 78–81
transitional justice in, 10, 23, 63,
    77–81
truth trials in, 123–124
Argentine Forensic Anthropology
    Team (EAAF), 91, 96–98, 194
accountability and, 96, 98
Chile and, 217
countries worked in, 97, 101–102
Cyprus and, 155
DNA and, 99–100
families of disappeared and, 103
forensic epistemic community and,
    96–98
Aronson, Jay, 186
Asian Federation against Involuntary
    Disappearances in Chile (AFAD),
    82, 117, 120–121
Asociación Civil Abuelas de Plaza
    de Mayo (Association of
    Grandmothers of May Square).
    See Grandmothers
Asociación Madres de Plaza de Mayo
    (Association of Mothers of May
    Square). See Mothers
Association of Relatives of Detained-
    Disappeared (Agrupación de
    Familiares de Detenidos
    Desaparecidos, AFDD), 213–214,
    230–231
AUC. See United Self Defense forces of
    Colombia
Aylwin, Patricio, 215–216, 232

Bakiner, O., 225
Balkans, exhumations in, 36
de Baravalle, Marta, 75
de Bazze, Dora, 69
Benedetti, Mario, 120
Benford, R., 64
Biko, Steve, 199–200
Bolivia, 210
Bomberger, Kathryne, 99

de Bonafini, Hebe, 63–64, 74, 75
Bosnia, 90, 99–100
Boss, Pauline, 85, 86
Boston tapes, 176
Van Boven, Theo, 114, 115
Brazil, 42
Brewer, John, 205
bridge figures, 113–114, 117–118
Britain, 70
broader truth, 32, 38–39, 49, 51,
    173, 239
Brysk, Alison, 22, 67
Bureau of Human Rights, 68

Cabezas, Diego, 220, 228
Cardenas, Sonia, 25
Carlotto, Estela, 80, 83
Carter administration, 68
case selection, 54–57
Center for Legal and Social Studies
    (CELS), 68, 78–79, 124
Chaftari, Assaad, 144
Chamoun, Dany, 141
Chile, 114, 208–232. See also
    Association of Relatives of
    Detained-Disappeared; Conjunto
    Folclor; Cuecas; Medical Legal
    Service; Rettig Commission;
    Revolutionary Left Movement;
    Roundtable; Vicaria de
    Solidaridad
amnesty in, 12, 116, 225–226
Argentina and, 209
democratization and, 225
disappearances in, 1, 46, 203,
    208–213, 217–218, 221
DNA and, 218
EAAF and, 217
executions in, 61, 211, 218
exhumations in, 171, 217–224
families of disappeared in, 227–228
forensic truth in, 50–51, 216–224
hunger strikes in, 213
judiciary in, 47, 151, 210, 223,
    225–231, 241
mobilization of families in, 2, 12–13,
    88, 208–209, 213–215
mothers in, 213

Chile (cont.)
  negotiated transitions in, 209
  perpetrators in, 220–221, 222,
    224–225
  political opportunities in, 224
  politics of measurement in, 211
  reparations in, 216–217, 219
  retributive justice and, 57, 224–231,
    242–243
  secret police in, 209, 212, 220
  transitional justice in, 7–8
  trials in, 229–231
  truth commissions and, 215–219,
    221–224
  truth recovery in, 42, 47, 209–210,
    215–224, 231–232
Chilean Forensic Anthropology Team
  (GAF), 97
Christians, Lebanon and, 133
Cingranelli and Richards database
  (CIRI), 18, 21–23
Citroni, Gabriella, 120
civil war, Lebanon and, 129, 132–135
CLAMOR. See Committee for the
  Defense of HR in Southern Cone
Clark, Anne Marie, 22–23, 89, 113
Clerides, Glafkos, 170
Clinton, Bill, 98–99
CMP. See Committee on Missing
  Persons
CNRR. See National Corporation for
  Reparations and Reconciliation
CODEH. See Comite para la Defensa
  de los Derechos Humanos en
  Honduras
Cold War, 93
Colombia, 50, 177–179, 243. See also
  Peace and Justice Law; United Self
  Defense forces of Colombia
Comisión Económica para América
  Latina (ECLAC), 213–214
Comite para la Defensea de los Derechos
  Humanos en Honduras
  (CODEH), 115
Commission of Inquiry into
  Complaints by Former African
  Congress Prisoners and
  Detainees, 189

commissions of inquiry, 32, 139, 189
Committee for the Defense of HR in
  Southern Cone (CLAMOR), 70
Committee of the Families of the
  Kidnapped and Disappeared in
  Lebanon, 135–137, 153
Committee on Missing Persons (CMP),
  11, 50, 51, 56, 87, 156, 163–174
  accountability and, 172–174
  broader truth and, 173
  DNA and, 171
  exhumations and, 170–171, 222
  families of disappeared and, 172–173
  forensic truth and, 155, 174, 242
  ICRC and, 169
  perpetrators and, 171
  right to truth and, 172–173
  timing and, 243–244
  Turkish Cypriots and, 170
  UN and, 169–170
CONADEP. See National Commission
  on the Disappearance of Persons
Concertación, 215
Concha, Sergio, 227
Conjunto Folclor, 213
contentious politics, 51–52, 64
country-disappearances-years, 27–29
Cuecas, 213
Cyprus, 154–180. See also Committee
  on Missing Persons; Ethniki
  Organosis Kyprion Agoniston;
  London-Zurich Agreements;
  Republic of Cyprus; Taksim
  democratization and, 175
  depoliticization in, 51
  disappearances in, 1, 23, 156–158
  DNA and, 166–167
  EAAF and, 155
  ECtHR and, 109, 158, 167
  exhumations in, 12, 72, 88, 90, 161,
    163–164, 165
  forensic truth in, 154, 155–156,
    163–164, 169–174
  frozen conflicts and, 56, 154
  Greece and, 156–157
  ICMP and, 155
  institutionalized silence in, 11,
    155–156, 160–162

international allies and, 175
invasion/peace operation in,
    154–155, 156–157
Lebanon and, 154–155, 175
mobilization of families in, 2,
    158–164
mothers in, 159
political opportunities in, 158
politics of measurement in, 165–166
retributive justice and, 73
transitional justice in, 7, 17
truth recovery in, 11–12, 42, 46, 62
Turkey and, 154–155, 156–157,
    160–162

databases, 9–10, 24–25. *See also*
    Cingranelli and Richards database;
    Disappeared and Missing
    Database
exhumations and, 26–27
qualitative studies and, 30, 54
qualitative-driven, 18–19
theory testing and, 30–36
transitional justice and, 7, 17–36
death certificates, disappearances
    and, 87
death rituals, mourning and, 86–87
Declaration (1992), 118
democratization
    Argentina and, 70–71
    Chile and, 225
    Cyprus and, 175
    exhumations and, 146
    Lebanon and, 142, 146–147, 152
    mobilization of families and, 52, 147
    transitional justice and, 40–41
    truth recovery and, 231
Denktas, Rauf, 169, 170
depoliticization, 51
Derian, Patricia, 117–118
Díaz, Viviana, 212–214, 227
Diez-Bacalso, Mary Aileen, 120–121
DIMIDA. *See* Disappeared and Missing
    Database
DINA. *See* secret police
disappearances, 1–2, 14, 85–89, 112. *See*
    also abductions
amnesty and, 115, 116

Amnesty International and, 21, 22,
    25, 88, 89, 112
ANC and, 186–187
in Argentina, 46, 61–62, 64–65, 66,
    69, 210
boomerang effect of, 208–209,
    233–234
in Chile, 1, 46, 203, 208–213,
    217–218, 221
CIRI and, 21–23
in Colombia, 177–178
in Cyprus, 1, 23, 156–158
death certificates and, 87
documentation of, 67–68
families of disappeared and, 85–89
forensic cascade and, 84–85
IACHR and, 122–123
Israel and, 134
Latin America and, 112, 210
in Lebanon, 1, 11, 132–135
legal framework for, 112–113,
    115–116, 117–122
missing and, 13–14, 182–183
of Mothers, 67
mourning and, 85–88
in Northern Ireland, 22, 23, 175
Pinochet and, 208–209, 212
post-authoritarian societies and,
    47–48
post-conflict societies and, 47–48
right to truth and, 122–123
RoC and, 164–167
in South Africa, 1, 185–188
in Spain, 62
trauma and, 85–86
TRC and, 191–192, 196–199, 206
truth commissions and, 105,
    106–107, 234
Turkey and, 167–169
universal instrument and, 117–122
victims and, 188, 233–234
Disappeared and Missing Database
    (DIMIDA), 7, 24, 25–27
country-disappearances-years in,
    27–29
sources for, 25, 29, 32
Dlamini, Adelaide, 203–204
DNA, 80

DNA (cont.)
  Chile and, 218
  CMP and, 171
  Cyprus and, 166–167
  EAAF and, 99–100
  ICMP and, 99–100
  TRC and, 192–193, 194
documentation, 114
  by Amnesty International, 114
  of disappearances, 67–68
Dorfman, Ariel, 208, 212
Due Obedience Law, 74
Dulitzky, Ariel, 69–70, 81, 116, 123

EAAF. *See* Argentine Forensic
  Anthropology Team
ECLAC. *See* Comisión Económica para
  América Latina
ECtHR. *See* European Court of Human
  Rights
El Salvador, 82
EOKA. *See Ethniki Organosis Kyprion
  Agoniston*
EPAF. *See* Peruvian Forensic
  Anthropology Team
epistemic communities, 93, 94. *See also*
  forensic epistemic community
ethnic violence, truth recovery and, 177
Ethniki Organosis Kyprion Agoniston
  (EOKA), 156
EU. *See* European Union
European Convention of Human
  Rights, 38
European Court of Human Rights
  (ECtHR), 2, 119
  Cyprus and, 109, 158, 167
  Turkey and, 167
European Union (EU), 164, 175
executions, Chile and, 61, 211, 218
exhumations, 5, 8, 42, 235. *See also*
  forensic exhumations;
  humanitarian exhumations
  in Balkans, 36
  in Chile, 171, 217–224
  CMP and, 170–171, 222
  in Cyprus, 12, 72, 88, 90, 161,
    163–164, 165
  databases and, 26–27

democratization and, 146
destructive, 219–221
Grandmothers and, 73
groups conducting, 26
International Convention for the
  Protection of All Persons from
  Enforced Disappearance and, 26
in Lebanon, 135–137
Mothers and, 72
Mothers and Grandmothers and, 72
Nazis and, 94
perpetrators and, 89
security and stability and, 144
in South Africa, 171
in Spain, 72, 82, 92
transitional justice and, 29–30
TRC and, 192–193, 194–196
truth commissions and, 52–53,
  108–109, 221–224
truth recovery and, 42
in Yugoslavia, former, 98–99
external actors, 55
  Lebanon and, 130
  Mothers and Grandmothers and,
    68–70
  TRC and, 183–184
  truth recovery and, 35–36, 41, 179
extraordinary renditions, 25

FAFG. *See* Guatemalan Forensic
  Anthropology Foundation
Falkland Islands, 70
families of disappeared, 119–120. *See
  also* mobilization of families
  accountability and, 111–126
  in Chile, 227–228
  CMP and, 172–173
  disappearances and, 85–89
  EAAF and, 103
  human rights and, 125–126
  in Lebanon, 132
  in South Africa, 2, 138, 203, 205
  TRC and, 182–183, 184, 193–194
  truth recovery and, 53
FEDEFAM. *See* Latin American
  Federation of Associations of
  Relatives of Detained-
  Disappeared

Fighters for Peace, 144
Finnemore, M., 93
Follow-Up Committee, 137
Fonderbrider, Luis, 96, 221–222
forensic cascade, 84, 89, 103–104,
    235–237
  disappearances and, 84–85
  justice cascade and, 109, 235–236
  transitional justice and, 91
  truth recovery and, 10
forensic epistemic community, 84,
    92–94, 96, 100–104
  EAAF and, 96–98
  funding and, 102–103
  ICMP and, 100
forensic exhumations, 90–91, 95–96,
    99, 103
forensic sciences. *See* technologies of
    truth
forensic truth, 32, 37–38, 48–49, 179
  in Chile, 50–51, 216–224
  CMP and, 155, 174, 242
  in Cyprus, 154, 155–156, 163–164,
    169–174
  depoliticization and, 51
  Latin America and, 94–95
  in Lebanon, 142–143
  mobilization of families and, 174
  in Northern Ireland, 50
  perpetrators and, 50–51
  policy and, 50–51
  post-authoritarian societies and,
    47, 195
  post-conflict societies and, 47
  security and stability and, 50,
    151–152, 238–239
  TRC and, 185, 191–196
Founding Line, 75
framing strategies, 52, 64–67, 75,
    113
France, 118
Franco, Francisco, 92
Freedom House, 40
Freeman, Mark, 181
Frei Ruiz-Tagle, Eduardo, 217
de Frouville, Olivier, 117
frozen conflicts, Cyprus and, 56, 154
Full Stop (*Punto Final*) law, 74, 116

funding, forensic epistemic community
    and, 102–103

GAF. *See* Chilean Forensic
    Anthropology Team
Gahona, Evelyn, 213
Garcia, Maria Ines, 80
García Lorca, Federico, 72
Garzon, Baltazar, 226, 227
Geagea, Samir, 141–142
Goldstone Commission, 189
Good Friday Agreement, 176
Grandmothers of the Disappeared,
    65–66, 70, 75–77
  CONADEP and, 71–72
  exhumations and, 73
  forensic exhumations and, 95–96
  framing strategies and, 75
  right to identity and, 81–82
  truth recovery and, 78–80
Grant, Stefanie, 68, 81, 112, 124–125
Greece, Cyprus and, 156–157
Greek Cypriots, 1, 88, 156–162
de Greiff, Pablo, 125
Guatemala, 45
Guatemalan Forensic Anthropology
    Foundation (FAFG), 97
Guelke, Adrian, 196
Guevara, Ernesto "Che," 210
Guzmán Tapia, Juan, 226

Haas, P. M., 93, 94
Haglund, William, 102
Halwani, Wadad, 129, 153
Hariri, Rafic, 145
Hashisho, Muhieddine, 146–147
Hashisho, Nacouzi, 146–147
Hayner, Priscilla, 191
headscarves, Mothers and
    Grandmothers and, 66
heroicization, TRC and, 198
Herzegovina, 90, 99
Hezbollah, 135
HIJOS, 76
Hirsch, M., 93
Homer, 212
human rights, 68–69
  families of disappeared and, 125–126

human rights (cont.)
  Lebanon and, 149–150
  transitional justice and, 20
  TRC and, 197
Human Rights Institute of the Paris Bar
  Association, 118
Human Rights Watch, 117, 178
humanitarian exhumations, 89–90,
  99, 236
hunger strikes, Chile and, 213
Huntington, Samuel, 3
Hussein, Saddam, 48

IACHR. See Interamerican
  Commission for Human Rights
IACtHR. See Inter-American Court of
  Human Rights
ICLVR. See Independent Commission
  for the Location of Victims'
  Remains
ICMP. See International Commission
  on Missing Persons
ICoJ. See International Commission of
  Jurists
ICRC. See International Committee of
  the Red Cross
ICTJ. See International Center for
  Transitional Justice
ICTY. See International Criminal
  Tribunal for the former
  Yugoslavia
ideal victims, Mothers and
  Grandmothers as, 82
idealist scholars, 36, 53–54, 241–242
IFP. See Inkatha Freedom Party
Iliad, 212
Independent Commission for the
  Location of Victims' Remains
  (ICLVR), 176–177
Inkatha Freedom Party (IFP),
  186–187, 190
institutionalized silence, 8, 32, 37,
  41–42, 48
  amnesty, 131
  in Cyprus, 11, 155–156, 160–162
  in Lebanon, 11, 130–131, 142–148
institutions of truth, 84, 104–109. See
  also truth commissions

technologies of truth and, 85
Interamerican Commission for Human
  Rights (IACHR), 69–70, 81, 118,
  122–123
Inter-American Convention on
  Enforced Disappearance of
  Persons, 119
Inter-American Court of Human
  Rights (IACtHR), 78–79, 115–116,
  123, 125, 229
international actors. See external actors
international allies
  Cyprus and, 175
  Lebanon and, 142–143, 147–151,
  152–153
  mobilization of families and, 52
International Center for Transitional
  Justice (ICTJ), 150, 178
International Commission for Human
  Rights on Colombia, 178
International Commission of Jurists
  (ICoJ), 113, 117, 118
International Commission on Missing
  Persons (ICMP), 98–101
  accountability and, 103
  Cyprus and, 155
  DNA and, 99–100
  forensic epistemic community
  and, 100
  forensic exhumations and, 99
International Committee of the Red
  Cross (ICRC), 13, 101–102, 103,
  122, 132
  CMP and, 169
  Lebanon and, 132, 134
International Convention for the
  Protection of All Persons from
  Enforced Disappearance, 14, 113,
  120–122, 242
  on exhumations, 26
  mobilization of families and, 117,
  120–121
  as universal instrument, 117
International Criminal Investigative
  Training Assistance Program, 178
International Criminal Tribunal
  for the former Yugoslavia (ICTY),
  98–99

invasion/peace operation, Cyprus and, 154–155, 156–157
Iran-Iraq war, 48
Iraq, truth recovery in, 36
Israel, 134–136, 145

Jameleddine, Hassana, 144–145
Jobson, Marjorie, 202, 205
judiciary
 in Argentina, 146
 in Chile, 47, 151, 210, 223, 225–231, 241
 in Lebanon, 146–147
 in South Africa, 200–201
 truth recovery and, 230
Justice and Development Party (AKP), 168
justice cascade, 4, 36
 forensic cascade and, 109, 235–236
 mobilization of families and, 126
 Sikkink on, 31, 90–91, 109, 233, 235

Kataeb, 133
Katyn massacre, 94
Keck, Margaret, 93, 113
Khulumani, 186, 202, 204, 205
King, Mary-Claire, 76, 95–96
Kleiser, Andreas, 100–101
de Kock, Eugene, 183, 199
Küçük, Plümer, 173

Lagos, Ricardo, 217
Lange, Matthew, 24–25
Laqueur, Thomas, 86
Latin America. See also specific countries
 disappearances and, 112, 210
 forensic truth and, 94–95
 regional learning and, 36, 45
 truth commissions and, 91
Latin American Federation of Associations of Relatives of Detained-Disappeared (FEDEFAM), 82, 117, 118, 214
Latin American Forensic Anthropology Association (ALAF), 97
Lebanon, 129–153. See also Committee of the Families of the Kidnapped and Disappeared in Lebanon;

Hezbollah; Kataeb; National Liberal Party; National Pact (1943); Shi'a Amal; Special Tribunal for Lebanon; Ta'if Agreement
 amnesty in, 56, 129–130, 139–142
 Amnesty International and, 141–142
 Christians in, 133
 civil war in, 129, 132–135
 commissions of inquiry in, 139
 Cyprus and, 154–155, 175
 democratization and, 142, 146–147, 152
 disappearances in, 1, 11, 132–135
 exhumations in, 135–137
 external actors and, 130
 families of disappeared in, 132
 forensic truth in, 142–143
 human rights and, 149–150
 ICRC and, 132, 134
 institutionalized silence in, 11, 130–131, 142–148
 international allies and, 142–143, 147–151, 152–153
 Israel and, 134–136, 145
 judiciary in, 146–147
 mobilization of families in, 2, 129–130, 131–132, 135–139, 143–144, 146–150
 mothers in, 138
 Muslims in, 133
 Palestinians in, 133–134
 perpetrators in, 135–136
 political opportunities in, 131–132
 post-transitional justice in, 130
 right to truth and, 150
 security and stability and, 143–145, 151–152
 security apparatus in, 142, 143–145, 152
 state-sponsored amnesia in, 140
 Syria and, 134–136, 145
 timing and, 130
 transitional justice in, 7
 truth recovery in, 11, 140, 141–142
 victims groups in, 135–136
Leebaw, Bronwyn, 190, 197, 198
Legal Agenda, 150

legal framework, disappearances and, 112–113, 115–116, 117–122
legal norms, 125, 126
Lieberman, E., 24, 25
Linking Solidarity, 121
London-Zurich Agreements, 156

Maalouf, L., 141
Mahoney, J., 19
Malan, Magnus, 201
Mandela, Nelson, 203
Mandela, Winnie, 201
Mansfield, E., 25
Marrizcurrena, Raquel, 61
McCarthy, Thomas, 114, 115
McConville, Jean, 176
Medical Legal Service (MLS), 218
Menem, Carlos, 74, 78
Milosevic, Slobodan, 4
minors, abductions of, 79, 116
MIR. See Revolutionary Left Movement
missing, disappearances and, 13–14, 182–183
Missing Persons Task Team (MPTT), 192, 194–196, 200
MK. See Umkhonto we Sizwe
Mladic, Radko, 91
MLS. See Medical Legal Service
mobilization of families, 1–3, 6, 10, 86, 87–88, 180. See also Founding Line; Grandmothers; Mothers; Mothers and Grandmothers; victims groups
    accountability and, 12–13
    in Argentina, 61–77
    broader truth and, 51
    in Chile, 2, 12–13, 88, 208–209, 213–215
    in Cyprus, 2, 158–164
    democratization and, 52, 147
    forensic truth and, 174
    framing strategies and, 52
    Greek Cypriots and, 158–162
    international allies and, 52
    International Convention for the Protection of All Persons from Enforced Disappearance and, 117, 120–121

justice cascade and, 126
in Lebanon, 2, 129–130, 131–132, 135–139, 143–144, 146–150
political opportunities and, 51–52
post-conflict societies and, 180
right to truth and, 122–125
in South Africa, 2, 201, 204–206
transitional justice and, 3, 10–11, 13, 125–126, 233–234
truth commissions and, 107–108
truth recovery and, 8–9, 51–53, 239–240
Montt, Ríos, 4
Morudu, Moss, 193–194
mothers
    in Chile, 213
    in Cyprus, 159
    in Lebanon, 138
Mothers, 65–66, 78
    CONADEP and, 71–72
    disappearances of, 67
    exhumations and, 72
    split within, 74–75
Mothers and Grandmothers of the Disappeared, 62–64, 81–83, 88, 233. See also Founding Line; Grandmothers; Mothers
    CONADEP and, 71–72
    contentious politics and, 64
    exhumations and, 72
    external actors and, 68–70
    framing strategies and, 64–67
    headscarves and, 66
    as ideal victims, 82
    Plaza de Mayo and, 65–66
    political opportunities and, 70–71
    retributive justice and, 73–74
mourning, 85–88
MPTT. See Missing Persons Task Team
Muslims, Lebanon and, 133

Nadelmann, Ethan, 113
National Commission on the Disappearance of Persons (CONADEP), 70–71, 77, 92, 95, 105, 232
    AAAS and, 107
    Grandmothers and, 71–72

Mothers and, 71–72
Mothers and Grandmothers and,
    71–72
National Corporation for Reparations
    and Reconciliation (CNRR),
    216–217, 223, 228
National Liberal Party, 141
National Pact (1943), 133
National Party (NP), 190
National Prosecutorial Authority
    (NPA), 200
National Reconciliation Accord. *See*
    Ta'if Agreement
National Unity and Reconciliation
    Act, 191
Nazis, exhumations and, 94
negotiated transitions
    in Chile, 209
    in South Africa, 184, 188–189
    truth recovery in, 33, 34–35
9/11, 101
Nkadimeng, Thembi, 182
Northern Ireland. *See also* Boston tapes;
    Good Friday Agreement;
    Independent Commission for the
    Location of Victims' Remains;
    Sinn Fein; Troubles
    disappearances in, 22, 23, 175
    forensic truth in, 50
    truth recovery in, 175–177
Northern Ireland Act, 176
Nowak, Manfred, 119–120, 121
NP. *See* National Party
NPA. *See* National Prosecutorial
    Authority

Organization of American States
    (OAS), 70, 119
D'Orival, Roberto, 221, 227
Our Unity is Our Salvation
    (*Wahdatouna Khalasouna*),
    144–145

Palestinian Liberation
    Organization, 133
Palestinians, Lebanon and, 133–134
Pan-Cyprian Organization of Parent
    and Relatives of Undeclared

Prisoners and Missing Persons,
    159, 160–162, 165
Papadopoulos, Tassos, 164
Parashos, Andreas, 163
PCLU. *See* Priority Crimes Litigation
    Unit
Peace and Justice Law, 178–179, 243
Pebco. *See* Port Elizabeth Black Civic
    Organization
Penchaszadeh, Victor, 76, 95
Pérez Esquivel, Adolfo, 68, 71, 120
Permanent Assembly for Human
    Rights (APDH), 68
perpetrators
    in Chile, 220–221, 222, 224–225
    CMP and, 171
    exhumations and, 89
    forensic truth and, 50–51
    in Lebanon, 135–136
    prosecution of, 38, 39
    transitional justice and, 3
    TRC and, 193–194
    truth recovery and, 53
Peru, truth recovery in, 45
Peruvian Forensic Anthropology Team
    (EPAF), 97
phase-based theory, truth recovery and,
    48–54, 238–239
Physicians for Human Rights (PHR),
    98, 101–102
Pinochet, Augusto, 47, 57, 88, 151,
    209, 218
    disappearances and, 208–209, 212
    popularity of, 209
    Spain and, 226
Plate, Ewoud, 88, 120, 121
Plaza de Mayo, Mothers and
    Grandmothers and, 65–66
Poblete, Claudia, 79, 227
policy, forensic truth and, 50–51
political opportunities
    in Chile, 224
    in Cyprus, 158
    in Lebanon, 131–132
    mobilization of families and, 51–52
    Mothers and Grandmothers and,
        70–71
    in South Africa, 204–205, 206–207

politics of measurement, 165–166, 211
Port Elizabeth Black Civic
    Organization (Pebco), 200
post-authoritarian societies
    broader truth and, 49
    disappearances and, 47–48
    forensic truth and, 47, 195
    idealist scholars and, 53–54, 241–242
    truth recovery and, 44–45, 46–47, 48,
        53–54, 151, 240–241
    victims groups and, 188
post-conflict societies
    disappearances and, 47–48
    forensic truth and, 47
    mobilization of families and, 180
    realist scholars and, 53–54, 241
    truth recovery and, 44, 45, 46–47,
        53–54, 151–153, 179–180, 240
post-transitional justice, 4–5, 19
    in Lebanon, 130
    technologies of truth and, 92–105
Priority Crimes Litigation Unit
    (PCLU), 202
Pro-Búsqueda, 82
prosecution
    of perpetrators, 38, 39
    reparations and, 242
    right to truth and, 237
public hearings, TRC and, 181–182,
    190–191, 193–194, 197, 206
Punto Final (Full Stop) law, 74, 116

qualitative studies, 6–7, 17, 20–21,
    30, 54
quantitative studies, transitional justice
    and, 6–7, 17–18, 19–24
Quinteros v. Uruguay, 121

realist scholars, 36, 53–54, 241
reconciliation, TRC and, 181–182,
    197–198
regional learning, 36, 45, 83
reparations, 200, 216–217, 219, 242
Republic of Cyprus (RoC), 156,
    164–167, 175
restorative justice, 31, 200–204
retributive justice
    amnesty and, 206

ANC and, 185
Chile and, 57, 224–231, 242–243
Cyprus and, 73
Mothers and Grandmothers and,
    73–74
South Africa and, 183, 184–185,
    199–206
technologies of truth and, 236–237
transitional justice and, 30–31
truth recovery and, 232
Rettig Commission, 215–216
Revolutionary Left Movement
    (MIR), 212
right to identity, Grandmothers and,
    81–82
right to truth, 121–122, 174, 229
    Argentina and, 79, 81
    CMP and, 172–173
    disappearances and, 122–123
    IACHR and, 123
    Lebanon and, 150
    mobilization of families and,
        122–125
    prosecution and, 237
    transitional justice and, 125
Robben, Antonius, 82–83, 87–88, 210
Robins, Simon, 85–86
RoC. See Republic of Cyprus
Rome Statute of the International
    Criminal Court, 119
Rosenblatt, Adam, 96
Roundtable, 217, 221–223, 229
Rousseau, Nicky, 186, 203
ruptured transition, truth recovery and,
    33, 34

Sandal, N., 93
Sant Cassia, Paul, 88, 157–158
Sarkin, Jeremy, 197
secret police, Chile and, 209, 212, 220
security and stability
    exhumations and, 144
    forensic truth and, 50, 151–152,
        238–239
    Lebanon and, 143–145, 151–152
security apparatus, Lebanon and, 142,
    143–145, 152
Shi'a Amal, 133

Shikegane, Rachel, 98
Sikkink, Kathryn, 4, 22–23, 93,
    103–104, 113
  on Argentina, 81
  on justice cascade, 31, 90–91, 109,
    233, 235
Simelane, Nokuthula, 182, 201–202
Sinn Fein, 177
Snow, Clyde, 72, 73, 78, 93–94, 95
Snow, D., 64
Snyder, J., 3, 25, 237
social peace, South Africa and, 205, 207
SOLIDE. See Support of the Lebanese in
    Detention and Exile
South Africa, 181–207. See also
    Commission of Inquiry into
    Complaints by Former African
    Congress Prisoners and Detainees;
    Goldstone Commission; Missing
    Persons Task Team; Truth and
    Reconciliation Commission
  amnesty in, 188–189, 199–200
  disappearances in, 1, 185–188
  exhumations in, 171
  families of disappeared in, 2, 138,
    203, 205
  judiciary in, 200–201
  mobilization of families in, 2, 201,
    204–206
  negotiated transitions in, 184,
    188–189
  political opportunities in, 204–205,
    206–207
  reparations in, 200
  retributive justice and, 183, 184–185,
    199–206
  social peace in, 205, 207
  transitional justice in, 8, 12
  truth commissions and, 56
Spain
  disappearances in, 62
  exhumations in, 72, 82,
    92
  Pinochet and, 226
  transitional justice in, 19
  truth recovery in, 42, 45
Special Tribunal for Lebanon
    (STL), 142

State Department, US, 21, 22, 25, 26, 68,
    117–118
state-sponsored amnesia, Lebanon
    and, 140
STL. See Special Tribunal for Lebanon
Stover, Eric, 95, 98, 102
de Suarez, Aida, 66
Subotic, Jelena, 207
Support of the Lebanese in Detention
    and Exile (SOLIDE), 137, 147
Syria, Lebanon and, 134–136, 145

Ta'if Agreement, 129–130,
    139–140, 143
Taksim, 156
Tanzania, 189
Tayler, Wilder, 113, 117
technologies of truth, 84, 94–104, 126.
    See also exhumations
  accountability and, 109–110
  institutions of truth and, 85
  post-transitional justice and, 92–105
  retributive justice and, 236–237
  transitional justice and, 89–92, 109,
    235–237
  truth commissions and, 91–92
theory testing, databases and, 30–36
Tilly, Charles, 19
timing
  Argentina and, 63, 78–81
  CMP and, 243–244
  Lebanon and, 130
  transitional justice and, 4–5, 8, 13,
    19–20, 179, 238–239
  truth recovery and, 40–43, 91, 231
Timor, 87
transitional justice
  amnesty and, 3–4, 29, 31–32, 40
  in Argentina, 10, 23, 63, 77–81
  in Chile, 7–8
  in Cyprus, 7, 17
  databases and, 7, 17–36
  democratization and, 40–41
  exhumations and, 29–30
  forensic cascade and, 91
  forms of violence and, 240–242
  human rights and, 20
  in Lebanon, 7

transitional justice (cont.)
  literature on, 3–5
  mobilization of families and, 3,
      10–11, 13, 125–126, 233–234
  moral and legal tensions in, 242–244
  perpetrators and, 3
  qualitative studies of, 6–7, 17, 20–21
  quantitative studies of, 6–7, 17–18,
      19–24
  retributive justice and, 30–31
  right to truth and, 125
  in South Africa, 8, 12
  in Spain, 19
  technologies of truth and, 89–92,
      109, 235–237
  timing and, 4–5, 8, 13, 19–20, 63,
      78–81, 179, 238–239
  victims groups and, 5–6, 11, 20, 30
transnational advocacy networks,
      112–113
trauma, disappearances and, 85–86
TRC. See Truth and Reconciliation
      Commission
trials, 42, 229–231. See also truth trials,
      Argentinian
Troubles, 23, 175
truth, TRC and, 191, 196–197
Truth and Reconciliation Commission
      (TRC), 2, 8, 93, 105–106, 181–207
  amnesty and, 190, 193
  ANC and, 189–190, 198
  disappearances and, 191–192,
      196–199, 206
  DNA and, 192–193, 194
  exhumations and, 192–193, 194–196
  external actors and, 183–184
  families of disappeared and,
      182–183, 184, 193–194
  forensic truth and, 185, 191–196
  heroicization and, 198
  human rights and, 197
  investigative powers of, 190
  perpetrators and, 193–194
  public hearings and, 181–182,
      190–191, 193–194, 197, 206
  reconciliation and, 181–182,
      197–198
  restorative justice and, 31

  truth and, 191, 196–197
  truth recovery and, 12, 56
truth commissions, 10–11, 31, 104–109,
      181. See also National
      Commission on the
      Disappearance of Persons; Rettig
      Commission; Truth and
      Reconciliation Commission
  amnesty and, 104
  Chile and, 215–219, 221–224
  disappearances and, 105,
      106–107, 234
  evolution of, 105–108
  exhumations and, 52–53, 108–109,
      221–224
  Latin America and, 91
  mobilization of families and,
      107–108
  South Africa and, 56
  technologies of truth and, 91–92
  truth recovery and, 42
  Uganda and, 104
truth recovery, 8–9, 32, 37, 39, 55. See
      also broader truth; forensic truth;
      institutionalized silence
  amnesty and, 41, 42, 140, 206,
      238–239
  in Chile, 42, 47, 209–210, 215–224,
      231–232
  in Colombia, 178–179
  in Cyprus, 11–12, 42, 46, 62
  democratization and, 231
  ethnic violence and, 177
  exhumations and, 42
  external actors and, 35–36, 41, 179
  families of disappeared and, 53
  forensic cascade and, 10
  forms of violence and, 43–48
  Grandmothers and, 78–80
  in Iraq, 36
  judiciary and, 230
  in Lebanon, 11, 140, 141–142
  mobilization of families and, 8–9,
      51–53, 239–240
  in negotiated transitions, 33, 34–35
  in Northern Ireland, 175–177
  perpetrators and, 53
  in Peru, 45

phase-based theory of, 48–54,
238–239
post-authoritarian societies and,
44–45, 46–47, 48, 53–54, 151,
240–241
post-conflict societies and, 44, 45,
46–47, 53–54, 151–153,
179–180, 240
regional learning and, 36
retributive justice and, 232
in ruptured transition, 33, 34
in Spain, 42, 45
timing and, 40–43, 91, 231
TRC and, 12, 56
trials and, 42
truth commissions and, 42
Turkey and, 46
truth trials, Argentinian, 123–124
Turkey. *See also* Justice and
Development Party
Cyprus and, 154–155, 156–157,
160–162
disappearances and, 167–169
ECtHR and, 167
EU and, 167–168, 175
truth recovery and, 46
Turkish Cypriots, 1, 156–158, 162, 166,
168–169, 170

Ubuntu, 190
Uganda, truth commissions and, 104
Uludag, Sevgul, 163
Umkhonto we Sizwe (MK), 186
UN Basic Principles and
Guidelines, 242
UN Commission on Human Rights,
118, 119–120
UN Convention on the Rights of the
Child, 82
UN Universal Declaration of Human
Rights, 139
UN Working Group of Human
Rights, 214
UN Working Group on Enforced or
Involuntary Disappearances
(UNWGEID), 81, 114–115,
118, 219
UNESCO, 93
United Nations (UN), CMP and,
169–170
United Self Defense forces of Colombia
(AUC), 178
universal instrument, 117–122
International Convention for the
Protection of All Persons from
Enforced Disappearance as, 117
UNWGEID. *See* UN Working Group
on Enforced or Involuntary
Disappearances
Uribe, Álvaro, 178
Uruguay, 243

Velasquez Rodriquez v. Honduras, 115,
118, 121, 123
Vicaria de Solidaridad, 114, 214,
227, 228
victimhood, ANC and, 202–204, 207
victims, disappearances and, 188,
233–234
victims groups. *See also* families of
disappeared
in Lebanon, 135–136
post-authoritarian societies
and, 188
transitional justice and, 5–6, 11,
20, 30
Vietnam, 97
de Vincenti, Azucena Villaflor, 66, 67
Vinjamuri, L., 3, 237
violence, forms of, 43–48, 240–242

Wiebelhaus-Brahm, E., 24–25
The Work of the Dead
(Laqueur), 86

Yugoslavia, former, 98–99. *See also*
International Criminal Tribunal
for the former Yugoslavia

Zalaquett, Jose, 113